T0326954

THE MIRROR OF LANGUAGE

Revised Edition

Marcia L. Colish

A Study in the Medieval Theory of Knowledge

University of Nebraska Press

Lincoln & London

Library of Congress Cataloging
in Publication Data

Colish, Marcia L.
The mirror of language.

Bibliography: p.
Includes index.
1. Knowledge, Theory of –
History.   2. Semantics
(Philosophy) – History.
3. Philosophy, Medieval.
I. Title.
BD161.C635 1983
121'.09'02   83-3599
ISBN 0-8032-6447-X

Contents

Preface

Videmus nunc per speculum in aenigmate,
tunc autem facie ad faciem. [I Cor. 13:12]

People who read books on the medieval mind are familiar with the dictum usually found on page one of any book on this subject: "Medieval man thought in terms of symbols." People who write books on the medieval mind acknowledge the symbolic mentality of the period with impartial and relentless frequency. Whether cited to attest to the clairvoyance or obscurantism, the subtlety or primitivism, the uniqueness or the universality of the Middle Ages, the symbolic attributes of the medieval mind have by now acquired the unexcogitated and prescriptive status of an *idée reçue*. The assertion that medieval men thought in terms of symbols is usually treated as a canon of explanation. It has rarely been treated as susceptible of explanation itself. More rarely still have those who study the place of symbols in medieval epistemology avoided the tendency to interpret them in anachronistic or otherwise extraneous terms. The study which follows is a partial attempt to remedy this situation. My aim throughout has been twofold. I have tried to examine how four major medieval figures actually thought that signs functioned in the acquisition and transmission of knowledge, and I have sought to place their theories of signification in the historical context of their specific interests, ways of thinking, and intellectual environments.

The thesis which this examination has yielded will be demonstrated throughout the book, but I would like also to state it briefly in these prefatory remarks. To begin with, many western medieval thinkers from the patristic period until the rise of propositional logic in the high Middle Ages were greatly influenced by a common theory of signs. Formulated by Augustine, this theory has two principal features: it treats signs not merely as intramental entities but as indices of realities that exist outside of and prior to the knowing subject, and it regards signs as fundamentally verbal in nature. These characteristics result from a blending of classical and Christian ideas. The Stoic and Aristotelian contributions to sign theory and epistemology, rooted as they are in an empirical approach to human knowledge, were of particular importance in the development of this theory. For the Stoics, all real beings are corporeal. Words, being physically produced and physically received, are themselves corporeal and accurate signs of the realities they represent. Aristotle also stresses the capacity of sense data, in this case words as sonic forms that are aurally perceived, to signify their objects accurately. But, unlike the Stoics, he held that the world contained incorporeal as well as corporeal realities, metaphysically prior to the sensible order, to which sensible signs could also refer with accuracy. The assumption that these nonsensible realities were truly prior in the order of being although they were posterior in the order of knowledge was one that the Peripatetics shared with the Platonists and Neoplatonists. The metaphysical bias that this view entails was fully capable of undergirding the conception of signs found in many medieval thinkers, whichever school of ancient thought they preferred in other respects. At the same time, while classical philosophers certainly discussed the theme of language, their sign theories were not particularly verbal in orientation. They tended to treat words as signs as one species within the broader genus of sensible signs in general. On the other hand, Augustine and the medieval thinkers influenced by him tended to view signification per se in primarily verbal terms.

While this approach entailed a shift in the emphasis of classical philosophy, classical culture still supplied the forms in which the medieval redefinition of signs as words was expressed. These forms were the verbal disciplines of the seven liberal arts: the trivium, consisting of grammar, rhetoric, and dialectic. The seven liberal arts were the basis of the medieval educational curriculum. Grammar, rhetoric, and dialectic not only taught medieval men how to read, write, and think in Latin in logical order. These disciplines also provided them with epistemological methods, linguistic forms, and criteria which they used in theorizing how words functioned as cognitive intermediaries between subject and object and between speaker and audience. The same basic verbal epistemology could be expressed through any of the three modes of the trivium. At various times during the Middle Ages it was expressed through each of them.

Christianity, no less than the classical tradition, was an important source of the theory of verbal signs that stemmed from Augustine. The medieval thinkers treated in this study developed their sign theory in the first instance to analyze and explain the functions of theological discourse and the reception and transmission of religious knowledge. This theological focus and imperative remained basic to their epistemology even in cases where they concerned themselves with objects of knowledge other than God or the contents of the Christian faith. As Christian thinkers they were thus forced to grapple with problems that had not been on the agenda of the classical philosophers. At the same time, Christianity itself supplied them with a number of doctrines that strongly supported the plausibility of a verbal theory of knowledge. The Stoic conviction that words are real entities that naturally signify the physical and metaphysical realities for which they stand and the Aristotelian certainty that sensory data lead to a knowledge of prior and nonsensible realities was paralleled by the scriptural assertions that God can be known through his creation, which he is believed to resemble. Yet, the kind of knowledge of God which the Christian regarded as normative in this life was faith. Knowledge by faith was firm and certain, but partial. It could be acquired only by an infusion of God's grace in the mind of the subject, and it involved his moral conversion as well as his intellectual assent. This set of beliefs predisposed medieval Christians to the view that cognition should be mediated through signs. At the same time, it led them to expect the knowledge of God to be mediated through signs *per speculum in aenigmate.* Signs, they held, would always be limited in their cognitive function, both in the degree to which they could represent the transcendent God at all and in the degree to which they could convey the knowledge of God to the subject in the first instance. They always disting-uished the reflection of God in the mirror of faith from God himself. They never confused signification with an identity between sign and object. They always regarded signs as instrumental, not heuristic; no one, they held, could acquire the religious knowledge necessary for salvation without the assistance of God.

Christianity also supplied medieval thinkers with a strong motive for a sign theory conceived in expressly verbal terms. This motive was the doctrine of the Incarnation. Medieval Christians believed that Christ the Word was God's perfect expression of himself to man. Having taken on a human nature and having expiated man's sin, Christ had restored man to God. Previously vitiated by sin, the human mind could now come to a knowledge of God in Christ; and the human faculty of speech could now participate in the Incarnation by helping to spread the Word to the world. Medieval thinkers thus stressed verbal signs as the primary media of religious knowledge because they saw in Christ the Word the mediator between God and man, whose redemption enabled them to know God and to bear God to each other in human words, as well as because their habits of mind were derived from the verbal disciplines of the trivium.

This book treats four medieval thinkers—Augustine, Anselm, Aquinas, and Dante—as exponents of a common conception of words as signs in a theory developed by Augustine and expressed by him and by his successors in the modes of the trivium. Augustine originally formulates this theory in the mode of rhetoric; Anselm recasts it in terms of grammar; Aquinas displays it in the mode of dialectic; and Dante presents it in the mode of a poetics conceived in rhetorical terms. These differences reflect as much the varying historical circumstances in which each of the four men lived and the particular status of the disciplines of the trivium in his day as they do his professional concern, the scope and directionality of his thought, and his personal tastes and affinities. This study will explore their similarities as well as their differences and will seek to elucidate the role that sign theory plays in the thought of each of them. It is not sufficient to present the theories themselves and to comment on their sources. It is also important to show how each thinker applied his theory to his work as a practicing theologian or man of letters, as the case may be. If the theory were set forth without the practice, the reader would be given a false impression of Augustine, Anselm, Aquinas, and Dante and might be inclined to think that they were more concerned with formulating a sign theory as an end in itself than with addressing the questions whose solution prompted them to speculate on signs in the first place.

At the same time, it has not proved possible to discuss all of the contexts where this application was made. Aesthetic theory, sacramental theology, and the language of mysticism are topics by no means absent from the thought of some or all of our figures. A detailed treatment of these topics would, indeed, be a logical extension of the present study. Considerations of space, however, militate against adding these subjects to the revised edition of this book, which the revisions themselves have already made more ample. For the same reason, consideration of analogous theories on the part of Greek Christian thinkers have not been included, apart from the brief remarks on the theory of the Byzantine icon retained in the Introduction from the first edition.

In choosing the four Latin thinkers discussed in this book, I have been guided by their standing as exponents of the medieval culture of their respective centuries and as outstanding exemplars of the use of the disciplines of the trivium in the solution of theological problems. Yet even while acknowledging that some of them were far more influential than others in this connection, I am by no means claiming that medieval sign theory, epistemology, or theology can be reduced to their particular approaches. The Middle Ages is no monolith, and no individual medieval thinker or group of thinkers can function as a code word for the period, on whatever subject. Augustine, Anselm, Aquinas, and

Dante produced noteworthy answers to ongoing questions on which the Middle Ages achieved no universal consensus. Their positions were not always greeted by the applause of their contemporaries, and their capacity to function as models for later thinkers was conditioned by their own idiosyncracies or by historical developments which they were incapable of predicting or controlling. Each of these men lived at a crucial time in medieval intellectual history, when new approaches were emerging and when older views no longer seemed completely adequate. The historical circumstances in which each of them lived help to explain why each uses the particular discipline of the trivium which he happens to use; in turn, each of the four, in the formulation of his own answer to the problem of knowledge, illustrates and specifies the intellectual circumstances of his age no less than his own personality and interests. In this sense, four very different men may be taken as representatives of a civilization marked by as many diversities as uniformities.

Given the fact that a fairly wide range of classical sources influenced medieval thought, I would like to clarify my reasons for emphasizing the influence of the trivium. This emphasis is quite deliberate, and it reflects what I think is a new approach to the treatment of classical influences in medieval thought. One of the most frequently encountered traditional approaches to the medieval mind has been to seek out the classical backgrounds of medieval Christian treatments of philosophical problems. One might focus, for example, on Ambrose's appropriation of Ciceronian ethics in his *De officiis ministrorum,* or on Augustine's appropriation of Neoplatonic metaphysics. This book deals with epistemology, but it does not adopt a strictly analogous method. Without losing oneself in the question of the subconscious versus conscious choices and intentions of thinkers—a question that is rarely soluble unless the historian is willing to forfeit his reliance on documentable facts for the insights and uncertainties of retroactive psychoanalysis—it can still be said that some influences are more inadvertent than others. Specifically, the rules of speech and thought which comprise the trivium, along with their epistemological implications, cannot be treated in exactly the same way as classical ethical or metaphysical ideas. Medieval men were not as free to accept or reject the trivium as they were to accept or reject other aspects of the classical tradition. Their education saw to it that the trivium was as much a part of their mental equipment as their Christian faith. In the few cases where the presuppositions of classical grammar, rhetoric, or dialectic came into conflict with the content of the Christian ideas which they were used to express, they were either reinterpreted or used inconsistently. As intellectual methods, however, the modes of the trivium emerged as real options only when medieval thought was on the verge of shifting its emphasis from one of them to another. My treatment of the trivium in this study will, I hope, illustrate this point.

I would also like to call the reader's attention to the methods I have used to construct the four major sections of this study. The reader will note that the organization of these sections is not invariably parallel. In the sections dealing with Augustine and Anselm, particular works of theirs are singled out for commentary or are made the *point d'appui* of the chapter. With Dante, the development of his ideas on signification has been studied chronologically. With Aquinas, I have attempted to select those ideas of his which are relevant to signification and to present them in a logical order. In all four cases, I have paid a good deal of attention to the historical circumstances and general epistemology of the thinker at issue. This manner of arranging the material, no less than the scope and emphasis, is deliberate. Many mistaken impressions of medieval thought have been fostered by the practice of abstracting ideas from their contexts in the works of their authors, to be compared with other ideas similarly abstracted from the works of other thinkers, as if thought existed in a historical vacuum. The four men whose ideas on signs I am concerned with exhibit tremendous differences in personality, in the range of their interests, in the amount and the kind of importance they accord to sign theory, and in the ways that they illustrate this theory in their works. It is necessary to come to grips with these personal and contextual considerations if one is to grasp the historical importance of their sign theory. I have therefore made a conscious effort to reconstruct, so far as I can, the texture and emphasis, as well as the content, of Augustinian, Anselmian, Thomistic, and Dantean epistemology. The organization of each chapter represents my attempt to achieve such a reconstruction.

I have prefaced my treatment of Augustine with a discussion of the ancient philosophy and rhetoric pertinent to his sign theory. The new edition of this book has enabled me to rectify my earlier handling of the Stoic component in this classical background, which was seriously deficient in the first edition. As before, I have used the *Confessions* of Augustine as the organizing principle of Chapter 1, and for the same reasons: the *Confessions* is a distillation of the epistemology of Augustine, summarizing all the ideas on the role of signs in religious knowledge that he elaborates in his earlier and later works. Second, and equally important, the whole tenor of Augustine's thought on knowledge is personal, developmental, and concrete. His own individual growth and the exigencies of his intellectual and moral life dominate his work and lend it an intense vitality and a lived reality. As the story of his spiritual struggles and changing mental states, the *Confessions* thus provides an unparalleled construct—and one constructed deliberately by Augustine himself—displaying the inner pulse of his thought. It is thus a far better axis around which to organize his ideas than could be provided by an abstract logical arrangement of them, which, while preserving the letter, would destroy the spirit. Finally, the interpretation of the *Confessions* from the standpoint of Augustine's sign theory provides a cogent way to relate the portions of the work dealing with the period after his conversion to the more overtly autobiographical material in the first nine books.

In the case of Anselm I have continued to concentrate my attention on his proofs for the existence of God, since they embody his most critical contribution to the problem of theological discourse. I remain convinced that his achievement in the *Monologion, Proslogion,* and *Contra Gaunilonem* can be grasped only in the light of his intentions and the meaning he imparts to such terms as truth, necessary reasons, and *intellectus fidei,* which he defines in other segments of his theological oeuvre. At the same time, I have payed greater attention in this revised edition to the linguistic theory that Anselm elaborates in some of his nontheological works, on which recent scholarship has shed considerable new light. Anselm has been revealed more clearly as a thinker with an appreciation for certain technical features of semantics, and he uses Stoic as well as Aristotelian and Boethian strategies for dealing with them in both theological and nontheological contexts. Keeping all this in mind, my focus in Chapter 2 still remains the role of grammar in the theological enterprise as it was understood in Anselm's day. In the present text I have substituted new and more accurate English translations of Anselm's work for those available when the first edition was published. The second edition also devotes more attention to the Carolingian forerunners of Anselm's grammatical method and to the question of why, despite the contribution made by his technique to the thought of the next generation, his approach to theology declined with relative rapidity in the twelfth century. These are topics enriched by important new scholarship that clarifies the genesis and nature of Anselm's proofs as well as their backgrounds and their immediate medieval fortunes.

In contrast with Augustine and Anselm, Aquinas wrote no treatises dealing comprehensively with the function of signs in religious knowledge. His commentary on Dionysius the Areopagite's *On the Divine Names* is the closest he comes to such a work, and it deals with the *via negativa,* a very small facet of the subject in general. Sign theory, per se, is clearly not a topic which Thomas felt called upon to discuss *ex professo.* On the other hand, and despite the fact that he places much of his treatment of how the human mind works in theological contexts, such as the nature of the Trinity, he is far more concerned than Augustine or Anselm with understanding how man knows the natural world, as well as God and the soul. While his epistemology is quite broad-gauged, it is also true that Thomas does not profess a systematic epistemology independent from his theology, despite the attribution of such a philosophy to him by modern neoscholastic commentators. When Chapter 3 was originally written, a hyperintellectualistic and overly abstract interpretation of his ideas was virtually canonical among Thomas scholars. Since then, the cumulative effect of the revisionism catalyzed by the Second Vatican Council has broken the hold of the neo-Thomists of the strict observance and has encouraged a view of Thomas's work that is much more sensitive to his own intentions and to the historical setting in which he lived. This tendency was already reflected in some of the scholarship cited in the first edition, and it has been amplified considerably by the wave of soul-searching on the part of Thomas scholars prompted by the seventh centenary of his death in 1974. These changes notwithstanding, the revisionists cannot be said to have made a clean sweep of the field in the early 1980s. Thus I have felt that there is some merit in retaining the distinctly polemical tone adopted in Chapter 3 in the first edition. Aside from incorporating the more recent scholarship and correcting some serious weaknesses in my original treatment of thirteenth-century logic, my approach to Thomas in the second edition has therefore been altered very little.

Since Thomas scatters his ideas on signs throughout his works, I have attempted to collect them and to set them forth in logical order. It is true that Thomas's thought undergoes a certain amount of change over time, at least on some topics. But sign theory is not one of them; his views on this subject and related matters remain more or less constant throughout his career. Thus his ideas on signs may be presented in a logical rather than a chronological or thematic order without doing violence to them. While organizing Aquinas's sign theory logically, I have nonetheless tried to underline carefully the contextual qualifications that must be made in discussing them. Since Thomas himself insists that the knowledge of God begins with the knowledge of the natural world, I have followed the same pattern in organizing Chapter 3, seeking at the same time to show the limiting conditions which Thomas imposes on signs as well as the logical and theological powers that he grants them.

The chapter on Dante is designed to illustrate the application of Augustinian sign theory to literature by analyzing Dante's poetic theory and the manner in which he expresses it in the *Divine Comedy*. This chapter subdivides itself naturally into three main sections. The first deals with the classical tradition of poetic theory inherited by the Middle Ages and elaborated by medieval literary theorists. The second treats the chronological development of Dante's theological poetics during the course of his career through his theoretical treatises and lyric poetry, charting his changing relationship to the medieval poetic tradition. The last part is an analysis of the *Divine Comedy*, which aims at discovering the extent to which Dante uses his theory in practice. Since Dante connects both his poetry and his literary theory to the linguistic, political, ecclesiastical, and moral reform of the Europe of his own day, I have discussed these questions as they appear in his works in an effort to indicate the nature of this connection.

Aside from substituting newer and better editions and translations of Dante's works for some of the texts used in the first edition, Chapter 4 in the revised edition remains substantially the same, despite the flood of commentary flowing from the seventh centenary of Dante's death in 1965, which swelled a modern Dante bibliography already of oceanic proportions. It is, however, distressing to have to note the repetitiousness that afflicts so much of the Dante criticism of the intervening years. Daunted, perhaps, by the magnitude of the scholarly literature on the poet, all too many practitioners have ignored the work of their predecessors and have published as new ideas insights that have been in print for quite some time. It would be equally redundant of me to provide an exhaustive citation of the Dante criticism between the mid 1960s and the early 1980s that, in effect, reinvents the wheel. Consequently, in bringing Chapter 4 up to date for the new edition, I have concentrated on those scholars who best exemplify particular critical positions, who have something genuinely new to say, and who provide useful guides to the studies published during that period pertinent to the themes treated in this chapter.

Before leaving the subject of methodological principles, I would like to insert a word of caution regarding my use of certain terms. The reader will frequently encounter such words as "sign," "symbol," "dialectic," "intuition," "allegory," as well as a number like them which have been used with specific technical meanings by various branches of recent or contemporary philosophy and literary criticism. If the reader comes to this book with a mind trained in contemporary epistemology, whether philosophical or literary, he should proceed with care. I have expressly avoided using philosophical and literary terms with the technical meanings and connotations that contemporary thought attributes to them. The meanings I give to such terms derive from the definitions given to them by the classical and medieval thinkers under consideration. Where no such definitions appear, the reader should understand epistemological terms in a general, not a technical, sense. This procedure admittedly lacks the verbal finesse that is characteristic of much contemporary logical and literary analysis. I have chosen it deliberately because I think that the application of anachronistic terminology or criteria of definition to medieval thought has at times had a disastrous tendency to distort the meanings and intentions of medieval thinkers. To impose a modern style of verbal precision on thinkers who may not have been particularly prone to it is generally as nugatory in its results as asking a past philosopher for answers to questions into which, for one reason or another, it never occurred to him to inquire. All of this is fully self-evident to the historian, who is less interested in assessing the tenability of past theories in modern terms than in understanding what past theories meant to past ages. However, it may be to the point to mention it for the sake of philosophers or literary critics who may conceivably be interested in reading this book. The sole exception to my antianachronism rule is the term "epistemology" and its variants, which, the reader will note, I have already used several times in this preface and which I continue to use frequently throughout the book. I am aware of the fact that I am violating my own canons in using this term. My justification is simply that its suppression would entail the repeated use of wordy synonymous circumlocutions. To avoid this I have retained "epistemology," but the reader should understand the term simply as a way of describing speculation on knowledge, not necessarily as a separate, technical branch of philosophy in the modern sense.

I would next like to comment on the bibliographical orientation of the book, which holds just as true for the second as for the first edition. In the last three chapters I devote considerable attention both in the text and in the notes to issues debated in the literature on which I wish to take a stand. The chapter on Augustine is not characterized by as much bibliographical analysis and comment. This is not because there is any lack of controversy surrounding the bishop of Hippo, but because the controversies tend to be located at points in the landscape different from the ones I am addressing in Chapter 1. On the comparatively rare occasions where I wish to outline controversies or to situate my own position in the context of a scholarly debate on Augustine, I have not included the material in the text, but have confined it to the notes. The scholars writing on the subjects treated in this book since the first edition was published have sometimes taken account of it and sometimes not. The updating of the notes in the new edition makes no distinction between authors influenced by my work and those who arrive at similar conclusions independently.

In coming to the end of this preface, I would like to renew the thanks extended to the institutions and individuals mentioned in the preface to the first edition. The debts I owe them have deepened over the years, and it is a pleasure to acknowledge them once again. I would also like to record the new debts that are added to the old, most especially to the reviewers and readers whose combination of generosity and exigence has brought to my attention the weaknesses, omissions, and errors found in the first edition of this book and who, at the same time, have emboldened me to think that a revised edition would continue to be of use. Equally important has been the assistance of the Yale University Press, whose gracious release of the copyright to the author made possible the publication of the new edition. The National Humanities Center in Research Triangle Park, North Carolina, has provided a tranquil and hospitable setting for the process of revision itself. As before, I alone remain responsible for the views expressed in the book and for any flaws it may contain.

Introduction

From the patristic period roughly until the end of the thirteenth century, the period encompassed by this study, western European thinkers produced a number of different yet reciprocal expressions of one basic mental universe. This mental universe embodied certain standard preconceptions about the nature of reality which in turn entailed standard preconceptions about the nature and methodology of knowledge. It will be useful at the outset to enumerate these preconceptions. We may thus orient our discussion of what is to follow by considering here the fundamental epistemological perspectives of medieval thinkers during these centuries.

Most of the classical philosophers whom the Middle Ages knew and regarded as authoritative held that there was an objective order of being prior to the subjective order of knowing. Following their lead, medieval philosophers endorsed the idea of an epistemology grounded in and controlled by its objects of knowledge with equal assurance and vigor. And, notwithstanding the scholastic demand for a theory of cognition explaining man's knowledge of the world of nature, the object to which medieval thinkers normally addressed themselves was the world of spiritual reality, with preeminent attention to God. The theory of knowledge professed by the thinkers treated in this study was a direct consequence of this radically ontological emphasis. Epistemology was conceived as a function of metaphysics. The existence of an objective order of being was the primary condition which was held to make human thought possible at all. Furthermore, medieval thinkers identified being par excellence with the God of the Bible. Thus, they held, the being of God himself was the guarantee, the criterion, and the *conditio sine qua non* of whatever men might know about him, or about anything else.

The relationship between man as knower and God as object of knowledge depended not only on God's absolute and transcendent existence. It also depended on his decisive intervention into the mutable world of his creation.

The belief that God had manifested his presence, inchoately in the history of Israel, consummately in the Incarnation of Christ, and continuously since Pentecost in his living extension in time and space, the church, held for medieval thinkers specific epistemological consequences. On the one hand, God in his entirety remained unequivocally beyond the scope of the human mind. But, on the other hand, God had made such knowledge of himself as he wished to communicate generally accessible to man. He had done this, however, solely on his own terms. The knowledge of God demanded from man the prior and unreserved acceptance of him just as he had revealed himself to be. Man might achieve the combined intellectual assent and loving personal adhesion which this acceptance required only on the basis of God's gracious gift of faith. Given through the church, faith made possible to man his primary mental contact with God in the person of Jesus Christ. Medieval men believed that Christ's redemptive action had been projected in time and that it was currently operative in the church, his mystical body. Moreover, they believed that Christ had chosen to manifest himself under the ecclesiastical dispensation, which would endure until the end of time, for the express purpose of enabling man to know and love God and other men through an integral union with him in the life of the church. Even as Christ on earth had joined the Transfiguration to the Incarnation in the economy of his redemption, so, in his mystical body, he continued to affiliate man to God and thereby to transfigure the ordinary modes of human cognition and expression, while yet in time, into worthy vessels of his revelation.

The new covenant of Christ, in which all major medieval thinkers believed themselves to participate, carried professional responsibilities as well as rewards. This was a condition duly recognized by the medieval commentators on the subject, most of whom had been ordained to preach and to teach the Word of God. They had been called, they believed, not only to attain a knowledge of God themselves but also to convey the knowledge of God to the world. To this task they bent at once the resources of their divine commission and the various techniques of thought and communication that human nature and their historical situation had imposed upon them and placed at their disposal. The acutely paradoxical implications of their mission did not fail to inspire in them mingled feelings of enthusiasm and unworthiness. God had commanded them to express the inexpressible, in terms accessible to the speaker and the audience alike. These very terms, however, would remain permanently inadequate to the assignment. Neither their logical rigor nor their verbal precision or eloquence could compass the mystery of the Godhead. The hearer's intellectual entry into the life of the Trinity would be initiated and accomplished by God, through grace. This notion was a matter of faith. Yet, at the same time, this faith emphasized the possibility of active human cooperation with God's grace in the process of learning and teaching about him. The tension between God's ineffability and the divine mandate to preach the Word to all nations remained a permanent one in the minds of medieval thinkers concerned with religious knowledge. To the extent that they found a resolution of this tension, they found it in the doctrine of the Incarnation. The ineffable God had revealed himself to man in Christ. Christ had taken on human nature and human faculties. By his life, death, and resurrection, he had renewed and restored these human faculties, reenabling them to become Godlike. Medieval thinkers drew an important epistemological corollary from this doctrine. In the Christian dispensation, human modes of thought and expression, although still limited by the human condition, could now worthily take on the tasks assigned to them by God. Human language, reborn through the Incarnation, could now assist God in spreading the effects of the Incarnation to the world. The medieval confidence that Babel had been redeemed in the gift of tongues was the immediate context in which men of this period judged, understood, and pressed into service the symbolic forms of human discourse.

Medieval thinkers combined their Christian heritage with a common educational tradition in their search for a theoretical explanation of the function of signs in the knowledge of God. In their formative years these thinkers all learned the basic techniques of reading, speaking, and thinking clearly from the textbooks of grammar, rhetoric, and dialectic more or less standard throughout the Latin west. The permanent effects of this discipline were apparent in their general approach to the problem of religious knowledge. Medieval sign theory was fundamentally linguistic. Crystallized in the categories of the trivium, the discussions of medieval epistemologists focused in the first instance on the role of language, literature, and logical statements in the cognition of being. The high medieval extensions of their symbolic doctrine to nature, by the school of Chartres and the Franciscans, and to the visual arts, by the proponents of the Gothic aesthetic, were advanced and justified in the idiom of this essentially verbal mode of thought. The symbolic theory of knowledge developed in the Middle Ages was cast in terms of the relationship between words, on the one hand, and reality, on the other. It was the attempt of medieval men to reflect, in the mirror of the trivium, what they believed to be the one normative epistemological relationship between man and God.

The operation of language as a cognitive intermediary between the knower and the object of knowledge, and between the speaker and the listener, required full-scale analysis and description. Medieval thinkers conceded that a word might signify truly, if partially, a really existing thing. According to this theory, a real relation may obtain between the word and the thing, although significance and identity, meaning and being, are by no means to be confused. The accuracy of any verbal formulation depends on its correspondence to the object it seeks to describe: *vox sequitur rem*. The object of knowledge always remains the yardstick against which any statement about it must be measured. Statements are thus held to be not heuristic, or productive of knowledge in the first instance, but expressive of a knowledge already existing in the mind of the knower. Axiomatic to this epistemology is the assurance of the subject's anterior knowledge of the object, a knowledge indispensable to his recognition of the truth of the words expressing it.

The second concern of the theory was the function of verbal signs in the mind of the knowing subject. If the subject has a prior knowledge of the object and can measure the accuracy of a verbal formulation by comparing it with the object to which it refers, then the function of language on the subjective level is either indicative or commemorative. The word of the speaker, although it cannot produce knowledge of the object, can point to it if it is not already in the mind of the subject. If the subject already knows the object, the word of the speaker can recall it to him, making it vividly present in his mind.

The subjective facet of this analysis of verbal signification bears a certain resemblance both to the Platonic doctrine of reminiscence and to the episte-mology of the icon developed in eastern Christendom. It also differs from these theories in a number of important respects. In the *Meno*, Platonic dialectic is employed to bring to the forefront of the subject's mind a knowledge which has always been there. [1] In its medieval use, on the other hand, the commemorative function of language recalls to the subject a knowledge of the object which had previously been introduced into his mind at some specific point by the object itself. This is the condition which enables the subject to judge whether or not the linguistic medium is truly significant.

The resemblance of this theory to Byzantine iconic epistemology is some-what less superficial, although, in comparison with visual symbols, the cogni-tive functions of words are wider and more variegated. Icons share with verbal signs an acknowledged real relation to their objects, precluding identity with them. They are likewise designed to draw the believer into a deepened and reawakened mental relationship with the spiritual realities they represent. [2] The effect that icons produce in the subject, however, is strictly evocative. Intended primarily for the use of the faithful in a specifically devotional context, they do not generally lend themselves to the needs of extraecclesiasti-cal polemic or apology. Words, on the other hand, play an indicative as well as a commemorative role in the theory of cognition posited by the medieval thinkers of the west. These western thinkers were faced with two correlative questions. How could a word which they regarded as a *flatus vocis* with no objective referent be used by the nonbeliever as if it were a true *vox significans rem?* Conversely, how could a word which they regarded as a *vox significans rem* be, in the mouth of the nonbeliever or the heterodox, a hollow reverberation or a false note failing to harmonize with the reality as they believed it to be? In contrast to Byzantine iconic theory, the linguistic epistemology formulated by western thinkers was simultaneously extramural and intramural. It extended beyond the realm of devotion because it had to account for the thinking of those outside the church in their encounter with orthodox doctrine. It also turned inward in seeking to explain how words could inspire and sustain their own contemplative experience, and how they could communicate its fruits to their fellow Christians.

In the west, this central theory of religious knowledge was created in the early Middle Ages, and it remained normative until the development of formal logic, starting in the twelfth century and reaching its high-water mark in the fourteenth century, effected a decisive split between reality, thought, and language. Before and outside of that event, however, the *aenigma* of language was generally recognized as the key to the cognition and communication of objective reality. The verbal sign theory of the Middle Ages was translated into the three basic modes of the trivium—grammar, rhetoric, and dialectic— and, at the end of the period, into the mode of rhetorical poetics. From Augustine to Dante, its prime exponents worked in terms of verbal definitions, figures of speech, logical and analogical statements. In their choice of form they took into account the vocabulary of the milieux in which they lived as well as their own intellectual solvency. The distinctive texture of the medieval linguistic epistemology which is the subject of this book was hence a result of the period's corporate response to a uniform mental environment, mediated through the shifting configurations of individual temperament and concrete cultural situation. The concern of this study is to set several major medieval solutions to the problem of the knowledge of God in the historical framework of personality and circumstance which gave rise to them.

One

Augustine: The Expression of the Word

The thought of Augustine occupies a position of central importance in the development of linguistic epistemology in the medieval west. The most profound and prolific of the Latin fathers of the church, in the Middle Ages he became an authoritative source second only to the Bible. Standing as he does at the end of the classical age, he brought his habitual techniques of late antique thought and expression to the problems of Christian theology and pastoral concern. One of the products of this merging of classicism and Christianity was the formation of a verbal theory of the knowledge of God destined to exercise a profound influence in European thought for almost a thousand years. At the same time, he succeeded in presenting, in theory and in practice, one of the basic modulations of that epistemology in the form of Christian rhetoric.

As a professional rhetorician thoroughly trained in the oratorical techniques of Cicero, Augustine already had a philosophy of verbal signification at his disposal before he became a Christian. Derived originally from Platonic, Stoic, and Aristotelian sources, this theory had been welded effectively to the art of exposition and persuasion by the tradition of Roman rhetoric. When he became a Christian, Augustine decided that his intellectual methods would have to be converted as well as his overall objectives. The manner in which he understood this intellectual conversion was thus of seminal importance to his later career as a pastor and a theologian. Augustine's conversion gave him the theoretical foundations for a positive theology. At the same time, it forced him to develop his views on the functions of language in the knowledge of God and in the Christian life. Augustine's speculations on language bequeathed to his medieval successors a clearly outlined verbal epistemology, firmly grounded in both classical language study and the theology of the Incarnation. His extensive writings contain many practical applications of this epistemology. Armed with the works of Augustine, his followers in the Middle Ages proceeded to absorb and to adapt his theory of language in the light of contemporary issues and their own interests. Augustine's contribution to this development was large and twofold. First, he constructed the basic medieval theory of words as signs in the enterprise of acquiring and transmitting religious knowledge; and second, he expressed this verbal epistemology in the mode of rhetoric. Concerned with establishing a theory of knowledge suitable for the work of the theologian and consistent with his own experience, Augustine focused his attention on the problem of the expression of the Word, a problem at the same time posed and solved for him in the first instance by his conversion to Christianity.

Although the theory of signs which Augustine eventually developed was his own creation, he by no means formulated it in a vacuum. In searching for an understanding of words as signs he could draw on the heritage of Greek philosophy as well as on his training in Roman rhetoric. The classical age, to be sure, was not lacking in highly penetrating analyses of language and signification. What was this tradition like? Here, as in so many other areas of philosophical discussion, the first major contribution was made by Plato, and alternative conceptions were offered by Aristotle and by the Stoics.

Plato's view of the function of language in the process of knowledge has both a positive and a negative side. Words certainly play an important cognitive role in his philosophy. Plato's antisophistic insistence that rhetoric should be joined to wisdom and virtue implies the idea that words can adumbrate truth and that they can therefore serve as vehicles of instruction.[1] It is evident from Plato's incessant use of the dialogue form that he considers the spoken word the best method of teaching and of evoking truth. He also confirms this preference in the *Phaedrus*.[2] While, for Plato, words can reflect realities, he nevertheless stresses that words are temporal entities perceived with the senses. Thus they are epistemological underlings, which can be relegated to the category of probability and opinion.[3] Just as time, for Plato, is a moving shadow of eternity, so language is a moving shadow of reality. And if the reality which a word happens to signify is itself transient and sensory, the word is the shadow of a shadow.

In Plato's philosophy, then, language is distinctly ambiguous. The locus classicus for his explanation of this ambiguity is the *Cratylus*. This dialogue includes three speakers: Cratylus and Hermogenes, who maintain opposed and mutually exclusive positions on the subject of language, and Socrates, who moderates between them. Cratylus consistently argues that words refer naturally and necessarily to realities. Names, he says, have by nature a truth. If they did not, it would be impossible to make true statements. Since true statements are in fact possible, names must logically indicate the nature of the things they represent.[4] Hermogenes, on the contrary, insists that the truth of names is by no means automatic. If words were necessarily true, he states, it would be impossible to make false statements; and false statements evidently can be made. The relationship between words and realities is not logical, he argues, but purely conventional and arbitrary.[5]

The controversy between these two speakers is settled, if settlement it may be called, by Socrates. With a bow in the direction of Cratylus, he observes that words do have a logical relationship to reality, as revealed by the study of etymology and verbal classification. All existing things, he says, have their correlative signs and names. The relationship between words and things is one of imitation; and this verbal mimesis would not be possible unless there really were a natural resemblance between words and things.[6] However, he adds, with a nod to Hermogenes, there are some words and letters that are synonymous or homonymous, and in such a case, men may apply them to different things by convention, for the sake of clarity.[7]

Their logical or conventional characteristics notwithstanding, continues Socrates, all words have cognitive limitations. Since they are images, words are metaphysically one step removed from realities. Their mimetic capacities are qualitative, not quantitative. Thus they cannot express their referents totally; if they could, they would be identical to them and would hence no longer be images of them. This limitation is even greater in the case of words that purport to imitate atemporal abstract ideas or ideal forms.[8] There is yet another problem. All realities, as Socrates has already observed, have their correlative signs and names. Words, however, are not similarly privileged. Not all of them have objective referents. In short, it is quite possible to utter gibberish. How can one tell whether or not a given word is truly expressive? Fortunately, Socrates notes, men already possess the transverbal criterion of truth. This observation suggests the principle that changeless realities may be known without benefit of verbal intermediaries. Clearly, the direct knowledge of real existence would be infinitely preferable to the partial and derivative information about it which language supplies. According to Plato, words are transient. But the knower, the human soul, and the supreme objects of knowledge, the ideal forms, are eternal. It would therefore be grossly imprudent for the man of intelligence to place any great confidence in the knowledge he can obtain through words, despite the fact that they may be accurate so far as they go. One who trusts in language, concludes Socrates, "condemns himself and other existences to an unhealthy state of unreality."[9]

For Plato the sensuousness and ambiguity of verbal signs is understood in the context of a philosophy of two worlds, a world of ideal forms and a world of tangible realities, which mirror the ideal forms imperfectly at best. Aristotle also sees signs as sensory, and at times as ambiguous, but for entirely different reasons. The Stagirite is not faced with the problem of bridging the gap between two worlds. He finds one world quite sufficient. It is, moreover, a world which is thoroughly real in itself, and which can be known empirically. This being so, it is no surprise to find that Aristotle regards the signs of sensible realities as themselves sensible, an idea which he illustrates liberally in practice by sprinkling his discussion of signification with examples of empirically verifiable signs, drawn from his wide-ranging studies of natural history. On the whole, Aristotle shows great confidence in the ability of sensible signs to denote realities, and in his epistemology he therefore puts them to work as straightforward inferential tools. At the same time, he admits that signs may be ambiguous. This ambiguity, however, occurs simply because men have a tendency to misinterpret and to abuse signs, or because signs may refer to things which are themselves dubious; it does not indicate any inability on the part of signs to correspond satisfactorily to objective reality.[10]

The context in which Aristotle discusses signs is, in the first instance, logical rather than verbal. He nevertheless by no means divorces thought from language, language being for him the medium in which the logician operates. In order for a sign to be introduced as evidence in a proof, for Aristotle, it must be converted into a statement so that it may be discussed in relationship to other statements. This condition obtains equally whether the sign is natural or conventional. Hence Aristotle's definition of a sign: "A sign means a demonstrative proposition, necessary or generally approved: for anything such that when it is another thing is, or when it has come into being the other has come into being, before or after, is a sign of the other's being or having come into being."[11] The logical form in which Aristotle verifies these demonstrative propositions is the syllogism, whether inductive or deductive: "The proper object of unqualified knowledge is something which cannot be other than it is. . . . By demonstration I mean a syllogism productive of scientific knowledge, a syllogism, that is, the grasp of which is *eo ipso* such knowledge."[12]

For Aristotle the art of demonstrative proof, properly speaking, is the domain of logic. Rhetoric, on the other hand, is the art of persuasion. Rhetoric and logic alike are faculties for providing arguments, rhetorical persuasion being a subordinate branch of logical demonstration. Where logic employs the syllogism, rhetoric employs the enthymeme. Syllogisms and enthymemes differ in that syllogisms deal with facts, which can be established with necessity. Enthymemes, however, generally deal with decisions about actions. They present us with alternative possibilities because of the contingent nature of actions, very few of which are determined necessarily. Although, Aristotle

notes, the propositions on which enthymenes are based are sometimes necessarily true, most of the time they are only usually true. Enthymemes are thus
constructed out of probabilities as well as signs. Probabilities, according to
Aristotle, correspond to propositions that are generally true, if they can be
classified as contingent or variable. The definition of sign which he uses in the
Rhetoric echoes his definition of sign in the *Prior Analytics:* signs correspond to
propositions that are necessarily true.

Signs, Aristotle continues, may be fallible or infallible. The infallible sign
constitutes a complete proof. It has the same relationship to the statement it
supports as the particular has to the universal. That is to say, it necessarily leads
to one, and to only one, conclusion. Syllogisms proper may be based on this
kind of proof; if the evidence adduced by the sign is empirically verifiable, it
will terminate in a scientific and irrefutable demonstration. Conversely, the
fallible sign has the same relationship to the statement it supports as the
universal has to the particular. That is to say, it involves empirical evidence
which may indicate more than one condition, and which thus may lead to more
than one conclusion. [13] While Aristotle does observe that words themselves
may be signs, [14] he is basically interested in significant phenomena or events, as
translated into propositional form, for the purposes of persuasion and demonstration.

Among the post-Aristotelian philosophers, the Stoics developed a sign
theory, a linguistics, a logic, and an epistemology that have some points of
contact with both the Platonic and the Peripatetic schools while displaying a
distinctive character of their own. The Stoic point of departure was a monistic
view of the world, which they saw as permeated by and identified with a deity
that is simultaneously the *logos* of the universe and the creative and animating
pneuma composed of the more rarefied of the material elements. They viewed
man also as a psychosomatic monism, all of whose activities are controlled by a
material pneumatic ruling principle which is a fragment of the divine *logos*. For
the Stoics, matter is fully real and all real beings are corporeal; everything that
acts is a body. Thus they materialized agents, such as God and the human soul,
which Plato and Aristotle viewed as immaterial. The Stoics' physical and
psychological monism is the context in which they elaborated their conception
of language, logic, and cognition. [15]

Human speech, clearly differentiated from the inarticulate sounds made by
animals is, for the Stoics, the expressive side of the human *logos*. Produced and
received by the body, words are acoustic forms, physical realities that signify
authentically the corporeal realities to which they refer. The Stoics thus treat
language as a natural phenomenon. Both the denotations of words, their

grammatical declinations, and their etymological derivations are accurate indices of real being. [16] This position makes the Stoics energetic supporters of the natural versus conventional theory of language expounded by Plato's Cratylus. At the same time, they share Aristotle's confidence that sensible signs, in this case words, can lead to a true knowledge of their significata. The Stoics' chief departure from both Platonism and Aristotelianism at this point stems from the fact that the significata in their system are invariably sensible and corporeal realities themselves. Further, and again in contrast with Plato and Aristotle, the Stoics' theory of how signs are perceived and appropriated by the human mind is located in their psychological monism. For the Stoics the human mind is not the passive recipient of sense data impressed on the organs of sensation by external objects. Nor does the mind possess any innate ideas. All human knowledge results from the interaction between the *pneuma* emitted by sensory objects with the psychic *pneuma* that activates the subject's sense organs and flows from them, producing a material bridge on which the sense data are carried back to the mind. This theory of sensation may be called intromissive and extramissive at the same time because of the double directionality of the *pneuma* responsible for it. The Stoics borrowed the former notion from Aristotle and the latter from Plato and combined them, while simultaneously materializing them. Once the images of sensible objects have arrived in the mind, the ruling *logos* evaluates them, and if it renders a positive judgment concerning their truth, it converts them into *kataleptic* presentations, or knowledge held with certainty. [17] The achievement of this certitude, for the Stoics, involves an exercise of intellect and will that lies within the subject's control. In that sense, the judgmental phase of the cognitive process is not an automatic, reflexive function of the human mind. Unlike Plato, they locate the criterion of truth within the process of cognition itself, not in a realm of transcendent prototypes seen as more real than the sensible objects man knows or the sensible signs by which he knows them. Unlike Aristotle, the Stoics do not see the empirical mode of knowing that they espouse as the pathway to nonsensible realities, since, in their philosophy, nonsensible entities are not real beings. Further, their test of certitude does not entail the capacity of the propositions formed from *kataleptic* presentations to function as terms in a demonstrative syllogism.

This last point reflects the sharp departure made by the Stoics from Aristotelian logic. Their own logic introduces a clear distinction between the referential power of the mental signs with which logic deals and the natural significance of words and other sensible signs. Stoic logic, while it may be regarded as metalinguistic from a modern perspective, is infralinguistic from the Stoics' own standpoint, in that it is made up of entities called *lekta,* which, unlike words, are not real beings.[18] *Lekta* are one subdivision of a group of entities which the Stoics call incorporeals, along with time, space, and the void. *Lekta* are defined as intellectual intentions, having a purely intramental character and validity. But, lacking corporeity, *lekta* do not really exist; they merely subsist. While the Stoics elevated logic to the status of an independent branch of philosophical investigation and developed it with considerable sophistication, they held that the predications, arguments, syllogisms, and fallacies that make it up are composed of *lekta.* The tenability of logical conclusions depends on the internal rules governing that discipline. But, since logical propositions are composed of *lekta,* they do not mirror the real, corporeal world. Unlike words, logical propositions may have meaning, but they do not possess full being. Thus logical constructs cannot be used to discover, to order, or to validate the phenomena of the extramental world. Stoic *lekta,* or intramental signs, may be said to have even greater limits than Plato imposes on sensible signs as means to the knowledge of the real world. And Stoic logic, being strictly formal, cannot function as a connecting link between the intramental and the extramental orders as the logic of Aristotle does.

As we mentioned earlier, Roman rhetoric, as well as Greek philosophy, dealt with the question of words as signs. The most authoritative source of Roman rhetorical ideas is Cicero. In turning from Plato, Aristotle, and the Stoics to Cicero, we move from the realm of philosophical sign theory of the first magnitude to the realm of intellectual transmission. Cicero's ideas on signs are wholly derivative, and, in this case, it is largely Aristotle from whom he borrows. He does so, however, without sharing Aristotle's interest in the relationship of signification to the broader issues of epistemology. Cicero adopts Aristotle's definition of sign as well as the Stagirite's empirical emphasis. "A sign," says Cicero, "is something apprehended by one of the senses and indicating something that seems to follow logically as a result of it: the sign may have occurred before the event or in immediate connexion with, or have followed after it, and yet needs further evidence and corroboration."[19] Cicero retains Aristotle's general distinction between rhetoric and dialectic, the enthymeme and the syllogism, and repeats the further distinction between the probability, the fallible sign, and the infallible sign. For the most part, Cicero restricts his discussion to probabilities and fallible signs. Still, he retains the Aristotelian certainty that signs, including words, may be accurate tokens of the things they represent.[20]

By discussing signs in a primarily forensic context, however, Cicero makes a major departure from Aristotelian usage.[21] While Aristotle views rhetoric as a subordinate branch of dialectic, Cicero subordinates logic to rhetoric, making demonstration ancillary to persuasion. According to Cicero, the orator has three aims, "to prove, to please, to sway."[22] Of these three objectives, persuasion is the most important: "The supreme orator, then, is the one whose speech instructs, delights, and moves the minds of his audience. The orator is duty bound to instruct; giving pleasure is a free gift to the audience; to move them is indispensable."[23] This stress on persuasion seems to have outweighed any interest Cicero may have had in exploring the connections between epistemology and linguistic theory. His treatment of the ambiguity of language typifies this approach. Both Plato, Aristotle, and the Stoics, as we have seen, hold that words or signs may be ambiguous, Plato on the grounds of the relative reality of sensible signs, Aristotle on the grounds of logic and human fallibility, and the Stoics on the grounds of the metaphysical gap between logical intentionality, on the one hand, and language and extramental beings, on the other. Cicero also observes that signs and words may be ambiguous, but he draws no epistemological conclusions from this insight. The ambiguity of language, for Cicero, is simply one of the operative conditions of rhetorical technique. The orator, he says, can and should take advantage of the multiple meanings of words in adapting his presentation to the ethos of his audience and in selecting the style, whether elevated, moderate, or plain, appropriate to the contents of his speech.[24] Indeed, were it not for the ambiguity of language, it would only be possible for the Ciceronian orator to give one kind of speech to one kind of audience.

Cicero's divorce of epistemology from linguistic theory is particularly evident in the *Academica,* where he shows his leanings toward mild skepticism. On the face of it, the primary implications of this view would seem to lie in the field of logic. Cicero, however, is not particularly interested in the effects of skepticism on induction, deduction, and inference. It is the moral consequences of skepticism which concern him. In the *Academica,* Cicero concludes that uncertainty as to what is true forces the skeptic to withhold his assent to the validity of any given moral code. He wishes to prove, further, that this conclusion does not necessarily force the skeptic into a position of apathy or social irresponsibility. The attitude that Cicero recommends to the reader is one of *dégagé* adherence to conventional morality.[25] Throughout this discussion Cicero displays no interest in the effects that Academic skepticism might have in the realm of inference and persuasion. It may be just as well. If he had applied his skepticism consistently to rhetoric, the results would have been disastrous, both to his oratorical technique and to the ethical context in which he places it. His easy assurance that the facts of a case at issue can actually be determined would have been severely undermined, and his insistence on the possibility of uniting eloquence with wisdom and virtue would have been rendered farcical.

Notwithstanding this inconsistency, Cicero's thought was an important ingredient in the classical theories of language which Augustine inherited and one, like others, that was available to him in the Latin tongue. Roman writers such as Varro and Aulus Gellius could communicate the Platonic and Stoic views,[26] while Cicero could transmit Aristotle's sign theory, a theory which Cicero in turn made available within the framework of rhetoric. Outside of his importance as a transmitter of Greek philosophy, Cicero also presented to Augustine and to posterity the classic portrait of the Roman orator, a figure whom we shall meet again shortly, with some modifications, in Augustine's *De doctrina christiana*. Finally, Cicero made a valuable contribution to the discussion of linguistic symbolism in his analysis of figurative language. In the standard list of metaphors and rhetorical tropes which Cicero includes in the *De oratore* we find the term *aenigma*. He defines it as a species of metaphor: "Something resembling the real thing is taken, and the words that properly belong to it are then . . . applied metaphorically to the other thing. This is a valuable stylistic ornament; but care must be taken to avoid obscurity — and in fact it is usually the way in which what are called riddles (*aenigmata*) are constructed."[27] This conception of *aenigma* as a kind of figure of speech, a usage also common in late Latin literature,[28] was to prove extremely influential in Augustine's theory of signification.

The heritage of classical sign theory was, as is evident, both rich and varied, and, as we shall see, Augustine incorporated a good deal of it in his own linguistic epistemology. Yet, for all their richness and profundity, the classical approaches to the question of how signs function in the process of knowledge could not handle the kinds of epistemological problems which beset Augustine after his conversion to Christianity. Augustine leaves no doubt in the reader's mind as to the exact nature of these problems. At the outset of one of his earliest works, the *Soliloquia*, he describes his epistemological aims. At the same time, he portrays the conditions which he thinks are appropriate to them. In book 1 of the *Soliloquia*, Augustine depicts the troubled state of mind in which he had first broached the problem of knowledge. He alludes to his brooding and protracted quest of self, of the good he ought to seek, and of the evil he ought to avoid. At this juncture, the author's reason intervenes. Augustine's reason counsels him to begin by seeking God's aid. He takes his reason's advice.

Prayer clarifies Augustine's thinking; having addressed himself to God, he then finds himself ready to answer his reason's request for a brief statement of purpose:

> R: What, then, do you want to know?
> A: The very things for which I have prayed.
> R: Summarize them concisely.
> A: I want to know God and the soul.
> R: Nothing else?
> A: Nothing else at all.[29]

Both the point in question and the way that Augustine arranges the inquiry in this brief excerpt from the *Soliloquia* neatly define his conception of the epistemological enterprise. The meditation in which he outlines his goal is a dialogue laced with prayer. Despite its title, the *Soliloquia* is not a monologue. Rather, it is an internal conversation, whose speakers are known in and through each other. The objects of knowledge are the participants themselves; their personal communication is both the end of knowledge and its means. Discourse helps to bring their relationship to consciousness, heightens that consciousness, and serves as the vehicle for its external expression.

A note sounded in one of his first works, the idea of cognition through speech became the underlying theme on which Augustine orchestrated the problem of knowledge during a long and diversified literary career. The circumstances prompting him to develop this idea were his conversion to Christianity and his consecration to the tasks of a priest and a bishop. He formulated it by renovating his intellectual heritage of classical eloquence and philosophy to suit the occasions of a new profession and to meet the demands of a new kind of epistemology. Augustine projected a redeemed rhetoric as the outcome of a revealed wisdom. On the basis of this theory, a twofold linguistic transformation was in order: the faculty of human speech was to be recast as a Pauline mirror, faithfully mediating God to man in the present life; and the agencies appointed for the translation of man's partial knowledge by faith into his complete knowledge of God by direct vision were to be redefined as modes of verbal expression.

This new covenant between speech and knowledge was both the link and the point of demarcation between Augustine the pagan orator and Augustine the fluent Doctor of Grace. It is an idea running through his collected works, touching every facet of his theology. Augustine gives his linguistic epistemology express analysis in two of his works, the *De magistro* and the *De doctrina christiana*. An unparalleled illustration of this epistemology in action, however, can be found in his *Confessions*, since his sign theory serves as the structural basis of the work. In the *Confessions*, the spiritual autobiography in which he charts his journey from paganism to Christianity, Augustine links his changing states of self-awareness and his comprehension of the outside world with his growing ability to learn through language and to express himself verbally. The crisis leading up to his conversion, he says, was inspired by his rejection of a sterile rhetoric, which lacked cognitive content and moral relevance, in favor of a rhetoric put to the service of God and men. In the treatment of his conversion itself, Augustine illustrates the function of the spoken and written word as media of revealed wisdom, and he concludes the work with a schematic outline of the various uses of redeemed speech.[30]

When he wrote the *Confessions*, Augustine had been active in ecclesiastical circles for almost ten years and had already set forth his rhetorical theology in some of his earlier works. In his later writings he continued to illustrate in broad strokes aspects of linguistic theory and redeemed rhetoric which he had sketched lightly in the *Confessions*. In the *Confessions* Augustine stresses the importance of learning and teaching through speech and outlines the divinely constituted sanctions and regulations of these processes with all the immediacy of direct experience. Vivid and concrete, the work is also constructed with a degree of circumspection and doctrinal rigor which make it a paradigm of Augustine's idea of knowledge through speech. These same qualities also make it an index of the ways in which he relates his theological pursuits to his epistemology and to one another.

Since the *Confessions* so aptly summarizes Augustine's philosophy of language as well as illustrates his interpretation of his spiritual history, this work is particularly well suited to serve as a framework for our discussion of Augustine's theory of words as signs in religious knowledge. It will therefore be used as the organizing principle of this chapter, with other works of Augustine related to it when they supply his more fully developed views on the matters at hand. This approach will allow us both to appreciate Augustine's own summary of his linguistic epistemology presented in developmental terms and to read the *Confessions* itself in a fresh light, which will also illuminate some of its problematic sections.

From the very beginning of the *Confessions* Augustine makes perfectly clear the manner in which he plans to handle the problem of knowledge. He prefaces the story of his life with a long contemplative prayer. In the middle of this prayer he interrupts himself and ruminates for a moment on the equivocal task of speaking about God: "And what do we say, my God, my life, my holy sweetness; what does anyone say when he speaks of You? Yet woe to him who is silent concerning You, of Whom the most eloquent man stands mute."[31] Set as it is in the midst of a long and fluent passage praising God, Augustine's statement about the poverty of language and his confession of his own literary ineptitude strike a paradoxical note. While the fact that God is ineffable presents Augustine with inescapable difficulties, it does not prescind from the urgency of his mandate to express what he knows; nor, apparently, does it hinder him particularly from doing so. But as Augustine takes pains to suggest even earlier in the *Confessions,* the paradox he has presented here can be understood in terms of a still greater paradox. He directs the reader's attention to the *aenigma* which animates and sustains his attempts to express the Word: "I call upon You, Lord, by my faith," he says, "which You gave me when You inspired me by the humanity of Your Son, through the ministry of your preacher."[32] The crux of the matter is Augustine's faith, its content, and the way he received it. The doctrine of the Incarnation and the manner in which Augustine understands his conversion to it are thus essential to his conception of the redemption of language, which, he holds, makes theology possible. His deliberate juxtaposition of the ideas of Incarnation and expression at the beginning of the *Confessions* is hence a directive. It instructs the reader to pay close attention to these ideas in Augustine's autobiography and in his work as a whole.

Having proffered this advice, Augustine launches forthwith into a description of his period of unregeneracy. This includes his infancy, childhood, youth, and professional career up until his conversion at the age of thirty-three (354–87), a period during which he moves from his native Thagaste to study and then to teach in Carthage, Rome, and Milan. From the very beginning of the *Confessions,* Augustine interprets his moral and intellectual failings in terms of the misuse of his linguistic faculties. The only exception to this rule concerns Augustine as a newborn baby. In this stage of development, he was incapable of perverting his verbal skills, a situation explained by the fact that as yet he did not have any. The infancy which ushered him into the "dying life and living death" of his unredeemed state,[33] he observes, was marked by a lack of conscious life, a condition signified by his inability to speak. As a baby, he says, he could only grasp physically the presence or absence of physical well-being. His inner life seems to have been composed of a random agglomeration of sensations. He was devoid of any awareness of himself as a person who senses, acts, or is acted upon. Although Augustine seems otherwise afflicted with total recall, it is understandable that, for his treatment of this part of his childhood, he is forced to rely on his later observation of babies and the testimony of others about himself at the same age.[34]

As an older infant, Augustine notes, the range of his physical perceptions gradually widened; he sensed, little by little, where he was. At the same time, he began to connect the care of his body with the presence of people outside of it and made his first attempts to communicate with them. His principal concern at this time was the gratification of his physical needs. The incoherent sounds and gestures he was now capable of producing, however, were an ineffectual means of bending his environment to his own will.[35] Referring to his endowments and strivings at the point when infancy was about to give way to childhood, Augustine states, "I existed then and I lived, and, already, at the end of my infancy, looked for signs with which to express my feelings to others."[36] Augustine now possessed being and life, but not consciousness; will and sensation, but no articulate means of expression. He therefore attributes his infant selfishness to original sin, since, in his isolation from the world of words, he lacked the means of conscious knowledge necessary for morally good or evil actions.[37]

Augustine gives a concise description of his passage into the age of reason: "For I was no longer a speechless infant; I was now a speaking child."[38] As a boy, articulate and reasonable, Augustine found himself faced with new moral responsibilities, a challenge which he holds himself to have met without success. He learned to speak naturally, he observes, by listening to his elders, imitating them, and noting their habitual association of certain sounds with certain things. As Augustine analyzes it, learning how to speak and learning how to think go hand in hand. Both, he holds, occurred at the point in his own life when he realized that he existed in a social and religious context. The response he made to this state of affairs, from the vantage point of the Confessions, was morally negative. He regarded his newly acquired powers of thought and language primarily as devices for getting his own way.[39] He resented the fact that he lived among adults who could legitimately prescribe his activities and who could make authoritative demands on him. When his parents sent him to grammar school, he disobeyed his teachers and shirked his lessons, preferring play to study.[40] This childhood peccadillo may seem harmless, but Augustine refuses to discount it, seeing in his boyhood misdeeds the same vices that motivate the serious defections of grown men.[41] His opposition to the will of his parents and teachers sprang less from idleness, he says, than from the pride of self-aggrandizement, the desire to surpass and manipulate his peers, which induced him to steal and cheat in his games and which he refused to admit when detected.[42] At the same time, he opposed his will to God by seeking to manipulate him. In attempting to escape the punishment provoked by his disobedience, Augustine tried to form a vocal pact with God, by which the Almighty might be placed at his disposal: "In calling upon You, I broke the bonds of my tongue, and I asked You . . . that I might not be beaten in school."[43] This request, needless to say, received no answer. As Augustine sees it, he had distorted his faculty of speech on this occasion by praying selfishly. Instead of asking God to help him use his talents fitly, he had arrogantly sought a sanction for his willful failure to do so.[44]

The perversion of language is a defect that Augustine sees in his grammatical studies as well as in his personal life. He by no means regrets that he was taught to read, write, and speak correctly. Nor does he consider these disciplines useless or evil in themselves. Rather, he condemns the grammar schools for teaching such valuable arts through the study of pagan poetry. Augustine explains his rejection of the *auctores* here in terms of their abuse of language and the deleterious morality which he feels that this abuse encourages. The poets, he says, use words erroneously, since they use them to refer to things and ideas which are nonexistent or untrue. Furthermore, he adds, the poets depict ignorant and irresponsible actions in their fictitious characters, who operate in accordance with the unreal universe of the authors' creation. The beauty of this poetry is doubly dangerous, according to Augustine, since it is used to construct a world of shadows and to make the fantastic morality of that world attractive and convincing.[45]

Augustine takes issue with not only the materials used as teaching devices in the grammar schools but also with the grammarians' shallow and formalistic approach to learning. He notes that his teachers devoted more attention to the laws of language than to the conduct of life. Although he was aware that he had moral obligations to others, his training thus led him to be more concerned with avoiding barbarisms than avoiding barbarous behavior.[46]

Augustine's grammatical studies, unsatisfactory from the perspective of the *Confessions,* lasted until he was sixteen years old. By that time, as he surveys his development, his personality had begun to crystallize. His self-consciousness had expanded to include a grasp of the unity of his senses and of his person. His tastes had also begun to form; he notes that he delighted in truth and friendship and that he detested deception, pain, baseness, and ignorance. His education up to this point, he says, had made him well spoken and retentive. But it had provided him with techniques rather than values. His grammar school days had increased his boyhood selfishness and had further deflected his budding talents and aspirations from moral ends. As he approached adolescence, Augustine concludes, his desires for sublimity, pleasure, and truth were to become increasingly directed away from God and toward his creatures, both himself and other men. [47]

At this point in the *Confessions* Augustine takes up a new stage in the story of his life, encompassing the years from sixteen to twenty-eight. During this time he was preoccupied at Carthage with rhetoric, first as a student and then as a teacher. In his progression from grammar to rhetoric, his linguistic abilities were embellished and sophisticated. His ex post facto self-criticism in the *Confessions* grows commensurately in range and intensity. Rhetoric, he states, was taught in as much of a moral vacuum as grammar. Detached from truth and goodness, the eloquence in which Augustine now rapidly excelled became the framework for his rich endowment of intellect and emotion, which he began to misdirect with all the freedom and power of adulthood. In general, Augustine interprets this period of his life as a movement away from divine unity toward a multiplicity of transient and self-centered goals. [48] He subdivides the period into two chronological sections. In the first one, which covers his student years from sixteen to nineteen, he portrays his behavior as a parody on human love and the love of God. In the second part, which includes his professional career up to the age of twenty-eight, he recasts his analysis, stressing the contrast between the temporal and corporeal, on the one hand, and the spiritual and eternal, on the other. In this latter section, too, he gives the first intimation in the *Confessions* of his projected Incarnational reconciliation of love, time, and language.

Part one of this section, the years from sixteen to nineteen, shows Augustine studying a rhetoric clearly devoid of moral considerations. [49] He opens this part of the *Confessions* with the famous affair of the green pears, the wanton theft which Augustine committed with a group of other boys during a year of enforced idleness at the age of sixteen. This crime is at first perplexing. Except for the fact that it enhanced Augustine's status among his peers, it does not seem to fit into his usual catalog of sinful motives. After analyzing it, however, he concludes that this apparently inexplicable misdemeanor is a paradigm of the very mystery of sin. Augustine begins by eliminating the motives that he feels are irrelevant to the theft. He notes that he did not need or want the pears and that he could not enjoy them, since they were unripe; he did not steal out of a desire for power, out of an inordinate longing for attractive things, or out of the fear of losing them. Nor was the act a means to some other end. [50] The sin, he says, lay precisely in the fact that it was an end in itself, committed simply for the joy of a shared wantonness. [51] Augustine sees this love of sin for its own sake as an inverted reflection of the perfect love of God. [52] In both cases what is loved is the object itself, not its by-products. A travesty of the love of God, the theft was also a caricature of Christian charity. Sinfulness, like blessedness, observes Augustine, is not a solitary condition. Both are social in their nature and in their consequences. In this case, Augustine and his companions reinforced each other's downfall by their complicity in evil. Thus their behavior was the perversion of a perfect friendship, whose members reinforce their love of God and of each other through their mutual joy in the good. In its defiance of God's love, in its distortion of human love, the theft of the pears was thus a perfect parody of a perfectly virtuous act.

Having used the pear-stealing incident as an occasion to specify the nature of sin, Augustine goes on to analyze some of the other defections of his adolescence. These acts, he thinks, were characterized by disobedience, the misuse of his faculties, and the distortion of right relationships with other people. They all reflect a mistaken attitude toward God and man. Augustine identifies the motivation of these sins as his desire to please himself and to be pleasing in the eyes of others.[53] He expressed these motives by rejoicing in his body, his emotions, and his mind as ends in themselves.

Two of Augustine's major temptations between the ages of sixteen and nineteen were women and the drama. In interpreting his sexual licentiousness and his fondness for the theater, Augustine finds that the same fault, the abuse of emotion, underlies both of them. Misdirected love also made both of them occasions for the abuse of friendship. His relations with women, Augustine confesses, were not inspired by reverence for their persons. He did not love his partners, but sought instead only the feelings of pleasure that they could produce in him. He quickly grasped that this cult of his own sensations would not yield happiness, for it at once mingled its insatiable sweetness with suspicion, jealousy, and pain.[54] Still, Augustine did not abandon or restrain his sexual exploits. The pain of love, he discovered, has its own subjective attractions; as Augustine loved to love, he also loved to grieve.

He sees his addiction to theatrical tragedies as rooted in the same kind of emotional introversion. Unlike sexuality, the stage produces its stimulus vicariously. According to Augustine, this very artificiality is the key to its perversity. The feeling of grief is sorry enough if one is forced to suffer it in one's own life, he states. If one's grief is aroused by the sufferings of others, the appropriate response is one of outgoing compassion. The theater, however, produces a solicitous relish for the fictionalized counterparts of grief and suffering, encouraging the viewer to turn inward and to revel irresponsibly in the illusion of his own compassion.[55] Thus, argues Augustine, his taste for the theater, like his licentiousness, distorted his personal morality by focusing upon himself emotions of pleasure and pain which should have signalized his obligations to others.

While Augustine interprets his sins of sense and feeling mainly as an opportunity for the selfish indulgence of emotion—although he does note that his licentiousness was also encouraged by the admiration of his peers[56]—his desire for praise and preeminence, he notes, was achieved primarily through his intellectual life. Instead of overriding and manipulating his fellows outside of school, as he had done in childhood, he now fed his ambition by becoming the star pupil in rhetoric.[57] Also, at the age of nineteen, he read the *Hortensius,* a protreptic work by Cicero. This work influenced him deeply, directing his attention to philosophy. Augustine's response to the *Hortensius* can be seen as a parody on his later conversion to Christianity. While the reading of the *Hortensius* inspired him to shift his emphasis from rhetorical form to philosophical content, it did not involve any basic change in his moral attitudes. Philosophy, like rhetoric, appealed to him at this point largely as a discipline in which he could expand his pride of intellect. As he puts it, he broadened the vanity which motivated his rhetorical strivings to include the equally vain desire for a personal immortality of wisdom.[58]

As if to specify the immediate outcome of such a misconception of wisdom, Augustine notes, he became a Manichee at this time. Manicheism seems apposite because, according to Augustine, this doctrine abuses both the form and the content of language. As he describes them in the *Confessions,* the Manichees understand neither the function of language nor the nature of reality. In their mouths, the names of the Persons of the Trinity are *flatus vocis,* since they use these names to designate myths and materialistic falsehoods.[59] As a philosophy with claims to literal truth, Manicheism, he holds, is hence more misleading than the seductive fables of the poets. The latter, although incidentally didactic, are at least useful for constructive training in grammar.[60] Manicheism, on the other hand, lacks the aesthetic and educational values of poetry. As with poetry, it perverts language as a means of communicating the truth and of conducing the hearer to the good, but it lacks the redeeming features of literature, since these distortions can never be excused as unintentional decorations. Thus, he concludes, the Manichees' false notion of God, like the falsehoods of the poets, leads to an unrealistic and distorted morality.[61]

This judgment is based on Augustine's view that an erroneous conception of reality can hinder a person from acting rightly, and conversely, that a person's moral state affects his ability to know the truth, by either permitting or preventing him from recognizing the channels through which it can be known.

At various points in this section of the *Confessions,* Augustine points out a number of these channels and admits that his moral obtuseness held him back as yet from hearing the voice of God through them. Characteristically, he thinks of God's communication to man in terms of speech. God speaks, as Augustine later observes in the events leading up to his conversion, through the precept and example of individual Christians, through Holy Scripture, and through the *magisterium* of the bishops of the church. Augustine deals with precept and example first. He brings forward his mother, Monica, a chaste and devout Christian, who begs Augustine to give up his sexual incontinence, or at least to marry; "and what were these but Your words, singing in my ears through my mother, Your faithful servant?" he asks.[62] Augustine also interprets Monica's dream that her Manichean son would one day join her in the *regula* of Christianity as a message from God, confessing that he thought this piece of evidence foolish at the time.[63] In the first flush of his reading of the *Hortensius,* he picked up the Bible in his search for wisdom, but his literary sensibility made him shrink from the crude style of the inspired writers.[64] Finally, the bishop whom Monica begged to exhort Augustine out of heresy perceived that the youth was too morally beclouded to be teachable and so declined to speak to him.[65] Thus the frame of mind in which Augustine had begun his quest for wisdom had closed his ears to it.

Before developing the next section of the *Confessions,* Augustine stops to summarize the caliber of his moral life at the beginning of the first nine years as a professional rhetorician. He notes that he still loved rhetoric because it brought him praise. Now, however, he intensified his misuse of the faculty of speech by becoming a teacher. He sold the art of persuasion out of cupidity, he says, despite his knowledge that it might well be used by his students for vain and unjust purposes. He also confined his sexual activities at this stage by installing a permanent mistress. Augustine interprets these sins as an expanded version of false friendship, widening the context of his analysis from personal to civic obligations. By failing to consider the values of the eloquence he taught and the uses to which his students might put it, and in shunning the duties of lawful wedlock, he was shirking his social responsibilities. He now sees his behavior as a parody on good citizenship, judging civic life by the same criteria which he thinks should guide personal morality.[66]

As the *Confessions* reveal, Augustine is a man of naturally gregarious habits.[67] He always sees himself as participating, whether morally or immorally, in a community. It is virtually impossible to conceive of him as a solitary and isolated individual. Throughout his life, and especially at its most crucial points, he shows himself surrounded by friends. Before his conversion, he observes, he usually misconstrued the nature of friendship, thus distorting the relationship in some way. In this section of the *Confessions*, the problem of false friendship is as pervasive as ever, but Augustine treats it in a new light. The occasion for the change is the sudden death of a friend whom Augustine had loved inordinately. This loss left him utterly desolate. He responded first by selfishly nursing his grief, and then by plunging headlong into the society of his other friends, attaching himself to them with a love equally intense and excessive.[68] The pain of his first loss had evidently taught him nothing. Friendship, he stops to note, cannot be truly human unless its nexus is the love of God. When a friend is loved in God, he can never be lost.[69] But, he says, he did not possess this insight at the time. Consequently, his inordinate love could only leave him wretched. "I was miserable," he says, "for every soul chained by friendship to mortal things is miserable, and is torn to pieces when it loses them, so that it even feels the misery before it has lost them."[70] The crux of his mistake, he observes, lay in his enslavement to transitory things and in his search for an infinite consolation in pleasures which are good, but which are necessarily finite.

Augustine employs this same contrast between the transitory and the eternal to recast his interpretation of language. Up to this point in the *Confessions* he generally regards his former attitude toward language as perverse, since he had oriented his eloquence to a variety of selfish goals and had detached it from the cognition of reality. But, he says, when language operates as God intended, it functions as a medium of truth. It should be used to deepen one's own knowledge of reality and also for the instruction of others.

But how is it possible for men to use language as God intended? Rightly ordered speech, according to Augustine, is a consequence of the Incarnation. The key to the linguistic epistemology which he posits is Christ, whom he sees as the verbal and actual reconciliation of God and man. To begin with, he notes, speech is a man-made art, which is part of the created universe of time and corporeal nature. Words are transient auditory forms, whose sensuous reverberations are continually falling into nothingness in order to make way for each other.[71] As a means of adumbrating sustained and nondiscursive realities, even on the purely human level, language is thus full of inadequacies. There always remains an opaque residuum of inexpressibility when a man tries to signify verbally his internal states of being.[72] In the face of the ineffable mystery of God, human language labors under crushing limitations. The possibility of intellectual contact with God through words would seem inadmissible. Yet the role which God assigns to speech in the economy of his redemption demands a real and dynamic relationship between language and objective truth. This problem springs from the disparity between divine and human nature. God overcomes it by uniting divinity and humanity in the Word made flesh. In Christ, says Augustine, God speaks to man as man, "proclaiming aloud by words," through the sensible, temporal media of his life, deeds, death, descent, and ascension.[73] The Incarnation conveys the knowledge of God to the world by communicating God himself. It also enables man to respond to God in human terms, by restoring man's words to God in Christ. Augustine explains this central idea most fully in one of his sermons on the Psalms:

Before you perceived God, you believed that thought could express God. Now you are beginning to perceive Him, and you think that you cannot express what you perceive. But, having found that you cannot express what you perceive, will you be silent, will you not praise God? . . . Honor is due Him, reverence is due Him, great praise is due Him. . . . "How," you ask, "shall I praise Him?" I cannot now explain the small amount which I can perceive in part, through a glass darkly (in aenigmate per speculum). . . . All other things may be expressed in some way; he alone is ineffable, Who spoke, and all things were made. He spoke, and we were made; but we are unable to speak of Him. His Word, by Whom we were spoken, is His Son. He was made weak, so that He might be spoken by us, despite our weakness.[74]

For Augustine, then, God creates the world and man through his Word, and he takes on humanity in the Word made flesh so that human words may take on divinity, thereby bringing man and the world back to God. In his redemptive plan, God has already solved for man the problem of his own ineffability. Once joined to God in Christ, human nature is restored in mind and body, and man's faculty of speech is empowered to carry on the work of Incarnation in expressing the Word to the world. For Augustine, redeemed speech becomes a mirror through which men may know God in this life by faith. And Christian eloquence becomes, both literally and figuratively, a vessel of the Spirit, bearing the Word to mankind, incorporating men into the new covenant of Christ and preparing them through its mediation for the face-to-face knowledge of God in the beatific vision.[75]

The solution to man's verbal and moral problems that Augustine intimates at this point in the *Confessions* and expands in his sermon on the Psalms is a retroactive one. It was not part of Augustine's mental equipment in his twenties. There are still several years of misguided activity that he wishes to relate and to interpret linguistically in the *Confessions*. As he observes, his inordinate and by now habitual emphasis on himself and the created universe continued to motivate the burgeoning intellectual pursuits of his twenties. During this period Augustine wrote a treatise on aesthetics, no longer extant,

De pulchro et apto, which he dedicated to a prominent orator whom his vanity urged him to imitate. The aesthetic theory expressed in this work was strictly sensuous, an offshoot of Manichean dualism, which encouraged Augustine to translate a material idea of God into a physical conception of beauty.[76] During these years, Augustine completed his formal education and became a teacher. Graduation, he says, found him mentally well equipped but poorly oriented morally. Philosophy, currently in the shape of Aristotle's *Categories,* continued to attract his interest, but it did not implement his quest for wisdom. He was able to understand Aristotle by himself, which only enriched his pride, while his attempts to understand God in terms of substance and predication, he feels, both demonstrated and encouraged his intellectual blindness.[77] On the whole, Augustine thinks that his ready mastery of the late classical curriculum refined his tendency to delight in his own excellence. Failing to perceive the source of his gifts or the value of his knowledge, he dissipated his accomplishments, neither profiting from them himself nor applying them to the needs of others less talented.[78]

We now move to the climactic portion of the *Confessions,* the section of the work in which Augustine describes the ideas and events leading up to his conversion. Between the ages of twenty-nine and thirty-three, he indicates, his desire for a solution to his intellectual problems became more and more compelling. Under the constant pressure of philosophical criticism, his belief in Manicheism grew weaker, although he still hoped to resolve his doubts within the Manichean system. When Faustus, a prominent Manichean adept, appeared in Carthage for a series of public debates, Augustine listened to him enthusiastically and later interrogated him in detail. He left the debates feeling that his hopes had been betrayed. Although superficially brilliant, Faustus's eloquence, he discovered, was only a mask for the Manichee's ignorance and affectation.[79] Augustine was disappointed, but he was not disappointed enough to abandon Manicheism altogether. A move from Carthage to Rome for the sake of professional advantage at that time entangled him briefly in Academic skepticism. But, for the most part, he retained his association with the Manichees, largely out of habit, despite his increasing dissatisfaction with their interpretation of Scripture, creation, and goodness and their general inability to explain adequately what he wanted to know.[80]

Just at the point when shallow eloquence, fantastic exegesis, and vacuous personal example were beginning to precipitate Augustine's defection from Manicheism, his appointment to the municipal chair of rhetoric at Milan put him in a position to experience these same occasions of knowledge in a Christian setting. He met Ambrose, the bishop of the city, and immediately noticed his warmth and cordiality, an impression that deepened in time into a profound respect for his exemplary life as a pastor and a teacher.[81] Still more impressive was Ambrose's example as a preacher. The bishop was a renowned orator. Augustine was first drawn to his sermons by his rhetorical technique rather than by his teachings. But an alarming change soon began to take place. Augustine was transformed from an observer into a hearer. He grasped the bishop's message, and also the fact that it was inseparable from its rhetorical form: "At the same time with the words, which I loved, there came into my soul the very things that I wanted to refuse. Moreover, I could not separate the one from the other. And, when I opened my heart to receive the eloquence of his speech, little by little the truth of what he said also entered." Particularly gripping for Augustine were Ambrose's expositions of knotty passages in the Bible: "I heard several passages in the Old Testament explained, often figuratively; and when I understood them literally, I was undone."[82] The bishop spoke, the words of revelation were made clear; the listener understood and was spiritually slain. The importance of this episode for the development of Augustine's philosophy of language cannot be overestimated. This experience, his first contact with redeemed eloquence, revolutionized his conception of rhetoric and religion alike. Shaken from his erstwhile prejudiced rejection of Christianity, he resolved to give the church an equal hearing and enrolled himself as a catechumen.[83]

Shortly afterward, an incident took place which substantiated Augustine's new awareness of the function of language in the knowledge of God and which gave that awareness an added dimension. To his surprise, he discovered that his own words could serve inadvertently as vehicles of Christian instruction. One day in his classroom he illustrated the topic under discussion with a satirical reference to the Circensian races. The offhand comment struck to the heart of Alypius, one of his students. The youth took the remark personally and at once wrested himself from the brutalities of the arena, to which he had formerly been addicted. No one was more startled than Augustine in noting that "You made burning coals of my heart and tongue, with which You cauterized and healed this eager but diseased mind."[84] Without having intended it, he found that he had been a mouthpiece for God. He also could see that while moral instruction had come through his words, its effectiveness derived from a source beyond himself.

In the two years immediately preceding his conversion, Augustine experienced a number of occasions—the Christian community at Milan, his companions who were now beginning to act as true friends, moral example, the reading of philosophy and of Scripture, and his own meditation—through which God spoke to him. It will be remembered that he had unsuccessfully encountered many of the same occasions earlier and that he interpreted their function in a similarly linguistic fashion. But now, he says, he was capable of receiving instruction through these channels. He continued to attend Ambrose's sermons and assembled most of the central beliefs of Christianity through the bishop's magisterial eloquence. [85] At the same time, he continued his philosophical inquiries and revised some of his views in the context of friendly debate. In a discussion with his companion Nebridius, the inconsistency of his spatial, quantitative idea of God was laid bare. Nebridius and another friend, Firmianus, were also able to demonstrate to his satisfaction the untenability of astronomical determinism, two positions which Augustine then predictably rejected as using words and ideas falsely. [86]

There remained a major philosophical question to which Augustine now directed his attention—the problem of evil. His discussion of the problem of evil indicates that at this point his Manicheism had already been tinctured considerably by Christian ideas. God, he held, is good; matter is evil. Yet God creates and dwells immanently in the material universe. [87] The difficulty here arises from Augustine's conception of the relationship between God and creation. As immanent, God is in matter, he held. Yet matter is evil. Since God, as identified with the material creation, cannot act against his will, he must therefore will and participate in evil. This conclusion Augustine could not reconcile with his initial postulate of God's goodness. A possible alternative to this inconsistency seemed to be provided by Neoplatonism, with its doctrine of divine transcendence over the transient world of material existence. Augustine began to study the works of the Platonists and was encouraged to note that their doctrine of emanation compared favorably at a number of points with the Christian beliefs he already possessed. In order to determine just how far the truth of Platonism went, to "spoil the Egyptians of their gold," [88] he withdrew to meditate on the Platonic concept of God and on its relationship to the problem of evil. In moments of intuition, he reached the certainty of God as absolute being, immutable, unmixed with evil. With this realization came the certainty that the created universe, including himself, was radically different and separate from God, and that he was still capable of knowing a being radically different from himself, even if briefly. [89] Augustine interprets this intuition, appropriated by spiritual experience, in verbal terms, as he interprets all forms of the temporal knowledge of God. He describes this kind of cognition as the voice of God speaking to him: "I heard, as it were, your voice from on high," he says. [90] The information which this intuition brought him enabled Augustine to solve the problem of evil while avoiding the difficulties of materialistic dualism. The solution he arrived at indicates that his Platonism, too contained a certain amount of Christianity at this point. Since, he reasoned, it has being, order, and harmony, the material creation is good, although imperfect; and it may conduce man to God, since the world is derived from him and reflects his sovereign glory. Evil is not a substance, he concluded, because being is good; rather, it is a perversion of the will—a distinctly biblical notion—whereby men love the created universe with improper reference to God.[91]

But, if Platonism helped Augustine to differentiate the world's goodness from God's goodness, it did not provide him with a way to attain to God in any sustained fashion while living in the world. The Platonists, he notes, lack the doctrine of the Incarnation, by which man may receive the power to share in the life of God in and through the conditions of temporal existence.[92] This is another passage in the *Confessions* where Augustine proffers a retroactive insight. At the point when he was plagued by the problem of evil, he says, he did not have an accurate understanding of the doctrine of the Incarnation. He observes that his current idea of Christ was a rationalization. Thus, he thinks, his attempts to transcend the limitations of creation and human nature through Christ failed because he had created Christ in the image of his own mind.[93] He had not yet realized that in the biblical Christ he would find a focal principle, capable of counterweighing his tendencies toward an immanental pantheism, with its identification of God and the material world, on the one hand, and a Platonized idealism, abstracting God from the material world, on the other.

The final stage of Augustine's conversion, as he understands it, was dependent on his grasp of the Incarnation in the metaphysical and moral order. He achieved this insight when he grasped the meaning of the Incarnation for his own personal life. Two verbal media of God's Word, the Bible and the eloquence of moral example, played a determining role in sealing Augustine's conversion. Just as his metaphysical position dictated the conditions of his ethical philosophy, so his moral state affected his ability to learn about Christ.

Augustine shows himself beset by three moral problems at this time: intellectual pride, the desire for worldly fame, and sensuality. His pride, he says, was dealt with first. Taking up the study of Scripture, he read the Epistles of Paul. As soon as he acknowledged that the apostle's fulminations against pride applied to himself, he began to understand the doctrine of Christ which Paul sets forth.[94] Held back by his desire for fame, however, he still shrank from applying the directives of this doctrine to his own life completely. Appealing for aid to Simplicianus, a circumspect elder of the Milanese Christian community, he learned of the conversion of Victorinus, a famous Roman rhetorician and the translator of some of the Neoplatonic works that Augustine had been reading. When Augustine heard that "the tongue of Victorinus, that great and sharp sword, with which he had slain many, . . . had been taken from him and purified, made fitting to Your honor and useful to the Lord for every good work,"[95] he compared himself, "a vendor of the art of speaking,"[96] to the courageous orator. Victorinus knew of the imperial decree forbidding Christians to teach rhetoric and the liberal arts, and, "in obedience to this law, preferred to abandon the wordy school rather than Your Word."[97] Augustine's own cupidity and desire for professional acclaim were put to shame, he says, and he was overcome by the desire to imitate Victorinus's example.

The third problem, sensuality, still remained. It was not unrelated to the other two. Augustine had already been persuaded by Alypius and by Monica, who had by this time joined him in Milan, to abandon his concubine. As alternatives he saw either marriage or celibacy. At Monica's urging and by her arrangement he had affianced himself to a girl from a wealthy and prominent family, whose position would be an asset in his career.[98] The same alternatives, marriage and celibacy, now stood before him, but he realized that he could adopt neither of them within a Christian ethic if he acted out of selfish motives.[99] Just at this point, Pontitianus, a visiting compatriot, told Augustine the story of the monk Antony, who had undertaken a life of extreme asceticism in the Egyptian desert. Pontitianus also related that a number of prominent young men, counseled by Scripture, had been inspired to follow Antony's example.[100] Contrasting himself to them, Augustine was struck by his own irresolution, his ties to wealth, fame, and sensual pleasure, and his unwillingness to take a moral stand on these matters that would conform to the dictates of his conscience.[101] In this state of internal division, he withdrew to the garden of his home with Alypius, where, self-condemned, he prayed for God's help. The famous cry, "Take up and read," turned his thoughts once again to Antony:

For I had heard of Antony, who was admonished by reading the Gospel which he came upon by chance, as if what he read was being addressed to him personally: "Go, sell all you have, give to the poor, and you will have treasure in heaven; and come, follow Me" [Matt. 19:21]; and this oracle converted him to You at once.

Augustine could procrastinate no longer. He took up Paul's Epistle to the Romans, and the book fell open to the text which specified the solution to his own particular moral dilemma: "Not in rioting and drunkenness, not in chambering and wantonness, not in strife and envying: but put on the Lord Jesus Christ, and make no provision for the flesh in its lusts" [Rom. 13:13–14]. At once he was suffused with the certainty that he could and should live in this way: "At the end of this sentence, a light, as of security, instantly irradiated my heart, and all the clouds of doubt dissolved."[102]

Augustine's conversion to Christianity had been achieved.[103] In his decision to read these biblical words and to accept what they said as the foundation of his personal morality, he assented to the Incarnation as the criterion of his life and his metaphysical and moral speculation. The relevance of Christian ethics and Christian theology would have been unthinkable without the actuality of the Incarnation, and Augustine found that the doctrine and the task required the same humility of spirit. It is this humility, this reverence for the object of knowledge, as well as the alteration of his ideas, which is the keynote of the cognitive experience underlying Augustine's conversion, and his whole theology. And it is through speech — literally, the words of Scripture, and figuratively, the eloquence of moral example — that he grasped a distinctive methodology of knowledge which he saw as a corollary of the distinctive doctrinal content and system of values of the Christian faith.

Many commentators on the *Confessions* come to a halt at this point. After shepherding Augustine safely through his conversion, they seem to lose interest in him. But from the point of view of Augustine's theory of words as signs in the knowledge of God, the last four books of the *Confessions* are as important as the first part of the work, since it is here that he shows how words served to deepen his knowledge of God and to express it to others after he had received the gift of faith. Thus, in books 9 and 10 of the *Confessions,* where Augustine presents himself as a neophyte Christian, he also begins to illustrate the functions of redeemed speech in the Christian life. The first function of words to and about God is prayer, which Augustine describes as a confession of faith and an offering of praise and thanksgiving: "You have broken my bonds . . . I offer You the sacrifice of praise. My heart and my tongue praise You, and all my bones say, 'Lord, who is like You?'"[104] Augustine then depicts the new birth in faith which he experienced as a linguistic rejuvenation. He could now speak to God as unabashedly as a child: "I prattled to You," he says.[105] As a Christian, he no longer found it possible in good conscience to continue the profession of a *vendor verborum,*[106] although legally he might have done so until his baptism. He decided, therefore, to retire with some like-minded friends to a country house in Cassiciacum, outside Milan, so that they could prepare themselves for their reception into the church.

In books 9 and 10 of the *Confessions* Augustine centers his treatment of redeemed speech on its intensifying functions, its role in deepening the believer's knowledge of God and of himself, and its uses in communicating the fruits of contemplation to other believers. The verbal media which Augustine stresses here are prayer, the reading of the Bible, Christian conversation, and the meditation of the believer. It will be noted that all of these channels of knowledge had been significant occasions of grace in the story of Augustine's conversion. He continues to view them as channels of Christian instruction within the Christian life. Or, put another way, for Augustine the Christian life is a continuous process of conversion.

Prayer, largely inspired by the reading of the Bible, and the Scriptures themselves figure predominantly in book 9 of the *Confessions* as types of religious dialogue which help Augustine to know God and himself.[107] Conversation with other Christians is still another verbal means of deepening these kinds of knowledge. Once established at Cassiciacum, Augustine wrote a series of five dialogues, which, he says, reproduce actual discussions that he held with the group or with himself.[108] The *Contra academicos, De beata vita, De ordine, Soliloquia,* and *De immortalitate animae* were Augustine's first compositions as a Christian. Written in the dialogue form and involving the participation of his companions, they reflect his desire to reinforce his faith by philosophical debate, since they deal with a number of currently mooted ethical and epistemological questions which his recent conversion had solved for him on a religious basis. The five dialogues, read in chronological order, also reveal a progressive spiritual growth among the interlocutors themselves.[109]

Even more remarkable is Augustine's conversation with Monica, which takes place shortly after his baptism and a few days before her death. The passage deserves to be quoted at length:

We were conversing together very sweetly. . . . Between ourselves we wondered . . . what the future eternal life of the saints would be like. . . . And when speech had brought us to the point where no sensuous delight and no corporeal light whatever could compare with the joy of that life, . . . lifting ourselves with a more ardent yearning to that life, we traveled gradually through corporeal things and through heaven itself. . . . And still we ascended, by inward thought, by speech, and by marveling at Your works. And we came to our own minds and transcended them, in order to arrive at the place . . . where life is that Wisdom by Whom all these things were made. . . . And while we were speaking and longing for it, we attained it, in some slight degree, with the undivided striving of the heart. . . . Then we returned to the noise of our mouth, where words both begin and end.[110]

During this discussion Augustine and Monica receive a momentary intimation of the joyful state that transcends the created universe, the mind of man, and human language, all of which come into being and pass away. Heaven, they speculate, must be the state in which men can know and love God without the need for the modes of indirect discourse through which He addresses them on earth:

If, for any man, the tumult of the flesh were silent; if the image of the earth, the waters, and the air were silent; if the poles were silent; if the soul itself were silent, and transcended itself by not thinking about itself; if dreams and imaginary revelations were silent—for to him who listens, they all say, "We did not make ourselves, but He Who abides in eternity made us"—if, having said this, they were silent and He spoke, raising our ears to Himself Who made them, not by the voices of angels, nor by the noise of the thundercloud, nor by the riddles of a simile (*per aenigma similitudinis*), but by Himself, Whom we love in these things; were we to hear Him without them, . . . and if it continued like this, . . . would it not be entering into the joy of the Lord?[111]

This passage has a strongly Neoplatonic cast, particularly in its stress on the ascent beyond the temporal and material modes of knowledge to the level of timeless, nondiscursive contemplation through a series of graduated steps. The passage is also strongly Pauline, and it illustrates Augustine's tendency to view all channels of religious knowledge in verbal terms. For Augustine, created things of all kinds, various signs and symbols, are spoken media through which men may know God in this life. They provide the Christian striving to mature in Christ with a means of growth in the knowledge of God on a day-to-day basis. At the same time, the knowledge of God which they afford is necessarily limited, since earthly life is itself limited. Furthermore, it is conditioned by its propaedeutic role. The function of life on earth, according to Augustine, is to prepare the Christian for the vision of God in the life to come. Earthly ways of knowing are necessary, but they have a term. They reach the end of their usefulness in the life of the Christian when he leaves his earthly life and enters into life eternal. Augustine and Monica perceive the quality of this eternal life in their brief foretaste of heaven. In heaven, the things which serve on earth as cognitive channels between God and man fall silent, for their work is done. All languages, whether literally or figuratively verbal, will cease, for the heavenly communion is beyond language.

It is a deep and intimate conversation between Augustine and Monica which is the setting for their foretaste of heaven. From the point of view of Augustine's Incarnational theology, it is through words that we move from verbal to transverbal knowledge of God. As we have seen, a dynamic relationship between God and man is initiated and sustained, for Augustine, in and through the temporal, material conditions of human existence, by virtue of the Incarnation. This in no sense means that in moving from earth to heaven the Christian leaves the Incarnation behind him. In the knowledge of God, Christ is the beginning, the way, and the end. In his repeated encounters with the Christ who acts in time, the Christian grows in the knowledge and love of God through verbal means, broadly conceived. In his eternal communion with God in heaven, the Christian knows and loves the Christ who is at once the timeless principle of creation and the resurrected Lord, through nothing other than himself.

The conversation with Monica which suggests these thoughts, then, considerably enhances Augustine's understanding of the importance of life on earth for the Christian. He portrays his developing spirituality in describing his reaction to the death of Monica. Death cannot be made incidental, and Augustine mourns for Monica effusively. At the same time, he knows now that her death is her initiation into life everlasting, in which Monica, Augustine, and all the saved may be united.[112]

The believer's knowledge of God may be deepened by meditation as well as by conversation. This idea occupies most of book 10 of the *Confessions*. Augustine also takes this occasion to point out that meditation has a social function within the community of believers. The contemplative, he says, must serve others with his voice and pen; he must share his words with others so that all may share the same knowledge and joy.[113] The theology arising from meditation, he explains, helps others by presenting them with the example of the theologian's mind at work as well as with the fruits of its labors. Since it is a way of knowing God, meditation is a form of verbal expression; Augustine defines thought as interior speech.[114] Underlining the contrast between the postlinguistic knowledge of God in eternity and the knowledge of God through speech on earth, he prefaces this meditative section of the *Confessions* by restating Paul's maxim emphatically: "And truly we see now as in a glass darkly (*per speculum in aenigmate*), not yet face to face."[115]

Augustine's meditations in book 10 are concerned with three questions: "What is God?," "How do we know God?," and "Why do we seek God?" He answers the first of these questions in a metaphorical dialogue. In order to establish that God is the creator of the universe, he addresses the earth, the heavens, the self, the whole created universe, asking them if they are God. When necessary, he personifies the respondents so that they can reply, "I am not He; He made me."[116] Next, Augustine takes up the question of how we know God. He solves this problem by turning the discussion back upon himself, centering his meditation on the nature of man, God's most wondrous and mysterious creature. The aspect of human nature on which this meditation comes to rest is the memory, since the knowledge of God can be found within it. [117]

Here follows Augustine's famous passage on memory, a section of the *Confessions* so often interpreted as a rich, though irrelevant, digression. Augustine, however, has good reason to discuss the memory and to discuss it just at this point in the work. He is concerned here with the methodology of the knowledge of God. It is characteristic for him to advise the seeker to look within himself for this knowledge. But, once the searcher's gaze has been directed within, why should it fasten on the memory, rather than on some other faculty of the soul? At the end of the passage on memory Augustine suggests an answer to this question. The knowledge of God requires the use of memory, he states, because it is a knowledge learned as the truth at a particular point in time. Since the time when it was first learned, the knowledge of God, like the rest of man's knowledge, has been stored away in his memory. The memory also makes knowledge accessible, on call, to his present attention. [118] Augustine is attempting to distinguish here between his view, that the knowledge of God is learned in time and is accessible to the mind thereafter through the memory, and the Platonic view, that truth preexists in the mind from eternity and is made present to the mind through dialectically aroused reminiscence. [119]

Augustine's epistemology requires the active participation of the memory in any case. Since he holds that learning takes place through the transient, sensory medium of language, the memory is essential to the existence of sustained cognition of any kind. This notion is one he derived from the theory of man's perception of musical sound originally developed by Aristoxenus, a Peripatetic of the fourth century B.C., whose teachings were transmitted to the Romans by Aristides Quintilianus and used by Augustine in his early treatise, *De musica*. [120] Aristoxenus stresses the empirical nature of music in opposition to the Pythagorean and Platonic view that the essence of music lies in its abstract, mathematical structure. Since individual musical notes are sounds whose reverberations must cease in order for the human ear to perceive the next note in the musical phrase, the faculty of memory is needed so that the subject can retain an entire musical idea in his mind at once, despite the necessarily successive manner in which its individual elements are produced and received. In his *De musica* Augustine repeats this idea and also uses rhetorical formulas for the analysis of music, which reflects his tendency to treat nonverbal signs in verbal terms. In the *Confessions* he expands this doctrine considerably, understanding all forms of signification, thought, and communication under the heading of speech and treating the faculty of memory as likewise necessary in all cases. Here too he states that the memory creates a kind of artificial simultaneity. Words, phrases, and longer stretches of discourse represent, sensuously speaking, a series of sounds, which can neither be enunciated nor received aurally at the same time as each other. Through the memory, sounds which have already ceased to reverberate in time can still be retained in the present consciousness of the mind. Were it not for this function of memory, the receptive powers of the mind would be crippled. The mind would only be capable of perceiving the concrete single sound actually being spoken to it at any given moment. Man's ability to learn and to contemplate would thus be reduced to the intellectual appropriation and retention of things and ideas capable of being expressed in words of one syllable. Of all the faculties of the soul, therefore, the memory is supremely relevant to Augustine's discussion of the methodology of knowledge.

Augustine answers the third question, "Why seek God?," by developing the idea that the knowledge of God is equivalent to the happy life. Indeed, he defines beatitude as *gaudium de veritate,* joy in the truth. All men naturally seek a happiness that can never be lost, he states. If his definition of beatitude is accepted, he argues, it is easy enough to prove that they will find it perfectly in God alone. [121] Augustine's definition of beatitude bears some examination. Joy in the truth is an arresting idea, but from a logical point of view it is slightly out of order. Why should joy and truth be linked in this way? One tends to think of joy primarily in a moral context, as the concomitant of the possession of the good. On the other hand, one tends to think of truth primarily in an epistemological context, as the goal of knowledge. Augustine's combination of these two notions is not accidental. By interweaving truth and joy in his definition of beatitude, he is expressing in terminal form one of his favorite ideas, the interdependence of morality and cognition. Since he stresses this interdependence frequently, it is not surprising that he should conclude his discussion of meditation as a means to the knowledge of God by noting that a deepened consciousness of God will result in a deepened consciousness of the self in relation to God. The better a Christian knows himself, Augustine asserts, the more he realizes his sinfulness before God. [122] The struggle against sin is a permanent feature of his life on earth. Augustine adds a lengthy passage in which he catalogs the various temptations that the Christian must expect to face, organizing them under the Johannine headings of *concupiscentia carnis, concupiscentia oculorum,* and *ambitione saeculi.* [123] The present life, the time of faith, is also a time of trial. This situation, Augustine stresses, should inspire hope rather than despair. The Incarnation, which makes possible the redemption of language on which man's present knowledge and expression of God are based, also encompasses the Passion and the Resurrection, which enable man to die to sin and to live again in Christ. [124] The proximate and ultimate goal of Christian ethics and Christian epistemology, therefore, is newness of life, a life that is both goodness and truth.

Augustine has already outlined the social function of redeemed speech on the intramural level. It commemorates for the believer and his audience a prepossessed knowledge of God, and it raises that knowledge through words to the present awareness of the mind. After his ordination to the priesthood, Augustine notes, the scope of his theological activities widened to include the extramural use of speech, not only in preaching but also in evangelizing men ignorant of God and in attempting to convince his doctrinal adversaries, both inside and outside the church. [125] Augustine gives us a picture of himself as an apologist in those passages in the *Confessions* where he censures the heterodox use of words about God as *flatus vocis*. We are given a glimpse of his budding zeal to correct the putative errors of others with the curious amalgam of solicitude and righteous indignation characteristic of the later Augustine in his polemical stance. [126] Faced with the problem of speaking about God with people who disagreed with him, Augustine was forced to conclude that although redeemed speech may be truly expressive, it is not always completely efficacious in conveying the knowledge of God. [127] Words, he had to acknowledge, have both cognitive powers and cognitive limitations.

In becoming a catechist, an exegete, and a preacher, then, and in assuming the responsibility for training other men for these tasks, Augustine found it desirable to analyze at some length just how extensive these powers and limitations were. He does this most directly in his *De dialectica*, his *De magistro*, and his *De doctrina christiana*. The first two treatises reflect his work as a pedagogue and were written shortly after his conversion, while the latter is a work of his maturity, showing his wish as a bishop to guide his clergy in the arts of biblical hermeneutics and homiletics. All three are of great importance to his sign theory and epistemology. At this point, then, it is desirable to take a detour from the *Confessions* in order to give these works the attention they deserve.

Augustine's first ex professo treatment of verbal signification appears in his *De dialectica*, written, along with the *De musica*, as part of a group of textbooks on the liberal arts which he projected just after his conversion. In the *De dialectica* he presents clearly the Stoic distinction between words as *lekta* and words as natural signs of real beings, using it to underline the differences between language and logic as taught by that school.[128] Speech, he states, is corporeal, while logic deals with intentions, which are incorporeal. A word (*verbum*) is an acoustic form, in contrast to an intention (*dicibile*), which is an immaterial entity perceived by the mind and not by the ear. Intramental intentions, he continues, are the proper subjects of logic. Although *verba* refer accurately to the things they signify, a feature of language that makes etymology a respectable intellectual technique, different meanings can be attached to the same words, a fact resulting from their use by speakers who have different intentions.

Clearly dependent on the *De dialectica* although much less narrowly cast, the *De magistro* is a dialogue between Augustine and his son Adeodatus.[129] Their discussion of the cognitive function of language is prefaced by a description of how words signify. Augustine quickly establishes that words are acoustic signs, which correspond accurately to the realities they represent. This correspondence, however, is partial, and it does not constitute identity with the things signified. Nevertheless, he says, signs are not inferior to their significata. Of all the various kinds of signs, states Augustine, words are the most universally useful and necessary. While other signs can only signify things, words can signify other words as well as things. Indeed, any part of speech can be treated as a name when it functions as a noun in a sentence.[130] Words also adapt more readily than do other kinds of signs to the task of showing the nature of realities accurately, since they can be used to describe the limitations inherent in any given instance of signification, thus helping the reader to correct for error. The real significance of words is so thoroughgoing that a person may even speak the truth without knowing it. It is also possible to tell lies and to make false statements, Augustine notes. But the responsibility for this falls entirely upon men. Lying occurs when a speaker deliberately perverts the true significance of words, and a falsehood is uttered when a speaker errs or is so inept as to define his terms too poorly for them to express what he means to say.[131]

Having described the nature of words as signs, Augustine moves on to discuss their function in knowledge. Speech, he says, serves the hearer either by commemorating or by indicating a knowledge that God provides. In neither case is language cognitive in the first instance:

The import of words . . . consists in this: they serve merely to suggest that we look for realities. These they do not exhibit to us for our knowledge. . . . It is indeed purest logic and most truly said that when words are uttered we either know what they signify, or we do not know. If we know, we recall rather than learn; but if we do not know, we do not even recall, though perhaps we receive the impulse to inquire.[132]

Augustine illustrates the commemorative function of speech in the *De magistro* in terms of two activities carried on by the Christian believer, prayer and the reading of Scripture. Speech in prayer, according to Augustine, is not used to convey information to God, who has no need of this service. Rather, it is used for the benefit of men. It reminds them to whom to pray and what to pray for. It recalls from their memories the reality of God as they believe him to be, and encourages them to rededicate themselves willingly to him. [133] Implicit in this interpetation of speech in prayer is the idea that the believer has an anterior knowledge of God, which his memory stores away for him. This previously acquired knowledge of God is also brought to bear on the believer's study of the Bible. Here again, notes Augustine, the words on the sacred page would have no meaning for the reader without his anterior faith. [134] He reads the Bible to deepen his knowledge of God. He already believes what he reads, but in order for faith to ripen into understanding, the believer depends on the intervention of Christ, teaching him from within. Augustine stresses that Christ distributes this illumination as he sees fit. But, he adds, underlining again the importance of morality to knowledge, only as much enlightenment is granted to each man as he is capable of receiving because of his good or bad will. Before leaving this subject, Augustine also observes that it is necessary to believe many things even though one may not yet, or may not ever, attain to an understanding of them. [135]

The action of Christ, the Interior Teacher, assisted by the words of human teachers, is equally essential in cases where language functions indicatively. Here Augustine brings forward a knowing subject who is not a believer. Unlike the subject in Platonic dialectic, he has no anterior knowledge of God implanted in his soul from all eternity on which to draw. The speaker's words serve only to show him in what direction the realities they represent lie. [136] The subject will not become a believer by perceiving the sign, but by perceiving the reality. This can take place only if Christ wills to teach it to him from within. Nonetheless, human speech remains necessary. Its importance is commensurate to the kind of nonbeliever whom the speaker is addressing. All things that men know, states Augustine, are perceived either through the body or through the mind. With respect to the knowledge of God, the vast majority of men require large quantities of human speech to get them oriented in a Godly direction. The minority need not rely on sensory data in the perception of intellectual entities. They may acquire faith through the reception of God's Word in that inward speech which is personal meditation, rather than by listening at length to other people's descriptions of God. [137] This latter type of person will hence be dependent on an external human speaker to a far lesser degree than the former type, but he will still require some brief indications of Christian doctrine on which to begin his meditations.

In his discussion of Christ as the Interior Teacher, Augustine thus presents a theory of words as signs in the knowledge of God which specifies their status as true, though partial, representations of their objects, and which also clarifies their functions in conveying knowledge to two different kinds of subjects, believers and nonbelievers. Before leaving the *De magistro,* it may be noted that Augustine is so concerned here with emphasizing the links between verbal epistemology and the Incarnation that he assigns to Christ in this work a role that some Christian theologians accord to the Holy Spirit.

In the *De magistro,* as we have seen, Augustine touches on the Bible as a source of the believer's deepened knowledge of God. In the *De doctrina christiana,* his second major treatment of words as signs, he takes up the subject of the Bible at much greater length. There he sets forth the requirements for the biblical exegete and preacher. The work treats verbal signs as means of the discovery of the Word in the interpretation of the Bible and as means of expressing the Word from the pulpit. As one would expect in any work of Augustine's dealing with epistemological matters, the whole discussion is set in the context of morality.

Before elaborating his version of the *modus inveniendi* and *modus proferendi* as applied to Scripture, Augustine introduces the distinction between use and enjoyment. Some things, he says, are to be used; others are to be enjoyed. The things that are to be used are not ends in themselves. They are used rightly only when they are ordered to the things that are to be enjoyed. Actually Augustine only points to one reality that is to be enjoyed—God himself. To the enjoyment of God, the exegete and preacher must direct all his knowledge and talent. [138] In order for him to do this it is necessary for him to purify his soul. In this connection Augustine inserts a résumé of the theology of salvation, concluding with a passage on the church, in which, he holds, it is currently available. [139] The specific aspect of moral regeneration that he emphasizes here is the love of self and of other men rightly ordered to God. For the aspiring exegete and preacher, this virtue involves his commitment to serve God and his fellow man through his words. This task requires the dedication of all his technical skill to the study and teaching of Scripture and the recognition that his motive and the norm of his achievement must be charity, the only one of the theological virtues that endures forever. [140] From the moral point of view, then, these are the principles which Augustine thinks should guide the minister of the Word.

The stage is now set for his unfolding of the linguistic principles on which the ministry of the Word likewise depends. The first question that Augustine takes up is the *modus inveniendi,* the method of acquiring a correct understanding of the Bible. Exegetical technique, he says, depends on the reader's recognition of the facts, events, and words that he finds in the text as signs of divine realities and, in turn, on his treatment of signification as a whole in verbal terms. At this juncture, Augustine provides a definition of sign reminiscent of Aristotle: "A sign is a thing which causes us to think of something beyond the impression that the thing itself makes upon the senses."[141] At the same time, he presents an analysis of signs that owes much to Stoic linguistics, despite the shift in the apposite terminology.[142] There are several kinds of signs, he states: natural, conventional, and linguistic. Of these kinds of signs, words can be applied most generally. Natural and conventional signs are susceptible of verbal description, but words cannot be described with equal success by signs of any other kind.[143] Thus, Augustine concludes, it is possible to reduce signification as such to verbal signification.

In the reading of Scripture, the exegete encounters signs and things. Things, according to Augustine, require no interpretation. They simply stand for themselves and do not signify anything else. Signs, he says, are essentially things, which, in addition to being things themselves, also refer to other things. Their original character as things remains more or less noticeable even while they are functioning as signs. The degree to which a *res significativa* noticeably retains its original character depends on whether it is a *signum proprium* or a *signum translatum.* The *signum proprium* signifies literally. Signs in this category begin and end as words. In their capacity as things, words are sounds, but this original character is, on the whole, subsumed by their significative function. The *signum translatum,* on the other hand, signifies figuratively. In essence it is a nonverbal sign that is conceived in verbal terms by being treated as a metaphor, or a figure of speech with transferred meaning. In practice it retains a large measure of its original character, making the subject aware that it is an independent thing at the same time that it is acting as a sign of something else. Examples of *signa translata* in the Bible, cited by Augustine, are such symbolic objects and events as the lamb and the story of Abraham and Isaac, both of which refer to the Passion of Christ as well as to themselves.[144]

Augustine thinks that *signa propria* may best be understood by the study of languages and textual criticism.[145] Languages are also helpful in understanding *signa translata,* but even more important to the exegete here is a knowledge of arts, sciences, and institutions of all kinds. This factual knowledge will enable him to grasp the similarity between the reality to which the sign refers and the thing from which meaning has been transferred. The exegete is thus licensed to "spoil the Egyptians," to avail himself of the classical heritage, while of course remembering the end to which this knowledge is to be applied. [146] In finding the meaning of a passage in Scripture he should also make use of previous handbooks on hermeneutics, and here Augustine cites Tyconius, a contemporary Donatist exegete, with qualified approval. The principle of charity, which Augustine may have derived indirectly from the exegetical tradition of Philo and Origen, is also invoked. One should not attribute immoral motives either to God or to holy persons, he states; nor should Old Testament figures be held accountable for behavior which enjoyed divine sanction before the Christian era but which has since been proscribed. [147]

Augustine completes the *De doctrina christiana* with a discussion of the *modus proferendi,* the way of expressing one's knowledge effectively. For the most part this is a restatement of Ciceronian rhetoric, but with a new twist. While Cicero recommends the choice of one out of three styles, the elevated, the moderate, or the plain, depending on the content of one's speech, Augustine notes that Christian oratory always deals with subjects having to do with God, which are thus of equal or comparable grandeur. Hence he recommends the selection of the style that will make the speaker comprehensible to the widest possible audience. [148] Cicero's stress on the necessity of persuasion is matched by Augustine's insistence on the preacher's apostolic mandate to teach and his willingness in charity to subordinate elegance to effectiveness. [149] Classical rhetoric relates the orator's ethos to his eloquence, an idea that does not escape Augustine. Aware of the limitations of human language, both in the preacher's understanding of God's Word in Scripture and in his congregation's reception of the Word through his sermons, he concludes by advocating that the Christian teacher reinforce his technical competence with an exemplary moral character and with prayer. [150]

The *De dialectica* shows Augustine's clear grasp of the difference between words and intramental intentions, while the *De magistro* and *De doctrina christiana* firmly anchor Augustine's theory of the function of words in the knowledge of God. As we have seen from our examination of these latter two works, he holds that words may signify God truly, if partially, and that they may signify him literally or figuratively. This signification is literal when the medium of knowledge is verbal in the first instance. It is figurative when the sign is originally nonverbal, but is verbalized by being treated as a metaphor. Whether literal or figurative, no word, for Augustine, conveys the knowledge of God to the subject by itself. The word may make the subject remember God if he is already a believer, or it may orient the subject toward God if he is not a believer. Christ must act in the subject's mind if the speaker's words are to serve as a catalyst, either for his acquisition of faith or for a deeper understanding of what he already believes. By interpreting all signs as linguistic Augustine makes it possible for himself to interpret all cognitive intermediaries between God and man as modes of verbal expression. This conception of knowledge as fundamentally verbal is a central principle of Augustine's theology, and, indeed, it is one of his major justifications for having become a theologian in the first place.

It would be quite possible to construct a verbal theory of knowledge, complete with epistemological guarantees and limitations, strictly on the basis of Christian doctrine. If one brought together, for example, the doctrine of the Incarnation as the guarantee that one's words may truly signify God, Christ's mandate to preach the Gospel to all nations, the Pauline idea that men know God on earth by faith, the idea that faith is a partial form of knowledge acquired through human intermediaries, and the belief that faith is a gift of God, one would have in a nutshell both the apostolic motive for the expression of the Word and its methodological problems. Augustine does, in fact, bring these doctrines together. They are at the core of his verbal epistemology and the verbal epistemologies of his medieval successors. In compounding his sign theory and in formulating it in the mode of rhetoric, however, Augustine drew on the classical as well as the Christian tradition. We have already indicated by way of background the discussions of sign theory carried on by classical thinkers. Some comment on the channels by which these classical doctrines came to Augustine is required, although it should be stated plainly that this matter is a less problematic one than it has sometimes been made to appear.

Augustine repeatedly indicates his familiarity with the Platonic theory that language, as a feature of the transient, sensory world, can be compared, to its detriment, with an eternal, spiritual world in which unmediated communication is possible. He also reflects the Stoic confidence in the capacity of words, as sensible signs, to lead man to a true knowledge of the real world. At the same time, with Aristotle, the real world that he sees as mediated by sensible signs includes immaterial as well as material significata. As is well known, Augustine read substantial portions of the Neoplatonic philosophers Plotinus and Porphyry, Plotinus having been translated into Latin by Marius Victorinus in the fourth century. Victorinus had also translated Aristotle's *Categories,* which Augustine reports having read as a youth. The relevant Stoic materials were available in a number of Latin authors. As a professional rhetorician Augustine was familiar with the whole corpus of Cicero's works and thoroughly conversant with them and was thus in a position to absorb the elements of classical sign theory that Cicero transmits as well as the overall aims, values, and stylistic strategies of Ciceronian rhetoric. Augustine's rhetorical approach to these questions is something that he expresses over and over again, both by precept and example.[151] There is no reason to suppose that those elements of Platonic and Aristotelian sign theory that were not available either in translation or in the work of the followers of those schools were therefore inaccessible to him. An important source of instruction during Augustine's time was the oral tradition as well as the *catenae,* manuals, and doxographies that transmitted Greek philosophy to Latin readers.[152] Equally to the point, while a number of scholars have argued that Augustine forgot the Greek he learned as a schoolboy and read no Greek in his later years, there is much more evidence to support the claim that he refurbished his Greek after he embarked on his ecclesiastical career.[153] While this brush-up of his Greek reflected Augustine's need to familiarize himself with the writings of the Greek church fathers and the Greek text of the Bible for the purpose of theological speculation and polemic, it was equally capable of equipping him to absorb those aspects of Greek philosophy that interested him, whether he did so by way of Greek patristic intermediaries or directly. The debates of the *Quellenforscher* on this question show no sign of abating. But this need not prevent intellectual historians from recognizing the various strains of classical sign theory that play a discernible part in Augustine's thought, whether he mentions his sources by name or not and whether his precise point of contact with them can be proved conclusively or not.

Just as important as the sources of Augustine's classical ideas, however derived, are the uses to which he put them. It is here that the originality of Augustine is most clearly visible. All discussions of signification previous to his time, whether entrenched in a particular epistemology, as with Plato, Aristotle, and the Stoics, or separated from epistemological considerations, as with Cicero, began by analyzing sensible data as signs. Words, as a species of sensible signs, were also analyzed by classical thinkers, but they were not held to be of primary importance. Augustine's theory of signification is the first to have concentrated exclusively on verbal signs.[154] His treatment of other kinds of signs is ancillary; he includes it in order to clarify his doctrine of verbal signification. While he retains Aristotle's definition of sign and the Stoics' doctrine of the natural significance of words, he combines these two theories, reducing all signs to words and using the resultant theory of verbal signs, so conceived, to try to bridge the metaphysical and epistemological gap between Plato's two worlds. As the *Confessions* testifies, Augustine eventually concluded that the Incarnation was the only viable bridge. His theory of sign as word is thus firmly correlated with his Christology, and it is on this basis that he unites those aspects of classical sign theory which he adopts with the Christian doctrines relating to redeemed speech. While, in some respects, this conjunction of ideas sets classical sign theory in a broader context, it also narrows and focuses its range. Since the objects of knowledge which interest Augustine and about which he theorizes are God and the human soul, he limits the application of his sign theory to religious knowledge. This is a type of knowledge which, for Augustine, is acquired less through the natural world as a whole than through man. Thus he did not intend his linguistic epistemology to be either a general theory of signs or a general theory of knowledge.[155] He created it explicitly to cope with the knowledge and expression of the Word in and through human nature.

With the sign theory elaborated by Augustine in the *De dialectica, De magistro,* and *De doctrina christiana* clearly in mind, we may return to the last three books of the *Confessions,* where he brings it to bear on the pastoral activities which he shows himself performing after his ordination. In the *De doctrina christiana,* as we have seen, Augustine lays down his rules for the interpretation of the Bible. Scriptural exegesis is undoubtedly one of his favorite occupations, filling as it does the vast bulk of his collected sermons as well as a number of treatises and tracts. It is also one of the interests that he illustrates in the portion of the *Confessions* devoted to his clerical career. The last three books of the *Confessions* are largely given over to a literal and anagogical analysis of the first few chapters of Genesis. This text was evidently one of Augustine's favorites, or at least one that he considered problematic or important for polemical reasons, for he commented on it on three separate occasions, in the *De Genesi adversus Manichaeos,* the *De Genesi ad litteram imperfectum,* and the *De Genesi ad litteram.* In fact, Augustine's predilection for Genesis has enabled students of his hermeneutical technique to trace his gradual shift from a more to a less figurative type of interpretation.[156] In the books of the *Confessions* devoted to Genesis, Augustine interprets it literally most of the time and is interested in showing that it may have more than one literal sense.[157] He does not neglect to note the commemorative function of language and the role of the Interior Teacher in the study of the Bible.[158]

Augustine's interpretation of Genesis in the *Confessions* is also the setting for his famous discussion of time, a passage which, like the passage on memory, has often been regarded as profound but irrelevant to the work. His analysis of time, however, is clearly connected to his exegesis of Genesis, for it is designed to deal with the question "What was God doing before he created the universe?" Augustine answers that God lives in the eternal present, that time did not exist before the creation, and that the question is hence beside the point. The way in which he arrives at this conclusion is characteristic of his stress on verbal explanations. The reason why the question of God's activities before the creation occurs to people in the first place, he says, is that they think that time comes packaged in three parts, the past, the present, and the future. This preconceived idea is embedded in their minds at an early age thanks to their linguistic training. As children in grammar school they are taught that there are three tenses of the verb, past, present, and future. As a result, they assume uncritically that time itself is likewise tripartite. Actually, observes Augustine, all time is reducible to the present. The past, he says, is the soul's present remembrance; the present is the soul's present attention; and the future is the soul's present expectation. Since this is true for men, he concludes, it should not be so difficult to appreciate the idea of the eternal present when it comes to God. [159]

After interpreting Genesis literally, pausing to discuss the nature of time, Augustine continues with an anagogical treatment of the same text. The anagogical interpretation is one of the three figurative levels of meaning which patristic and medieval exegetes saw in the Bible, in addition to its literal or historical level. [160] The typological application of Augustine's theory of signification is clearly visible in cases where he adopts the fourfold method of scriptural exegesis. In such interpretations, Augustine treats the persons, places, objects, events, and cryptic utterances found in the Bible as *signa translata*. There is only one basic difference between the ordinary run of Augustinian *signa translata* and his typological signs. Typological signs, like *signa translata,* involve the metaphorical transference of meaning from one thing to another. But typological signs also involve the transference of meaning across a span of time or from one mode of discourse to another. In the case of allegorical and anagogical interpretations, all that is involved is the transference of meaning in time. The allegorical method views persons, things, and events in the Old Testament as types of persons, things, and events that occur later, in New Testament times, with particular reference to the life of Christ. The anagogical method views persons, things and events occurring in the Bible as types of the church of the saints at the end of time. In the case of the moral or tropological method, both transference of meaning in time and the shift from one mode of discourse to another are involved. The moral state of the believer in the present time is the point of reference, and that is a state which is subject to change. Hence there is a transference of rhetorical styles, usually from the expository to the hortatory.

Important as it is, Augustine does not see the Bible as the only means by which men can know God in the Christian life. Nor does he emphasize Holy

Scripture to the extent of excluding other means of this knowledge, which he thinks should be associated with it. In the *Confessions,* he links extrascriptural knowledge to cognition through Scripture by including them under the same verbal rubric. For Augustine the reduction of signs to words or to figures of speech has an application that extends far beyond the science of hermeneutics. In fact, he holds that all of man's knowledge of God in the life of faith can be treated according to the very same principle of explanation. When communication between God and man takes place by means of what Augustine regards as words, as in prayer, meditation, intellectual intuition, Christian conversation, the writing and reading of theology, and the reception of the Gospel through preaching, he describes this communication as taking place literally. When the knowledge of God is expressed through things, persons, and actions, such as the mirror of the Trinity in the human soul, the sacraments, confessions of faith, and the witness of Christian example, Augustine regards it as operating figuratively. Whether literal or figurative, he holds, the verbal knowledge of God is correlative to the believer's moral transformation in Christ.

The anagogical interpretation of Genesis with which Augustine opens the last book of the *Confessions* is thus a preface to his discussion of the evangelical, liturgical, devotional, and charitable functions of the church. Elsewhere he defines the church as "the people of God throughout all nations, which is His body, in which are joined and numbered all the saints, who lived in this world even before His coming, and who believed that He would come, just as we believe that He has come."[161] According to Augustine, the function of the church on earth is to transmit the Christian faith to mankind and to bring the faithful to a shared joy in the vision of God, through the medium of language.[162] As we have seen, his definition of language is a broad one. Thus, for Augustine, the church, as the corporate extension of the Word into the present, provides a variety of agencies for the verbal interrelationship of God and man. These agencies are a résumé of the literal and figurative signs in the Christian life described above. This life, says Augustine, begins with faith and baptism, which incorporate the individual into the church.[163] Once enrolled in the church, he gains access to a new language, with new modes of learning and expression.[164] Thus, in the creed, the Christian can profess the faith that he holds.[165] He can deepen and share his faith through prayer, through biblical exegesis, and through theology, "interpreting, expounding, discussing, considering, blessing, and invoking You,"[166] as well as in the communal sacrifice of the Eucharist.[167] This growth in knowledge, Augustine states, must be matched by moral purification, which should be manifested by a vital concern for the good of the church, as a whole and in all her members. This concern should be expressed through charity, exemplary behavior, works of mercy, and the witness to God commensurate to one's vocation in the church. All these practices, he says, strengthen the brethren and show forth to the world the things of God.[168] Christian virtue, he thinks, includes obedience to spiritual authority, in the sense of the norm of faith. The believer should submit willingly to it, says Augustine, even when he does not understand its contents.[169]

It will be noticed that there is nothing particularly unusual either in Augustine's ecclesiology or in his description of the attitudes and practices that make up the Christian life. What is new, however, is the fact that he interprets the various things that Christians say and do in expressing their knowledge and love of God as verbal signs of one kind or another.

According to Augustine, then, the whole of the life of faith provides man with the knowledge of God *per speculum in aenigmate*.[170] Many "words," both literal and figurative, are at work in this process. But of all of them, he singles out one for very extensive treatment—the soul of man. Genesis, says Augustine, presents us with the doctrine of the Trinity, the most imponderable of all Christian beliefs. As an aid to the understanding of this mystery of faith, he adduces the soul of man, the most mysterious of God's creations.[171] This is a line of argument which Augustine touches on only briefly in the *Confessions*, but which he develops at great length in the *De trinitate*, his most mature speculative work. From the point of view of Augustine's sign theory, the *De trinitate* bears comparison with the *De magistro* and the *De doctrina christiana*, even though it is a different kind of treatise from either of them. Each of these three works is important enough to warrant extended discussion in its own right. Also, each of them has a limited epistemological objective. In the case of the section of the *De trinitate* that concerns us most, Augustine confines himself to the question of how God may be known through the Trinitarian analogies in the human soul. Concerned solely with religious knowledge, the *De trinitate*, like the *De magistro* and the *De doctrina christiana*, does not try to present a general theory of language and signification.[172]

In the *De trinitate* Augustine illustrates the strengths and weaknesses of his chosen line of argument obliquely, through the structure of the work, as well as directly. In the first fourteen books, working from the beliefs that man is made in the image of God and that God is triune, he argues that a study of the created trinities in the human soul will enlighten us as to the uncreated Trinity which they signify. Then, in the last book, after summarizing his previous arguments, he systematically breaks down all the Trinitarian analogies he has just established, thereby emphasizing the idea that God transcends all comparisons.

Augustine opens the *De trinitate* with a caveat, reminding the reader of the difficulty of comprehending the changeless Godhead through changeable human speech and stressing the need for faith, spiritual purification, and recourse to Holy Scripture.[173] Books 1 through 7 are then given over to a positive exposition of the doctrine of the Trinity, liberally documented from the Old and New Testaments. After describing the nature of the Trinity *in se* and *quoad nos,* Augustine devotes the rest of the treatise to the question of how the Trinity can be known. The thesis of the *De trinitate* is that man, since he is made in the image of God, can learn about God by examining himself. Augustine supports this assertion by outlining a series of Trinitarian analogies in the human soul. The first one that he presents is the analogy of fraternal love. We cannot love God unless we love our neighbor, Augustine notes, and this love, though one, is also three: "Now love is the action of a lover; and, through love, something is loved. There are three things here: the lover, the beloved, and love. For what is love but a kind of life, which unites two beings or strives to unite them, namely, the lover and the beloved? . . . And thus there are three things: the lover, the beloved, and love."[174]

The terms of this trinity, love, the lover, and the beloved, are discernible when one loves another person. However, when one loves oneself, they would seem to be reducible to two, since in this case the lover and the beloved are identical. Now love of self, according to Augustine, may properly be charitable. A rightly ordered love of self is a precondition of the charitable love of others. But, how can love of self reflect the Trinity if it is not threefold? Augustine solves this problem by pointing to another Trinitarian analogy within the soul of man. Love of self, he says, can be understood in the interaction of the soul, its knowledge, and its love. The soul must know itself before it can love itself, and, concurrently, it must possess the desire of a lover in order to seek self-knowledge in the first place. A second Trinitarian analogy, that of *mens, notitia,* and *amor,* may thus be added to the first one.[175]

By elaborating this second analogy, Augustine provides a further elucidation of the Trinitarian lineaments of the soul's knowledge and love of itself. When the soul knows sensible things, he notes, it forms sensible images of them, which it then stores in the memory and recalls to mind when it wants to think or to talk about them. As an object of knowledge, however, the soul is not sensible. It gains knowledge of itself by intuition, by pure intellection, and it forms a strictly intellectual image of itself. Any self-knowledge which the soul wishes to convey to others it must express through sensible language. The term that Augustine applies to the soul's intellectual image of itself, or its image of any other object known by intuition, is *verbum mentis*. This notion is ultimately of Stoic derivation, going back to the distinction between the inner word, or intramental intention, and the word as outwardly expressed. The inner word is a *lekton*, immaterial and obedient to the rules of thought alone. For Augustine, in the present setting, the inner word's lack of corporeity is an asset rather than a metaphysical liability. When the thinker wishes to communicate his inner word outwardly, he uses the sensible speech which Augustine elsewhere calls *verbum*. Apart from his formulation of this distinction in his *De dialectica,* Augustine had invoked it frequently in other works in which he had considered its semantic implications for such topics as the meaning of negative or privative statements, lies, falsehoods, errors, heresies, fables, and fictions and the significance of words in languages not known to one's audience. Equally to the point, he was aware of the fact that a number of Greek patristic writers had used the same distinction to explore the doctrine of the eternal filiation of the Word in relation to the Word made flesh. While Augustine's use of the term *verbum mentis* as an analogy of the generation and loving contemplation of the Son by the Father within the eternal Trinitarian family may be initially confusing in the light of his definition of *verbum* in the *De dialectica,* the Trinitarian context in which he now develops the theme accounts for the shift in terminology involved. [176]

The interplay of love and knowledge is Augustine's point of departure for his third Trinitarian analogy, that of *memoria, intellectus,* and *voluntas.* In practice, he observes, the memory, the intellect, and the will operate in and through each other; and the soul knows and loves itself through all of them. The soul, he says, gains knowledge of itself through the intellect; the soul retains knowledge of itself through the memory; the soul loves itself through the will. The life of the soul, he adds, is manifested integrally in the activities of its memory, intellect, and will. These three faculties are mutually contained in each other. With the memory, the soul remembers that it has memory, intellect, and will. With the intellect, the soul knows that it knows, remembers, and wills. With the will, the soul wills to will, to know, and to remember. Each faculty independently is hence fully equal to the other two, and each as a whole is equal to all three taken together. Thus, concludes Augustine, the three are one: one life, one soul, one essence. [177]

Up until this point in the *De trinitate* Augustine has concentrated his attention on the soul's knowledge and love of other men and of itself. Now he goes on to note that the soul can also know and love the created universe and God. According to Augustine, the soul, for the most part, comes into contact with the created universe through sensory experience. He stresses that man's physical nature, unlike his spiritual nature, is not made in the image of God. Properly speaking, therefore, man's knowledge and love of physical objects through his physical senses cannot be treated as an analogy of the Trinity.[178] Nevertheless, Augustine finds it possible to suggest in the case of sensory experience two partial and very weak analogies which are Trinitarian, if only because they include three terms which function as one. In this passage of the *De trinitate* Augustine reiterates and modulates the theory of sensation which he had developed earlier in his *De Genesi ad litteram* and which he derived from the Stoics.[179] For Augustine sensation is both an intromissive and an extramissive process, with the soul taking an active part in directing the sense organs toward their objects as well as receiving the data which they transmit back to the mind. In Augustine's theory of knowledge, both the affective and the cognitive faculties of the soul are employed when it lovingly grasps or lovingly contemplates a sensible object of knowledge. When the soul grasps a physical object, the will actively directs the senses to form a sensible image of it. The three terms here are the object, its sensible image, and the will.[180] When the soul contemplates a physical object, the will actively evokes its sensible image from the memory, the three terms in this case being the sensible image, the memory, and the will.[181]

It is, however, in the soul's knowledge and love of God that Augustine sees its interrelated functions of memory, intellect, and will as the best possible analogy of the Trinity. Augustine defines the knowledge and love of God as wisdom (*sapientia*), in contrast to knowledge (*scientia*), a term which he applies to the knowledge and love of created things.[182] Wisdom and beatitude, he states, are correlative, and they are achieved through knowledge. The believer acquires them by virtue of the Incarnation, for God offers in Christ the perfect union between *scientia* and *sapientia*: "For Christ is our knowledge (*scientia*), and the same Christ is our wisdom (*sapientia*). He engrafts faith into us through temporal things; He shows forth the truth of eternal things. Through Him we proceed to Him; we aspire to wisdom through knowledge. But we do not depart from the one, same Christ."[183] As the believer grows in wisdom, as the image of God within him is progressively purified and enlightened, the temporal analogy of *memoria-intellectus-voluntas* is replaced by the eternal analogy of *memoria Dei—intellectus Dei—amor Dei*. In the final books of the *De trinitate*, also, Augustine introduces a shift in this formula, deemphasizing the nouns *memoria, intellectus,* and *voluntas* and stressing instead the verbs *meminit, intellegit,* and *diligit* in order to underscore the idea that the closest possible analogy between God and man can be found in the dynamic activity of man's mental faculties.[184] The action and the process involved represent the believer's transformation in Christ. For Augustine it is also identical to his faithful journey through words to the translinguistic vision of God, and of all things in God.[185] In the state of beatitude, then, the human soul resembles the Trinity as closely as anything can. The three interrelated faculties of the soul have God as their object, and, like the Trinity, the soul in this condition knows and loves God through God himself.

Having built up the foregoing analogies with great care and profundity, Augustine occupies himself with breaking them down in the final book of the *De trinitate*. His aim here is to restate the point that God is ineffable and that he towers infinitely over anything men can say about him. Our knowledge of God in this life, reaffirms Augustine, is partial and shadowy. It is the knowledge of faith, *per speculum in aenigmate,* and it is acquired and expressed through speech. Augustine's use of the term *aenigma* in this connection is quite important. It will be remembered that Cicero defined an *aenigma* as a figure of speech. At the close of the *De trinitate* Augustine also reminds the reader that an *aenigma* is a rhetorical trope, one of the subdivisions within the category of allegory.[186] He describes *aenigma* as "a kind of simile, but obscure and difficult to understand," and adds, "by the terms 'mirror' and 'aenigma' we understand the apostle to have signified certain similes, which are accommodated to our understanding of God, in the way in which this is possible."[187]

As figures of speech go, *aenigmata* are admittedly difficult to grasp. But their very obscurity may also enable them to function as accurate signs. For Augustine, verbal signs, whether literal or figurative, truly, if partially, represent really existing things. While literal signification is a suitable way to express fairly straightforward realities, metaphorical signification is far better suited to express realities that are themselves intrinsically obscure and difficult to understand.[188] An *aenigma,* like any other figure of speech, and like speech itself, is designed to communicate information. Its built-in difficulties thus enhance, rather than reduce, its expressive power. In attempting to convey the infinite incomprehensibility of God, then, an *aenigma* is a most suitable *vox significans rem*.

The specific *aenigma* that Augustine has in mind here is, as we have seen, the human soul, with its various structural and functional similarities to the Trinity.[189] In the context of Augustine's sign theory, the soul, as an *aenigma,* can be treated as a *signum translatum,* a thing acting as a sign. Once he has conceived of it in this way, he can place the same limitations on the soul as an analogy of the Trinity as he places on words as signs of nonsensible realities. Hence he circumscribes the soul as created, mutable, and temporal; it is inextricably bound up with the life of the body; it is subject to the gaps between meaning and being and between being and expression. The soul, he concludes, therefore cannot represent perfectly the eternal, uncreated Godhead, in whom meaning and being, expression and existence, are simultaneous and identical.[190] But, notwithstanding these limitations, Augustine thinks that the *aenigma* of the human soul provides the fullest knowledge of God that is available in the earthly life, a knowledge, he hastens to add, which would remain extrinsic but for the action of God himself within the knower. As a means of summarizing the powers and limits that he ascribes to speech in the knowledge of God, Augustine restates one of the central paradoxes in his theory of knowledge at the end of the *De trinitate.* We can know God as he is only if we become like him, he says; and we can become like him only by knowing him. This appears to be a tautology, but, for Augustine, it is instead a dynamic opportunity, an opportunity which God makes possible by incorporating man into the life of the Trinity through the gift of the Holy Spirit.[191]

As his envoi to the reader of the *De trinitate,* Augustine poses once more the theologian's dilemma, which he also refers to at the beginning of the *Confessions.* In view of the topic that he has set out to discuss, he confesses, he has said nothing of value. Still, he perforce must speak, and so he offers his words to God and to the reader, in a spirit of prayer.[192] Augustine's conception of the problem of expressing the inexpressible, and his response to it, sum up his attitude toward redeemed rhetoric. In his own eyes, it would have been impossible for him to have been a Christian or a theologian without the understanding of the ties between speech and knowledge which the exigencies of his personal life gave him. Once in possession of this understanding, he was moved to formulate it theoretically and to use it in practice in his writings. In doing this, he fused a classical conception of words, both literal and figurative, as the authentic, sensible signs of knowable realities, with the Christian belief that language, redeemed through the Incarnation, was both a necessary and an inadequate means to the knowledge of God. This constellation of ideas is basic to Augustine's epistemology, and it was to become authoritative to many later theorists on the knowledge of God and the problem of theological discourse. Augustine conceived this linguistic epistemology, and, at the same time, he exemplified it in the mode of rhetoric. In his theological writings, and in his very conception of himself as a theologian, Augustine typifies the Christian orator who interprets his vocation as an apostolic expression of the Word.

Anselm: The Definition of the Word

The place of eminence occupied by Anselm of Canterbury in the intellectual history of the Middle Ages has never been in doubt. Both the range of his interests as a theologian, philosopher, and ecclesiastical statesman and the rigor and profundity of his thought mark him as a speculative mind of the highest rank, the first such mind to appear in western Europe since the days of the church fathers. Anselm was also the first thinker since the Carolingian age to make the patristic inheritance fully his own, to rethink it creatively, and to strike out in new directions. If his innovations seem impressive for their suddenness, the questions Anselm addressed can be numbered among the great classic themes in medieval Christian thought—the existence of God, the nature of the Trinity, the Incarnation, Mariology, the foreknowledge and providence of God in relation to the free will of created beings, the theological tension between the Greek and Roman churches, and the respective spheres of *regnum* and *sacerdotium*. He contributed as well to the literature of devotion and to the technical study and teaching of grammar and logic. Anselm had a broad understanding of the theological enterprise. He saw it as nourishing the meditative vocation of the monk and, equally, as informing the church in its apologetic and magisterial mandate, enabling the believer to render a cogent account of his faith to the nonbeliever and guiding the prelate in opposing heresy, schism, and royal attacks on ecclesiastical liberties. Anselm manifested these concerns in a series of writings reflecting his successive and sometimes overlapping roles as a Benedictine monk, the prior and abbot of the Norman abbey of Bec, the archbishop of Canterbury, a political exile owing to his conflict with the crown over lay investiture, and a leading participant at the Council of Bari, convened in the closing years of the eleventh century to set ecclesiastical policy toward the Byzantines in the wake of the schism between the Greek and Roman churches.

Another characteristic feature of Anselm's thought, pervasive throughout his works although it has received a far too restricted appreciation, is his fascination with the problem of the significative capacities of language and his taste for verbal arguments. These traits appear in his theological and nontheological works alike across his entire career and reflect Anselm's successful recasting of Augustine's verbal epistemology in the particular academic terminology of the eleventh century. Anselm's writings supply extensive documentation to support this fact. Yet, regrettably enough, the bulk of the literature devoted to Anselm as an epistemologist and theorist on the nature of theological language has confined itself to the proofs of God's existence found in his three earliest works, the *Monologion, Proslogion,* and *Contra Gaunilonem.* More typical still has been the further narrowing of the focus to the first four chapters of the *Proslogion* and selected passages of the *Contra Gaunilonem,* the latter work being an effort on Anselm's part to refute the criticisms of the *Proslogion* proof set forth by Gaunilo, a contemporary monk from the abbey of Marmoutiers. This deliberate exclusion of the evidence that Anselm's other works provide about his sign theory, his intellectual formation, and his broader theological and philosophical objectives is as unsettling as it is misleading. At the same time, it can be explained, at least in part, as a consequence of the view of Anselm's importance that had become canonical by the end of the Middle Ages. Both Anselm's *Proslogion* proof and Gaunilo's objections to it caught the attention of thirteenth and fourteenth-century scholastics, Thomas Aquinas rephrasing and approving Gaunilo while opponents of Thomism rephrased and supported Anselm. On all sides, however, the arguments for and against the *Proslogion* proof were reconceived in terms of the philosophical language then current, in such a way as to make their force, and even their meaning, increasingly remote from what Anselm had had in mind.

The postmedieval commentators contributed even more substantially to this tendency. The most signal and influential case in point was Immanuel Kant, whose late eighteenth-century reading of the *Proslogion* proof as an ontological argument imposed a cumbersome new burden of anachronism upon its interpreters. Kant succeeded in shifting the grounds on which later scholars attacked and defended the proof for well over a century. While the ontological understanding of the proof was later generally abandoned, the twentieth-century scholars whose continuing interest in Anselm has made publication on the *Proslogion* a growth industry have invoked a barrage of newer, and equally anachronistic, criteria. The point has long since been reached where their inspiration reflects more strongly their desire to discuss each other's versions of the proof than their wish to understand Anselm himself.

While sharply skewed in these ways, the emphasis which Anselm's *Proslo-*

gion has been accorded in the literature still reflects a fact of central importance: this treatise, along with the *Monologion* and *Contra Gaunilonem* with which it is associated, are indeed prime locations in Anselm's oeuvre where he distills the ideas on the cognitive status of theological statements which he treats as well in other works. It is here, too, that he applies most systematically the specific methodology of argumentation which he developed as an expression of that theory. These three works, then, rightly hold pride of place in any consideration of Anselm's epistemology and sign theory. But it must be stressed that a proper understanding of Anselm can be neither achieved nor exhausted by a preclusive concentration on the handful of texts traditionally extrapolated from these works on which so much scholarly ingenuity has been lavished. The proofs of God's existence found in these three treatises are comprehended best when they are read in conjunction with the rest of the works in which Anselm placed them. Further, the task of interpreting the proofs is lightened considerably when the general sense of his verbal epistemology is brought to bear on it. Finally, Anselm's linguistic strategies, in the proofs and elsewhere, can be grasped most fully only in connection with the important changes in the disciplines of grammar and logic that were taking place in the late eleventh century. These contemporary developments gave a particular point and currency to Anselm's theological style and to some of its particular applications. At the same time, they help to explain why the appeal of Anselm's approach declined almost as rapidly after his death as it had arisen in his lifetime and why, when later medieval scholastics revived his *Prologion* proof, his friends were as likely to misconstrue it as his foes.

This chapter, then, has two parallel goals. First, it aims at resituating Anselm's proofs of God's existence, or more accurately, his notion of the signification of statements referring to God's existence and nature, in their literary and historical contexts. Three kinds of contextual reorientation are required, tasks, that, in the body of the chapter, will be addressed in an order inverse to the one mentioned here. First, the apposite passages in the *Monologion, Proslogion,* and *Contra Gaunilonem* need to be read in the context of the entire works in which they appear. Next, these three works must be read in the context of Anselm's oeuvre as a whole, drawing on his other writings for the light they can shed on the objectives and conditions attached to his arguments for God's existence. Finally, Anselm's conception of words as signs in the knowledge of God must be placed in the context of the intellectual milieu in which he studied and taught and to which he spoke. The achievement of the second major goal of this chapter will emerge in the attaining of the first. Anselm's verbal mode of argument and the attitude toward the powers and limits of theological language that appear in his proofs of God's existence and in his handling of related questions will also show his assimilation of the verbal theory of knowledge developed originally by Augustine and, simultaneously, his reformulation of it in a distinctively eleventh-century grammatical idiom.

It will be remembered that in this Augustinian theory of religious knowledge words may represent really existing things truly, if partially, and that they function either commemoratively or indicatively in the subject's mind, depending on his previous relationship to the object. Although seen as an epistemological necessity, verbal signs are never held to be cognitive in the first instance. They must be energized by the action of God in the mind of the knower in order for them to lead to the knowledge of their significata. These conditions obtain whether the subject be an infidel moving from unbelief to faith or a believer whose faith is deepening into an understanding of what he believes.

This Augustinian doctrine of the significative possibilities of redeemed speech, of the warrants and limitations of language with reference to God, and of its cognitive operations and restrictions on the level of the subject had been so thoroughly absorbed in western Christian thought by Anselm's time that it became the implicit and unquestioned ambience in which religious epistemology was conceived. The received tradition of the trivium, moreover, although doubtless a pale imitation of the linguistic arts at Augustine's disposal, served nonetheless to make Anselm's conception of knowledge as ineluctably verbal as Augustine's was. At the same time, owing to the cultural developments, problems, and interests of postpatristic Europe, there was a gradual dissociation of Augustine's theory of signs from the rhetorical context in which he had expressed it. The theory was translated from rhetoric into the mode of grammar, a grammar derived originally from Donatus and Priscian, passed on in diluted form by Carolingian scholars, and growing increasingly rationalized in the eleventh century under the impact of a revived interest in Boethian-Aristotelian logic and in the semantics of the Stoa that had been transmitted in Latin during the early Middle Ages.

The real meaning and importance of Anselm's proof is rooted immovably in these facts of intellectual history. His general ideas of theology and of religious knowledge are derived from Augustine's verbal theory of signs, and the verbal medium in which Anselm himself thinks and works is grammar. Most of his writings, including those containing the proof, manifest his sense of the urgent need to adjust the current notions of grammatical signification to the new and disturbing insights of eleventh-century logic. This quasi-logical grammar is Anselm's basic theological tool; its peculiar, and as events were to prove, highly transitory methods and presuppositions dictate the operative conditions of his thought as a whole. Like Augustine, then, Anselm's major epistemological concern is the theological problem of speaking about God. But, where Augustine sees the task of theology as the eloquent expression of the Word, Anselm sees it as the conscientious and faithful definition of the Word.[1]

The need to survey the immediate intellectual background of Anselm's thought and to establish the contemporary meaning of his famous proof is impossible to deny. It becomes even more urgent when we survey the conflicting interpretations of Anselm which the anachronistic presuppositions of recent scholarship have provided. To place oneself in the hands of most twentieth-century exegetes is to plunge precipitously into a morass of contradictions, which do a fair job of illustrating some of the intellectual concerns of the twentieth, if not the eleventh, century. Categorizing the commentators into the friends and the foes of Anselm is no way out of the maze, because the reasons adduced in favor of the proof by some of Anselm's adherents are freely disparaged by other, equally vigorous, supporters, while those critics holding the proof untenable are as likely to betray antithetical grounds for rejecting it. It is extremely difficult to classify the views of Anselm scholars; this question has itself already become an issue of learned debate. Acceptance or rejection of Anselm's proof has become virtually meaningless as an index of opinion. It has been suggested that Anselm commentators fall into the two groups — or between the two stools — of exaggerated rationalism and exaggerated fideism.[2] While moderately helpful, this rationalist-fideist distinction is still an oversimplification. Before addressing ourselves to Anselm, then, it may be useful to give some indication of the range of modern points of view on his proof; the classical critiques of Thomas Aquinas, Locke, and Kant, on the one hand, and of Descartes, Leibniz, and Hegel, on the other, are too well known to warrant repetition here.[3] While the positions to be cited below are, in our opinion, defective in some way or other, they nevertheless do make some positive contribution to the understanding of Anselm. In most cases they err by perceiving only part of the picture and by mistaking the part for the whole. Notwithstanding the fact that this may lead to conclusions about Anselm so tangential as to be almost irrelevant, each of these commentators still manages to illuminate some central truth about him.

By far the largest group of commentators on Anselm is that whose philosophical or theological presuppositions may loosely be described as springing from the tradition of neoscholasticism. Whether agreeing or disagreeing with the proof, the members of this group possess a vocabulary and a conception of the nature of theological and philosophical problems which derive indirectly from the thirteenth century. Generally speaking, the neoscholastics can be divided into two broad subcategories. The first, who perceive correctly, and with much gratification, that Anselm deliberately tries to argue his proof on extrascriptural grounds, see him in consequence as a "precursor of Aquinas" or as "the father of scholasticism" because of his alleged interest in proving the compatibility between revelation and reason, reason in this context being assumed to mean Aristotelian logic.[4] Anselm's proof thus emerges as natural theology, as an exercise in pure philosophy. Exercises of this type are generally held by the neoscholastics to be cognitive. Anselm is therefore praised for having formulated a heuristic apology for the reasonableness of Christianity, such apologetic criteria being deemed normative for the work of the discursive theologian.[5] Paradoxically enough, this judgment is still capable of being harmonized in some cases with the standard Thomistic rejection of the proof.[6]

The second wing within the neoscholastic camp is composed of scholars who, while adhering to the canon of Aristotelian logic as the normative tool for discursive theology, still manage to grant a cognitive value to Anselm's proof, while simultaneously emphasizing the non-Aristotelian and nonlogical elements in it. This turnabout is accomplished by underlining the scholastic distinction between discursive and speculative theology. Although they do not admit Anselm to the ranks of the purely philosophical discursive theologians, these commentators readily underwrite the value of the proof, on grounds that Anselm is a mystic,[7] and ultrarealist[8] and/or a Neoplatonist.[9] While correct in noting the strongly devotional tendencies in Anselm, these scholars make the mistake of equating uncritically any and all kinds of religious experience with mysticism and thus preserve the neoscholastic assumption that mysticism and logic, Platonism and Aristotelianism, are the only two alternatives for the Catholic theologian and that they are parallel roads which never meet.[10]

The devotional timbre of Anselm's thought to which this latter wing of neoscholastics testifies links them with a second major group of commentators, who manifest neither the presuppositions nor the uniformities of neoscholasticism. Despite their heterogeneity, however, the members of this group are united in assuming the priority of experienced faith as the exclusive and irreducible criterion of all theological positions. They extend this assumption to Anselm either for philosophical or for theological reasons, and sometimes for both. We may find this presupposition expressed in the form of a strictly Kantian rejection of Anselm's proof, on the shopworn allegation that it is an ontological proof.[11] We may also find it underlying the arguments of non-Kantian critics who accept the cognitive value of the proof. We have, for example, an Aristotelian who claims, by a somewhat non-Aristotelian distortion of the meaning of "empiricism" so that it is made to include data beyond the limits of the senses, that Anselm has provided an empirical a posteriori proof based on the evidence of his own psychic experience. [12] An analogous argument, without benefit of Aristotle and without sweeping claims, puts forth the view that the proof is valid on the basis of religious empiricism— valid, that is, on the level of knowledge, although noncommittal on the level of being. [13]

Emphasis on the preclusive authority of individual religious experience and the certainty that it is an authentic guide to exterior realities is heaviest and most intense in the interpretations of scholars whose point of departure is *sola fide* Protestantism. The requirements of this position incline them to see Anselm as a "precursor of the Reformation" and encourage them to reject out of hand any explanation of the proof smacking of pagan rationalism. [14] In modern times, thinkers of this latter school have emerged who applaud Anselm's proof as a nonphilosophical, purely religious foundation for a new, constructive approach to Protestant theology. [15] Moving still farther afield, some of them claim Anselm as a "precursor" of twentieth-century neo-orthodox Protestant "crisis" theology, a position which, oddly enough, reaffirms fideism and excoriates philosophical arguments with a vengeance, notwithstanding its own extensive reliance on categories of thought appropriated from Kant, the existentialists, and the phenomenologists. The leader of this movement is Karl Barth. [16] A similar reliance on Kantian epistemology may also be found, mutatis mutandis, in an interesting discussion of Anselm by Robert S. Hartman. Despite his debt to Barth, Hartman ends by denying the validity of Anselm's proof, terming it a reductio ad absurdum. Nevertheless, for Hartman the proof holds out the tantalizing possibility of being truly ontological, on the basis of an as yet undisclosed "meta-Anselmian axiomatic" matrix, which would make logical modes of predication the criterion of God's existence. [17]

This, however, does not by any means bring our catalog of critics to an end. Another group of commentators to direct their attention to Anselm is one that generally derives its insights and assumptions from logical positivism and linguistic analysis, which, for the purposes of Anselm exegesis, may be treated as one movement. These philosophers are correct in noting the importance of grammar in Anselm's proof; this, indeed, explains why the proof has excited such interest within their ranks. Although claiming to be epistemologists and speculative grammarians, the linguistic analysts tend to make insinuations about the real order, since, in virtue of the limitations which their point of view entails, they are forced to deny the authenticity of anything which proves recalcitrant in the face of their methodological assumptions. Some linguistic analysts reject Anselm's proof, usually conceiving it as an ontological proof, and, as such, inadmissible because ontologism would make existence a predicate. Their insistence on the idea that no existential proposition is true on the basis of its terms alone sounds remarkably like a restatement of the scholastic maxim *a nosse ad esse non valet consequentia.* Despite a shift in terminology, they conclude, as did Thomas, that Anselm's proof is a tautology.[18]

Similar presuppositions also inform critics from this school who support the proof. Their grounds are, simply, that linguistic analysis is concerned only with arguments and not with beings, and that, on the level of argument, Anselm's proof holds so long as it is suitably redefined in empirical, linguistic terms.[19] A peculiar variant of the linguistic analysts' position, finally, is one which holds that Anselm's proof is untenable, that it begs the question, but that it still may be meaningful, or at least useful. It may function either as a consolation to the believer, who is presumed not to need logic,[20] or as a means of making Kantians, logical positivists, and linguistic analysts realize that if they accept on principle that God's existence cannot be thought of as a logical necessity a priori, they must also accept the complementary principle that God's nonexistence cannot be thought of as a logical necessity a priori.[21]

There are two other positions that more or less support Anselm's proof and that do not fit into any of the categories previously discussed. Armando Cicchetti, interpreting the proof as ontological, upholds Anselm on the basis of "the new ontological idealism," a position to which he attaches the authority of Augustine and one which, the reader is not surprised to learn, he holds himself. Unfortunately, Cicchetti does not elaborate the nature of this new ontologism in any detail in his book on Anselm, but the philosophical bias he exhibits betrays his affinities to Hegelianism in its modern Italianate form.[22] Charles Hartshorne also emerges as a qualified defender of the proof. He considers it heuristic, although he does not think that it exhausts God's reality. According to Hartshorne, the proof proves God's being without proving God. "God" is understood here as more than simple being; he is also, and preeminently, becoming.[23] This analysis is set in the context of a Whiteheadean metaphysics, in which the supreme reality is change and development; consequently God, for Hartshorne, can be grasped adequately, but only in part, through concepts that denote static absolutes. The grain of truth which lies all but concealed in these two interpretations is the fact that Anselm did think that, so far as he went, he was saying something accurate about God.

Yet another new trend in the ongoing analysis of the *Proslogion* proof has been to shift attention away from the question of whether Anselm's argument is acceptable according to the canons of twentieth-century philosophy and to move instead to the question of how many proofs there are in that work, where they are located, and which are the most important.[24] A mere sampling of the extensive debates on this issue shows that some scholars find a single argument in the *Proslogion,* located in its second and third chapters read together;[25] others see Anselm developing an argument in chapter 3 distinct from the one in chapter 2;[26] while some see the fourth chapter as the critical one.[27]

It is refreshing indeed to turn from Anselm as seen through the clouded filters of modern critics to Anselm as seen in the context of his own age. Paul Vignaux is quite correct in stating that "St. Anselm did not categorize his work according to our concepts."[28] Gillian Evans is equally correct in emphasizing as the salient quality of Anselm's theology his success in "keeping what he had to say simple and easily comprehensible."[29] For the medievalist, at any rate, Anselm is much more accessible than he has been made to seem by commentators who have sought to reclothe his thought in forms that were not his own. In addressing the problem of theological discourse, Anselm's primary mode of thought is grammar. Just as the Middle Ages has been divided chronologically into an age of Vergil, an age of Horace, and an age of Ovid, so it may also be divided chronologically into an age of rhetoric, an age of grammar, and an age of dialectic, as the disciplines of the trivium gradually replace each other in preeminence over the course of the centuries.[30]

The pervasiveness and importance of grammatical studies between the seventh and the twelfth centuries was a result of two major conditions. The first was the Germanic migrations and the struggle between Islam and Byzantium for the European shore of the Mediterranean. The Lombard conquest of Italy and the Muslim conquest of Spain and parts of southern France led to the waning of civic order and to the closing of the classical public schools in most of the heavily Romanized sections of southern Europe. The result was to shift Europe's intellectual center of gravity from the south to the north, particularly to the British Isles. In practical terms, this meant that, for the first time in early medieval history, the burden of Christian Latin culture after the seventh and eighth centuries fell on the shoulders of men to whom Latin was not a native language. Under these circumstances the immediate relevance of grammar was obvious. Grammar was the introductory subject in the trivium; it had to be mastered before the seals could be lifted from the books of the other arts and before any official business in church or state could be transacted. Thus Rabanus Maurus in the ninth century stresses the importance of grammar in the contemporary curriculum: "Grammar is the science of interpreting the poets and the historians, and the method of writing and speaking correctly. It is both the source and the foundation of the liberal arts."[31] Early medieval educators were not innovators. Their tools for conveying the rudiments of the Latin language to the Germanic peoples were the grammatical compendia of the late imperial period, particularly those of Donatus and Priscian. Often enough the grammars of Donatus and Priscian proved to be too extensive and sophisticated for the uses to which they were put, and they had to be condensed, abridged, and reformulated in scrupulously simple language. Grammar was the favorite topic among Carolingian textbook writers. Their educational efforts can be summed up as an attempt to preserve the grammatical traditions of Rome by progressive dilution,[32] a procedure dictated by the exigencies of the time.

A second reason why grammar outstripped rhetoric and dialectic after the age of the church fathers and transmitters lies in the fact that the principal purveyor of Latin letters in western Europe up to the twelfth century was the Benedictine monastery. The *Rule* of Benedict presupposes literate monks, since one of their standard daily occupations, after the *opus dei*, is *lectio divina*. The meditative reading of Holy Scripture is to be supplemented by the perusal of scriptural commentaries and other edifying patristic works. These activities demand both a prayerful and contemplative attitude toward learning and a knowledge of how to read and to construe the texts. The monastic vocation may be presumed to have supplied the first requirement; for the second, the monks relied upon the classical discipline of grammar. The seven liberal arts were kept alive in the monastery, but grammar remained paramount. It was the means to the understanding of the sacred writings, and so it was intrinsic to the spiritual efforts of the monks. Grammar was even identified with the form of the writings composed by the inspired authors of the Bible. Rabanus Maurus makes this clear in the rhymed preface to his *De clericorum institutione:*

> Know, brethren, what the law requires
> > Which fitly commands us to know the Word of God.
> It asks that he who has ears, should hear
> > What the Holy Spirit speaks in the Church.
> Through grammar the Psalmist brings this to the people,
> > Duly confirming their grasp of the law of God.
> So, brethren, we should strive always,
> > With eyes and ears intent, to learn the Word of God.[33]

Rabanus's contemporary, Smaragdus of Saint-Mihiel, sums up the value of grammar in still stronger terms in his own treatise on that subject. Observing that grammar unlocks the meaning of Holy Scripture and that it is thus the key to real being, he describes grammar as an instrument of salvation.[34]

During periods of monastic reform, when Rabanus and Smaragdus wrote, "good letters" were stressed because they were seen as essential to the maintenance or restoration of accurate texts of the Bible, the liturgical books, the church fathers, and the transmitters. Grammar, which included not merely the knowledge of the Latin language but also the techniques of the gloss, the concordance, and the allegorical method, was the necessary introduction to the science of Holy Scripture. As such, it was quite natural for it to become the basis of the monastic thinker's intellectual style.[35]

Since this was so, it is not surprising to find early medieval thinkers applying explanations drawn from grammatical modes of thought to their discussions of theology and other topics of current interest. To be sure, some tendencies of the earlier rhetorical method survived into the ninth century. Thus, in the Eucharistic controversy between Paschasius Radbertus and Ratramnus Maurus, we find Paschasius supporting his case in favor of the real presence of Christ in the sacrament by an argument that turns on a rhetorical figure, the metaphor involving a transferred meaning. He compares the relationship between the matter of the Eucharist, the bread and wine, and its spiritual content, the Body and Blood of Christ, to the relationship between persons or events in the Old Testament that prefigure persons or events in the New Testament and their New Testament counterparts. Just as passages in the Old Testament may be allegorized in the light of the New Testament while still retaining their literal, historical meaning, he argues, so the matter of the Eucharist remains sensible in the sacrament notwithstanding the change in its spiritual content effected by the consecration.[36] Such rhetorical explanations, however, tend to disappear rapidly from view after the patristic period. Grammatical elucidations of the Eucharist, and of other theological and philosophical questions, are much more typical of Carolingian thought.

Two significant examples may be used to illustrate this point. The first was the debate on the Trinity between Gottschalk of Orbais and Hincmar, archbishop of Rheims, which was a theological cause célèbre of the ninth century. Relations between the two men had already been strained by their opposition in the earlier controversy over predestination launched by Gottschalk and by his repeated evasions of ecclesiastical discipline. Despite their antagonism, the positions on the Trinity taken by both thinkers turn on a grammatical analysis of the terms used to describe or denote God.[37] Gottschalk's argument, based on the idea that the structure of language can and should show forth the structure of being, asserts that a perfect being should be denoted by an abstract noun. Thus, *trina et una deitas* is an appropriate name for the Trinity. The term *trina* indicates that there are three divine Persons while the noun *deitas,* being abstract, shows that they are perfect. If other nouns, such as *pax* or *lux,* are applied to God, says Gottschalk, they must be used in the singular rather than in the plural form to indicate that God is one. For his part, Hincmar rejects the formula *trina deitas* because it uses a singular noun, *deitas,* to denote three Persons. He accuses Gottschalk of equating the grammatical with the metaphysical order, although, at the same time, he himself tries to correlate them. Hincmar points out that the Latin language contains nouns that are singular in form but plural in meaning. A similar convention applies to the adjectives referring to number, including *trina. Trina* can thus be applied appropriately to a threefold subject such as the Trinity, even though it is an adjective that is grammatically singular. On the other hand, the word *deitas* is a singular noun of the type that can denote only a singular subject. Hence, Hincmar concludes, the term *deitas* is inadmissible with reference to the Trinity. While the foregoing debate was eventually settled by episcopal authority rather than by the successful confutation of Gottschalk, it is striking for the belief in the explanatory power of grammatical conventions in theological argument which both contestants display.

A second example of the speculative problems that Carolingian scholars addressed in grammatical terms was the question of how negative or privative language can be meaningful. How can a word like the noun *nihil* have any significance when it has no objective referent? This question itself, and the answer it evoked in the Carolingian era, reflects the continuing influence of Stoic semantics on two points: the idea that words, as real beings, truly represent significata that are likewise real beings, and the distinction between words and *lekta,* or intramental intentions which subsist in the mind but which, as incorporeals, have no real existence. Augustine had raised the same question concerning *nihil* in his *De magistro,* and several ninth-century thinkers, from Fredigisus of Tours to John the Scot, wrestled with it again. Fredigisus devotes an entire treatise to the problem, *De substantia nihili et tenebrarum,* while John addresses it both in his *Periphyseon* and his sermon on the preface of the fourth Gospel, where he treats the theological language appropriate to the *via negativa.* Both Fredigisus and John agree that *nihil* and related terms possess a comprehensible grammatical meaning, as the opposite of *aliud* and related terms, to whatever degree they apply this analysis to the explication of a metaphysics of nonbeing.[38]

A concern with the significance of negative terminology as applied to God persisted in the post-Carolingian age. In the tenth century, Abbo of Fleury compiled a list of difficulties of all kinds in a volume entitled *Quaestiones grammaticales.* In *Quaestio* 21, Abbo deals with a problem in Trinitarian theology, the procession of the Holy Spirit. The Father is unbegotten; the Son is begotten; but the Holy Spirit is neither begotten nor unbegotten. How can this be? Abbo answers this question by first discussing the grammatical effects of negation. A negative statement, he explains, does not always denote unqualified privation. Some negations do signify the complete nonexistence of the things to which they refer. Thus a man called "unjust" is never just of necessity; and a man called "blind" cannot see at all. But, he says, other negations are relative, and do not denote absolute privation by grammatical necessity. Thus not everyone who does not see is blind; and not everyone who is not just is invariably unjust. Abbo's criterion for drawing this distinction seems to be that if a negative word, like *non,* is used in an adjectival phrase, the privative significance of the phrase is relative, but that if the adjective is itself grammatically negative, as in the case of *caecus* and *injustus,* it signifies complete privation necessarily. Now Abbo declares that the Holy Spirit is *nec genitum nec ingenitum.* On the basis of the grammatical principle which he has just elucidated, he concludes that the Holy Spirit, although absolutely unbegotten, is also begotten in a relative sense, since he proceeds eternally from the Father and the Son.[39] Hence, far from being a digression in a book ostensibly given over to matters grammatical, the nature of the Holy Spirit is clearly a theological question which Abbo thinks can be explained by grammatical reasoning.

The tenth century provides us with additional evidence that grammar was called upon to play a role which we might ordinarily expect to find assigned to rhetoric or dialectic. In the year 964–65, one Gunzo, a noted Italian grammarian, was brought from Rome to Germany by the emperor Otto I. During the month of January he stopped at the monastery of Saint Gall. This visit provided the occasion for his *Epistola ad Augienses,* Gunzo's sole extant work and our only source of information about him.[40] It seems that one day Gunzo used an accusative instead of an ablative case ending, a faux pas which raised an outcry among the monks. One of the younger monks, or a student at the cloister school, decided to gloss the lapse in verse. His teacher forwarded this poem to Gunzo, who had already proceeded on his journey, thus beginning the literary feud between Gunzo and Saint Gall which is contained in the *Epistola.* The *Epistola* may seem gratuitously turgid unless one perceives its underlying structure—it is a grammatical treatise converted to the uses of polemic. Although stressing pointedly at the outset that words and grammatical forms, unlike the sense and meaning of the thoughts they express, do not lead one to truth and wisdom, Gunzo nevertheless proceeds to combat his opponent's usage and to confirm his own accuracy in grammatical style. His principal method of argument is quotation. The *Epistola* is liberally sprinkled with choice passages from Servius, Donatus, Priscian, Vergil, Horace, Cicero, Plato, Aristotle, Boethius, Martianus Capella, the Bible, the liturgy, and Gregory the Great, to name only Gunzo's favorites. These extensive citations, in fact, form the bulk of the *Epistola*, and they are adduced to vindicate the correctness of Gunzo's usage. The author intrudes only to arrange the quotations in a plausible sequence and to comment on their contents. Lest the point escape the reader, he affirms in closing that grammar is the basic art. It would be difficult, however, to mistake Gunzo, for throughout the work he has applied the grammarian's technique of elucidating a grammatical usage by reference to hand-picked *exempla* drawn from the writings of unimpeachable stylistic authorities.

This intense interest in grammar continued into the eleventh century, as the incidence of contemporary commentaries on Priscian attests.[41] At the same time, grammatical thinkers were faced by a new problem, which was presented by a revival of interest in the Aristotelian *logica vetus* through the medium of Boethius's translations and translations ascribed to him.[42] There are no traces before the twelfth century of any of the logical works of Aristotle translated by Boethius except the *Categories* and the *De interpretatione*. A treatise on the *Categories* based on Themistius and credited to Augustine existed in the early Middle Ages. It had been known and used since at least 780, although it was far removed from Aristotle's original text. In the tenth century this pseudonymous and inaccurate reading of Aristotle's logic was displaced by an anonymous translation of the *Categories* attributed to Boethius, and, in the first quarter of the eleventh century, by Boethius's own translation of the *Categories*. Scholars in the late tenth and early eleventh centuries were quick to perceive the superiority of these recently available texts. By comparing the anonymous tenth-century translation with Boethius's own version of the *Categories* and with his commentary on that work they were able to reconstruct an accurate Aristotelian-Boethian tradition. This tradition and the manuscript evidence behind it were familiar to such influential contemporary teachers as Notker of Saint Gall, Abbo of Fleury, Gerbert of Aurillac, and Fulbert of Chartres. Some of the same pedagogues were also conversant with Boethius's *Topics*, which includes information on categorical and hypothetical syllogisms. By the late eleventh century the renaissance of the Aristotelian-Boethian *Categories* had been achieved, and manuscripts reflecting this fact were widely available at such major monastic and cathedral schools as Chartres, Corbie, and Fleury in France, Saint Emmeran, Weihenstephan, Tegernsee, and Echternach in Germany, and Monte Cassino in Italy. The interest of so many leading schools and scholars in these materials testifies to the depth and extent of the demand for accurate translations and guides to Aristotelian logic and certainly supports the conception of this period as an "age of Boethius,"[43] philosophically speaking. It is by no means surprising, for example, that the eleventh century should witness the beginning of the realism-nominalism controversy, a problem suggested by Boethius's commentary on the *Isagoge* of Porphyry.

While the potential impact of a revival of interest in the *logica vetus* of Aristotle on philosophy is not difficult to appreciate, it is less immediately apparent why this revival should have created problems for grammarians. Yet, problems it did create, and they were serious ones. The issue centered in the fact that the *Categories* forcibly and inescapably introduced eleventh-century grammarians to the concepts of substance and accident, genera and species. The idea that a given thing might be looked at in a variety of ways called into question the classical definition of the part of speech used to denote a thing, the noun. Previous to this time, the noun had excited very little anxiety in western Europe. Its definition was a fairly standard received tradition, originating in Donatus and Priscian and reiterated more or less coherently by Carolingian writers. Donatus on the noun reads: "The noun is a part of speech signifying the accidence of a thing whether properly or in general. . . . The quality of a noun is twofold, for nouns may be proper or appellative."[44] Priscian recapitulates Donatus: "The noun is a part of speech which distributes the quality of some subject, body, or thing, generally or properly."[45] He adds that "it is proper for the noun to signify substance and quality."[46]

This late classical definition was retained by ninth-century grammarians. Remigius of Auxerre tells us:

The noun is used, in the first instance, to demonstrate a substance. . . . The definition [of the noun] includes several parts. It asks of what number, name, and substance a thing is. It is a part of speech under the surveillance of Latinity. Thus, the noun is defined. As we said above, the definition starts with the genus (*a genere*) and moves to the proper through species (*per species ad proprium tendat*).[47]

Alcuin proceeds more concisely: "The noun is a part of speech, according to the grammarians, which distributes quality to some body or thing generally or properly";[48] and he adds that nouns may be proper or appellative.[49]

The grammarians, in short, assert that a noun defines a thing both substantially and accidentally, both generically and specifically. They lump these two types of designation together, without providing any insights into what changes nominal signification undergoes, if any, when it moves from the one to the other. Boethius, on the other hand, is quite precise in defining these distinctions. In his translation of the *Categories* it appears plainly that nouns do not all signify in the same way. If they signify with respect to accidents, they cannot properly signify with respect to substance, and vice versa. He further elaborates in his translation of *De interpretatione* that a noun must signify one or the other, but not both.[50] Hence the problem: Who is right, Donatus and Priscian or Boethius?

In general, we can say that the testimony of Boethius was accepted, but it was not allowed to overthrow the massive authority of grammar. The Boethian-Aristotelian concepts of substance and accident, genus and species, were integrated into Priscian's theory of the noun by commentators on the disciplines of the trivium in the eleventh century, despite the intellectual contortions which this occasionally required, and the peculiar amalgam of "categorized" grammar that resulted made its way thence into the intellectual gear of scholars and controversialists. It is no accident that the examples of scholarship and controversy most illustrative of the problems entailed by the new grammar of the eleventh century, and the uses to which it was put, are to be found in the works of Anselm, his teacher Lanfranc of Bec, and Lanfranc's principal opponent, Berengarius of Tours. The issues it raised were considered vital to the most outstanding minds of the age.

On the face of it, it is also no accident that eleventh-century monastic thinkers could have made this bizarre amalgam of logic and grammar in the first place. It is worth remembering that the practice of distinguishing rigorously among the seven liberal arts dates from the twelfth and thirteenth centuries, when individual scholars began to specialize in one, and only one, art. We can attribute this development not only to the wider range of classical materials which the renaissance of the twelfth century made available but also to the fact that the most important centers of education had then become the burgeoning cathedral schools and universities. These new schools, which served an expanding urban population and which attracted many foreigners, tended to be much larger than their monastic counterparts, and, unlike them, they were dedicated to full-time study and teaching. The instructors on their enlarged staffs were given specific curricular assignments, on which they were supposed to concentrate all their attention. These academic responsibilities, and their correlative limitations, usually paralleled the level of higher education that had been attained by the individual instructor, and his major field of interest as well. This was especially true of university education, the bachelor's, master's, and doctor's degrees being licenses to teach a particular subject at a particular level. Such a degree of academic specialization cannot be found in most eleventh-century monastic schools. Although, as we have seen, the monks required a certain amount and type of training, education was neither the exclusive nor even the primary function of the monastery as an institution. The average monastery could count itself lucky if it managed to attract or to develop educators with specialized talents; their presence in any number, however small, was by no means a foregone conclusion. While it is true that great houses such as Cluny tended to develop a comparatively large and distinguished staff of teachers, smaller and less eminent houses usually had to rely on the services of one or two instructors, whose responsibilities encompassed all of the arts that were taught.

In the case of the monastery of Bec, which had been founded in 1041 and which was just emerging from relative obscurity thanks to the patronage of several rising Norman barons[51] and the presence of Lanfranc, we find clear-cut distinctions among the arts absent. Lanfranc himself was generally acclaimed by his contemporaries for having relit the lamps of the liberal arts in the west. Even though his educational writings, the *Quaestiones Lanfranci* and the *De dialectica,* which are frequently listed in eleventh-century library catalogs but which are, unfortunately, no longer extant, might lead us to assume that logic was his exclusive speciality, this is not the case. In actuality, he taught all the arts.[52] Anselm also falls into the category of the nonspecialist. If we were to draw inferences from his educational works alone, it would be easy to conclude that he, like Lanfranc, taught only logic. Yet we find contemporaries anxious to send their protégés to Anselm to be instructed in grammar.[53] The lack of academic specialization at the school of Bec is further attested by the description of it, and of Anselm as an educator, left by Ordericus Vitalis, the Anglo-Norman monk and chronicler of Saint-Evroult in the early twelfth century. At first Ordericus seems to regard Anselm as a logician. He describes Lanfranc and Anselm both, in one breath, as "profundi sophistae."[54] Yet, he notes, the abbey school under Lanfranc was led by a generalist, not a specialist. Lanfranc taught philosophy, the liberal arts, and the Bible, producing alumni well versed in both sacred and secular learning.[55] In the same way, in judging the impact of Anselm on education at Bec, Ordericus does not limit his preeminence to any one of the arts:

The fame of this master's learning was spread all over the Latin world, and the western Church was wonderfully refreshed by the nectar of his true knowledge. A great store of learning in both the liberal arts and theology was assembled by Lanfranc in the abbey of Bec, and magnificently increased by Anselm so that the school sent out many distinguished scholars and also prudent pilots and spiritual charioteers, who have been entrusted by divine providence with holding the reins of the churches in the arena of this world. So by good custom the monks of Bec are so devoted to the study of letters, so eager to solve theological problems and compose edifying treatises, that almost all of them seem to be philosophers; and by association with them, even with those who pass as illiterates and are called rustics at Bec, the most erudite doctors (*grammatici*) can learn things to their advantage.[56]

The habit of mind in which the liberal arts were not compartmentalized is faithfully reflected by Ordericus's lack of an exact vocabulary with which to describe learned men or disciplinary specialists in this passage. Given that same habit of mind, it is not difficult to see why late eleventh-century scholars should have injected Aristotelian ideas into grammar, or why logical as well as theological works should reveal a grammatical bias in this period.

It has been observed that Lanfranc and Berengarius of Tours, two of the most important theological controversialists of the late eleventh century, were grammarians at heart. This fact has been brought into clear focus by Margaret Gibson's study of Lanfranc's grammatical approach to theology, from doctrinal debate to Biblical exegesis,[57] and by R. W. Southern's analysis of Lanfranc's conflict with Berengarius over the real presence of Christ in the Eucharist.[58] For our purposes the most interesting aspect of this controversy is the opponents' style of argument, rather than their teachings on sacramental theology. Berengarius's case against the doctrine of the real presence is a manifest expression of the new Aristotelianized grammar. It turns entirely on the difference between nouns and pronouns, a distinction which the idea of substance and accidents had forced grammarians to accept. The current view was that a noun, with a nod to Priscian, signifies its object substantially and accidentally, but that a pronoun, *pace* Boethius, signifies its object only substantially. A pronoun has the grammatical function of standing for a noun in a sentence. However, it does not share the significative function of the noun which it replaces; in order to signify a thing both substantially and accidently, it would have to be a noun itself. Since a pronoun is only a grammatical substitute for a noun, it can signify the object bequeathed to it by the noun it replaces only substantially, but not accidently as well.[59]

Now what relationship does this theory of the pronoun have to the Eucharist? Berengarius's whole argument turns on an analysis of the formula which the celebrant uses to consecrate the Eucharist during the mass, "Hoc est enim corpus meum." Now "hoc" in this sentence is a pronoun, and its grammatical function is to signify the Eucharistic bread on the altar. "Corpus," signifying Christ's body, is, to be sure, a noun. However, it functions as a predicate nominative in the sentence, and, as such, is controlled by "hoc," the subject of the sentence, with which it must agree. Since the pronoun "hoc" has limited significative possibilities, good grammar dictates that these limitations must also extend to "corpus" in the context of the sentence. If, as the opposition claims, the substance of the bread were actually changed into Christ's body during the consecration, the subject of the sentence would be annulled and destroyed by its own predicate nominative, a manifest grammatical impossibility.

Formidable as this argument must have seemed to thinkers well schooled in eleventh-century grammar, it did not daunt Lanfranc. He developed on his own behalf a rebuttal of Berengarius which is equally verbal in nature. This rebuttal is particularly interesting as an index of Lanfranc's mentality. While it is ostensibly logical, it is in fact based on grammar. Logic, for Lanfranc, does not automatically connote the apparatus of the syllogism. Instead, his argument employs a term and a technique which he calls "equipollent propositions."[60] Lanfranc is the first medieval thinker known to have used this term and mode of argument. Its ultimate provenance is thought to be Apuleius, a Platonist of the Middle Academy born about A.D. 125, whose work, according to Southern, was coming into use in the eleventh century. Equipollency means the detection of equivalent forms of a proposition. If equivalent forms can be produced, the initial proposition is conceded to have earned more cognitive weight than it had before. In an argument carried on by the use of equipollency, the speaker's aim is therefore to demonstrate this equivalency. He does this by taking a proposition and redefining it several times, each time expanding, focusing, or channeling the definition so that, when the final definition has been reached, the initial proposition has actually been converted into the one to which he wishes to prove it is equivalent. In short, this redefinition of a given proposition replaces it bit by bit with equivalent propositions, until it literally becomes what one is trying to prove it to be. The way in which an equipollent proof functions may be clarified by contrasting it with a diagram of the classic syllogistic proof. Where the syllogism would read:

> All A is D,
> But B is A
> Therefore all B is D

the equipollent proof would read:

> $A = B = C = D$
> Therefore $A = D$.

To the modern mind Lanfranc's method may appear to be no more compelling than Berengarius's. However, contemporaries found both arguments convincing, a fact which stems largely from the prominence of grammar in each proof. Berengarius, as we have seen, is dependent on the new theory of the pronoun conceived by eleventh-century grammarians under the impact of the *Categories*. Lanfranc is dependent on grammar in the more general sense of the word. His approach has clear affinities to the monastic grammarians' method of elucidating a text or an individual word,[61] and he shares their confidence in the significative power of the noun by assuming that definition in itself is somehow not only explanatory but intellectually convincing.

The controversy between Berengarius and Lanfranc was at its peak when the young Anselm left his native Aosta and went to Bec to study with Lanfranc. Anselm was thus in an excellent position to familiarize himself with the methods of both of the disputants, an opportunity which he did not waste. Although he towers over Berengarius and Lanfranc in ability and in theological importance, he learned a great deal from both of them; it is thus incorrect to describe him as "a sudden emergence, a Melchisedech without father or mother or genealogy."[62] Southern has made the trenchant suggestion that Anselm may be an even better source of examples of the equipollency technique than Lanfranc, and that he shared Berengarius's concern with developing proofs according to the contemporary rules of language.[63] It is this suggestion that remains to be documented in detail. Anselm was a man of his times; the problems of the new grammar were ones that he studied and wrote about as an educator, and the methods it provided were the tools he used in his famous proof and throughout his theological writings as a whole.

In using language as a tool, Anselm treats it less as a universal criterion than as a means of solving the particular problems that interest him, whether in the liberal arts, philosophy, or theology. He is not concerned with developing a linguistic theory as an end in itself. Nor does he apply linguistic modes of analysis uniformly to every issue he addresses. His approach is multiform, and he feels perfectly free to use different and even antithetical strategies of argument in different contexts, sometimes in passages within the same treatises, depending on what he thinks will be most helpful in resolving the particular dilemma before him.[64] While, in this sense, Anselm is certainly unsystematic as a philosopher of language, he shows at the same time a considerable sensitivity to the internal semantic issues and difficulties connected with the use of contemporary Latin as an instrument of philosophical and theological reasoning, a sensitivity that sees him searching for a precise, technical, and artificial language, even a metalanguage, that transcends the limits and ambiguities of the ordinary *usus loquendi*. Anselm does not hesitate to coin neologisms, such as the world *pervelle* in his *De casu diaboli,* although they may be barbarisms according to the contemporary grammatical rules, if they express his meaning more clearly; he argues that meaning is more important than adherence to grammatical conventions. He is also interested in such technical aspects of language and logic as negation, which he develops far beyond the scope it attains in Augustine and in his Carolingian predecessors. Anselm's handling of this issue reflects his appreciation of the Stoic logical principle that a negative particle, such as *non,* negates a statement more exhaustively if it is placed before the whole proposition than if it is placed before the verb, a point that he explores repeatedly and at length in his analysis of the propositions *non possit malum facere* and *non posse peccare* as applied, respectively, to God and to angels in his philosophical fragments, his *De libertate arbitrii,* and his *De casu diaboli.* Anselm devotes sustained attention not only to the significance of negative and privative statements but also to the semantic character of lying statements and to problems in formal logic such as inference, infinite regress, paronymy, and modal propositions, whether their uses lie outside the domain of grammar and dialectic or not.[65]

Yet it would be just as much a mistake to view Anselm primarily as a forerunner of the systematic formal logic of the later Middle Ages or of modern times as it would be to underrate this element in his handling of language and linguistic arguments. While he sometimes concerns himself with purely formal matters, he is just as likely to treat the *usus loquendi* as an adequate index of extramental realities, both created and uncreated. And, on those occasions when he abandons this approach, he does so because, for the purpose at hand, it is simply not useful. In such cases, Anselm comes to this conclusion not only because he is aware of the limitations of the contemporary *usus loquendi* on semantic grounds but also because he sees it as limited from the broader perspective of the ways that human language as such falls short in speaking about the world and God, which he inherited from the Augustinian tradition. Anselm's approach to words as signs in theological discourse thus reflects simultaneously his commitment to grammar as a cogent way of grasping and explicating reality, both intramental and extramental, and his conviction that statements about God must be measured by their appropriateness and their correspondence to the God known by faith. Within this framework, Anselm also develops a technique of deepening that faith into *intellectus fidei* in terms of the particular grammar available to him, a grammar which he taught as a pedagogue as well as employed as a theologian.

We might begin by examining Anselm's educational works, the *De gramma-*

tico and the unfinished *De potestate et impotentia*. . . . Both are ostensibly logical treatises. Anselm himself describes the *De grammatico* as a discussion of problems currently mooted among dialecticians and as useful for students in that discipline;[66] elsewhere he recommends it as an introduction to logic.[67] Eadmer, the monk of Canterbury who was Anselm's biographer, secretary, and close friend,[68] catalogs it in his list of Anselm's writings as a work which propounds and solves many dialectical questions.[69] Several modern scholars, however, have observed that the problem contained in the *De grammatico* is not purely logical, since it results from the impact of Boethius on Priscian's definition of the noun.[70] In fact both works are as much grammatical as logical, if not more so. This is true not only of the questions which they ask but also of Anselm's method of answering them. It is important to give particular attention to this method. The *discipulus* in the *De grammatico* requests the *magister* to prove his answers by necessary reasons,[71] and at the end of the dialogue he appears to be satisfied that his terms have been met. The work will thus begin to give us some idea of what Anselm thought necessary reasons were, a topic highly relevant to his epistemology and one to which we will have occasion to return in some detail below.

The basic question in the *De grammatico* is: "Whether a grammarian is a substance or a quality." This is an issue whose investigation promises at first glance to be as enervating as the redoubtable "How many angels can stand on the head of a pin?" and "How many steps did Saint Denis take with his head tucked under his arm?," which used to be attributed regularly to medieval savants before the advent of revisionist historiography. The problem that the *De grammatico* raises is, however, both plausible and concrete. The *discipulus* asks this question because he wants to know the denominative status of *grammarian* and words like it, a dilemma suggested to him by Boethius's *In Categorias Aristotelis,* where we read: "Denominatives are defined as those words that derive their appellation from the noun, with any single difference in case, as 'grammarian' from 'grammar' and 'strong' from 'strength.' "[72] The issue is located in the fact that the word *grammarian* is derived grammatically from the discipline of grammar. But it is equally true that grammarians are chronologically and logically derived from the human race, since it is necessary to be a man before one can become a grammarian, and *grammaticus* is a species of the genus *homo.* Sensing that the *discipulus* will have difficulty understanding this logical relationship, the *magister* has recourse to a grammatical example in order to clarify it. The genus *homo,* and the species *grammaticus,* he points out, are related in logic the way that the adjective *hodiernum,* and the adverb *hodie* are related in grammar.[73]

This still leaves open the status of the word *grammaticus* with respect both to man, on the one hand, and to grammar, on the other. Now words, Anselm states, represent things. What kind of thing does *grammaticus* represent? It represents a flesh and blood grammarian. This grammarian, according to Anselm, is a quality, and *grammarian* is therefore a *vox significans qualitatem*.[74] Quality, he adds, is one of Aristotle's accidents, and in order to explain what an accident is and how it compares with substance, he falls back once again on a grammatical analogy. Substance is to accident as a word which can either stand alone or be modified is to a word which is grammatically dependent on the word it modifies.[75] Words may signify either substantially or accidentally. Those signifying substantially are *voces significativae per se;* those signifying accidentally are *voces significativae per aliud.* The word *grammaticus* does not signify the human being occupied with the study of language and the agent whose name is derived from the discipline of grammar in the same way. It signifies the nominal derivative *per se* and the man *per aliud.* In the first case the word is properly significative; in the second case it is appellative.[76] For Anselm, thus, grammatical relationships are prior to, and more comprehensible than, logical and chronological relationships. The grammatical derivation of a word is substantial and independent, while the logical derivation remains accidental and dependent.

In the case of the *De potestate et impotentia* we find a similar tendency on Anselm's part to pose or to answer logical questions grammatically, although this is visible far less systematically than in the *De grammatico.* In one series of questions he takes up the implications of negation. What does not exist, he says, has no power at all. It has neither the power to be nor the power not to be, and hence, paradoxically, it is both necessarily nonexistent and necessarily existent. Anselm admits that this conclusion is absurd even though it is logically plausible.[77] Another series of questions deals with the problem of attributing negative or apparently privative terminology to God. We may say, Anselm notes, that there are some acts that are impossible to God, such as lying, or that some of God's characteristics are necessary, such as justice. However, impossibility connotes impotence and necessity connotes coercion, both of which are imperfections, and cannot therefore be attributed to God. If we say that he serves truth by his inability to lie and that he serves justice by coercion, this would mean that he can neither be truthful nor just freely, a conclusion which is plausible but which cannot be true because it conflicts with God's nature. If we try to avoid this conclusion by stating that, so far as God is concerned, necessity and impossibility signify perfections rather than defects, we are faced with the paradox of words that signify their opposites: "Why," asks Anselm, "is this strength indicated by names signifying weakness?"[78] It would be interesting indeed to know how Anselm planned to answer this question, but he does not do so in this work, which is unfinished, although he does address and resolve the problem elsewhere.

Anselm's taste for explaining logical relationships in terms of grammatical relationships is also visible in the De potestate et impotentia, particularly with respect to causality. He compares causes to effects by analogizing them to nouns and predicate nominatives. As the noun governs the predicate nominative, he says, so the cause governs the effect.[79] In the case of efficient causality Anselm's illustrative example is drawn from metaphorical signification. The efficient cause, although it is not the effect, can still be affirmed of it, just as the foot, although it is not the eye, is, figuratively speaking, the eye of a blind man.[80] In its fragmentary state, the De potestate et impotentia gives us much less to work with than does the De grammatico. Yet it is worthy of notice in that it provides us with some insight into the kinds of questions Anselm was asking, and it reinforces our impression of him as a man whose primary mode of thought was grammar.

The grammatical mode of thought is freely exploited by Anselm in his epistemological and theological works. It will be seen in the case of Anselm's theory of knowledge that he is in full command of the Augustinian view of the cognitive functions, possibilities, and limitations of words and that he frequently explores epistemological relationships in terms of grammatical concepts. Like Augustine, Anselm sees a definite connection between love and knowledge, and his epistemology is formulated in such a way as to be applicable primarily, if not exclusively, to theological objects of knowledge. Anselm's epistemological preoccupations are fairly few in number. What concerns him most is the nature of truth, the tenability of proofs, and the cognitive function of proofs. These interest are explored, more or less respectively, in his dialogue De veritate, in his analysis of necessary reasons, and in his theory of fides quaerens intellectum. An understanding of these points is essential to an understanding of his views on the theology of God's existence in the Monologion, Proslogion, and Contra Gaunilonem.

The intimate connection between Anselm's theory of knowledge and his religious aims is made manifest in the prologue of the De veritate, the only one of his major works expressly devoted to epistemology. Here he states that the purpose of the dialogue is to aid the reader in the study of Scripture and to discuss the nature of truth, the things of which truth is ordinarily predicated, and justice.[81] At the outset, the discipulus poses the question of truth in the following terms: We believe that God is the truth. Yet, at the same time, there are many other things which we call true. Must we say that anything that is true is therefore God? This is an implausible notion in view of the fact that God is eternal, while other things are not. A definition of truth is hence required which will explain in what sense the finite things we call true are true.[82]

The discipulus and magister accordingly turn their attention to the truth of signification, beginning with the significative function of statements. Their dialogue reveals Anselm's interest in both the relation of the sign to its significatum and the relation of the sign to the speaker.[83] This point reflects his familiarity with the Stoic distinction between intramental intentions, or *lekta*, and the words that men use to express them. There is, according to Anselm, an intrinsic, natural truth in speech, a *veritas enuntiationis*, in virtue of the fact that a statement signifies truly what its speaker means. This natural significative function pertains to all statements, whether or not they are factually accurate. If they are in fact accurate in addition to expressing the intention of their speakers, they are accidentally true. It is this latter type of truth that Anselm dignifies with the name "rectitude." Statements that are intrinsically erroneous may yet be naturally true, but only statements which signify that what is, is, and that what is not, is not, possess both truth and rectitude. Rectitude, the correct relation of the sign to the thing it signifies, is the real criterion of its epistemological validity.[84] This being the case, it is clear that the hearer can perceive the rectitude of a sign only if he knows both the sign and the object it signifies. The sign, thus, does not bring to the hearer any knowledge which he does not already have. It is on the basis of his prior knowledge of the object that he judges the rectitude of the sign, the truth of a statement. This is completely consistent with Augustine's ideas on signification. The sign may be accurate, but it is not identical with its object. It is not cognitive in the first instance. Its objective accuracy is controlled by its object, and its subjective accuracy can be assessed only by a mind able to compare the sign with its object, which it already knows.

Anselm, like Augustine, begins with verbal signs: his explanation of rectitude is elaborated first with respect to the truth of statements and definitions. He then goes on to show that there are other types of signs which can be understood in the same way as statements.[85] After analyzing the truth of statements, he proceeds to discuss the truth of thought, the truth of will, the truth of action, the truth of the senses, and the truth of the essences of things. The same criteria which he applies to verbal signs are applied to these other types of signs. Thus, he notes, an idea may have rectitude if the thinker thinks that what is, is, and what is not, is not.[86] Just as the truth of thought lies in thinking what is right, so the truth of will lies in willing what is right, conforming the will to moral reality.[87] Moral rectitude includes truth of action, the doing of what is right. For Anselm, there is a direct parallel between the truth of statements and the truth of actions. Just as a statement may be naturally or accidentally true, depending on whether it merely expresses the speaker's meaning or it also expresses realities accurately, so an action may be necessarily or unnecessarily true, depending on whether the agent merely exercises its given nature unconsciously, or it acts, or permits itself to be acted upon, with conscious reference to its moral objectives.[88] The truth of the senses is natural; to the extent that the senses are healthy, they provide the judgment with accurate data. The judgment may interpret sense data truly or falsely, depending on how well informed it is on the science of sense perception. Thus, citing the conventional example of the straight stick that appears to be bent when seen through water, Anselm observes that an understanding of the physics of refraction will enable the judgment to correct for error and to retain the material truth of sensory data on the intellectual level.[89]

So far Anselm's discussion in the *De veritate* has shown that things which are not themselves eternal truth may still be true insofar as they are signs that signify their proper objects with rectitude. There still remains the question of whether God is the truth of all true things. This point is taken up by Anselm in commenting on the truth of the essences of things. The essences of things exist and are true, he says, because they are derived from the supreme truth. They are true insofar as this truth is in them and they are in it; for they are what they are in relation to supreme truth.[90] This means that "what exists, is true"; but it does not necessarily follow for Anselm that "whatever is, is right and ought to be." Unlike most Neoplatonists, Anselm does not extricate himself from this difficulty by means of a privative theory of evil. Rather, he attacks the problem while achieving in effect the same thing, in grammatical form. The verb *ought,* he states, may only be used properly in the active voice. Consequently, a knowledge of what is right obliges the agent to do it, but rectitude cannot be invoked as a justification of what happens to a person when he is acted upon.[91]

Supreme truth, however, is the basis for all other kinds of truth. Discourse, and by extension other kinds of signification, would have no rectitude unless its objects existed; and things exist only because God creates and sustains them. For Anselm, thus, truth is rectitude perceived with the reason; justice is rectitude sought consciously by the will and expressed in right action for the sake of, and by means of, justice itself.[92] The rectitude underlying all true signification is prior to its signs; it is independent of them, and they cannot confer being upon it or withdraw being from it: "Then, the rightness (*rectitudo*) in terms of which the signification is called correct, or right, neither exists through nor changes with the signification regardless of how the signification changes."[93] This rectitude—God—is the eternal truth toward which all other truths—truths of will, of intellect, of fact, of word, of action—are oriented.[94] This idea has very little to do with the exemplarism which some people find in Anselm.[95] It is, rather, a corollary of Anselm's belief that God is the creator of all things and the object of all human activity and that he makes it possible for men to know and to love him. For Anselm, as for Augustine, love and knowledge are correlative and inseparable. It is as impossible for Anselm to sever the cognitive from the affective faculties as to detach man's efforts toward intellectual and moral rectitude from God's initiative and assistance. "In Anselm's thought . . . the moral and intellectual virtues adumbrate an identical reality, and serve a single end."[96]

Anselm's second principal epistemological interest, necessary reasons, is somewhat more elusive, as it is a topic which he treats less extensively than the nature of truth. Nevertheless, the two ideas are inseparable. Anselm's notion of necessity is firmly embedded in the idea of rectitude which he elaborates in the *De veritate;* and the importance of necessary reasons to his theology as a whole is impossible to overlook. At the beginning of the *Monologion* Anselm states that he intends to support his position with necessary reasons, which he defines as rational arguments acceptable even if they are not supported by the greater authority of Scripture and tradition.[97] Although the term "necessity" is used only twice in the *Proslogion,* it is invoked and explained in a number of Anselm's works and is repeated several times in his refutation of Gaunilo.[98] In Anselm's own words, necessary reasons stand at the center of his proof of God's existence. It is therefore not surprising to find that scholarly opinions on the cognitive status of necessary reasons have sometimes been affected by scholarly conclusions as to the nature and validity of the proof.

There are a number of commentators who find some anomaly or imprecision in Anselm's conception and use of necessary reasons. Paul Vignaux confesses his puzzlement. Necessary reasons, he states, are "not . . . merely probabilities for the use of this or that questioner, but rather [they] aspire to the universality of the true." Yet Anselm employs them in writings that "leave aside the Incarnation but include the Trinity; they are not concerned with a philosopher's God;"[99] and, even stranger, their universal validating power is rather weak in practice in Anselm's arguments.[100] David Knowles solves this dilemma by observing that in Anselm's thought, "the adjective *necessarius* means 'formally admissible,' 'probable,' rather than 'compelling.'" However, he finds an Anselmian paradox of his own. Notwithstanding the cognitive limits of necessary reasoning, Anselm, he holds, thinks that the human mind can perceive the "inevitability" of the truths of faith. This pecularity lies, according to Knowles, not so much in Anselm's presumed attempt to use necessary reasons in a manner which their nature does not warrant as it does in his presumed failure to distinguish between "natural" and "supernatural" objects and modes of knowledge, a lapse not satisfactorily rectified until Aquinas, which therefore can be attributed to Anselm's philosophical naïveté. [101] While anxious, on the other hand, to assert that Anselm was no Pelagian of the mind, George S. Heyer, Jr., likewise concludes that Anselm uses necessary reasons unprofessionally because of the logical vagueness of his times. [102]

Besides tending to depict Anselm as fuzzy-minded and inconsistent, these opinions give rise to a major problem by focusing attention too exclusively on the function of necessary reasons in the proof of God's existence. To be sure, Anselm's own statement of purpose is responsible for this emphasis, and we shall also make the proof the terminus of our discussion of his epistemology. However, one must recognize that the *Monologion* definition of necessary reasons is neither the only source of information about them nor the only answer to all the relevant questions that they raise. In particular, two further questions remain to be settled: Where did Anselm get the idea of necessary reasons in the first place? What is Anselm's own criterion of necessity?

In answering the first question we are given substantial assistance by a helpful and strangely neglected article by A.-M. Jacquin, who traces the idea of necessary reasons to its ultimate source, the logic of Aristotle, and who gives us some notion of the filiation of this idea in the Latin Middle Ages up to Anselm's time. Aristotle talks about necessity most succinctly in his analysis of signs, which we have treated above. For Aristotle, it will be remembered, signs may be fallible or infallible. Infallible signs are proper to logic; they are used in syllogisms which entail scientific knowledge and necessary truth. Fallible signs are proper to rhetoric; they are used in enthymemes, which may be credited with probable, but not necessary truth. As Jacquin notes, this Aristotelian definition of probability and necessity was repeated by Cicero, Marius Victorinus, and Cassiodorus, its chief Latin transmitters. He thinks that Cassiodorus was most likely Anselm's source. [103] It must be emphasized that the works in which Aristotle expounds the syllogism-enthymeme distinction most thoroughly were not part of the *logica vetus* and were thus not available in Latin until the second half of the twelfth century. Anselm was thus incapable of knowing the complete context of Aristotle's original idea of necessity. In his own conception of necessity we note a significant shift in emphasis. Anselm is not at all concerned with the difference between probability and necessity. What does interest him is the fact that the derivative Latin discussions, in particular the discussion of Cassiodorus, emphasize the point that necessary reasons entail truth. Now, as we have seen, Anselm defines truth as rectitude, a quality indicating the accuracy of a sign vis-à-vis its object. It is not at all difficult for Anselm to assimilate the idea of necessity to the idea of rectitude, and this is precisely what he does. Thus, according to Anselm, an argument may be considered to have been proved by necessary reasons when it states that things are the way they really are, without invoking the support of a higher authority.[104]

Necessary reasons are therefore a mode of explaining the rectitude that exists between a sign and the object it signifies. They are not heuristic; their cognitive function is dependent on the hearer's prior knowledge of the object. In fact, the very same criteria apply to necessary reasons as apply to truth. All kinds of statements may be verified by means of necessary reasons. As we saw in the case of the *De grammatico,* they may be applied to purely academic questions. Apparently, their major practical limitation as epistemological tools seems to be the fact that they are usually grammatical in structure. In the case of theological questions, necessary reasons may likewise be used to verify statements about God, provided that these statements are consistent with God as he is. A concise definition of the nature, function, and limitations of necessary reasons may be found in the *Cur deus homo,* where Anselm, as magister, says to Boso, as discipulus:

Since in this inquiry you are assuming the role of those who prefer to believe nothing except what has been established in advance by reason, I would like for us to agree to accept, in the case of God, nothing that is in even the slightest degree unfitting and to reject nothing that is in even the slightest degree reasonable unless something more reasonable opposes it. For in the case of God, just as an impossibility results from any unfittingness, however slight, so necessity accompanies any degree of reasonableness, however small, provided it is not overridden by some other more weighty reason.[105]

It is in this sense that Boso can say to Anselm at the end of the dialogue: "You prove the necessity of God's becoming man, and you do so in such a way that . . . you would satisfy not only the Jews but also the pagans by reason alone."[106] Necessary reasoning, for Anselm, thus in no way implies that objects of knowledge can be altered, reified, or delimited by the human mind. What it does imply is that human words and ideas are validated and controlled by the objective realities they are designed to express and that they can express these realities, in their own terms, with rectitude.

Necessary reasons are linked not only to rectitude. They are linked also to Anselm's third major epistemological preoccupation, the idea of *fides quaerens intellectum. Fides quaerens intellectum* sums up Anselm's epistemology. It presupposes and includes necessary reasons and the principle of rectitude, and it specifies his conception of the cognitive status of theological statements. Comment on this important question has usually been limited to its role in Anselm's proof of God's existence. As in the case of necessary reasons, there is good warrant for this; it is a well-known fact that Anselm entitled the *Proslogion* as *Fides quaerens intellectum* before giving it its later name. [107] It is, however, necessary to explore the meaning he attaches to *fides quaerens intellectum* in his other writings as well in order to appreciate fully what he means by this term in the proof.

An excellent source of information on *fides quaerens intellectum* is a series of letters which Anselm wrote to combat the Trinitarian doctrine of Roscellinus, a contemporary logician, whose nominalism inclined him toward tritheism. Anselm's attack on Roscellinus is the closest he comes to out-and-out polemic. In this rebuttal he rejects Roscellinus's position on two counts—the logician's faulty methodology and his faulty moral and intellectual attitude toward his subject. In connection with these two objections, Anselm reveals once again his grammatical orientation, and he has ample opportunity to develop his views on the role of arguments derived from human thought in theological speculation. He also gives a clear statement of his purposes in combatting Roscellinus, which provides a certain amount of insight into the epistemological functions he attributes to his own arguments.

When it comes to the actual content of Roscellinus's teachings, Anselm presents an objection derived bodily from the eleventh-century grammar with which, as we have seen, he was so deeply concerned. In fact, his argument is quite reminiscent of the *De grammatico*. He holds Roscellinus to be in error because his attribution of the names "Father," "Son," and "Holy Spirit" to the Persons of the Trinity, as Anselm understands them, is grammatically inaccurate. In Roscellinus's mouth, he states, these names are *flatus vocis,* because they are applied to God in the way that such terms as "white," "just," "king," and "grammarian" are applied to an individual man. [108] With our knowledge of *De grammatico* behind us, it is not difficult to appreciate Anselm's reasoning at this point. He deplores the confusion of the proper, substantial application of words to their objects with their improper and accidental applications. It is clear that Anselm's whole approach to this problem is verbal rather than logical. He understands Roscellinus's position in terms of grammar rather than in terms of realism and nominalism.

Roscellinus's ideas are mistaken, according to Anselm. Even more noteworthy is his negative judgment on Roscellinus's moral and intellectual attitude. To Anselm it seems deplorable, almost inconceivable, that a man who is a Christian, and who thus may be assumed to know what he means when he uses the word *God*, should have failed to ground his theological speculations on that knowledge. A Christian who speaks of the three Persons of the Trinity as if they were three *res* must be either grossly impious or so intellectually confused that he does not know what he is saying.[109] Roscellinus, along with the dubious "modern dialecticians" whom he represents, is clearly an intelligent man. Yet he attempts to reduce God to the dimensions of his own logic, to leap from thought to existence.[110] This would be a questionable procedure in any case, since rectitude demands that we employ the realities that we know as the criteria of our thoughts about them. It is an especially inappropriate procedure when it comes to God. In dealing with God, says Anselm, intellectual and moral rectitude demand our humble acknowledgment that he is a transcendent mystery and that he takes the initiative in our acquisition of whatever knowledge we have of him: "By no means does God protect me if I dispute against the faith on how he does not exist. Through God's continual grace I believe, I love, I live for the disputation on how he does exist. If I am able to understand, I give thanks; if I cannot understand, I do not raise an outcry, but bow my head in worship."[111] In short, says Anselm, if one wishes to know God, one must first believe. Once firmly grounded in faith, the believer may investigate his beliefs with the greatest possible rigor; but this questioning is designed to explicate the rectitude of his beliefs, not to establish them in the first place.[112] This being the case, what value does Anselm attach to his own theological arguments against Roscellinus? His aims are limited; his comments are addressed to believers since, as he notes, he has written in response to the request of his monastic brethren.[113] Anselm explains what this response involves in a letter to Fulco, bishop of Beauvais, written after Roscellinus's condemnation:

For our faith ought to be rationally defended against the impious, but not against those who admit that they delight in the honor of the name "Christian." From these latter it must rightly be demanded that they hold firmly to the pledge made at baptism, but to the former, it must be demonstrated rationally how irrationally they despise us. For a Christian ought to advance from faith to understanding, instead of proceeding through understanding to faith or withdrawing from faith if he cannot understand.[114]

Judging from what Anselm has to say in this controversy, it might seem that he conceives of theology as functioning exclusively as a series of correct statements about God, which, in showing the believer the rectitude of what he believes, serve to intensify his moral and intellectual appreciation of what he already knows by faith. It is undeniable that Anselm was an intramural theologian, and this is a fact which has been stressed by a number of scholars in their zeal to counteract the claims which others have made for the alleged apologetic character of his proof of God's existence. Most of the commentators who have advanced the purely intramural argument have cited the nature of Anselm's human environment to support their case. He lived, they note, in a world where atheism, skepticism, and religions other than Christianity were not well known enough to present a problem. Furthermore, he did most of his important theological work in the nondisputative, devotionally oriented atmosphere of the monastery.[115]

All of these conditions are real, and their significance should not be underestimated. However, in themselves they do not completely explain why Anselm thinks that theology can assist the believer; and they utterly fail to explain what Anselm thinks theology can do for the nonbeliever. It is necessary to point out that the nonbeliever exists in Anselm's writings. He is irreducibly there. It is probable, of course, that Anselm never met him in the flesh. One can only praise Gustave Weigel and Arthur G. Madden for their acute observation that

the non-believer for Anselm is the non-believer of the order of Original Sin. Before that time [the Fall] man was in loving and familiar contact with God, and . . . would have seen the question [of God's existence and nature] lucidly. Of the man of pure nature, a later Scholastic conception, Anselm shows no awareness.[116]

We would certainly be the first to agree that Anselm saw the nonbeliever as a hypothetical straw man rather than as an organized contemporary threat to the Christian faith. On the whole, his controversial writings show that he was far more troubled by impiety and heterodoxy within the fold than by atheism. To the extent that he attacks individuals who disagree with him, he sees them not as Satanic intellects but as misguided Christians who have unaccountably gotten their heads screwed on backwards. Both in theory and in practice, Anselm's theology is weighted heavily in favor of the believer. Nevertheless, he does speak to, as well as about, the nonbeliever, and he does think that the nonbeliever will be able to learn something from the argument of *fides quaerens intellectum*. It would be a gross mistake to overlook this fact, as it would prejudice one's understanding of Anselm's theory of knowledge from the outset. For Anselm, theological statements do not always function the same way. Their objective powers and limitations are permanent, for they are dictated by the intrinsic nature of correct signification. But their subjective powers and limitations are fluctuating; they are dictated by the moral and intellectual status of their audience with respect to their object and are hence dependent on the individual and on God.

If we find in Anselm's *Epistolae* on the Trinity a case for intramural theology, his *Cur deus homo* provides us with a broader perspective. Here Anselm delineates the extramural role of theology as well and analyzes theological arguments by necessary reasons in relation both to their significata and to their hearers. He began to write the *Cur deus homo* when he was archbishop of Canterbury and finished it during his Italian exile, which resulted from his conflict with King William II over lay investiture. This enforced travel may have widened Anselm's horizons; in any case, the preface of the work shows him to be quite serious about nonbelief. The *Cur deus homo*, he notes, is divided into two books:

The first of these contains the answers of believers to the objections of unbelievers who repudiate the Christian faith because they regard it as incompatible with reason. And this book goes on to prove by rational necessity (*rationibus necessariis*)—Christ being removed from sight, as if there had never been anything known about Him—that no man can possibly be saved without Him. However, in the second book—likewise proceeding as if nothing were known of Christ—I show with equally clear reasoning and truth (*aperta ratione et veritate*) that human nature was created in order that the whole man . . . would some day enjoy a happy immortality. And I show the necessity of man's attaining this end for which he was created, and [that it can be attained] only by means of a God-man. [117]

Nonbelievers must be shown that Christianity is not irrational, an undertaking which demands arguments that do not depend on revelation. Anselm thinks that arguments by necessary reasons will also be useful to the believer faced with the task of answering the objections of the infidel. He explains this point further:

In reply to those who make inquiry, I am accustomed to give the rational bases of a particular problem of our faith. . . . They make their request not in order to approach faith by way of reason but in order to delight in the comprehension and contemplation of the doctrines which they believe, as well as in order to be ready, as best they can, always to give a satisfactory answer to everyone who asks of them a reason for the hope that is in us [1 Pet. 3:15]. Unbelievers habitually raise this particular problem as an objection to us, while derisively terming Christian simplicity a foolish simplicity; and many believers repeatedly mull over this same problem: For what reason and on the basis of what necessity did God become man? . . . Many individuals, then, keep asking that this problem be dealt with; and in spite of the fact that the investigation seems very difficult, the solution is intelligible to everyone and is commendable because of the utility and elegance of the reasoning. Therefore, even though the holy Fathers have said about this problem what ought to be adequate, nevertheless what God will deign to disclose to me about this topic I will endeavor to show to those who are inquiring.[118]

This is a very rich passage, and Anselm explores its implications at various points throughout the work. As he sees it, rational proofs can show the nonbeliever that Christian teachings are not absurd; but faith cannot be achieved by reason. Neither can reason dissolve the doubts of the faithful. Within the fold its task is to gladden the heart of the believer by helping him to understand the reason for his confidence and to prepare him to defend the faith before nonbelievers.[119] In both cases, that of the believer and that of the nonbeliever, the same technique, argument by necessary reasons, is to be used.

According to Anselm, necessary reasons have several epistemological advantages. Like all signs possessing rectitude, they are accurate representations of their objects, so far as they go; and they are more useful than authoritative statements, which are not decisive for the nonbeliever.[120] They also have several epistemological limitations. Like all signs possessing rectitude, they are controlled by their objects. And, in the case of theology, statements cannot be correct or necessary if they attribute to God anything unjust, uncharitable, unfitting, lacking in harmonious proportions, or, in a word, inconsistent with his divinity.[121] It must further be understood that, for Anselm, necessary reasons are auxiliary, but not essential, foundations of faith. Faith does not depend on rational proofs.[122] It is a gift of God;[123] and it is expressed sufficiently in the teachings of the fathers of the church. So embodied, it is the criterion of the necessity of any reasons invoked with respect to its contents. Finally, necessary reasons in theological questions are limited by the fact that their object cannot be known completely by the human mind; and, furthermore, that this object, God, must be loved in order to be known. Theological speculation, although true so far as it goes, must therefore combine moral and intellectual rectitude, and it can thus only be truly necessary if it reverently acknowledges its inadequacies in the face of divine transcendence.[124]

We thus have in theological statements reasons which are necessary because they correspond to God, as previously known by faith on the part of the theologian. It should be noted that *fides*, for Anselm, means both the teachings of the church as an objective norm of what is to be believed and the subjective state of full, personal assent to it; there is no discrepancy between the two.[125] *Intellectus* is the believer's deepened awareness of the meaning of his faith, achieved by the quest for necessary reasons to fit the propositions of his creed. *Intellectus fidei* has been described as a form of contemplation which advances the believer on the road from faith to the vision of God.[126] A more complete definition of *intellectus fidei* would have to take into account the fact that it entails moral as well as mental transformation. Just as faith itself is a gift of God, so also *intellectus fidei* can take place only with the assistance of grace; its aim is beatitude, which is the consummation of the believer's love and knowledge of God.[127]

This aim, and the correlative method of *fides quaerens intellectum,* seem eminently plausible in the case of the believer. Anselm's confidence that they may plausibly be applied to the nonbeliever as well is based on the fact that the necessary reasons on which *fides quaerens intellectum* depends are not drawn from authority. Nonbelievers and believers are expected to listen to the same theological arguments. But they are not expected to profit from them in the same way. Necessary reasons cannot produce faith; the most they can do for a nonbeliever is to show him that Christian beliefs are not entirely incoherent. Anselm's preferred method for doing this, in the *Cur deus homo* as elsewhere, is by means of grammatical explanations,[128] although he also cites the persuasive power of the single argument.[129] For the believer, then, theology has an intensifying and commemorative function; it gives him understanding and helps him to grow in the Christian life. For the nonbeliever, the same theology has a function which is purely indicative.[130] And, for the theologian, the question which his professional activity raises is not whether he can make meaningful statements about God or whether he can show that the Christian faith is true but, rather, how to do so simultaneously for these differing audiences.

In discussing the historical importance of Anselm, R. W. Southern has pointed out that "Augustine's thought was the pervading atmosphere in which Anselm moved. . . . Anselm, at his first appearance as a writer, was and claimed to be an *Augustinus minor;* but he was an Augustine formed by the logic, grammar and monastic life of the eleventh century."[131] From the point of view of the epistemology of theological statements, nothing could be more true than this observation. Working as he is in a different intellectual environment, with a much narrower range of antique sources, Anselm still manages to reiterate all of the salient aspects of Augustine's theory of signification—the accurate and yet limited status of signs in relation to their objects, and the differing subjective functions of signs, depending on the cognitive and affective status of their hearers vis-à-vis God—although he detaches the theory from its Augustinian framework of rhetoric, preferring to express it through grammar. Anselm's intellectual dependence upon and stylistic differences from Augustine have been noted in a variety of his works. They are nowhere more systematically revealed than in the three treatises which comprise his theology of God's existence; and it is to the *Monologion, Proslogion,* and *Contra Gaunilonem* that we now turn.

The first thing to be noticed about this series of works is their intention. The philosophical interest which they have aroused since the eleventh century has inclined people to focus attention on the proofs of God's existence which they contain. Strictly speaking, however, the *Monologion* and *Proslogion* are not exclusively, or even primarily, proofs of God's existence. A simple glance at the contents of these works should make this clear. The *Monologion* contains eighty chapters, of which 1 through 4 deal with the existence of God; 5 through 28 deal with the nature of God and his relationships to the created universe; while chapters 29 through 80, by far the largest portion of the work, deal with the Trinity. Among the twenty-six chapters of the *Proslogion,* 1 through 4 discuss the existence of God; 5 through 22, the bulk of the treatise, examine God's nature; 23 is devoted to the Trinity; and 24 through 26 form a prayer directed to God as the end of man.

Anselm himself indicates what he thinks the *Monologion* and *Proslogion* are about in the prefaces of these two works. The *Monologion,* he states, represents his thoughts "regarding meditating on the Divine Being and regarding various other themes related to a meditation of this kind."[132] He describes the *Proslogion* as a continuation of the *Monologion,* a meditation "in the role of someone endeavoring to elevate his mind toward contemplating God and seeking to understand what he believes."[133] The similarities in subject and method are further visible in the titles he first selected for the two works, *Exemplum meditandi de ratione fidei* and *Fides quaerens intellectum.*[134] Nowhere in Anselm's work does he refer to the *Monologion* and *Proslogion* as proofs of God's existence. Rather, he sees them functioning together as attempts at Trinitarian speculation. In his *Epistola de incarnatione verbi,* he states that he wrote them to show "that what we hold by faith regarding the divine nature and its persons—excluding the topic of incarnation—can be proven by compelling reasons (*necessariis rationibus*) apart from [appeal to] the authority of Scripture."[135] In his private correspondence, he further identifies the *Monologion* as a *De trinitate.*[136]

Certainly, Anselm's contemporaries shared his own views about his works. In discussing Anselm's writings, his biographer has this to say about the *Monologion* and *Proslogion:*

Here [in the *Monologion*], putting aside all authority of Holy Scripture, he enquired into and discovered by reason alone what God is, and proved by invincible reason that God's nature is what the true faith holds it to be, and that it could not be other than it is.

Afterwards it came into his mind [in the *Proslogion*] to try to prove by one single and short argument the things which are believed and preached about God, that He is eternal, unchangeable, omnipotent, omnipresent, incomprehensible, just, righteous, merciful, true, as well as truth, goodness, and so on; and to show how all these qualities are united in Him. [137]

Eadmer does not analyze the *Proslogion* any further, merely noting that after it was written a monk in a nearby monastery criticized it and that Anselm had this critique and his reply to it attached to the body of the work. [138] Finally, in cataloging Anselm's theological contributions, Ordericus Vitalis mentions that he wrote, at the request of friends, on the Trinity, on free will, on the fall of the devil, and on why God was made man, [139] nowhere referring either to the *Monologion, Proslogion,* or *Contra Gaunilonem* by name or to the fact that these works contain proofs of God's existence.

As far as content, then, the proof is a *De trinitate,* which does not shrink from speculating on the most abstruse aspects of the divine nature. From the point of view of method, Anselm specifies that necessary reasoning is to be the technique of argument, so that "nothing at all in the meditation would be argued on scriptural authority, but that in unembellished style and by uncomplicated arguments and with simplifed discussion rational necessity (*rationis necessitas*) would tersely prove, and truth's clarity would openly manifest, whatever the conclusion of the distinct inquiries declared."[140]

There has been some confusion as to Anselm's meaning here, which arises from the fact that he cites the authority of Augustine's *De trinitate* immediately after he makes this statement. [141] Scholars, to be sure, have noticed Anselm's Augustinian tendency to argue the Trinitarian relations of the divine Persons on the analogy of the human mind as the image of God. [142] It is quite true that Anselm takes this style of argument, among others, from Augustine, not to mention his wholesale adoption of Augustine's epistemology of signs. However, it is important to understand exactly what kind of debt Anselm thought he owed to Augustine. When Anselm wrote the *Monologion,* he sent a copy to Lanfranc, then archbishop of Canterbury. [143] Lanfranc's reaction was negative. He deplored the fact that Anselm had not documented the treatise with proofs drawn from scriptural and traditional authority. That Anselm was well aware of the fact that he was making a new departure is evident in the placatory tone he adopts when explaining his intentions in the preface to the *Monologion.* [144] He also answers Lanfranc's objection by pointing out that his work is not totally devoid of precedents, citing Augustine's *De trinitate:* "For, since this is how blessed Augustine proved his great disputations in his book *De trinitate,* I may argue in the same way, finding, as it were, my brief arguments in his sure authority."[145] It may seem strange to think of Augustine's De trinitate as a work proved by disputation. Anselm, however, clearly thinks that it is, and thus he uses it as a justification for his own method. He refers to Augustine not only because he is an authority in the church but also because he thinks that Augustine's style of argument in the De trinitate validates and confirms his own technique of argument by necessary reasons.

The specific kind of necessary reasons which Anselm employs in the Monologion, Proslogion, and Contra Gaunilonem tend to be grammatical in nature. His principal methods for implementing necessary reasoning in these three works are equipollent proofs and explanations turning on the grammatical relationships among words. That equipollency is a sure path to the rectitude on which truth depends is underlined in the De veritate, where the discipulus at the beginning of the dialogue insists that the magister demonstrate his conclusions with a "definition of truth," as he had in the Monologion.[146] It has been appreciated that the Proslogion proof turns on the definition of a name[147] and the importance of nominal definitions has also been noted in the case of the Monologion.[148] The use of definition is basic to these works in the sense of the quest for names of God that possess rectitude. To find these names, Anselm moves from one definition to another by equipollency.

Anselm chooses proof by definition as the style of the Monologion and Proslogion not only because he thinks of it as the most plausible expression of necessary reasoning but also because he considers it the most appropriate style for the audience to which both works are addressed. Despite the intramural emphasis of these two works, they are both intended for nonbelievers as well as for believers. The statement in which Anselm explains that he wrote the Monologion because "certain brothers have persisted in urging me to write out for them, in the form of a meditation, a number of things which I had discussed in non-technical terms with them regarding meditation on the Divine Being" is well known.[149] Apparently less well known is the fact that he goes on to say, "They also desired that I not disdain to refute simple and almost foolish objections which would occur to me."[150] We find that at several points in the Monologion, Anselm has occasion to direct his attention to the "simple" and "foolish," who object to Christian teachings because of impudence, imprudence, falsehood, or impiety.[151] He also poses the problem of nonbelief at some length in the Monologion, explaining that his style of argument is tailored to the demands of that position.[152]

Similarly, in the Proslogion, we find Anselm repeating his intention of writing "upon the insistent adjurations of certain brothers,"[153] a plausible audience in view of the extensive use of prayer which he makes in this work. At the same time, he chooses the famous nonbelieving fool of the psalmist as the butt of his argument in chapters 2 through 4. It is evident that these works have a twofold intention. This is a point which Anselm takes pains to reemphasize in his *Epistola de incarnatione verbi,* when he discusses why he wrote the *Monologion* and *Proslogion:* "I advanced these points (1) in order to defend our faith against those who, while unwilling to believe what they do not understand, deride those who do believe, and (2) in order to assist the devout striving of those who humbly seek to understand what they most steadfastly believe."[154] The intramural and extramural functions of arguments by necessary reasons are thus visible in both the *Monologion* and the *Proslogion.* Here, as elsewhere, Anselm's confidence that the same arguments can function in two different ways for two different audiences at the same time is based on his concept of the cognitive strengths and weaknesses of linguistic, and particularly grammatical, signs. His frequent insistence on the necessity, truth, and persuasiveness of the arguments that he uses in these works, already noted, indicates his assurance that it is possible to speak about God with rectitude. The prayerful nature of the *Proslogion,* sometimes interpreted as a rejection of logic for devotion, is actually a refinement of Anselm's method. Just as he thinks that his proof in the *Proslogion* is enhanced because he has found a single demonstration to replace the several arguments for God's existence in the *Monologion,*[155] so the introduction of prayer in the later work should be seen as the decision to employ a research device that will result in a high degree of rectitude, considering the nature of the object of knowledge in question. As Anselm puts it: "Teach me to seek You, and reveal Yourself to me as I seek; for unless You instruct me I cannot seek You, and unless You reveal Yourself I cannot find You. Let me seek You in desiring You; let me desire You in seeking You. Let me find You in loving You; let me love You in finding You."[156]

With the proper attitude and technique, then, words about God can be true and thus necessary. At the same time, Anselm stresses, no statement about God can be totally accurate or totally convincing. Anselm insists that his intention as a theologian is purely utilitarian. He formulates his speculations, he says, with an eye to their practicality.[157] Yet, at the same time, we find him protesting his ineptitude and voicing the hope that his work will soon be obsolete.[158] The nonbeliever, he thinks, can be persuaded by reason for the most part, but not completely; and the arguments by necessary reasons directed at him are not omnipotent, but provisional:

Nevertheless, if in this investigation I say something that a greater authority does not mention, then even if my statement is a necessary consequence of reasons which will seem [good] to me, I want the statement to be accepted as follows: It is not thereby said to be absolutely necessary but is only said to be able to appear necessary for the time being. [159]

In both the *Monologion* and *Proslogion,* we find Anselm building up proofs about God's nature on the analogy of human phenomena. [160] At a certain point, however, he systematically breaks down these analogies in order to stress the uniqueness and transcendence of God. The functions of the human mind, human thought and language, he holds, must in the end stand abashed before God. [161] Both the building up and the breaking down of these analogies are Augustinian devices; and so are a number of the characteristics which Anselm analogizes to God, as we shall see below. The epistemological conclusions that Anselm reaches in the *Monologion* and *Proslogion* likewise reflect Augustine's view of the theological statement as an accurate, yet partial, *aenigma.* God is ineffable, Anselm agrees; yet we must speak about him in order to know him and to love him. [162] And, by extension, we must also speak about God in order to inspire this knowledge and love in others. When he wishes to convey the simultaneous expressiveness and poverty of language, Anselm occasionally has recourse to the sensuous imagery of the mystics. [163] Still, he does not avoid the difficult question: Given God's transcendence, how can men possibly say things about him that are valid? In answer, Anselm explains that theological statements may be valid without infringing on God's ineffability, so long as we remember that our words do not apply to God and to other things to which they may be applied in the same way. We know and express God, he says, through words, as through a reflection in a mirror:

For we often say many things which we do not express precisely as they are. Instead, we signify obliquely (*per aliud*) that which we either cannot or else do not want to express properly, as when we speak in riddles (*aenigmata*). And often we see a thing, though not properly, that is, not as the object itself but rather by means of a likeness or an image, as when we see someone's face in a mirror. Thus, we do and do not say one and the same thing; we do and do not see one and the same object. We speak and see obliquely; we do not speak and see in accordance with the respective reality. So, in this manner, if the Supreme Nature is not at all assumed to be expressed in accordance with the reality of its essence but is assumed to be somehow or other designated obliquely, then nothing precludes the truth of all that was earlier stated about the Supreme Nature, and nothing prevents this Nature from remaining as ineffable as ever. [164]

By its nature and in its operations, then, the human mind, for Anselm as for Augustine, is the most adequate *speculum Dei.* [165] Before meeting God in face-to-face vision, man may learn to know and to love him by contemplating his own mind. The human analogies by which he does this, though they are only reflections in a mirror, are still the best *aenigmata* of God available in this life. [166]

A closer look at the *Monologion, Proslogion,* and *Contra Gaunilonem* will provide a clearer idea of how Anselm puts into practice his concept of the powers and limitations of theological statements, which we have just examined from a theoretical point of view. Let us begin with the *Monologion,* the earliest work in this series of three. In the *Monologion,* Anselm alternates between the use of equipollent proofs and explanations drawn from grammatical analysis, although he is also heavily indebted to arguments borrowed from Augustine. He establishes the proof of God's existence at the beginning of the work by equipollency. Anselm opens the treatise with the statement that all men naturally desire the things which they judge to be good. From this assertion he infers that all men should want to know the ultimate cause of the goods which they desire. [167] This sounds as if Anselm is laying the foundation for an a posteriori proof of God's existence. But such is not the case. Rather, his proof is based on a theory of participation and proportionality. One can discern sensibly and intellectually, says Anselm, that not all things are equally good. There are degrees of goodness, which we understand in terms of the quality of goodness itself; a thing is good insofar as it participates in goodness. Above and beyond degrees of goodness, he notes, it can also be seen that things are good in different ways. They must therefore be judged not only in terms of the extent to which they participate in goodness but also by their relationship to goodness, that is, in terms of whether or not they promote goodness. [168] This reasoning depends on the existence of a quintessential good which serves as the norm of other, lesser goods, a notion reminiscent of Platonic idealism. It is just at this point, however, that Anselm interjects a series of equipollent definitions into his argument, by means of which this Greek abstraction is translated into an entity capable of being equated with the God of Abraham, Isaac, and Jacob.

The first shift in definition is the almost imperceptible conversion of this supreme good into a being. Next, since this being is indubitably very good, and since all other goods exist through it and in relation to it, it must therefore be self-existent, assuming the absurdity of infinite regress. As self-existent, it is not merely very good, but supremely good. Anselm's third step is to redefine the supremely good as the supremely great, the highest of all existing things. Its very self-existence, he says, shows that it exists in the greatest degree of all beings; and, as such, it is not difficult for him to add that it is unitary. [169] By the time Anselm has reached the end of chapter 4, which terminates the proof of God's existence in the *Monologion,* he has managed to expand and to specify his definition considerably:

Hence, there is a Nature, or Substance, or Being (*essentia*) which through itself is good and great, and through itself is what it is; and through this Nature exists whatever truly is good or great or something. And this Nature is the Supreme Good, the Supreme Greatness, the Supreme Being (*ens*) or Subsistence (*subsistens*)—in short, the highest of all existing things. [170]

Thus, by progressively redefining the idea of good, Anselm emerges with a Supreme Being, who can be called a nature, substance, or essence, who is great, one, and self-subsistent as well as good, and through whom all goodness, being, and truth exist. With this definition well in hand, he has a solid basis for his further equipollent elaborations on the nature of this being and his relationships with the existents for which he is responsible.

Actually, Anselm has more or less inferred the proof *that* a Supreme Being exists. There is, for example, no particular reason to assume at the outset that the various goods which men desire on earth do, in fact, have a single cause. However, as we have seen, by redefining goodness, Anselm works out the unity of the Supreme Being, as well as his aseity and supremacy over all other beings. *That* such a Supreme Being exists is established by equipollency. When it comes to establishing the *how* of his attributes, Anselm has recourse to grammatical explanations of several kinds. In the case of existence per se, he unfolds the relationship between essence and existence in the Supreme Being by comparing it to the relationship between a noun and the infinitive and participle of the verb derived from it:

How, then, in the last analysis, ought this Nature to be understood to exist through itself and from itself? . . . Should we perhaps understand how, by comparison with our saying that through itself and from itself light shines and is something shining? For in the way that light and to shine and shining (*lux et lucere et lucens*) are related to one another, so what is and to be and being (*essentia et esse et ens*) are related to one another. [171]

A second problem is that of creation *ex nihilo.* Its solution, according to Anselm, turns on the way in which the word *nothing* is understood. *Nothing,* says Anselm, may be understood in three ways: as a *façon de parler,* when we mean that what we are talking about has never really existed; as a real entity, capable of action or passion; and as the negative of *anything.* In the first case, he says, *nothing* may be true figuratively, but it is unintelligible when applied to real things literally. In the second case, *nothing* may have a natural truth in the sense that it expresses the intention of the speaker, but it is otherwise self-contradictory. If *nothing* is understood in the third sense, however, it may be said without inconsistency that the Supreme Being created the universe from nothing.[172]

In the next section of the *Monologion* Anselm extends his discussion of the relations between the Creator and the creation. He continues to employ equipollency and grammatical arguments here, but he also displays an increased use of Augustinian devices as well as an increased interest in the limitations to which human speech is subjected in reference to the Supreme Being. Pursuing further the mode of creation, Anselm states that created things had an existence in the mind of the Creator before they were made visible. He draws upon the Augustinian analogy of the formation of concepts in the human mind to explain this process. Just as a man has interior *locutiones mentis* before expressing himself in externally perceptible signs, he states, so the Creator has *locutiones* about the universe before he reifies it externally. Since this is so, the world exists in and through the creative expression of the Supreme Being.[173] Having noted this comparison, Anselm at once proceeds to depreciate the similarities between the operation of the human mind and that of the Creator, from which point he launches into an extensive discussion of the qualifications that must be made in speaking about the Supreme Being. He outlines three major limitations that pertain to the analogy based on human thought. Unlike men, says Anselm, the Creator needs no materials or images drawn from external sources in order to formulate his thoughts; he is absolutely original. Also, he can reify his thoughts at will. Finally, there is no gap in the Creator between either thought and expression or being and expression.[174]

The identity between the Creator and his *verbum mentis* means that man experiences the same general difficulties in trying to speak about either of them. These difficulties are considerable. The first one which Anselm attempts to solve concerns the sense in which different kinds of statements can be true of the Creator:

Now, I am especially and not unjustifiably moved to inquire . . . into what, from among whatever is predicable of something, can appropriately be predicated substantively of such a marvellous Nature as this. For I would be surprised if among the names or words (*nominibus vel verbis*) which we apply to things created from nothing, there could be found a term appropriately predicable of the Substance which created all other things.[175]

He concludes that relative statements, that is, statements involving comparative adjectives, cannot be attributed properly to the Creator. Comparisons, such as "supreme," "greatest," or "highest," he says, imply the ability on the part of the subject they modify to suffer addition or diminution. They also imply the necessity of the creation in terms of which the Creator is supreme, whereas in truth his nature is not changed by the presence or absence of other beings. Thus relative statements, whether positive or negative, do not describe him substantially. On the other hand, Anselm holds that nonrelative expresions, such as infinitive statements, may be properly and truly applied to the Creator, so long as the characteristics which these statements attribute to him are better than they are not. The accurate infinitive statement may be positive or negative, depending on its content.[176]

Anselm adds a series of further limitations to the strictures that he applies to relative and infinitive statements. These limitations pertain to the sense in which the terms "substance" and "quality" may be applied to the Supreme Being. Unlike other things, he observes, the Supreme Being is identical with his qualities. He does not participate in them, as this would entail the existence of entities prior to him. Since he is simple, he is not a composite of his attributes, a condition which presupposes a whole made up of parts.[177] Anselm establishes these conclusions equipollently, by deductions from the definition of the Supreme Being at which he has already arrived. He employs redefinitions, grammar, and Augustinian arguments in explaining the categories of time and space as they apply to the Supreme Being. This being, he says, is atemporal and aspatial, and is yet everywhere all the time. His atemporality is deduced from his self-subsistence, as well as from his status as truth. Nothing can precede him, infers Anselm; and truth must be eternal in order for any statement about eternity to be true.[178] Repeating his previous explanation of creation *ex nihilo,* Anselm notes that here too, *nothing* must be treated as the negative of *anything,* rather than as a real entity, in order for the reader to achieve a correct understanding of the statement that nothing preceded the Supreme Being.[179]

The nature of time itself is a problem which Anselm solves in an Augustinian fashion, although his speculations lack the psychological profundity of the *Confessions.* He notes that time comes in three dimensions, past, present, and future, which are understood in terms of the three tenses of the verb. He further observes that the present tense is the only one which really applies to the Supreme Being.[180] Similar considerations apply to space, but here it is the adverb whose nature Anselm scrutinizes.[181] In general, he concludes that the Supreme Being transcends the categories of time and space. We can speak correctly of time and space with respect to him only if we remember that they do not apply to him substantially: "For if the Supreme Being is said to be in space or time, then even though on account of our customary way of speaking this one expression applies both to the Supreme Being and to spatial and temporal natures, nonetheless on account of the dissimilarity of these beings the meaning of the expression is different in the two cases."[182] To complete his treatment of the attribution of "substance" and "accident" to the Supreme Being, Anselm redefines atemporality and aspatiality into immutability. From this vantage point he observes that "accident" may not be properly attributed to the Supreme Being, since he suffers no change.[183] "Substance" is also improper because it denotes something which can be affected by accidents.[184] Strictly speaking, then, neither these nor other words which we apply to the Supreme Being can be applied substantially. Although we do apply them to him, we must remember that he is unique and transcendent,[185] and "hence, if He ever has some name in common with others, without doubt a very different signification must be understood [in His case]."[186]

In the Trinitarian section of the *Monologion*, proofs based on the usage of words are absent, except where Anselm wishes to specify the limitations of language. Equipollency and Augustinian arguments predominate. Anselm begins his discussion of the Trinity by analyzing the Creator's *verbum mentis*, a definition already established. On the basis of this definition he deduces that the Word is one, coeternal, consubstantial, and coessential with the Creator.[187] The Word, he states, is not subject to the change and imperfection of the created universe, which is his image and which exists through him; in short, the Word is related to the creation in exactly the same manner as the Creator is.[188]

When it comes to the relations of the Three Persons of the Trinity among themselves, Anselm relies extensively on the Augustinian triad of *intellectus-memoria-voluntas*,[189] although here, as in his discussion of time, his analysis is not particularly profound. According to Anselm, man's difficulties in knowing the Trinity spring from defective comprehension on man's part as well as from ineffability on God's part. It is impossible, he notes, for man to grasp precisely how God knows his creation.[190] It is even more difficult for man to grasp precisely how the Creator and his Word can be two and yet one, although, he thinks, the terms "Father" and "Son" have a high degree of rectitude.[191] Most difficult of all is the relationship among the Father, the Son, and the Holy Spirit. This problem impels Anselm to reinforce his caveat against applying human words to the Supreme Being substantially.[192] Still, he argues, the gaps in man's knowledge of the Supreme Being should not lead to despair and loss of faith. Anselm attempts to provide some consolation by elaborating some of the positive features of human nature, on the basis of his definition of the human mind as the best *speculum* of the Trinity. Man, he states, was created to know and to love God. He may do this partially in his earthly life. But, given the kind of being man is and the kind of being God is, Anselm can deduce the immortality and the potential beatitude of the human soul. [193] Given the possibility of eternal beatitude, he argues, men should be able to believe and hope in God, even though they cannot know him completely in this life. Furthermore, they should love him, which entails a faith living in good works. [194]

The process of redefinition, then, terminates in this point, apparent from Anselm's reasoning: "It is clearly advantageous for every man to believe in an ineffable Unity which is trine and Trinity which is one." [195] But the real end of the *Monologion* is reached when Anselm states his final definition of the Supreme Being, in which he asserts that all the definitions and explanations that have gone before it, and the name itself, are true, proper, and necessary. "Therefore," he says, ". . . the name 'God' is properly assigned (*proprie nomen dei assignatur*) to this Supreme Being alone." [196] The whole treatise is a quest for a name of God that possesses rectitude.

Anselm carries on this quest for a name of God rather more concisely in the *Proslogion*. His principal technique in this work is equipollency, although there are a few important places where Anselm's point turns on the usage of words. Augustinian proofs are absent, although the temper of the devotion in the treatise, particularly the prefatory *Excitatio mentis ad contemplandum deum*, has Augustinian overtones. [197] From the brevity of many of Anselm's arguments in the *Proslogion*, he seems to be presupposing that the reader has first studied the *Monologion*, where all of the same problems are analyzed in greater detail. As in the *Monologion*, he addresses the believer seeking to understand his faith. His aim here is to find necessary reasons which will explain that God is *what* we believe him to be and *as* we believe him to be; God's nature as well as his existence is to be considered. He also addresses himself to the fool who says in his heart, "There is no God." For Anselm, the question raised by the fool is not "Is he right?" but "Why is he wrong?" In explaining why the fool is wrong, he is able to show that his own definition of God, "that than which nothing greater can be conceived (*aliquid quo maius nihil cogitari potest*)," [198] possesses rectitude vis-à-vis the God of faith.

This name of God does not imply that either God's existence or his nature is contingent in any way on the powers of the human mind. Rather, Anselm intends the formula to indicate, first, that God is the greatest being and, second, that we can conceive of him. By putting the definition in the negative, Anselm gains the advantage of being able to develop the first stage of his argument without having to prove that God is a being; he chooses this name because it is the simplest one he can find. From Anselm's point of view, the beauty of the name lies in the fact that it is a self-evident definition; it virtually proves itself. Only one major equipollent redefinition is needed to show that the name is an accurate designation of God. This step is based on the distinction between knowledge *in solo intellectu* and knowledge *et in intellectu et in re.*[199] If *aliquid quo maius nihil cogitari potest* exists only in the mind, says Anselm, it does not conform to its definition. In order for it to be truly that than which nothing greater can be conceived, it must exist both in the mind and in reality.[200] Thus the name proves the existence of the being which it defines.

According to Anselm, the reason why the fool is wrong is that he fails to make this distinction between *esse in solo intellectu* and *esse et in intellectu et in re.* He therefore confuses mental and extramental realities. He has in his mind the idea of God as *aliquid quo maius nihil cogitari potest,* and he must know what this phrase means; otherwise, it would not occur to him to reject it as false. He assumes, however, that his negation of God's existence is an accurate statement about the world outside his mind.[201] It is not Anselm, but the fool, who makes an unwarranted leap from thought to being. What Anselm does, on the other hand, is to move from being to thought in the formulation of a name of God that does not contradict the nature of God as he is. The key to the fool's mistake lies in the fact that there are two kinds, or degrees, of truth in Anselm's epistemology. A word may have a natural truth when it accurately signifies the intention of the speaker, even when it is a *flatus vocis* with respect to existing things outside of the speaker's mind. A word may have both truth and rectitude if it correctly signifies its real object as well as the intention of the speaker.[202] *Non est deus;* in the mouth of the fool, is an example of a sign with a truth that is merely natural. *Aliquid quo maius nihil cogitari potest,* on the other hand, is a sign possessing both truth and rectitude. Rectitude cannot be divorced from being, but this is because rectitude is dependent on being rather than vice versa. Anselm's name of God can be called "verissimum" because it conforms to its object, the being which exists most truly.[203]

Once having established the rectitude of the definition of God as *aliquid quo maius nihil cogitari potest,* it is a fairly simple matter for Anselm to redefine this name equipollently so as to work out the salient attributes of God. Most of the argumentation here is an abstract of the same points in the *Monologion.* Thus he shows God to be self-existent, the creator of the world *ex nihilo,* supremely good and hence just, truthful, and blessed, and, in short, whatever it is better to be than not to be.[204] God is consequently omniscient[205] and omnipotent. It is only on the subject of God's omnipotence that Anselm diverges from his equipollent arguments in favor of a strictly grammatical explanation. This explanation is identical to the discussion of relative and infinitive statements and their comparative applicability to God in *Monologion* 15, and the point at issue is one he addressed later in *De potestate et impotentia* and a number of other works. How, he asks, can we say that God is omnipotent when there are some things, namely evil things, which he cannot do? Are his inabilities in this respect a real curtailment of his power? Anselm answers that God's inability to do evil in no way qualifies his omnipotence, because *not* to be able to do evil is better than *to* be able to do evil, and is consequently true of God.[206]

Reverting to equipollency, Anselm further deduces that God is immutable and yet compassionate. This paradox can be explained, he says, by the fact that he is immutable *in se* but compassionate *ad nos*. His compassion extends to all, even to the wicked, because it operates in accordance with God's nature rather than being proportioned to our own just deserts. This idea may seem difficult for men to understand, says Anselm, but it is true, because the reverse would be impious. In any case, he points out, justice can be redefined as the will of God, which effectively takes care of the problem.[207] Continuing to deduce attributes from his definitions, Anselm goes on to show that God is simple,[208] unbounded by time and space,[209] that he is light, wisdom, goodness, truth, eternal blessedness and blessed eternity, and finally that he is known and yet unknown, both because the human mind is dazzled by God's brightness and because it is darkened by its own intellectual and moral infirmities.[210] Anselm ends this section of the *Proslogion* with the affirmation that he has, in fact, proved that his original definition holds up under scrutiny, and he moves in his conclusion to his last equipollent redefinition of his formula from negative into positive terms: "Therefore, O Lord, not only are You that than which a greater cannot be thought, but You are also something greater than can be thought (*non solum es quo maius cogitari nequit, sed es quidam maius quam cogitari possit*)."[211] The importance of this final definition is that it recognizes God's unknowability as an integral part of his existence and nature.[212]

The remainder of the *Proslogion* is devoted, in effect, to a commentary on the known unknowability of God. For this reason there is a shift in method; the necessary reasons which best express this situation and the attitude which it demands are reverent statements rather than equipollent definitions. Consequently, Anselm makes practically no attempt to prove the assertions he sets forth in *Proslogion* 16–26. Instead, we find an extended prayer in which he catalogs divine attributes, usually reiterating characteristics that he has already proved, in a tone of voice calculated to impress upon the reader the necessity of mental humility before God. He begins with the point that God is incomprehensible,[213] then modulates into a mystic key by describing him as ineffably beautiful, harmonious, fragrant, sweet, and pleasant.[214] God, continues Anselm, is atemporal, aspatial[215] and transcendent.[216] He is wisdom, life, truth, blessedness, and eternity existing as one.[217] God is simply who he is. For Anselm, this implies the personal dimensions of divinity best designated in the doctrine of the Trinity.[218] Paralleling his organization in the *Monologion*, Anselm ends the *Proslogion* by praising God as man's true delight, salvation, and eternal joy, by exhorting the reader to translate this conclusion into appropriate action, and by presenting himself as an example of one whose knowledge and love of God on earth inspire his hopes for the consummation of that love and knowledge in beatitude.[219]

Where the *Monologion* is an extended quest for a name of God that possesses rectitude, combined with a series of proofs which explain the nature of that rectitude, the *Proslogion* is a treatise in which the *rectum nomen* has already been found before the work begins. It is likewise written to explain the rectitude of the name.[220] Although less detailed and explicit than the *Monologion*, the *Proslogion* is in some respects a better demonstration, because of its greater economy and also because it illustrates Anselm's meaning by its shifts in form as well as by his use of equipollency and grammatical explanations. In this latter sense, one might consider the *Proslogion*, Anselm's most individual work, as more Augustinian in spirit than the *Monologion*, notwithstanding the fact that the *Monologion* contains a larger number of overtly Augustinian arguments. In the *Proslogion*, however, the reader is placed in the presence of the theologian with his mind and heart at work. For the believer, this technique dramatizes the importance of the questions discussed and increases the persuasiveness of the solutions reached. Anselm's interest in moving his audience shows that he could find a place for rhetoric even in his grammatically oriented necessary reasoning.

Before leaving Anselm, we must consider Gaunilo's objections to the *Proslogion* proof and Anselm's rebuttal in the *Contra Gaunilonem*. Although neither of these works adds anything new to Anselm's epistemology of signs, both are nevertheless of interest. In Gaunilo of Marmoutiers we find a mind of high caliber, illustrating the high level of philosophical culture in the average Benedictine house of the late eleventh century.[221] Many of Gaunilo's arguments have served as the touchstone for later rejections of Anselm. As for Anselm, the *Contra Gaunilonem* gives him an opportunity to restate his proof, and it indicates that he has a thorough awareness of his own methodological presuppositions.

Gaunilo presents four major objections in his *Pro insipiente*, of which the first is by far the most important. It is based on the supposition that Anselm has started from the realm of thought, and that he is treating his definition of the name of God and the proof which follows from it as if they were heuristic. Assuming that this is the case, Gaunilo finds it impossible to follow Anselm's distinction between *esse in solo intellectu* and *esse et in intellectu et in re*. They are both in the mind; and if we begin with the mind, he asks, what grounds have we for claiming that the latter is extramentally real while the former is not? Furthermore, he argues, if this distinction were so obvious as Anselm makes it, there would be no fools. In general, Gaunilo's perspective leads him to the conclusion that the proof is a tautology. [222] Next, he challenges the idea that God is actually *in intellectu*. If God is unknown—and, after all, Anselm does say that he is not completely knowable—how can his name tell one anything about him? The name is meaningless unless one knows what it signifies. [223] Even if we assume that the name of God is *in intellectu,* this does not prove the existence of God *in re,* an argument Gaunilo illustrates with the example of an imagined perfect island which has never been seen and whose existence cannot be proved on the basis of its intramental existence. [224] Finally, Gaunilo argues that it is possible to conceive hypothetically of the nonexistence of God, just as it is possible to conceive of the nonexistence of the self or of anything else. [225]

Anselm's response reaffirms his sense of audience and is intended to remind Gaunilo of it. His critic is a believer, and Anselm addresses him as such: "Since my arguments are not attacked by the Fool, against whom I directed my treatise, but by an intelligent and orthodox Christian (*catholicus*) on behalf of the Fool, it will suffice to reply to the orthodox Christian (*catholicus*). [226] This reproof is cushioned by a compliment; no fool, he observes, could have constructed objections as good as Gaunilo's. [227] Anselm begins by restating his proof verbatim, and then calls upon Gaunilo's faith and conscience to attest to its truth. [228] Having shown Gaunilo what his proper orientation should be, he follows by proceeding to answer his objections.

Anselm's first step is to establish his *Proslogion* proof all over again by translating it from the indicative to the subjunctive mood of the verb, in response to Gaunilo's recasting of his formula into a hypothetical syllogism. No one who doubts or denies the existence of a being than which nothing greater can be conceived, says Anselm, denies or doubts that *if it did exist,* its nonexistence, either in fact or in the mind, would be impossible; otherwise, it would still not conform to its own definition. [229] It is difficult at first to see what Anselm has gained by pushing the argument a step backward into the realm of conjecture. However, by means of this subtle redefinition, he is able to prove that there is some point, at least, at which even the doubters and deniers are forced to admit that the extramental reality of *aliquid quo maius nihil cogitari potest* is possible. This conclusion deals in part with Gaunilo's first objection as well as giving Anselm a basis for his further redefinitions in the rebuttal. Taking up next the difficulty found by Gaunilo in the distinction between *esse in solo intellectu* and *esse et in intellectu et in re,* he points out that the intellect and reality cannot be thought of as locations where God may be found sometimes but not always. This argument is geared to God's known relationship to time and space; as Anselm points out, he exists *semper et ubique.* [230]

With respect go Gaunilo's second objection, Anselm maintains that words are intrinsically meaningful, in one way or another. Unless the person one is addressing does not comprehend the language, what one says to him will be in his understanding, and he will consequently understand it. Further, he notes, it is irrational to deny the existence of something just because one does not understand it completely; one can grasp statements in part about what one knows partially. Just as lesser goods resemble greater goods, so statements, even if defective, resemble the things they signify, and they therefore provide some positive knowledge about them. [231] Next, Anselm rebuts the third objection by observing that Gaunilo's example of the perfect island is an invalid one. All islands, however perfect, are created things. They are contingent; they come into being and pass away. It is not particularly difficult to contemplate the nonexistence of an island. However, he states, the same reasoning that applies to islands does not apply to God, since he is not contingent. [232] This same argument is also directed against Gaunilo's last objection. The self and all other beings that are not God are contingent, says Anselm, and they are thus eminently conceivable as nonexistent. However, nonexistence cannot be conceived of the being which exists in the highest degree, even hypothetically. [233]

Even more interesting than this point-by-point rebuttal of Gaunilo's objections are the overarching criticisms of Gaunilo's methodological presuppositions which Anselm makes in order to show that Gaunilo has failed to grasp his own. Anselm makes the trenchant observation that Gaunilo has misquoted him by understanding him to say that *if* something exists in the mind it *therefore* exists in reality. [234] He wishes to underline the view that the object is always the norm of its sign in the intellect. He also slices through Gaunilo's query of how, from a purely formal perspective, one would differentiate *esse in solo intellectu* from *esse et in intellectu et in re.* It is an irrelevant question, he says, that "is not my concern." [235] The reason why the question is irrelevant to Anselm is that, in this context, he is concerned with showing the accuracy of the *Proslogion* formula as a sign of God as he is believed to be, not with analyzing the semantic cogency of a phrase whose grammatical form is perfectly comprehensible. Anselm leaves Gaunilo, after reasserting that his original proof has been demonstrated by necessary reasons, with the final principle that one must always attribute to God what it is better to be than not to be.[236] Whether Gaunilo was, in fact, brought around to an Anselmian way of thinking by these parting instructions we do not know. However, his approach is not without its significance as an index of contemporary speculative thought, as well as pointing to the future.

Gaunilo was the only contemporary thinker of a speculative temper who appears to have taken seriously Anselm's epistemology of signs in theological discourse. Anselm did not succeed in founding a theological school in the strict sense of the word. While it is true that a number of Englishmen and Frenchmen of greater or lesser renown in the early decades of the twelfth century either studied with Anselm at Bec, or imitated one or another of his works, or were inspired by personal association with him as a spiritual presence, his influence as a writer lay more in the areas of genre and style than in the field of theological method. Those of his disciples who absorbed his grammatical approach tended to apply it to concerns such as biblical exegesis, to which Anselm had made no signal contribution, rather than to epistemological questions or to the technique of theological discourse he had developed. Most of these figures in the generation following Anselm had died by 1130.[237] The waning of Anselmian influence can be partially reconstructed by a survey of the manuscript traditions of some of his major works. There are only nine extant manuscripts of the *Monologion,* seven of which date from the late eleventh and early twelfth centuries; by the end of the twelfth century, the textual tradition had died out altogether.[238] The tradition of the *De veritate* presents us with a similar story, although there are even fewer extant manuscripts in this case.[239] Of the nineteen extant manuscripts of the *Proslogion,* fourteen date from the eleventh and twelfth centuries, three from the thirteenth, and two from the fourteenth and fifteenth; already by the twelfth century people had begun to dismember the work, preserving only the first four chapters containing the proof of God's existence.[240]

To what can we attribute the dislocation and the rapid neglect of Anselm's works so soon after his death? The reason can be traced to a series of changes in intellectual history that began to set in even while Anselm was alive, as the writings of men like Roscellinus and Gaunilo make clear. Indeed, Anselm himself contributed to the development of grammar as a more technical instrument of logical and theological analysis, and his own efforts fostered that very movement. Yet while Anselm himself could comfortably and confidently combine "the language of devotion and the language of hard argument," these vocabularies had already come to a parting of the ways in his own day, and they were to move even farther apart in subsequent generations.[241] At the same time, internal developments within the disciplines of grammar and logic that had begun in the late eleventh century tended to undermine the particular conflation of these branches of the trivium that is so marked in Anselm and his contemporaries. The effect of these developments was to separate the two disciplines for the time being and to point them in different directions. Logicians were spurred on in the twelfth century not only by the recovery and more extensive study of Boethius's Aristotelian translations and commentaries and his own theological works but even more by the translation of Aristotle's *logica nova* from the Arabic, making the corpus of Peripatetic logic available in full by the end of the century. The revival of classical literature that marked the twelfth-century renaissance also permitted and encouraged the reemergence of grammar as a technique of literary criticism as well as a technical subject in its own right. Not only the new texts and the deeper study of texts already available but the expansion of schools and the specialization of pedagogical functions enlarged the curriculum of both grammar and logic, redirected their emphases, and altered their mutual relations, so that the distinctions between these disciplines grew more clearly marked than their similarities.[242] The grammatical interests of the post-Anselmian period differed sharply from those of the preceding age. Syntax now became a major concern.[243] There was a split along regional lines, whereby grammar tended to become an ancilla of disputation in France and an ancilla of jurisprudence in the *ars dictaminis* of Italy.[244]

By far the most striking new development in the grammar of Anselm's day, interesting both for its affinities and lack of affinities with his own thought and as a forerunner of the semantics and formal logic of the later Middle Ages though lacking its philosophical substratum, was the speculative grammar that emerged at the end of the eleventh century and that expanded in the early twelfth century. Its original exponents were the disciples of one Drogo, whose works are not extant. Our sole source of information about him is Anselm of Besate, one of his enemies, who provides some insight into the ideas of Drogo's school in the process of criticizing them. About Anselm of Besate we are more fortunate. According to one of his editors, he was born around 1020 and was probably a cleric of Milan, but traveled widely in Italy, France, and Germany in search of further education. These peregrinations, rather than any philosophical inclinations he may have had, won him the cognomen "the Peripatetic." In 1045 Anselm went to Germany, where he became a scribe at the court of the emperor Henry III; in 1047 he was promoted to the rank of imperial chaplain. It is not known exactly when Anselm died, but he is thought to have ended his days as chancellor to Opizo, bishop of Hildesheim from 1054 to

1067.[245] Anselm's chief works are his *Rhetorimachia,* his *Epistola ad Drogonem,* and his *Epistola ad Droconem magistrum et condiscipulos.* Written in the late eleventh century, they achieved their widest circulation in the middle of the twelfth century,[246] although Anselm notes that Drogoism is already widespread in the Italy, France, and Germany of his own day.[247] Anselm's general objection to Drogo and his disciples is their alleged confusion between language and truth and their excessive verbal sophistry. Drogoism, he states, is marked by deliberate ambiguities,[248] *flatus vocis,*[249] a disrespect for traditional grammar,[250] "incantations" and meaningless digressions,[251] the use of distinctions and definitions so subtle that they cease to be helpful or even meaningful in terms of normal discourse,[252] and a variegated host of additional verbal sins. Drogo, in short, is a grammar-chopper.[253] His overrefined and jargon-ridden grammar is not only useless but misleading, because he insists that it is the criterion of real existence.[254]

This grammatical abstractionism scorned by Anselm of Besate aroused a great deal of antipathy in the twelfth and thirteenth centuries. Although he is known to us only through the filter of Anselm of Besate's ire, it is clear that a major concern of Drogo was the quest for a technical language more precise than the *usus loquendi,* an interest we have also noted in Anselm of Canterbury. Drogo and his followers have been identified with the "Cornificians" excoriated so roundly by John of Salisbury in his *Metalogicon.*[255] On the other hand, their ideas received the support of so distinguished a twelfth-century educator as Bernard of Chartres, whom John praises so warmly.[256] The criticisms of twelfth-century logicians were even more decisive than John's plea for a balanced culture and for the union of wisdom and eloquence. Abelard and the school of dialecticians whom he trained rejected the epistemological claims of grammatical analysis as part of their general program of annexing and subordinating to logic the functions that grammar had exercised in the previous generation, substituting for grammar their own discipline of logic as the prime instrument of speculative thought.[257] The same note was sounded even more strongly in the early thirteenth century, this time by the theologians, now reacting against the speculative grammar of their own day, which had been applied to theology with disastrous results, they thought.[258] This, in part, inspired them to hasten the decline of grammar as a theological tool. Grammar was finally replaced by logic not only because of the excesses of the speculative grammarians; concurrently, the logicians were recovering the complete *Organon* of Aristotle, thus providing themselves with an epistemology which they considered to be far more thorough, precise, and reasonable than grammatical analysis.[259] Grammar had become too dry, too abstract, and too irrelevant;

logic had to be invoked to humanize the thought of the thirteenth century.

In conditions such as these, a theology grounded so thoroughly in grammar as Anselm's and a theology that combined so freely the technical apparatus and the tone of prayer, which were to diverge so sharply in the twelfth century, had little chance of survival in the immediate sequel. The very qualities that make Anselm so Anselmian also made his conception of the theological enterprise difficult to accept for most of his immediate successors and rendered it an obstacle to the thinkers of the next two centuries. The problem of the impact of Boethius on Priscian ceased to be meaningful. But, despite this shift from grammar to a predominantly logical mode of thought after the eleventh century, the Augustinian epistemology of signs in theological discourse was retained. Having been dissociated from rhetoric and clothed in grammar by Anselm in the eleventh century, it was dissociated from grammar and reemerged in the garb of logic in the thirteenth century.

Three

Thomas Aquinas: The Conception of the Word

It is a well-known fact that the thirteenth century marks an important milestone in intellectual history, as scholasticism became the dominant mode of thought in western Europe. The development of the university, the increased professionalism and systematization of teaching in all its faculties, the reception of Graeco-Arabic translations, and the existence of religious diversity on a wide scale — these innovations, occurring as they did in a period of political and social change, produced a situation of intense intellectual ferment in western Christendom, as it strove to deal with a flood of new and sometimes alien ideas as well as with its own internal stresses and strains. Under these circumstances it is not surprising that the thought of the thirteenth century should witness a marked change in scope, emphasis, and style. Epistemology is one of the areas of thought in which this change is most apparent, particularly as it touches on the knowledge of God and on the problem of theological discourse.

It is an equally well known fact that Thomas Aquinas made a major contribution to thirteenth-century scholasticism. Since this is the case, it may seem strange to find him ranged in the same epistemological category as Augustine and Anselm. There are, to be sure, distinctive differences between Thomas and his patristic and monastic predecessors, differences too wide and deep to be explained merely as the triumph of Aristotelian empiricism over Augustinian intuitionism or Anselmian apriorism. It is true that Aristotelian logic in its contemporary form, the need to train professional theologians able to survive the disputative rigors of university life and to hold their own against heresy and nonbelief, and the encyclopedic mentality characteristic of the age do give Thomas's thought a tenor that makes it impossible to confuse him with either Augustine or Anselm. At the same time, we must not mistake form for content in addressing the question at hand. Despite his cosmological emphasis, despite the deliberate impersonality of his style, despite the fact that by using the intellectual vocabulary of his century he was forced to express his views on the role of signs in the knowledge of God in the context of a general epistemology that was in some respects poorly suited to this purpose, Thomas nevertheless retains the salient features of the verbal theory of religious knowledge which we have already found in Augustine and Anselm. Translated into the mode of a logic originally formulated to analyze and to organize conceptually the structure and function of the sensible universe, this theory is interpreted by Thomas so as to stress ideas, and to some extent the created universe, as the principal *signa Dei*. Like Augustine and Anselm, Thomas is concerned with the task of finding the most suitable terms in which to express man's knowledge of God, and he is interested in why these terms make different subjective impressions on different audiences. But above all he is fascinated by the conception of the Word, by the attempt to understand how the knowledge of God enters the human mind.

Since Thomas recasts the Augustinian theory of signs in logical terms, it is necessary to devote some attention to the kind of logic he used and what the perceived options in this discipline were during his generation. In the century before Thomas there had been a marked revival of interest in logic, stemming both from the Aristotelian translations and commentaries of Boethius and the widening availability of the Stagirite's *logica vetus et nova* and from the growing awareness that there were semantic questions, signaled by earlier medieval authors yet underrated by the Aristotelians, that required systematic investigation. The excitement generated by these complementary impulses won for logic the priority over grammar and rhetoric as the basic preparatory discipline among the liberal arts, which it had achieved in the late twelfth and thirteenth centuries, with major teachers such as Abelard and Gilbert de la Porrée pointing the way to its application to the tasks of the theologian as well.[1] The first half of the thirteenth century witnessed at Paris a continued efflorescence of both these developments. The study and teaching of Aristotelian logic grew apace, especially after the university statutes of 1215 prescribed these works as set books that had to be mastered by all candidates for the degree of bachelor of arts. At the same time, there was a considerable growth of the post-Aristotelian dimension of scholastic logic represented by the terminist school.

Terminist logicians concentrated above all on certain aspects of logic that had been treated inadequately by Aristotle and were particularly concerned with the significative function of terms within the particular grammatical and propositional contexts in which they are used. They saw their work as supplementing, not as replacing, Aristotelian logic. On the other hand, while they shared with their Aristotelian sources the view that logic is not identical with epistemology, psychology, or ontology, the terminists of this half-century tended to move with great swiftness from the extramental reference of terms at the first stage of signification to the intramental reference they acquire when they are used in particular propositional settings. This emphasis is reflected in the distinction drawn by the terminists between *suppositio* and *significatio*. The *significatio* of a word is its natural or lexicographical meaning, while the *suppositio* is its actual meaning, that is, the meaning it acquires in the verbal context in which it is situated. For the terminists, the *significatio* is a prior type of signification, but it is far less interesting than the *suppositio,* since the latter could be used to develop what L. M. de Rijk has well described as "a logic of language based on the cardinal importance of the verbal context for the actual functioning and meaning of a word."[2] Another index of the terminists' fascination with supposition was their development of the theory of syn-categorematic signs, designed to account for the significative function of words such as *every, if, and,* and so on, which have no *significatio* in their own right since they do not stand for any real extramental things or events. While it would be inaccurate as well as anachronistic to describe thirteenth-century terminist logic as metalinguistic, or as a purely formal logic, it is also true that its chief focus moved increasingly away from the analysis of the powers and limits of words in relation to their significata and increasingly toward logical and semantic analysis itself, to which the truth conditions of propositions grew more and more attached. Thinkers trained in terminist logic who used it as a tool in other spheres of intellectual endeavor may have believed that they were doing natural philosophy or theology thereby. But their approach led them to depart in practice, if not in ultimate conviction, from the Aristotelian view of logic as a methodology of science and as a means of structuring the information that the human mind can gain about the objective order of reality.

Even as the achievements of the logicians of the first half of the thirteenth century, in both its Aristotelian and terminist dimensions, were being sythe-sized by Peter of Spain in his classic *Summulae logicales,* a new movement, the logic of the *modus significandi,* came to the fore in about 1250 in Paris, where it was to dominate the field for the next quarter of a century. The rise of modist logic coincided with a new interest in commenting on the logic of Aristotle on the part of theologians, above all the friars. This interest stemmed partly from their desire to relieve the professors in the arts faculty of the task of teaching material which the theologians wished to teach because of its theological implications and partly from the wish, manifested most consistently on the part of the Dominicans, to understand Aristotle's works in as integral a manner as possible, eliminating the interpretations of intermediary commentators, especially Averroës. Although some of the leading proponents of modist logic in mid-century Paris were Averroists in other respects, they and their mendicant contemporaries produced versions of scholastic logic which served as alternatives to terminism during Thomas's period of intellectual activity, despite their divergent starting points.[3]

The modists shared with the terminists the view that linguistic analysis was the chief area where Aristotle's logic was deficient. They also recognized a difference between the natural signification of words and the reference they acquire when placed in a grammatical context. However, they posited far less of a gap than the terminists did between the functions of words as signs in these two distinct settings. The modists began with the idea that the purpose of language is to signify existing realities. When man has ascertained the properties of the realities, he imposes names on them, which signify these properties. Once this has been done, the name stops being a mere word and becomes a sign, a *ratio significandi* of the thing it stands for. The *ratio significandi* is a specifically vocal type of sign, or a *dictio*. *Rationes significandi* may manifest themselves in more than one way, in cases where more than one expression signifies a common nature. In such instances, man assigns different modes of signification, or *modi significandi,* to them. When *dictiones* have *modi significandi* imposed upon them, they acquire the status of parts of speech. They also acquire a fixed meaning, derived both from the grammatical considerations involved in the imposition and from the nature of the realities of which the terms are signs. Hence, in the modist system, each term or concept denotes a real being, a *proprius modus essendi rei,* and conveys as well a meaning dictated by its grammatical function. The real beings signified may be individual or common natures, and the terms that signify them may be, correspondingly, individual or universal. In either case, the signification is both accurate, verifiable, and immutable, since neither the essences of things nor the rules of grammar are subject to change.

The modists' notion that the meaning of terms is always the same once they have received their assignments as *modi significandi* and their assumption "that language, thought, and things are isomorphic with one another" represent their chief points of debate with the terminists.[4] The terminists charged, not without cause, that modist logic lacked the flexibility of terminist semantics, which is better adapted to explain linguistic phenomena such as analogous, equivocal, and synonymous terms, circumlocutions, and complex meanings. The inability of the modist logicians to provide convincing answers to these criticisms accounts for the relative decline of modism in the late thirteenth century and the full and final flowering of medieval terminism in the sequel. There was another reason for this shift in taste as well. While both modism and terminism are ontologically neutral per se, the growing impatience with Aristotelian epistemology and metaphysics on the part of the fourteenth-century scholastics inclined them to reject modism because it had, on its first appearance, been attached to these philosophical doctrines.[5]

In the generation of Thomas Aquinas, however, it was precisely those features of modism that were to inspire the disesteem of later scholastics that made it congruent with the needs and interests of the Christian Aristotelians within whose ranks he bulked so prominently. Modism was a way of asserting the primacy of concepts and words as authentic signs of real beings. Modism was consistent with the Aristotelian notion that real beings are fixed essences whose intelligible components can be appropriated by the human mind by empirical observation and mental abstraction. Further, the modist approach made it possible to apply a rigorous logic to universals and causes, to metaphysical and theological realities that are not empirical, experienced not in themselves but through their effects. The rise of modist logic in his own day was one of the conditions making it possible for Thomas to recapture Augustine's sign theory and to reformulate it in the technical language of thirteenth-century logic and to attach it systematically to an Aristotelianized Christian theology.

At the same time, Thomas felt free to draw on the ideas of nonmodist logicians, whose work, in the form it had achieved by the middle of the century, also contributed to his own use of logic and sheds valuable light upon it. One important feature of this logic is the fact that it is almost exclusively syllogistic in emphasis. To all intents and purposes it reduces argument as such to syllogism.[6] Beyond this, however, contemporary logicians recognized that syllogisms do not all possess the same probative force. There is the demonstrative syllogism, which begins with the necessary and certain causes of the conclusion and which produces scientific knowledge, the dialectical syllogism, which begins with probable causes and produces tentative conclusions, and the sophistic syllogism, which begins with what appear to be probable causes and whose aim is not knowledge, but glory or triumph in discussion.[7] In practice the logicians rarely used the sophistic syllogism. The dialectical syllogism, as they defined it, is actually the Aristotelian enthymeme, or rhetorical syllogism, which the Stagirite treats in his *Rhetoric* and not in his logic. While the mid-thirteenth-century logicians emphasized clearly the difference between demonstration and dialectic and while they assigned full probative power only to the former, they insisted that both could be handled syllogistically and that both fall within the domain of logic. This is an important fact to keep in mind in considering Thomas's conception of logic and his use of probable arguments in his theological works. His arrangement of his arguments in syllogistic form should not mislead us into thinking that these arguments are always demonstrated with scientific certitude in his eyes or in the eyes of contemporaries.

As already indicated, the logicians of Aquinas's day felt free to reassign a rhetorical doctrine of Aristotle to the field of logic. They also depart at times from the Stagirite's suggested order in which this subject should be studied. They occasionally combine Aristotelian teachings with insights derived from other traditions of ancient logic and with innovations of their own that are often less compatible with the material to which they are assimilated than their authors seem to think they are. While including this new matter, they do not always reproduce the full contents of Aristotle's *Organon* in their own logical curricula.[8] It is hence not surprising that Thomas and other theologians who sought to recover the most authentic Aristotelian doctrine possible should turn their attention to the production of translations of and commentaries on Aristotelian logic or that they should engage in philosophical disputes concerning their findings. In so doing, they were also seeking an approach to logic that squared with their own avowed purposes as theologians. They were quite well equipped to add their own learning on this subject to the flow of logical studies emanating from the arts faculty, for thirteenth-century theologians were thoroughly trained in logic, whether as seculars who had received the license in arts that was required for admission to the theological course or as mendicants who received an analogous preparatory education in their own houses of study. The tendency of the theologians to formulate their ideas in logical terms was a natural consequence of their intellectual formation and of the techniques of scholarly inquiry and debate typical of the university setting in which they worked. They are correspondingly syllogistic in method.[9]

Aquinas reflects quite well the contemporary theologians' assimilation of logic as the *modus sciendi*, along with the current departures from a purely terminist approach to that subject. He uses the terms "logic" and "dialectic" more or less interchangeably with "reason" and employs syllogisms for constructing arguments, particularly the deductive syllogism, in both demonstration and dialectic. He ranks himself clearly among those logicians of the time whose teaching on the relations between words and concepts and the things they signify concurs with his own reading of Aristotle as a logician, epistemologist, and metaphysician.[10] It was just this combination of ideas that provoked Thomas's later medieval critics to object that he had confused logic with metaphysics and with theological discourse.[11] Yet Thomas's position derives rather from the conviction that real beings exist outside the mind and that, while logical signs are an accurate way of representing them, the sign is not the same thing as what it signifies. At the same time, and despite its trappings in the technicalities of contemporary scholastic logic, his position also reflects his adherence to the sign theory derived from the Augustinian tradition. While Thomas substitutes concepts for words as the primary signs, he endows the human ways of knowing by means of concepts with analogous and sometimes with identical powers and limitations.

The involvement of theologians in the study of Aristotelian logic in Thomas's day is perfectly comprehensible in the light of their awareness of the contemporary controversies over the scope and applications of logic, which were of direct relevance to them. In part this concern is of a piece with the more widespread enthusiasm for the study of Aristotle and the many new translations and commentaries on his works that were made in the mid-thirteenth century. In some cases this new wave of textual study can be explained by the fact that previous translations were inaccurate, or were clouded by the extrapolations of intermediary critics, as was true of the Averroized *Metaphysics*. But the mid-century also witnesses the restudy of Aristotle's logical works, even though they had already been translated satisfactorily for the most part and incorporated into the curriculum of the arts faculty for decades. The majority of these new commentaries on logic were made by theologians rather than by logicians, and quite a few of these theologians were friars. [12] Dominican contributions to this enterprise, which were extensive, began about 1240. This development apparently reflects the order's loosening of restrictions on secular studies as well as the interest of its leading members in gaining insight for themselves into the significance of Aristotle's logic as a technique for dealing with the philosophical and theological problems that they wished to address. [13]

Highly prolific in this vein was Albert the Great, the teacher of Thomas Aquinas, who produced eleven commentaries on various logical works of Aristotle in the course of commenting on most of the Aristotle that was available in Latin in his time. One of the noteworthy features of Albert's logical commentaries is his tendency to stress Neoplatonic and Arabic interpretations, either because they made sense to him or because they were more readily available to him than representatives of the Stoic and Megaritic traditions of Aristotle exegesis. [14] Thomas contributed two logical commentaries, on the *Analytica posteriora* and on part of the *Perihermenias*, in addition to his treatises on Aristotelian ethics, physics, metaphysics, and politics. The logical commentaries, written between 1268 and 1272, are works of his maturity. They became justly famous in his own day for the easy familiarity with Aristotle's thought and the critical use of previous commentaries which they reveal and for Thomas's comparative objectivity, remarkable as thirteenth-century commentaries go, in interpreting both the literal sense and the intention of his author and in his wish to defend the integrity of Aristotelian logic in a period when this subject was hotly debated. [15]

The caliber of these works indicates that Thomas had a thorough and integral knowledge of Aristotle's logic and a good idea of its context. At the same time, he made use of ideas derived from other sources. He drew on Stoic semantics and epistemology, whether by way of earlier Latin authors or as a component of the newly available Graeco-Arabic tradition. He was also open to Platonic influences, both through other works upon which he commented and through the Neoplatonic elements in the interpretations and commentaries of his teacher. Thomas produced a commentary on the *Liber de causis*, a work attributed to Aristotle in the thirteenth century, but which was actually written by an Arabic author who derived most of his ideas from Proclus. He also wrote a treatise explaining Boethius's *De hebdomadibus*, a work combining Aristotelianism and Neoplatonism. Probably most important is the fact that both Thomas and Albert regarded Dionysius the Areopagite as an authority. Thomas commented on Dionysius's *De divinis nominibus*, and Albert wrote an exposition of all of the Areopagite's writings, which Thomas cites extensively in his own theology. [16] Stoic, Platonic, and Neoplatonic ideas thus found their way into Thomas's thought and affected his epistemology at the points which concern us, as well as did an Aristotelianism somewhat broader and more inclusive than the formal logic of the arts faculty.

Aquinas made use of this inheritance in formulating his views on the role of signs in the knowledge of the Christian universe. The term "Christian *universe*" is apposite here because Thomas, unlike Augustine, was interested in knowing the world as well as God and the soul, a concern for which he found both logical and theological warrants. While Aquinas has a theory of signs and some definite ideas on the nature of the universe, he does not have a systematically articulated epistemology. As George Lindbeck has well put it, if Aquinas had a systematic philosophy at all, he never wrote it down. [17] Thomas's views on the subject of knowledge must be pieced together, for the most part out of passages in his writings where he discusses the operations of the human mind by way of illustrating some other question. The only works in which he confines himself to epistemological questions are his commentary on Dionysius's *De divinis nominibus*, which takes up the cognitive status of names of God, and his

Quaestiones disputatae de veritate, which deals with the truth of man's knowledge. However, in this latter work he devotes far more space to the metaphysical and theological than to the epistemological aspects of truth.

The fact that most of Thomas's teachings on knowledge are scattered through the body of his thought is rarely suggested by his commentators, many of whom are anxious to extrapolate a Thomistic epistemology by wrenching his ideas out of the contexts in which he originally placed them. This procedure is regrettable, since the contexts are often quite illuminating. It is also misleading in that it conveys the impression of a system where one does not exist, fostering the misapprehension that the world Thomas was interested in knowing was a purely philosophical or scientific Greek world, rather than a Christian one. This has resulted in a highly intellectualistic interpretation of Thomas's epistemology which overemphasizes the certainty and extensiveness of man's knowledge of nature. In a few cases, scholars interpret this intellectualism in a Platonic vein. [18] Most commentators, however, place Thomas in Aristotle's epistemological universe, and do not shrink from attributing to Thomas Aristotle's unbounded confidence that the world is totally intelligible and that the human mind is perfectly adequate to it. [19] The effect of this point of view on the analysis of signification is to produce an interpretation of Thomas's signs in which they have full cognitive powers but no cognitive limitations. In some instances scholars have gone so far as to claim that Thomistic signs are identical with their significata, [20] although, if pushed to its logical conclusion, this view would have to countenance either the assimilation of the mind to the world or the assimilation of the world to the mind.

The main ingredients in this overly confident construct of the powers of Thomistic signs are quite easy to assemble. There is substantial agreement on it among most scholars, and it can be located at will by consulting any standard study of Aquinas. [21] In outline, this theory is an explanation of how the exterior world comes to be known by the knowing subject. So far as it goes, it can be documented from Thomas without forcing the texts. Thomas, like Aristotle, begins with the assumption that the world is so constructed as to be knowable by the human mind, that the mind is able to gain true knowledge of the world, and that the mind is primarily passive in doing so. Knowledge of the world, for Thomas, begins with sensation. Sense impressions automatically signify the objects they represent; falsity occurs only accidentally, when the object happens to resemble something it is not. An accurate sensible sign, or phantasm, is formed out of sensory impressions; it is then transformed into an intelligible sign by a faculty of the mind which Thomas calls the active intellect. The active intellect in a sense distills the significative content out of the phantasm by abstracting from it its intelligible species, that is, the aspect of the phantasm which is capable of being conceptualized. The intelligible species is then impressed on the possible intellect, or the mind insofar as it can know all things, and the possible intellect responds by forming a *verbum mentis*, or conceptual sign of the original object. This *verbum mentis* is directly analogous to the phantasm. It is produced automatically and is naturally free from error unless the intelligible species of its object happens to be confusingly similar to something else.[22] It is primarily the conceptual level of signification with which Thomas is concerned. While concepts are dependent on phantasms to supply the raw materials out of which they are constructed, sensory data themselves do not really begin to play an effectual role in cognition at large until they have been processed to permit the extraction of their intelligible components.

It will be noted that Thomas uses the Augustinian term *verbum mentis* to describe a mental sign. However, this term, in Thomas's hands, undergoes a change of meaning. For Augustine, a *verbum mentis* is the sign of a purely intellectual object of knowledge, such as the soul and other nonsensible things which are known by intuition. He uses this term to indicate that even intuitive knowledge is mediated in this life by signs, as well as for the sake of the Trinitarian connotations which the term arouses.[23] While Thomas, as we shall see below, draws frequently on the *verbum mentis* when casting about for analogies of the Trinity, he does not confine its significative function to any particular kinds of objects of knowledge on principle.[24]

The presence of an accurate conceptual sign in the mind in the form of a *verbum mentis* represents only the first step in Thomas's theory of signification. The subject cannot use the sign coherently in any kind of logical construction unless he is able to acknowledge that it is, in fact, accurate. This requires another step, the formation of a judgment on the object by means of the sign. The validity of the sign must be evaluated and its truly representative character accepted before the mind can willingly employ the sign in composing negative or affirmative propositions concerning the object. The need for an independent rational judgment of the *verbum mentis* recalls the Stoic stress on the role of judgment in converting a proposition from a simple presentation to a *kataleptic* presentation which the mind holds with certitude. The role that Thomas assigns to the will in performing this act of intellectual assent, except in the case of scientific proofs that constrain the intellect, also suggests the place of that function in Stoic epistemology.[25] In itself the judgment is also a conceptual sign of the object, although it may also serve as the significatum of a verbal sign should the subject wish to express his knowledge externally. The intentionality of the judgment makes it capable of being true on a conscious and subjective level above and beyond the automatic signification of the *verbum mentis*. Thus, once the act of judgment has been completed and the *verbum mentis* has been verified, the judgment as a conceptual sign possesses both truth and rectitude, in Anselm's terms.[26] In the process of judgment the subject must be aware simultaneously of the object and of the contents of his mind. His judgment will be true only if it affirms that what is, is. Only then will it correspond with or, in Thomas's terms, be adequate to, the thing it signifies. The mind judges, not by measuring the object against the yardstick of its own intellectual sign of that object, but by measuring the sign against the yardstick of its object. As in the theory of signification we have already noted in Augustine and Anselm, the beings signified, for Thomas, are the criteria of the correspondence, and hence the truth, of the ideas that men have about them.[27]

According to Thomas, then, we can come to a true knowledge of things through conceptual signs. What limitations, if any, are there on the extent of this knowledge? In the conventional picture of Thomist epistemology, natural objects are so constructed as to enable the mind to acquire a quidditative or scientific knowledge of them by demonstrative logic. This scientific knowledge is perfect, because it affords a knowledge of the essential nature of a thing. In knowing the quiddity of a thing, one knows it in itself and in relation to its cause; one can form a precise sign of it, a definition of its intrinsic being and place in the universe.[28] Thomas's confidence in the ability of the human intellect to perceive the proper structure of the world is shown by his frequent explanations of the relations between things in nature by means of logical relationships.[29] It would seem, from this analysis, that man is limited in his knowledge of the universe only by the fact that man's days are numbered and there are a finite number of things in nature to be known.

This, however, is not all that there is to be said about the powers of concepts and their logical arrangements in the knowledge of the world in the thought of Thomas Aquinas. The difficulty with the conventional approach is that it tends to stop here. In order to gain a complete picture of the nature of Thomistic signs, it is necessary to point out that there are, for Thomas, some definite limitations to their powers. His theory is far less intellectualistic than most treatments of his epistemology would indicate. In contrast to the untinctured cognitive optimism which is frequently attributed to him, Thomas makes it perfectly plain that intellectual signs, however far advanced on the road to demonstrative knowledge they may be, are different from their objects. Men, he states, do not know natural objects perfectly, even those objects accessible to the senses, since they have made and can make mistakes about them.[30] The mind of man, he observes, runs into even more obstacles in attempting to know objects which are not sensible, such as the universal causes of things. These "separate substances," that is, entities devoid of matter, are the most actual, the least potential, and therefore the most intrinsically intelligible things in the universe. But they are the least known things as well. Since science and speculation require a knowledge of things through their causes, difficulties in the cognition of these causes cannot but impose limits on our knowledge of other, less general things. Yet, because these separate substances are not sensible, it is impossible to know them perfectly in their essences.[31] Furthermore, the first principles upon which all science rest are themselves nondemonstrable; they are either intuited or presumed to exist because of their explanatory power.[32]

The limitations of the human mind with respect to its natural objects are also clearly implied in Thomas's analysis of judgments of truth. He repeatedly states that things which are known are known according to the mode of the knower.[33] At the same time, he affirms that things are the criteria of the truth of men's thoughts about them. Being is evidently prior to knowing. Being is also evidently different from thought; one of Thomas's most frequent assertions is that the order of being is not the same as the order of knowing.[34] The human mode of knowing is by means of sensible things. This condition makes the mind better adapted to the knowledge of inferior beings than to the knowledge of superior beings; the more intelligible a thing is, the higher its grade of being, the less the mind can know about it. Intelligibility is a property of things in themselves; it is not a property of things which they acquire when they exist in the human mind and under no other circumstances. The foregoing line of reasoning raises some interesting questions: If men know whatever they know in terms of their limited, sense-bound mode of knowledge, how can they know that a mode of being exists which is different from their mode of knowledge? If man's judgment of truth, of the adequation of the mind to its object, is itself a conceptual sign, how can the subject perceive the accuracy of another mental sign by means of it?

The answer to these questions can be found if we avoid either a radically objectivist or a radically subjectivist interpretation of Thomistic signs.[35] Thomas shares with Augustine and Anselm a metaphysical bias. Before he starts to theorize, he knows a great deal more about the universe than his insistent empiricism would immediately lead one to suspect. In the case of the knowledge of nature, he has a large selection of presuppositions about reality, which permit him to measure the adequacy of a given intellectual sign to its object.[36] He should not be confused with postmedieval empiricists who assert that sense data, and/or ideas derived from them, are not only what we know first but that they are all we know. The Augustinian theory of signs which Thomas adopted avoids these problems by insisting that we begin with existing things, that we assent that the signs men make of them may be true, but incomplete, and that we can judge this fact by comparing the sign with the original. For Thomas, sensibly derived intellectual signs do not leave the knower trapped within his own mind. Neither does the priority of being render human cognition irrelevant. Signs are true, so far as they go, and the knower is capable of judging that they do not go the whole way.

Beyond the philosophical reasons for the limitations under which Thomistic signs labor, there are a host of qualifications on their powers which are a consequence of the Christian dimensions of both Thomas's universe and his knowing subject. It is in their failure to give adequate emphasis to this fact that the conventional commentaries go farthest afield in attempting to depict Thomas's epistemology. After perusing the literature on Aquinas, one is given the impression that most writers are primarily interested in delineating, organizing, and even extending in some cases the areas of knowledge in which the mind of man is supposed to be able to operate on its own. The older neoscholastic authors do so in the effort to show that Thomas's Christianity does not prevent him from being a philosopher. This interpretation, which has been challenged successfully by modern scholarship, has been achieved by editing and rearranging his ideas in a manner which fails to show the true nature of his aims. It is necessary to state strongly that Aquinas was first, last, and always a theologian.[37] He was a philosopher only incidentally, and his philosophical statements cannot be isolated from their theological contexts and treated independently. This is a point on which even some of the most eminent authorities are confused.[38] The "autonomy of philosophy" approach to Thomas is predicated on a rigid distinction between nature and supernature and on the styles of knowledge which are considered appropriate to these levels of being, each of which is assumed to be fundamentally self-contained. It is well to keep in mind that the idea of pure nature is not found in the works of Thomas Aquinas. It is an interpolation which appears to have been introduced into Thomism by Cardinal Cajetan in the sixteenth century.[39] The knowledge of nature in Thomas is not discrete; it is part of a theological and epistemological whole. It is also something which he talks about in different ways, depending on what he hopes to accomplish at the particular point where he is discussing it.

A full consideration of the limits as well as the aptitudes of signs will clarify Thomas's perspective on the role of logic in knowledge.

As we have seen, there are philosophical contraints on the exhaustiveness of Thomistic signs, based on his view that the origins of man's knowledge are empirical. In the process of formulating signs, in the judgment of truth, and in the acquisition of scientific knowledge of nature through signs, human concepts are further bounded for Thomas by the fact that both the knower and the world he knows are dependent on God. God operates in the human intellect, since he is the source of all intellectual power. Man is part of the creation; he owes everything he has to God. The natural light of his mind is given to him and sustained in him by God.[40] Thomas describes the active intellect, the mental faculty which abstracts the intelligible species from the phantasm and makes it possible for the mind to form a conceptual sign of its object, as a participation of God: "If we posit that the active intellect is a kind of power participated in our minds, as it were a kind of light, it is necessary to posit another external cause from which this light is participated. And this we call God, Who teaches from within."[41]

As the final words of this quotation indicate, Thomas shares with Augustine the doctrine of God as the Interior Teacher. While human teachers, he thinks, may assist a student in his acquisition of knowledge by proposing examples, by strengthening his mind through intellectual discipline, and even by causing him to know things by means of demonstrations, their assistance is purely external. It is God who implants in the student's mind the light of reason and the power to know; and it is God who uses the teacher instrumentally as a proximate cause in the student's instruction.[42] The principal difference between Augustine and Thomas here is that Augustine is exclusively concerned in his *De magistro* with the transmission of religious truths through preaching, while Thomas has in mind the acquisition of knowledge about the natural world through the agency of the university lecturer.[43] It should be clear from the above discussion, however, that what Thomas means by "natural knowledge" is not knowledge which man can acquire without the "intervention" of God, for there is no such thing, but rather, simply, the knowledge which the creature, man, has about the rest of creation.

In judging the truth of its ideas, the mind, for Thomas, must also rely on God, and in more than one way. Truth, according to Thomas, is not only an epistemological condition. It is also a metaphysical transcendental, which is convertible with being. All things have truth to the extent that they have being; and their truth and being are dependent on God. As the Supreme Being and the supreme truth, God is the ground and the cause of the truth and the being of the various things which exist in nature; and they, in turn, are the criteria of the truth of men's ideas about them.[44] This notion is highly reminiscent of Anselm's idea of truth.[45] The parallel does not end here. Anselm's definition of truth as rectitude bears with it moral implications; it entails rectitude of the will as well as rectitude of the intellect vis-à-vis the object. Truth also has a moral aspect for Thomas. He discusses truth as a virtue as well as a metaphysical and epistemological fact. When truthfulness is simply the adequation between the sign and its significatum, it is related to God as the supreme truth epistemologically and metaphysically. But when truthfulness is what prompts a man to speak what is true, to be a witness to the truth, it is a virtue by which he is related to God as the supreme good morally.[46]

Having acquired a true, if partial, knowledge of things with the assistance of God, men are still faced with the task of discovering the essential natures of things and their places in the universe. Since it is a Christian universe, scientific knowledge and even speculative understanding fall short of the perfection and exhaustiveness which they enjoy in an Aristotelian universe. The ultimate in knowledge for Aristotle is a knowledge not just of things but of the nature and interrelationships of the causes of things and of the universe known through its causes. This, Thomas agrees, is accessible to man by the light of reason in signate form, but it is exhaustive only up to a point. Beyond that point lies the knowledge of the universe as it really is. It is a world created in the pattern of Christ and restored to God through Christ.[47] It is a world that is ordered by the providence of God, who disposes all things and directs them to their rightful ends.[48] Prior to the world we know, to the extent that we can know it, is the world as it exists in the mind of God. In order for men to know the real world perfectly, it would be necessary for them to know perfectly Christ, God's providence, and God's ideas. This is impossible, even to the blessed in heaven, for Christ, providence, and the prototypes of creation in God's mind are identical with God. To know them perfectly would be to know God perfectly, and this is possible only to God himself.[49] In this sense, a world created by God and endowed with its nature and purpose by God always retains some of God's own inscrutability, which is not so much a darkness as a brightness that makes it too dazzling to be seen.[50]

The fact that the world is created by God, as well as the epistemology to which Thomas is committed, makes it imperative for him to proclaim the importance of the knowledge of nature. Epistemologically, as we have seen, he holds that all knowledge, with the exception of intuited first principles, enters the mind through the senses. One must therefore study natural objects in order to acquire an understanding of their universal causes. Far more important than this purely philosophical interest in nature are Thomas's theological motives for understanding the universe so far as is possible. The most accurate vision of the world, although it may employ philosophically obtained knowledge, is a vision which is dependent on God, not only because God is the reason why the world exists as it is and why it can be known by man but also because the world is part of the divine economy. According to Thomas, one would misinterpret the true nature and value of the universe unless one were to recognize this fact. The investigator must thus have a prior knowledge of God in order to appreciate fully the importance of the world.

In addition, the world, for Thomas, resembles God and provides men with a means of acquiring knowledge about him. On the level of philosophy, this may be said to be true insofar as effects resemble their causes and serve as an a posteriori way of knowing these causes. Theologically, however, this is true because God has expressly constructed the world to be more or less like him and to provide a set of *signa Dei* for man. Such signs are aids in the restoration of a correct relationship between man and God,[51] a relationship which is obstructed by man's sin and lack of faith. Where the person to whom these signs are addressed is a believer, they can help to deepen his understanding of what he believes. In this connection, Thomas frequently quotes Paul's dictum: "The invisible things of God are clearly seen, being understood by the things that are made" (Rom. 1:20).[52] It is important for Thomas, then, that we know the world accurately; otherwise, we might misconstrue the nature of God. For this reason, one may "spoil the Egyptians" of their science, while at the same time recognizing that the first cause of the philosophers is not the God of salvation, who can be known as such only by faith.[53]

This view is based on Thomas's acknowledgment that the knowledge of God required for salvation comes from faith. Faith is addressed to, and has consequences for, the whole man, and not just the intellect.[54] For Thomas, faith is not merely a revealed metaphysics, which endows the intellect with a set of facts that it would not otherwise possess. Faith is, rather, a bond between God and man, initiated by God as a gratuitous gift,[55] which demands a moral as well as an intellectual response from man. These conditions are entailed both by the fact that God is the object against whom man's judgment of faith is to be measured and by the manner in which the human mind functions. In religious knowledge, as in knowledge of all other kinds, the object is always the criterion of what may be known about it. Even in the philosophical sciences, Thomas notes, different methods of cognition and degrees of certitude apply to different sciences, depending on what they deal with.[56] Now faith deals with God.

Since God is the supreme good as well as the supreme being and the supreme truth, man cannot form an adequate judgment of him in the act of faith unless he apprehends him morally, acknowledging God as the object of his will as well as the object of his intellect. God's nature, in itself and as the final beatitude of man, demands that men love him as well as know him.[57] Anything less would reflect a conception of God lacking a true adequation to God as he is.

Actually, the metaphysical bias we have observed in Thomas is a corollary of his God-centeredness. He sees knowledge of the world and knowledge of God as both regulated by God, although in different ways, depending on the metaphysical distance between God and the particular object to be known. In the case of his creation, God is the criterion of man's knowledge generally and relatively. In the case of God himself, and of the creation as it is known through him, his initiative and control are specific and absolute. In the latter case, God, as both the object known and the intrinsic cause of that knowledge in men, may grant or withhold himself at will in a particular case. In the economy of redemption, to be sure, he appoints apostles, teachers, and preachers to spread the knowledge of God through the world. These intermediaries may be compared at some points with teachers in the field of natural knowledge, in that they are both extrinsic instruments of God in transmitting information to other men.[58] In both instances, they labor, but it is God who gives the increase. However, the teacher of natural knowledge may enact his role without necessarily realizing that he is, in fact, God's instrument, whereas the commissioned teachers and preachers of Christian truth are generally cognizant of the fact that they have been called and ordained for their work. Further, they may be aware that God has given them special graces, which enable them to interpret correctly the truth that they are expected to communicate, and to express it with an eloquence sufficient to touch the minds and hearts of their audiences.[59] In addition, while the student addressed by the teacher of natural knowledge actually appropriates the information put before him by the teacher by means of his God-given rational powers, these are powers in which all men share by definition. On the other hand, an individual in the audience of an ordained teacher or preacher of God's Word is able to recognize the truth of what he hears, or to gain a deeper insight into it if he is a believer, solely through a gift of God's grace to him in particular, whether it be a preparatory grace which sows the seeds of a future conversion, the gift of faith itself,[60] or, for the believer, the gifts of the Holy Spirit which enable him to penetrate further into the mysteries of God, to perceive their theological interrelations, and to become aware of their practical applications.[61] This specific and individual character of the inner workings of grace is attested by the fact that, although all men are potentially believers, not everyone actually does believe. Some men before whom Christian teachings are expounded receive the gift of faith and some do not. Nor do all believers receive the gifts of the Holy Spirit to the same degree or in the same particulars. On the contrary, all men with the same intellectual aptitude are potentially teachable to the same degree about nature. Furthermore, in accordance with the fact that different objects of knowledge are at issue, the successful student will become a knower and will grow in the perfection of his intellect, while the successful hearer of the Word will become a witness or will grow in his witness, thus expanding in the perfection of his whole being.

Faith, and the understanding of one's faith, entails love and knowledge not only because they are signs of God which must correspond to his nature but also because of the way in which the human mind operates. In analyzing the mind in general, Thomas observes that the intellect and the will are functionally interrelated. It is necessary to know something in order to desire it as good, he says; and the desire to know must precede the act of knowing.[62] These interrelations are assumed in all mental operations. But in some cases Thomas gives priority to one or the other faculty. He thinks that scientific knowledge, for example, is primarily the work of the intellect. This is so because the necessary truth of demonstrative conclusions rules out the need for choice. Scientific conclusions constrain the mind to accept them; the mind is not really free to weigh them or to reject them.[63] There is thus no need for the will to encourage the intellect to assent to demonstrations.

In the case of faith, however, the will plays a much more important role. The will finds no difficulty in attaching itself to God as the good. The fact that this good cannot be grasped completely is no obstacle, since the quality of yearning for an unfulfilled desire is basic to the will. The intellect, on the other hand, is more exigent. It hesitates to accept as true something which it cannot know quidditatively and which it cannot verify empirically. One may wonder at this point why the intellect has such a problem when it comes to God, since it readily accepts as self-evident first principles which cannot be demonstrated. Thomas's reasoning here is essentially descriptive and is geared to the exigencies of theological polemic. In actual fact, he thinks, few people have difficulty with first principles. On the other hand, there are many people to whom God is not at all self-evident. There are also some who assert that God is self-evident to them, but Thomas takes pains to derogate this view by asserting that this self-evidence is merely customary and unexcogitated.[64] It may, of course, be true that this judgment represents Thomas's considered opinion of persons he knew who argued that God was self-evident to them. However, a stronger imperative for criticizing this position is that, if one subscribes to it, one has no means of rebutting the objections of those to whom God simply is not self-evident.

Stayed from action by the demands of an intellect geared to scientific knowledge, the unbelieving mind is unable to acquire the perspective which would help it out of its dilemma. The believer, according to Thomas, is aware that faith transcends science. Faith, after all, deals with the noblest possible object of knowledge; it opens to the knower an infinitude of truth and goodness; and it is absolutely certain. The mind toying with belief, however, can only see that faith represents partial knowledge, a knowledge which cannot be verified in a manner leading to scientific certainty.[65] It is to overcome these intellectual scruples that the will now intervenes, silencing the doubts of the intellect. In the completed act of faith, the will supplies what is lacking to the intellect, carrying the mind into a realm which the intellect cannot chart, yet making the mind cling to the unknown God with a firm adhesion.

The act of faith is thus accomplished by the intellect through the agency of the will.[66] While grace must be present to move both intellect and will,[67] it does not constrain the believer as does a scientific demonstration, which forces assent. The reason for this, according to Thomas, is that faith is a virtue as well as an epistemological condition.[68] In fact, his most extensive discussions of faith in his works of general theology, the *Summa theologiae*, the *Summa contra gentiles*, and the *Compendium theologiae*, are found under the heading of virtue. Since faith is a virtue, it requires both an infusion of divine grace, without which man cannot do what is good nor even undergo a preparatory change of heart, and the freedom of man to accept or to resist grace. If faith were forced into the mind by grace under constraint, it would cease to be a virtue. Belief, then, is proper to both the will and the intellect because of their functional correlation in the act of faith and because faith has moral as well as epistemological characteristics and implications. Again, although faith, once received, may degenerate into a purely intellectual condition which renders it barely adequate to shoulder its religious weight, it is through the will, under the influence of grace, that faith achieves its proper form in becoming a living faith infused by charity.[69]

The interaction of love of God and knowledge of God which Thomas posits conserves the basic outlines of the Augustinian and Anselmian positions on this subject. One is impressed, however, by Thomas's comparative lack of straight-forwardness in expounding it. In part this is a result of his use of an epistemology and a doctrine of mental faculty which perhaps unnecessarily complicate his description of the act of faith by forcing him to milk texts of Aristotle of implications which are foreign to Aristotle's mind. That Thomas does manage to maintain this fundamentally Christian position, despite the intellectual gymnastics that it sometimes requires, attests to his simultaneous commitment to both Christianity and Aristotle, or his realization that Aristotelianism was the only language in which his contemporaries would hear him, if not both.[70]

In the light of Thomas's teaching on the superiority of the believer's love and knowledge of God to the philosopher's knowledge of the first cause as an adequate sign of God, it is clear why faith rather than philosophy should provide the normative relationship between man and God. Yet, despite this fact, Thomas is by no means averse to the use of philosophical arguments in theology, nor does he shun logic in the elaboration of his teachings. It is necessary to indicate the precise sense in which Thomas admits the use of human reason, as well as the reasons why he makes these admissions. It is equally important to indicate the kind of emphasis that he gives to reason in the various contexts in which he employs it. This is a question that requires the elucidation of Thomas's conception of theology: its aims, its methods, his view of the cognitive status of theological arguments, and the ways he expects them to affect particular audiences.

Thomas's reliance on logic is so obvious that it is unnecessary to belabor the point. His use of the *quaestio* form in the vast majority of his works gives him ample opportunity to employ syllogisms of various kinds in his *sed contras* and in his responses to the objections in each article. Deduction is his ordinary method of proof, and he uses it in the discussion of every kind of topic, including those topics having to do with the nature of God. In addition, he is strongly committed to the principles of contradiction, identity, and excluded middle, and he uses these and other logical rules freely as explanations of God's operations.[71]

More problematic, however, is Thomas's use of philosophical proofs of the existence of God. Such proofs are found in the *Compendium theologiae*, the *Quaestiones disputatae de potentia*, the *Summa contra gentiles*, and the *Summa theologiae*, the famous "five ways" in the latter work being their classical locus. What kind of accuracy as signs of God does Thomas attribute to the conclusions of these proofs, and why does he use them? It must be admitted that the majority of commentators on the proofs do not contribute very much to the discovery of Thomas's intentions. On the whole, they either confine themselves to expositions of the five ways which try to establish the priority of one or another of them,[72] or, insisting that the ways are fully heuristic, they try to show that Thomas solves in advance most of the major problems of postmedieval philosophy.[73] A variant of this latter tendency has been the attempt to translate the ways into the terminology of symbolic logic, presumably to make them more palatable to the modern mind.[74] In general, one can say that this approach to the proofs reflects the interest shared by many modern Thomists in abstracting the philosophical texts of Aquinas from their theological contexts. The impression one receives from much of their work is that they are trying to make Thomas vindicate the autonomy of metaphysics.

Nothing, however, could be further from Thomas's true intention. His aim, on the contrary, is to show that philosophical proofs, although they may have their uses, are fundamentally inadequate signs of God. It is important to note here that the amount of emphasis which Thomas places on the respective utility and inferiority of these proofs has a great deal to do with the nature of the works in which he locates them. Thus, in the *Compendium theologiae,* a straightforward piece of positive theology, organized under the headings of faith, hope, and charity and dedicated to a believer, his friend, secretary, and fellow Dominican Reginald of Piperno, Thomas gives one proof of God's existence: Aristotle's argument from motion to a prime mover. The proof is located at the beginning of the work under the heading of faith. In stating his reasons for including it, Thomas simply says that God's existence must be affirmed before anything else can be affirmed of him, and that reason can prove this.[75] The *Compendium* is in no sense apologetic; Thomas merely wishes to observe that reason provides an extrinsic support for faith.

A similar intention is visible in the *Quaestiones disputatae de potentia,* although here the discussion is set in a much more academic context. Thomas begins by posing the question whether anything can exist which is not created by God. His answer is predictably negative, and he lets his case rest on the *sed contra* by quoting Paul: "From Him and through Him and to Him are all things" (Rom. 11:36). In his response, he goes on to observe that a number of pre-Socratic philosophers attempted to locate the universal cause in matter. This is an approach which he deplores, and he indicates his disapproval by citing with evident appreciation three post-Socratic proofs which involve an immaterial universal cause. The first is derived from Plato and others, by way of Augustine, and is based on the inference of unity from multiplicity. The second is Aristotle's *primum in aliquo genere* argument. The third proof also comes from Aristotle, by way of Avicenna, and stresses the possibility of reducing effects to causes until one reaches unparticipated pure act. The function of these three proofs is both to beat the Greeks with their own stick and to provide a bit of orchestration for the dominant theme already provided by Paul; Thomas's conclusion is: "For thus it is demonstrated by reason and held by faith that all things are created by God."[76]

The case of the *Summa contra gentiles* is rather a different story. This work was written at the instance of Raymond of Peñafort, head of the Dominican order, for the use of Dominican missionaries in Muslim Spain. Thomas's immediate audience was a group of theological specialists attached to the order's *studium arabicum* whose concern was the presentation of Christian doctrine in a manner persuasive to non-Christians who possessed a sophisticated philosophical culture. The *Summa contra gentiles* is a good example of Thomas's sensitivity to the rhetorical needs of apology to this type of ultimate addressee. He treats Islam not as a revealed religion whose adherents, like the Christians, revere the testimony of the Bible. Rather, he approaches the Muslims primarily as philosophers and relies heavily on the formulation of current philosophical problems as they had been put forth by Muslim thinkers, so as to provide a common point of departure with them. Thus, in stating the cardinal principle that errors should be disproved from authorities accepted by one's opponents, he concludes that with Muslims one must rely on natural reason.[77] This conclusion notwithstanding, Thomas does not mince words about the limitations of his suggested approach. He states quite plainly that although reason can know God as the first cause, there is a great deal more to be said about him.[78] Faith, he adds, compensates for these limitations and also aids the lazy and the intellectually inept in acquiring even the knowledge of God as first cause.[79]

Thomas's principal aim in the *Contra gentiles* is to refute what he holds are Muslim errors by showing that the teachings of the Christian faith are not opposed to reason.[80] Having made a clear distinction between truths that apply to God as the first cause and truths that apply to him as the God of faith, he considers it expedient to emphasize the former in the first three-quarters of the work. It is in this context that he proceeds to prove the existence of God, after proving God's provability, as a necessary basis for what is to follow in books 1 through 3. Thomas cites only one major proof of God's existence, Aristotle's argument from motion. Actually, he devotes much more attention to the impossibility of infinite regress of causes, on which this argument is based, than to the proof itself.[81] The importance of proving God philosophically in the *Summa contra gentiles* is a consequence of the apologetic burden of the work. Philosophy, Thomas thinks, is the only way to reach the Muslims. Since he assumes that they are all thoroughly grounded in the teachings of the Greeks, he also assumes that a missionary would be foolish to assert either that God's existence is self-evident or that it cannot be proved.[82] The Muslims, he thinks, know as well as he does, and possibly even better, that the existence of the first cause can be proved. The situation is not a matter for conjecture; the first cause already *has* been proved by philosophers using only the light of natural reason.[83] Thomas wants to make certain that his readers give proper weight to this fact; if they do not, they are in danger of being booted out of Spain as illiterates.

It is only when we reach the fourth and last book of the *Summa contra gentiles* that the intrinsic, as opposed to the ad hoc, value of such philosophical proofs is explained. Here, in the context of exploring the truths which may be known only by faith, Thomas emphasizes the limitations of reason rather than its cognitive possibilities. Imperfect even in the acquisition of natural knowledge, reason must be supplanted by faith in the acquisition of the truths needed for salvation, of which it can catch only a vague and momentary glimpse.[84] Extensive as Thomas's exploitation of the philosophical stance is in the *Summa contra gentiles,* the overall impression he leaves with the reader is a theological one; even in the books dedicated to the treatment of Christian doctrines by natural reason, the organization follows the theological movement from God to creatures rather than the philosophical movement from creatures to God.[85]

Thomas's treatment of proofs of God in the *Summa theologiae* is somewhat more subtle; it is, even, initially ambiguous. This is not a work designed primarily to confute non-Christians, but rather a general introduction to theology intended for beginners, designed not only to launch them in this discipline but also to arm them with the positions espoused by Thomas, many of which were extremely controversial at the time. It is safe to assume that these students would not have been working for degrees in theology unless they were already believers. The *Summa* seems to begin harmlessly enough, but it suddenly brings the reader up short. Although the first article of the first question of the first part of the work is ostensibly designed to prove the inadequacy of philosophy and the need for revelation and faith, it does this by proclaiming not only that there are truths about God which can be known by reason but also that only the lethargic, preoccupied, and slow-witted need know them by faith.[86] The impression that Thomas places a high value on the knowledge of God acquired by philosophy is fortified when one turns to the second question of the fist part, there to discover that it contains, not one, not three, but five proofs of God's existence drawn from philosophical reasoning, more proofs, in short, than are found even in the overtly apologetic *Summa contra gentiles.*

It may seem, at the outset, that the *Summa theologiae* does provide a case for Thomistic metaphysics after all. Closer scrutiny, however, uncovers some details which do not square with this view. The amount of space which Thomas devotes to philosophically demonstrable truths about God is proportionately much smaller here than in the *Summa contra gentiles* and the *Compendium theologiae*. Further, the proofs for God's existence presented at the beginning of the work are stated in a laconic, matter-of-fact, and summary fashion, as if to suggest that the author sees them as a chore to be disposed of as swiftly as possible, as necessary but well-worn preliminaries, before he addresses the main task of the work in his own distinctive manner. The last thing that Thomas does is to offer the five ways as novelties or as proofs original to himself.

In understanding the place of these proofs in the *Summa theologiae* it is important to keep in mind the role that this work was intended to play in the education of its readers, which in turn involves an awareness of the intellectual milieu in which it was written. The *Summa theologiae* aims at preparing incipient doctors of divinity to handle the kinds of problems they are likely to encounter in their work as professional theologians, especially if they adhere to the theology of Thomas himself in the contemporary debates, even if they did not become members of his order. Their course in divinity was designed to train them, not for the pastoral ministry in the first instance, but for the career of scholarship and teaching. Thomas's disciples could look forward to lives devoted to study, lecture, and debate in a university environment electric with theological controversy. While some parts of the *Summa theologiae* were written in the comparative seclusion of Italy, where Thomas had been called to develop a plan for theological education in a land not hitherto noted for its *studia* in that field, most of it was composed in the teeth of a new round of hostility toward the mendicants at Paris, which occurred at the same time as the furor over Latin Averroism and the interpretation of Aristotle in the arts faculty, coupled with the continuing agitation over the nature and scope of theology as a discipline. The theologians with whom Thomas's disciples could expect to lock horns were, to be sure, believers. But many of them took strenuous exception to his ideas and regarded his entire approach to theology as radical, dangerous, and worthy of condemnation. The *Summa theologiae* was still in the process of completion in 1270 when some of Thomas's teachings were in fact condemned by Étienne Tempier, bishop of Paris, in response to strong pressures from various segments of the university community, who thus sought to yoke Thomas's thought with the positions of the Latin Averroists condemned at Paris in the same year. In addition, the Parisian atmosphere was by no means devoid of philosophically motivated heresy, agnosticism, and nonbelief. Standing side by side with heresies of a more popular nature, a renewed awareness that the Roman communion was not the only Christian church brought about by the collapse of the Latin kingdom of Constantinople and the reinstitution of Greek Orthodoxy in its territory, and the increasing sense of Christianity itself as a form of identity to be measured, and protected, against other religions such as Judaism and Islam — these questions all provoked the impressive range and intensity of theological activity characteristic of the University of Paris in the second half of the thirteenth century. Thomas himself had helped to lay down the lines which many of these conflicts took, and it is understandable that he should want to pass on his point of view to his students. Those neophytes who elected Thomas as their master were, for their part, anxious to follow in his footsteps; otherwise, they would have chosen a different professor.

Now one of the quarrels in which Thomas was involved was the dispute over whether God's existence needs to be proved rationally, and whether it can be so proved. This was a hotly contested question among Parisian theologians. For Thomas, what was at stake was the *aggiornamento* of theology; in the minds of his opponents, among whom were ranged many of the members of the conservative university establishment and a number of prominent friars, what was at stake was devotion to the older ways, the dignity of revelation, and, in some cases, the vindication of a mystical rather than logical epistemology. [87] While the *Summa theologiae* in itself is not an apology for Christianity, it is an apology for Thomas's theology. His theological organization of his material, which moves from God to creatures, does not prescind from the fact that the style and method of the *Summa* give every article, in effect, an apologetic structure and tone. Thomas shows his interest in silencing philosophers' objections. But it is also the objections of his fellow Christians, some philosophically motivated and some not, that he has in mind. The structure and arrangement of the work, as well as the fact that Thomas is arguing against a fairly wide range of philosophical and theological opponents, give the *Summa theologiae* an intramural ad hoc character.

The principal reason for the inclusion of the proofs, then, is didactic;[88] it is to train his students to cope with Thomas's critics. Some of these critics oppose him as philosophical agnostics, heretics, and nonbelievers, rejecting the need for revelation. To this group Thomas wishes to prove the plausibility and necessity of theology as a science learned through revelation rather than through metaphysics. Further, he wants to show that the first principles of theology, although undemonstrable, are not opposed to reason. [89] Insofar as the philosophers may be dislodged from their complacent rationalism, such an array of truths about God proved philosophically may serve as *praeambula fidei;* their prejudices may be shaken if they are encouraged to see the harmony between reason and revelation where it exists. [90]

Many of the opponents whom Thomas envisages, however, are his own confrères who claim that God's existence is self-evident, or who think it impossible or impious to try to prove it. In general, they wish to exclude the new philosophy from the theological enterprise. Thomas's approach here is to make his points while indicating that he shares their reverence for revelation and for the mystery of God. He begins by giving his assurances that faith transcends philosophy and that God in himself is supremely self-evident.[91] However, he goes on to show the absurdity of the statement that God's existence cannot be proved by natural reason. He does this by indicating that it has already been done, and that it has been done by thinkers using natural reason and natural reason alone. It is in this connection that Thomas cites the five ways, beginning from motion, efficient causality, contingency, *summum in aliquo genere,* and purposive order, and arriving at a necessary, intelligent, supreme being, which is the prime mover and the final cause of the universe.[92] We have encountered some of these arguments before in other works of Thomas. None of them is original. Nor are they meant to be. The fact that they would be familiar to anyone conversant with thirteenth-century philosophy is precisely why Thomas employs them. In this manner, he hopes to point out to his objectors that rational proofs for God's existence are not only possible but actual. His response to the claim "It can't be done" is to show that it can be done, in virtue of the empirical fact that it actually has been done already. Even before he thus underscores the reality of what his opponents deny, Thomas proposes a further justification for rational proofs of God, based on the fact that they use a posteriori arguments. Rather than taking this occasion to stress the resemblances between God and creation in order to validate the use of proofs that work from effect to cause, an idea to which Thomas alludes with respect to rational proofs of God in other contexts, he displays his apologetic intent here, stating that a posteriori arguments for God's existence give witness to God's otherness, by affirming that man cannot know God as he is in himself, but only through lesser, human ways of knowing.[93]

Thomas's conclusion that God is not self-evident to man is thus designed to accomplish several things at once. It is an argument against what he holds to be obscurantism, against his critics' failure to recognize the existence and the tenability of well-known philosophical demonstrations. It is also a plea for the rejection of a support for faith whose contrary is incontrovertible. Finally, it is a statement of the view that philosophical reasoning about God does not necessarily reflect impiety. This latter point is just as essential an ingredient in Thomas's position as the former two. In the context of his proofs for the existence of God, he stresses it once more, emphasizing the gap between God and man by asserting that men should not confuse their own fuzzy apperceptions, desires, and verbal intentions with facts.[94]

It is in this connection that Thomas restates and condemns Anselm's *Proslogion* proof. He rejects it because he is unaware of its nature.[95] This leads him to misconstrue the aim of the author of the proof. Thomas mistakenly thinks that Anselm is trying to provide a philosophical demonstration in terms of the truth criteria of first principles. He is unwittingly put off by the fact that he has a different conception of definition from Anselm. For Anselm, definition is a grammatical notion. It refers to the name of a person or a thing; it is, in short, simply a noun or a nominal phrase. His aim in the *Proslogion,* as we have seen, is to find and to explain a *rectum nomen* for God, with all that rectitude implies. On the other hand, a definition, for Thomas, is a judgment which signifies a quidditative grasp of its object and which can be used as a term in a demonstrative syllogism. It is thus out of the question, for Thomas, to try to define God. One of the most interesting paradoxes in Thomas Aquinas is that he argues the bulk of his own theology along lines resembling Anselm's more than he realizes, as will become clear below, although his logical presuppositions prevent him from perceiving this fact.[96]

The proofs of God's existence in the *Summa theologiae* are not ends in themselves. Thomas's mode of presenting them is conditioned by the fact that he is trying to address and to convince several groups of critics simultaneously, some orthodox and some heterodox, some rationalist and some antirationalist. As in the *Summa contra gentiles,* Thomas does not wish to leave the impression that the ad hoc presentation at the beginning of the first part of the *Summa theologiae* is all that there is to be said. In the second part of the *Summa,* where he treats things from a faith-oriented perspective, he indicates his overall views on the values and limits of the proofs. Philosophical knowledge of God, he states, is valid to some extent, but only because it is participated from the knowledge of God by faith.[97] Even though it is possible to know some things about God by reason, he says, it is better to know them by faith. Faith is more certain than reason, and, more importantly, faith is a virtue which reflects a right relation to God. Now the only truly virtuous motive for believing in God is the acceptance of the preambles of faith because they are proposed on God's authority. If one believes for this reason, one's faith has merit. The merit that attaches to this assent, however, does not attach to an assent to truths about God in the category of *praeambula fidei* which are held on the authority of reason. Since what is known demonstratively is not believed, at least not by the same person at the same time, a philosophical knowledge of God thus adds nothing to the merits of faith, but rather reduces the number of the truths of faith that are believed on God's authority. While a believer who can show that there are rationally demonstrable preambles of faith may indeed do a good work for the sake of the nonbeliever by pointing him in the right direction and by making it difficult for him to think that Christian belief is a form of obscurantism, the preambles of faith are not to be equated with the effort on the believer's part to understand more fully the beliefs he already possesses. For the process of *intellectus fidei* is largely accomplished by means of deductive and dialectical syllogisms whose conclusions are governed not only by their logical form but by the norm of theological appropriateness, unlike the five ways, which are presented as inductive and demonstrative syllogisms whose conclusions verify the existence of a philosopher's God. A believer would be seriously mistaken if he thought that the conclusions of the five ways enlarged his faith. A nonbeliever convinced by the proofs would still not possess the conviction necessary for a normative religious connection with the God of faith. But, for Thomas, as for Anselm, the greatest demerits go to those who refuse to believe what they cannot grasp scientifically by means of a demonstrative proof.[98]

Surveying in general Thomas's conclusions on the values and limits of philosophical statements about God proved by inductive logic as signs of God, it appears that he considers them most useful in apologetic contexts. Elsewhere they may provide extrinsic support for things that are believed. The prevailing impression one gets from the *Summa theologiae* is that such knowledge is valuable not only apologetically but also to counteract current theological approaches which Thomas thinks would make Christian faith appear irrelevant or indefensible to the *litterati*. On the whole, despite their uses, he maintains that a posteriori proofs of God's existence drawn from reason are weaker than they are strong. They bear only a shadowy resemblance to their object, both because the mind cannot know perfectly the creatures on which they are based and because the creatures themselves fall infinitely short of God. In any case, according to Thomas, it is possible only for a believer to recognize the existence and the extent of the resemblances between God and creatures,[99] and hence only a believer can judge the accuracy of philosophical proofs of God.

Helpful as these signs may be as *praeambula fidei* for the nonbeliever, Thomas does not neglect to note that they are purely external and indicative. The real and intrinsic *praeambula fidei* are the preparatory graces which God gives to a person whom he intends to convert,[100] without which the potential believer would be unable even to take these proofs seriously as indicative signs. And, finally, proofs of God's existence by natural reason cannot even achieve the heuristic, demonstrative status which they claim on their own basis. All judgments, for Thomas, require the knower's awareness of the thing to which his mental sign is to be compared. In order to make an intellectual judgment about something, one has to have some prior knowledge of its nature: "But we know that we cannot know whether a thing is unless we know in some way what it is, whether by perfect cognition or, at least, by confused cognition."[101] These conditions apply to God as well as to other things. In fact, they are especially applicable to God because he is supremely simple; his essence and existence are one. God's nature can be known, not, to be sure, perfectly, but in part, *per speculum in aenigmate*. But this is the knowledge of faith, not of philosophy. Notwithstanding Thomas's frequent assertions that philosophical knowledge is a preparation for faith, in the last analysis it appears to be not only extrinsic to faith but ex post facto. The kind of knowledge that would make the proofs work rests on faith.[102]

Although a great deal of emphasis is traditionally placed on such rational strategies as the proofs of God's existence as characteristic of the theology of Thomas Aquinas, in actual practice they play a very minor role in it. The vast majority of Thomas's work does not consist in the application of demonstrative reason to the world in order to induce truths about God, but rather in the deduction of conclusions from the truths of faith by dialectical reasoning. This is a procedure which Thomas calls *sacra doctrina*. *Sacra doctrina* must be carefully distinguished from metaphysics, or natural theology.[103] Although they both use reason, they employ it in different ways, to a different extent, and with different results. For our purposes, the most important consequence of this distinction is that *sacra doctrina*, or the science of theology, is concerned with signs of God which are more complete and accurate than those produced by natural reason. Also, where the function of philosophical signs in religious knowledge is largely indicative, the function of signs that are, strictly speaking, theological, is largely commemorative.

For Thomas, the science of theology is a science because it employs rational arguments and syllogisms. However, it is essential to note that Thomas uses the term *scientia* in a variety of ways: as the absolutely certain knowledge produced by demonstrative syllogisms, as the firm possession of certain knowledge, and as a gift of the Holy Spirit.[104] It is in the latter two senses, with a qualified admixture of syllogism, that Thomas considers theology a science. It is not a science in the strict Aristotelian sense of the word.[105] The science of theology, like other branches of science, is grounded on first principles, which are not demonstrable. In the case of the philosophical sciences, the first principles are not demonstrable because they are self-evident; in the case of theology, the first principles are not demonstrable because they are articles of faith which cannot be known by reason. [106] *Sacra doctrina* does not deal with the kind of articles of faith which may be known philosophically as *praeambula fidei*. Instead, it works with beliefs concerning the Trinity and the Incarnation, which are accessible only by faith. Thomas also includes in the category of *sacra doctrina* the problem of whether the universe is eternal, because he does not think that it can be solved philosophically. [107]

Scientific theology, as defined above, was not something new to Thomas. It was a development which began around 1130, with the arrival of Aristotle's *logica nova* in western Europe. [108] The second half of the twelfth century shows the gradual displacement of scriptural commentaries using grammatical techniques of exegesis, which up until this time had been the dominant style of theology, by the new discipline. The growing use of *quaestiones* at this time indicates the emergence of a more logical approach to theology, as does the shift in the meanings of some key words. *Sententiae,* for example, which traditionally had been statements of the church fathers used as the basis for glosses, or as the contents of *florilegia,* came to be systematically arranged compilations of theological interpretations. The standard work in this genre, the *Sentences* of Peter Lombard, became in turn the subject of innumerable commentaries in the thirteenth century. In general, the emergence of theology as a science marked a separation between speculative theology and biblical exegesis. Most of the progressive theologians began to use extrascriptural modes of proof; logical skill, rather than the extensive citation of authorities, came to dominate theological treatises.

There were some thirteenth-century opponents to these developments. Robert Grosseteste and Roger Bacon held out for a more scriptural emphasis, and the conservative secular theologians at the University of Paris were disturbed. However, by 1220, William of Auxerre had formulated at Paris the classic scholastic statement of the rights of reason in theology in his *Summa aurea.* William begins by affirming the priority and independence of faith. At the same time, he employs rational methods to develop his conclusions. He sees three different uses for reason in theology: to augment and to confirm the faith of believers, to convince heretics of error, and to incline the ignorant toward faith. William justifies his position by taking Paul's definition of faith as the *argumentum non apparentium,* as well as Aristotelian logic, as a warrant. This new view attained wide popularity in the years following the publication of the *Summa aurea,* particularly among the friars now making their way to Paris. Such prominent theologians as Eudes Rigaud, Simon of Tournai, the Franciscans Alexander of Hales and Bonaventura, and the Dominicans Albert the Great, Robert Kilwardby, and Thomas Aquinas adhered to it. The proponents of theology as a science in the thirteenth century all believed that its technique in no way altered the nature of theology as *sapientia,* as a quest for communion with God, and as an activity integrally related to the personal piety of the theologian, although some, with Bonaventura, emphasized the affective side of the theological enterprise more than others. None of them believed that the proofs used in scientific theology were conclusive demonstrations.

Thomas is an inheritor of this tradition, but he elaborates and refines it somewhat. The most noticeable difference between his own interpretation of theology and William's is Thomas's distinction between demonstration and dialectic, which goes back to scholastic logic. For Thomas, demonstration has no place in a science based on faith because demonstrative proofs can either be verified empirically or referred to self-evident first principles. However, God, the object of faith, is not available for empirical tests, and is not, in Thomas's view, self-evident to men. Therefore, he selects dialectics as the appropriate type of reasoning for theology, its function being to find probable arguments. [109] Within the general category of theological arguments, however, not all are dialectical. Some conclusions are only deducible from faith on divine authority, whether it be through Scripture or through another article of faith. These proofs, he states, are extremely convincing for the believer. They are more potent than scientific demonstrations, because the believer holds the first principles of faith with more certainty than he holds philosophical first principles. [110] One of Thomas's most frequently used types of the argument from divine authority is the argument from theological suitability. He employs this proof in discussing God in general, [111] but more often in connection with the Trinity[112] or the Incarnation. [113] Its basic criterion is the norm of what is fitting to God, in terms of what one already knows about his nature and operations by faith. This is something that a believer, and only a believer, can judge.

Thomas's second major source of arguments is the dialectical syllogism. Its conclusions are less probable than those derived from divine authority, but they can be accepted both by believers and nonbelievers. It is because of their wide appeal that Thomas advocates public debates on theology employing dialectical syllogisms before a heterogeneous audience. The rules he lays down for this kind of debate put one back in the intellectual world of the thirteenth-century university town. They also exemplify Thomas's concern for the social responsibilities of the theologian. One is struck by the level of dialectical skill he demands in his theologians. Although limited to the use of probable arguments, the theologian, says Thomas, may not convey the impression that the articles of faith are themselves doubtful. His stated reason for arguing, outside of jeu d'esprit, is to refute error, but he must do so without suggesting that his refutations have been demonstratively proved, for if he did this he would hold the Christian faith up to the ridicule of objectors capable of detecting such a logical faux pas.[114] His probable arguments also avail to the consolation of the faithful.[115] But here, Thomas notes, the theologian must exercise prudence and discretion, lest he bewilder and demoralize rather than edify. Thomas notes that the literate believer, who can be counted on to be theologically sophisticated, will enjoy the disputation and will profit from it. But in the case of weak or poorly instructed brethren, the theologian must rapidly discover whether they are beset by nonbelievers trying to corrupt their faith. If this is so, he must take the risk that they will be confused by theological debate; if not, it is best to leave them undisturbed.[116]

In addition to the needs of the people whom the theologian is commissioned to serve, he has personal requirements to meet in his work. According to Thomas, theology has an important practical side, but it is primarily a speculative science, which aims at beatitude.[117] Both the public and the private goals of theology make it essential that it be a living dialogue between the contemplator and God, and not merely an abstract discipline. Practical and speculative theology alike demand that the theologian's work be wedded to his spiritual life. The grace of God, piety, and personal holiness are required for the deepening of his understanding of what he believes,[118] an exercise of *fides quaerens intellectum* that contributes both to his external effectiveness and to his own contemplation. As an instructor, Thomas notes, the theologian needs the gifts of knowledge and understanding, which teach him how to make the faith known.[119] If he is a preacher, he also needs the gift of speech, in order to carry out successfully the Augustinian mission to teach, to delight, and to persuade.[120] Man's cognitive powers, Thomas observes, are affected by his moral status.[121] Since the end of contemplation is the vision of God, the theologian must strive to grow in wisdom and virtue. *Intellectus fidei*, as well as faith itself, demands the functional interaction of love and knowledge,[122] and the grace of prayer,[123] as well as the faculty for finding probable arguments.

For Thomas, the knowledge of God acquired through a deepened faith is the most adequate sign of God, short of mystic rapture, that is available to man in this life. Yet, he states, all knowledge by faith is essentially partial and confused. Theological speculation is just that: the knowledge of God *per speculum in aenigmate*.[124] It is in this context, the context of *sacra doctrina,* that

Thomas considers a final species of sign, which brings into sharp focus the tension between man's God-given ability to speak about God and the impossibility of his ever saying anything truly commensurate with him. One of the tasks of the theologian, Thomas states, is to provide likely similitudes about God, for the purpose of clarifying the divine truths which he teaches. [125] These similitudes must bear a resemblance to God; otherwise, they are useless. They cannot be anything but probable, because they are to be dealt with under the heading of *sacra doctrina* rather than natural theology. The problem of locating signs such as these was one that both Augustine and Anselm had to face. For Thomas, the quest was even more difficult because he was obstructed by his logical habits of mind and by the scholastic method of his theology from finding the easiest solution to it. Where Augustine and Anselm respond with apt figures of speech and are able to specify the paradox posed by the assignment of discussing the known yet unknown God in the programmatic arrangement of their works, Thomas is blocked by the impersonality and argumentativeness of the *quaestio* style and by the fact that his stylistic predilections incline him to replace figurative language with literal and discursive speech wherever possible. It is not that Thomas's poetic sensibilities were atrophied. His liturgical verse shows him a master at that art. But his poetic style is one of highly intellectualized verbal conceits and multiple layers of connotation rather than metaphor. [126] Given the problem of dealing with transferred meanings, Thomas's response was analogy. Analogy is his attempt to make logic do what can be done much more easily by metaphor, in speaking about God from the limited vocabulary provided by human ways of knowing.

Analogy, for Thomas, is essentially a *façon de parler*. It is necessary to make this point quite clearly at the outset because the prevailing approach is to regard Thomistic analogy as an *ex professo*, systematic, and metaphysical doctrine. In so doing, the neoscholastic commentators responsible for this interpretation have placed a far heavier philosophical weight upon analogy than Thomas ever engineered it to carry. It is not our intention here to enter the intramural disputes among Aquinas scholars on analogy; for our purposes, most of them have asked the wrong questions. [127] Before proceeding further, however, it may be useful to state the traditional conceptions of Thomistic analogy and to indicate why we think that the subject requires an approach different from the approaches usually accorded it.

It should be noted at the outset that analogy is a device used by Thomas to explain how we can think about two or more things that are not quite the same and yet not entirely different, and that therefore cannot be thought of either univocally or equivocally. Thomas is very unsystematic about analogy, which is the best he can do in trying to rationalize ambiguities while keeping them ambiguous at the same time.[128] He does not limit analogy to the relationships between God and creatures. Thus, not all the analogies that can be found in Thomas's works are directly relevant to the problem of theological discourse, although attention has usually been directed to those analogies which Thomas thinks can be used for this purpose. A second point that should be kept in mind is that there are two approaches to analogy in Thomas, the theoretical and the practical. Virtually all the commentary on this subject has been confined to the theoretical level. It has thus concentrated on what Thomas says about analogy. No attempt has been made to examine in detail the kinds of analogies that Thomas actually uses when he wants to elucidate the nature of God by reference to creatures. As we shall see, Thomas's use of analogy in practice goes a long way toward explaining his doctrine of analogy in theory.

Although a variety of different kinds of analogy have been found in Thomas's writings by the assiduous scholarship of his disciples,[129] the debates of the commentators have focused on two kinds, the analogy of attribution and the analogy of proper proportionality. In the analogy of attribution, a characteristic, such as being, is attributed to two or more entities, each of which bears a relationship to being that is different from the others. The prime analogate possesses being properly and intrinsically, while the secondary analogates possess being extrinsically, by attribution from the prime analogate. In the analogy of attribution, then, being is regarded as intrinsically one and as relatively diverse. Being is present in the various analogates *per prius et posterius*. The classic example used to illustrate the analogy of attribution is drawn from Aristotle: an animal, urine, and medicine are all called healthy. The health involved is the same in each case, but each of the analogates is related to it in a different way. Health is an attribute proper to an animal. Urine may be "healthy," since it is a sign of health; and medicine may be "healthy" because it is conducive to health. In general, the analogy of attribution tends to stress the similarities among the analogates rather than their differences. Scholars who follow Suarez on Thomistic analogy and those who wish to emphasize the Neoplatonic aspects of Thomism are inclined to consider the analogy of attribution the basic kind of analogy in Thomas, since it can be used in a participationist type of metaphysics more easily than can other kinds of analogy.

The chief contender for the title of basic Thomistic analogy is the analogy of proper proportionality. The analogy of proper proportionality sets up a four-term proportion. The classic example of such a proportion is: man's being: man as God's being: God. In contrast to the analogy of attribution, being is proper here to each of the analogates. In the case of both man and God, the mode of being in question is intrinsic to the entity in question, although the two modes of being are not equal to each other. As opposed to the analogy of attribution, the analogy of proper proportionality presents us with a situation in which being is regarded as intrinsically diverse, and only relatively one. The analogy of proper proportionality thus tends to emphasize the differences between the analogates rather than their similarities. Scholars who stand with Cajetan on Thomistic analogy are inclined to reject the claims of all kinds of analogy exept proper proportionality to be truly Thomistic.

The prevailing trend in analogy scholarship has been reductionism. It is the foregone conclusion of most of the commentators that there must be one and only one kind of analogy that is "properly Thomistic." On this point there is almost universal agreement; the debate among the commentators centers on whether the one, true Thomistic analogy is the analogy of attribution or the analogy of proper proportionality. There are a variety of reasons why scholars argue for the one or the other. They range from metaphysical bias to the adding up of all the instances where Thomas cites analogy and the conclusion that the analogy which appears most frequently is the "properly Thomistic" one. In reaction against reductionism, M. C. D'Arcy has urged that it is a mistake to emphasize either kind of analogy at the expense of the other. If we adhere too rigidly to attribution, he states, the result is pantheism; and if we adhere too rigidly to proper proportionality, the result is relativism. [130] Others have sought to heal the breach by arguing that analogy describes similarities which lie "halfway between equivocity and univocity." [131]

These positions, despite their differences, all reveal an approach to the understanding of Aquinas that is as noncontextual as it is unhistorical. Scholars whose preference for one kind of analogy or another rests on metaphysical grounds show their willingness to base their views on traditional sixteenth-century Thomistic authorities, often at the expense of the text of Thomas, or on their equally traditional unwillingness to believe that Thomas could have employed both Aristotelian and Neoplatonic ideas on analogy without choosing decisively between them on principle. Some think that one or another kind of analogy should be put forth as "properly Thomistic" because it permits them to address problems in post–thirteenth-century thought to which they think that Thomism, as a *philosophia perennis,* must have forecast a satisfying answer. Those who attempt to discover which type of analogy is "properly Thomistic" on the basis of a statistical or chronological study of Thomas's works make the mistake of attributing too much system to his thought.

George P. Klubertanz has quite rightly observed that Thomas only discusses analogy in specific contexts, vis-à-vis specific objections. [132] This insight leads to the conclusion that the frequency with which Thomas refers to a particular kind of analogy has more to do with the frequency with which he feels called upon to rebut particular objections than with his personal preference for one kind of analogy as opposed to another. Here as elsewhere in Thomas's thought it is necessary to remember that the structure of scholastic argument creates an apologetic tone that is not present to the same degree in other philosophical styles. It has been noted that the analogy of attribution inclines more toward a univocal concept of being and that the analogy of proper proportionality inclines more toward an equivocal concept of being. Thus the respective utility of these two approaches depends on whether one looks at the relationship between God and creatures from the point of view of nonbeing or from the point of view of being. [133] If one looks simply at the being of God vis-à-vis the being of creatures, one has to deal with two radically different modes of being. The analogy of proper proportionality is most useful in this context, because it stresses the differences rather than the similarities between the analogates. On the other hand, compared with nonbeing, both God and creatures possess being, although in different ways. The analogy of attribution is most useful in this context, because it stresses the similarities rather than the differences between the analogates.

Having said this, it is irrelevant to ask how often Thomas stresses the similarities between God and creation by means of the analogy of attribution and how often he stresses the differences between God and creation by means of the analogy of proper proportionality. It is sufficient to state that Thomas believes that both similarities and differences exist; thus he employs both kinds of analogies. His reason for citing one of them in a particular context usually depends on the nature of the objection it is designed to refute. Thomas tends to use the analogy of attribution, and, in general, a participationist type of argument, to combat thinkers who see nothing in common between God and creation. [134] Thomas opposes this view because he holds that, if it were permitted to stand, it would result in agnosticism, for both philosophical and theological reasons. As an empiricist, and as a firm supporter of the idea that causes and effects resemble each other, Thomas is philosophically certain that the world resembles God, its first cause. This belief is basic to his view that the world can provide man with information about God through a posteriori reasoning. As a Christian, Thomas takes seriously Paul's assertion that the invisible things of God can be seen through the visible things of his creation.

Both philosophy and theology, for Thomas, proclaim the existence of some resemblances between God and creation, however weak. Both philosophy and theology provide warrants for the doctrine that God can be known to some degree from creation, according to human ways of knowing. Now for Thomas human knowledge operates by means of ideas derived from sense data, which are provided by creation. But if the creation in no way resembles God, it cannot tell man anything about God. Man has no alternative but agnosticism. It may be noted that Thomas here omits faith as a possible means of knowledge about God in default of a creation that resembles him. This is because faith, for Thomas, is given through created intermediaries; it is proposed to men by the words and deeds of other men. If nothing that is created, whether it be the laws of nature or the words of preachers, resembled God, man would have no access whatever to the certainty that God is God.

On the other hand, Thomas uses the analogy of proper proportionality when he wants to combat thinkers who, he holds, find too much in common between God and creation.[135] Insufficient discrimination between God and creation, he thinks, leads to pantheism or monism. Pantheism and monism are mistaken positions primarily because they obliterate the transcendence of God. They also fail to do justice to the uniqueness of created beings, particularly human beings. Thus Thomas tends to use the analogy of proper proportionality in dealing with opponents who, he thinks, are overly emanationist in their metaphysics, and against proponents of the Averroist view of the unity of the intellect.[136] He finds just as many philosophical and theological warrants for stressing the differences between God and creation as for stressing their similarities. The same Aristotelianism which assures him that causes can be known through their effects provides him with the conviction that causes are always greater than their effects and that they are never identical with them. And the same theology which asserts that the creation proclaims the Creator also asserts that it falls infinitely short of him.

Attention to context, then, solves one of the difficulties in which many commentators on Thomistic analogy needlessly embroil themselves. Another problem, touched on at the outset of our discussion of analogy, results from the tendency of many scholars to treat Thomistic analogy as a metaphysical doctrine. According to this view, being is intrinsically analogous. Therefore, concepts about being must also be analogous. Analogous concepts tell us the truth about beings. It is thus possible to discover something about God through analogous concepts derived from creation. Further, analogous concepts derived from creation can tell us that God is transcendent over creation and that he possesses any perfections that we may find in creation in an absolutely preeminent way. This position on analogy contains two accurate perceptions about Thomas's epistemology: the priority of being over knowing and the idea that concepts based on sense data can be accurate signs of their objects. However, proponents of the view that analogy is a metaphysical doctrine fail to integrate these two notions successfully, thus confusing the order of being in Thomas with the order of knowing. This position, therefore, results in a paradox. Its supporters argue that analogical concepts are simply the intelligible representations of intrinsically analogical facts and that God possesses the characteristics being analogized in a unique and supreme way. At the same time, they argue that the analogical way of knowing moves from creation to God, since men derive the ideas on which analogies are based from their inspection of created things. This sounds like an attempt to eat one's cake and have it too. If, for Thomas, our knowledge were truly limited to what we can know by means of sense data, it would be impossible for us to know that God possesses his analogated attributes in a radically different way from sensible creatures. The argument that analogy can show us a transcendent God would thus fall. At the same time, if we begin with the mode of being instead of the mode of knowing, asserting that God's being transcends the being of creatures on the basis of metaphysical or theological first principles known by intuition or faith, the argument that analogical concepts can tell us something about God and creation that we did not already know would also fall. This notion of analogy, which demands that we begin with creation and work up to God, but which depends on God's movement down to creatures for its validity, is, in effect, a tautology. [137]

It would be a tautology, that is, if Thomistic analogy really were a metaphysical doctrine or if Thomas actually thought that his analogies of God provided heuristic foundations for a constructive metaphysics. The case, however, is quite otherwise. Analogies are never intended by Thomas to bring anyone to a knowledge that he does not already have. [138] Rather, they are a means of showing forth the relationships between things that are already known by faith, and are hence a species of *intellectus fidei*. To establish this point with the firmness that it deserves, it is necessary to underline three basic qualifications which Thomas applies to analogy. The first of these qualifications stems from the general limitations which Thomas places on all concepts, whether logical or analogical, as signs of nonsensible objects. The second can be deduced from his placement of analogical arguments in his works, which tells us whether or not he considers them demonstrative proofs from effects to causes. The third concerns the aspects of deity for which Thomas seeks analogies, and the nature of the analogies that he finds for them. With these latter two qualifications we move from the realm of analogical theory to the realm of analogical practice.

For Thomas, as we have seen, true concepts are accurate but partial signs. They always have cognitive limitations vis-à-vis their objects. The more immaterial the object the more extensive the limitations, for the human mind is so constructed that its ideas, with the exception of intuited first principles, derive from sense data. These conditions apply to analogical concepts no less than to logical concepts. It is just as necessary in analogical as in logical reasoning for the subject to have a prior knowledge of the object in order to be able to judge the truth of the analogy, its adequation to what it signifies. In this sense, no true judgment, whether logical or analogical, ever tells the subject something of which he was previously ignorant. Analogies are signs; so far as their adequation to their objects goes, they are no weaker or stronger than other kinds of signs. But, for Thomas, analogies have a special advantage. Because of their structure, they are able to signify the relationships between things as well as the things themselves.

Analogies, then, are not heuristic. In fact, if we examine Thomas's practical use of analogies, it appears that they have even fewer capacities for demonstrative use than do ordinary arguments about God. As we have noted earlier, Thomas employs both demonstrations and probable arguments in his theology. The vast majority of his arguments are probable ones. This is because he assigns to probable arguments a very large task, the discussion of articles of Christian doctrine which can be known only by faith. The number of such doctrines far outstrips the number of those which he thinks can be known by natural reason. Probable arguments fall under the purview of *sacra doctrina,* in which conclusions are deduced from theological principles. On the other hand, Thomas assigns to demonstration a comparatively small task, the discussion of God's existence and some of his primary attributes. Demonstration is responsible for the conclusions about God which natural philosophers have been able to prove about God by accurate induction. Demonstrative conclusions about God fall into the category of *praeambula fidei.* With this distinction in mind, we may ask whether Thomas uses analogical arguments in *sacra doctrina,* in the *praeambula fidei,* or in both. The answer is quite simple. There are no arguments from analogy whatever in those sections of Thomas's works devoted to the treatment of *praeambula fidei.* Analogical arguments appear only as a means of explaining those truths of the Christian faith which, according to Thomas, must be known by faith. It is thus impossible to regard analogy as a kind of philosophical demonstration from effects to causes or to place it in the same category as Thomas's proofs for the existence of God. Rather, analogy should be regarded as a kind of probable argument, by means of which Thomas deduces conclusions from articles of faith according to the norm of theological appropriateness, and whose resemblance to God can be judged only by believers.

Still greater insight into the uses to which Thomas puts analogy can be gained if we consider the specific articles of faith for which he formulates analogous arguments and the nature of the analogies which he chooses for this purpose. As we have seen, Thomas employs the theory of analogy in different contexts, depending on the objections he wants to refute and on the kind of relationship between God and creatures that he wants to stress. Despite his heavy emphasis on the idea that we derive analogical concepts about God from nature at large, when he is faced with the practical problem of finding likely similitudes of God, he has recourse to only one kind of analogy: the mind of man. He uses analogies drawn from human nature primarily in passages dealing with Trinitarian theology. Thus, in practice, Thomas emphasizes psychology over cosmology; and he does not shrink from analogizing man's mental processes to the deepest mystery of the Christian faith. He compares such phenomena as the interactions of man's mental faculties, the process of concept formation, and the relationship between man's inner ideas and his external expression of them to the relations among the Persons of the Trinity,[139] the procession of the Word,[140] and the Incarnation.[141] In fact, it is in the course of discussing these Trinitarian doctrines that Thomas develops a sizable proportion of his teachings on the operations of the human mind.

Both Thomas's methods and his examples are quite conventional. They follow faithfully the tradition of Augustine and Anselm. Equally conventional is Thomas's construction of analogies between God and the mind of man. He begins by building up the analogy, underlining the similarities between God and man. Then he breaks down the analogy, illustrating the immense gap between God and man. Analogy, like man himself, has both strengths and weaknesses as a sign of God. The human mind, which resembles God more closely than any other created thing, cannot represent him fully, even in the state of beatitude. Only Christ is the perfect image of God.[142] So analogy, which combines univocity and equivocity, adumbrates the mysterious relationship between two mysterious entities, God and man. The imprecise nature of analogy enables it to display the impenetrable as impenetrable.

For Thomas, then, analogical knowledge of God is one species within the general category of conceptual signs of God. Like all signs of God, analogies refer to a reality whose nature is already known in part by faith. Analogy is more serviceable than are straightforward names of God in displaying the doctrine of the Trinity because it can signify relationships as well as things and because it can elucidate the relationships between things that are both similar and different without identifying the similarities or making polar opposites of the differences. Analogies of God, for Thomas, are *aenigmata*. The lack of mathematical precision in his doctrine of analogy, his failure to state just how similar and just how different the analogates in his analogies are, his lack of interest in systematizing his theory of analogy, and his disinclination to tell the reader which, if any, of his types of analogy is "properly Thomistic" are hence deliberate. An *aenigma* by nature signifies through its obscurity rather than through its clarity and precision. Thomistic analogy is a pillar of cloud, not a pillar of fire.

As a theorist on the role of signs in the knowledge of God, Thomas Aquinas is in some respects harder to lay hands on than either Augustine or Anselm. Despite the extensive amount of space he devotes to topics related to this problem, Thomas never compiles all the relevant materials into one work, nor does he put forth his theory with either economy or overtness. Clearly, the question of signs did not interest Thomas as much as it interested Augustine and Anselm; and his efforts to harmonize Aristotle with Augustine on this point are not always felicitous. But, when there is a contest, it is generally Aristotle who is made to cede. For all Thomas's differences from Augustine and Anselm, it is possible to see that he agrees with the basic Augustinian theory of signs on all the important points. For Thomas, concepts, and by extension words, represent real things. They represent them truly but partially. This applies to all the signs he treats, from judgments about natural objects to God as represented by demonstration, dialectic, and analogy. In all cases, he sees the object as the criterion of the truth of its sign. The more adequately these signs signify God, the less they rely on reason, and the more closely correlated to the mystery of the Godhead they become. In the cognition of their objects, however, signs always remain extrinsic. No sign is perfectly heuristic in the first instance. All signs are appropriated mentally as representations of their objects on the basis of God's activity, in one way or another, in the mind of the subject, whether God's intrinsic causality be reflected in the light of the intellect, the gift of faith, the gifts of the Holy Spirit, or, ultimately, the light of glory. There are some Thomistic signs which are primarily indicative, such as inductions from nature to the first cause, and there are others which are primarily commemorative, such as deductions from faith as performed by *sacra doctrina,* although there is some degree of overlapping between these two types. And, finally, Thomas retains the Augustinian stress on the interrelationship of love and knowledge in the signification of God *per speculum in aenigmate,* in his analysis of the functions of the human mind, in his definition of faith, and in his notion of the nature and aims of theology.

Four

Dante: Poet of Rectitude

The linguistic epistemology which is the subject of this study was, as we have seen, both resilient and adaptable. Capable of assuming the garb of rhetoric, grammar, and dialectic in response to the shifting intellectual climates of the Middle Ages, it retained its Augustinian amalgam of classical sign theory and the theology of the Incarnation despite these permutations and their attendant shifts in emphasis. The durability of this theory during the Middle Ages can be explained not only because it bore Augustine's authoritative stamp but also because it appeared to satisfy the needs of theologians as diverse as Augustine, Anselm, and Aquinas for an explanation of how human powers of thought and expression could achieve and communicate the knowledge of God. This was a concern which appealed primarily to the professional theologians of the Middle Ages. Yet, if we confine ourselves exclusively to the history of theology, we will be unable to appreciate fully the range and flexibility which this theory attained. The Augustinian conception of words as signs in the knowledge of God was, in fact, applied to a number of forms of expression other than theological discourse. One of these forms of expression, which we propose to examine here, was poetry.

The extension of Augustinian sign theory to poetry can be seen in the poetics of Dante Alighieri and its consummation in the *Divine Comedy*. Our selection of Dante for this purpose does not necessarily imply that he is representative of all phases of medieval poetics. Nor is it meant to suggest that his view of poetry can be applied retroactively to his literary predecessors at all points. It may certainly be argued that Dante's poetics is original in conception and unique in accomplishment. Yet Dante's theory of poetry is related to traditional medieval poetics and to his immediate poetic background, the *dolce stil nuovo,* both by way of acceptance and by way of reaction. For Dante, the poet is a prophet and teacher. Poetic beauty becomes the means whereby he communicates God to man. Dante's treatment of poetry as an epistemic method thus parallels the rhetorical theology of Augustine, the grammatical theology of Anselm, and the dialectical theology of Thomas Aquinas, and it is based on the same fundamental conception of words as signs.

This attribution of cognitive and didactic functions to poetry springs in part from the subject matter of the *Divine Comedy* and from the heavenly inspiration which Dante believes warranted his writing it. It is derived also from his assimilation of poetics to rhetoric. This assimilation, a common practice among medieval educators, was perpetuated by Dante, although he departs from the tradition in several important respects, as we shall note below. Now the linguistic epistemology of the Middle Ages was also set in a rhetorical context, at least in its original Augustinian manifestation. Given a tradition in which poetry was treated from the point of view of rhetoric, and given the wide availability of Augustine's works, it would not be difficult for a medieval poet and intellectual to put them together, especially if he saw himself as a reformer with a message for his times. This, we maintain, is what Dante does. Appropriating for Christian poetry the role that Augustine entrusts to Christian rhetoric in the knowledge of God, Dante develops a poetics which aims to teach, to delight, to persuade: a poetics which, in attempting to express the Word and to move men toward God through its aesthetic, moral, and intellectual rectitude, retains the functional interrelations between wisdom, virtue, and eloquence assigned by Augustine to redeemed speech.

Given the retention of this interrelationship by Dante, it must be stressed that he sees the content and the corollaries of wisdom, virtue, and eloquence in a manner both broader and more specific than any of the thinkers whom we have already examined. For Dante, the pursuit of wisdom and virtue demands that he take an attitude toward the Europe of his own day. This attitude entails a thoroughgoing reform of Christian society at all its levels, from the most universal to the most particular. The need to unite wisdom and virtue is the focus around which Dante organizes his views on ethics, doctrine, and ecclesiastical and political theory. Out of this complex of ideas he posits an ideal of intellectual and moral rectitude, which correlates the salvation of the individual with the restoration of right order in church and state. Wisdom and virtue, in turn, must be related to eloquence. This Dante accomplishes by attaching his moral and intellectual ideals to a literary ideal, which entails a reform of language and the invention of a poetry of rectitude, and by expressing them in a poem which meets his own linguistic and literary criteria.

Dante's poetic epistemology, while grounded in the Augustinian tradition, is thus specified, as were its grammatical and dialectical counterparts, in terms of the conditions and needs of a particular historical environment as perceived by a particular mind. Dante's theories on human nature, the state, the church, language, and poetry, his interpretation of his own poetic development, his local and European loyalties, are fused aesthetically in the *Divine Comedy*. This work, then, in its conception, contents, and execution, is the specific mode in which Dante resets and reexpresses the Augustinian doctrine of signs.

In attempting to demonstrate this assertion, our first task is to set forth the poetic theory of Dante, to explain its development in his early works up to the *Divine Comedy*, and to ascertain the nature and extent of his debt to medieval poetics before his time. As one would expect in the case of an author who has been commented on unremittingly from his own age to the present, there exist a wide variety of interpretations of Dante's poetic theory. These variations, to the extent that they deal with Dante's relationship to medieval poetics, result in part from the fact that what is commonly regarded as medieval poetics is actually made up of several ingredients, which do not necessarily blend consistently into one coherent theory. There are theories of poetry expressed in textbooks on the liberal arts, and these may be taken to represent the school tradition. There are also theories of poetry put forth by figures whose contributions lie primarily in fields other than the writing and teaching of poetry. Both must be contrasted with attitudes toward poetry implicit in medieval poems whose authors were not interested in issuing theoretical analyses of their art.

When these various approaches are taken into account, several different views of poetry emerge. All of them possess classical antecedents. All of them contain the implicit idea that poetry, as a form of communication, can be judged according to rhetorical canons, although the type of rhetoric in each case may differ. Thus medieval poetics can assume a sophistical, or purely technical, orientation, in which primary stress is placed on decoration and style. Or, it can assume a broader, antisophistic orientation in which the good, the true, and the eloquent are linked and applied to poetry, by way of criticizing existing poetry or by way of establishing norms for the poetry that ought to be written. Some medieval theorists hold the view that poetry is wholly or partially false or fictitious, an interpretation which implies that poetry is didactic and persuasive. Thus some of them regard the characters, plot, or stylistic accoutrements of a poem as fictitious veils which stand between the reader and an edifying inner core. These fictitious veils may be pulled aside by literary analysis or left clothing the core of the poem, depending on the literary astuteness of the reader. For the less sophisticated reader, the veils may be regarded as a lure, a sugar coating over the pill within, which makes the edification provided by the poem more palatable. The more skillful reader will regard the veils as a series of obstacles, and his enjoyment of the poet's message will be enhanced by his feeling of success in having met and overcome them. Alternatively, the fictitious veils may be thought of as a shield protecting an esoteric inner truth from profane eyes, ensuring that it will be detected only by initiates whose intellects are equal to the task of penetrating the veils. Finally, following the tradition established by Plato when he ejected the poets from his *Republic* and seconded by Augustine in his *Confessions,* some medieval theorists thought that poetry was entirely false and fictitious in the ideas and attitudes it put forth and that it was dangerously seductive on account of its beauty. It must be kept in mind that when most medieval theorists said "poetry," they were referring to classical poetry, that is, to poetry written by pagans, which contained references to pagan gods and religions. The truth of such poetry could be treated in several ways. Although all of these approaches could be related to rhetoric, medieval poetic theory was by no means a homogeneous tradition. In constructing and exemplifying a specifically Christian poetic theory, Dante accepted some aspects of it while rejecting others.

Both the distinction between poetry and rhetoric and the tendency to assimilate the former to the latter can be traced to classical literary theory. Greek and Roman educators treated poetry and rhetoric as two separate arts requiring two different styles of composition. Where poetry utilized an imaginative mode of organization involving an emotional progression from image to image, rhetoric utilized an intellectual mode of organization involving a logical progression from idea to idea. Thus each demanded its own technique of composition.[1] For centuries rhetoric and poetic were kept apart. During the Augustan age, however, there was a marked tendency to conflate them, to the detriment of poetry's autonomy. This development has been attributed to the fact that Cicero and his contemporaries regarded rhetoric as the most important type of literature. This led them to treat poetry as an ancilla to rhetoric and to conceive of poetry in rhetorical terms. Thus, in his *Pro Archia,* Cicero defends poetry by arguing that it has didactic value and that it is a useful means of commemorating the great deeds of famous men. Poetry, like rhetoric, he holds, should instruct as well as delight the reader.[2]

The rhetorical attitude toward poetry dominated Roman criticism from Cicero's day until the end of the classical era. It is expressed most completely in Horace's *Ars poetica.* Horace, as J. W. H. Atkins describes him, succeeded in "applying to poetry a doctrine which by this time had become standard in the rhetorical schools."[3] The very title of *Ars poetica,* which was given to Horace's treatise by Quintilian, was perpetuated by grammarians who scarcely saw poetry as a separate technique. This indicates the degree to which poetry had become assimilated to rhetoric, for there is very little in this work that does not apply equally to Ciceronian prose.[4] Horace defines the aim of poetry as didactic and pleasurable; it should uplift the reader morally as well as delight him. Horace upholds Cicero's emphasis on persuasion and teaching, at the expense of pleasure if necessary. He also stresses the educational function of poetry, envisioning it as a civilizing agency in the broadest sense. Cicero's preoccupation with suiting the style of the oration to its subject matter is paralleled by Horace's ideal of congruity between the poem's theme, its organization, and its stylistic finish.[5]

The impression that Roman men of letters were merging poetry into rhetoric of a deliberately antisophistic sort is strengthened by a consideration of Plutarch. Plutarch stresses pointedly that the didactic and ethical aspects of poetry should be the poet's first concern. It is not enough, according to Plutarch, for a poem to produce pleasure in the reader. The real aim of the poet is to elevate the reader's character, to move him to follow the good, and to bring ethical principles to bear on his daily life. Plutarch emphasizes this idea to the point where he strains the Ciceronian harmony between wisdom, virtue, and eloquence by conceiving of the pleasing function of poetry in a purely utilitarian light, thus subordinating it rigorously to its moral ends.[6]

Late Latin critics, who were responsible for transmitting classical literary theory to the Middle Ages, preserved this assimilation of poetry to rhetoric. One way in which they did this can be seen in their treatment of Vergil. The Antonine rhetor Florus entitles a fragmentary work *Virgilius orator an poeta.* Donatus and Macrobius lend their authority to the rhetorical treatment of Vergil; and the minor rhetoricians of the Roman Empire follow suit, repeatedly citing passages from Vergil to illustrate the rhetorical usages which their works outline.[7] The assimilation of poetry to rhetoric was also susceptible of more synthetic treatment at the hands of Cassiodorus, who restates the principle that the poet can speak according to the rules of rhetoric. The poet's aim, according to Cassiodorus, is to move the conscience of the reader. It is not his subject matter but his technique which differentiates him from the orator.[8]

Scholars have frequently noted that this classical confusion between poetry and rhetoric was carried over into the medieval school tradition.[9] In part this was simply the result of the perpetuation of the ideas of Cicero and Horace by late classical critics, whose textbooks became the basic channels of literary education. In part it was the result of the fact that rhetoric tended to lose its forensic orientation during the Middle Ages. Except for its application to preaching, rhetoric was generally treated as a science of literary style. Latin poetry was also studied as a rhetorical production, and thus it was an easy matter to fuse the methods of these two arts.[10] Poetry, it is true, was taught as part of the grammatical curriculum, as it had been in classical times; in his definition of grammar Rabanus Maurus states that its concern is to interpret the poets and historians.[11] Yet, in practice, rhetorical canons of style came to be imposed upon poetry. Many medieval teachers of poetry concentrated on the *colores rhetorici*. Poetry, for them, was the study of style. They were chiefly interested in illustrating how to apply the appropriate stylistic decoration to poetic works, and extended rhetorical norms of literary decorum and beauty to poetic decoration.[12]

Scholars of late have frequently cited many examples of the application of rhetoric to poetics in the Middle Ages. In the seventh century, we find Isidore of Seville treating poets and rhetors as stylists, under the same general heading. According to Isidore, both poets and orators must suit their style to their audience. Thus he passes on to poetry the Augustinian redefinition of Cicero's three modes of discourse, the elevated, the middle, and the low. Poetry, like rhetoric, is a form of narration, which may also have didactic functions. Isidore adds that figurative language contributes to the beauty and decorum of poetry, just as it ornaments rhetoric.[13] The transference of the three Ciceronian styles to poetry is also evident in the writings of Bede in the eighth century and of Alcuin in the late eighth and early ninth; the Carolingian scholar Lupus of Ferrières repeats this principle and illustrates it from Vergil.[14] An anonymous Carolingian commentator on Horace's *Ars poetica* reiterates the idea that the aim of poetry is to charm and to instruct, while adding a new twist to the theory. The author assumes a normative point of view, affirming that the true poet ought to depict a moral ideal. The poem will be useful to the extent that it contains moral truths and moves the reader toward them. Only truth, according to the author, will really delight the audience. The charm of the poem thus depends on the wisdom of the poet as well as on his literary artistry. The most important criterion of a poem is the degree to which it conforms to the good, the true, and the beautiful. The style of the poem is thus assimilated to its content; the content itself determines the ability of the poem to please the reader. This interpretation marks a correlation of style to content new to the tradition of rhetorical poetry. The Carolingian anonymous, however, does not develop it systematically, for, in restating the Ciceronian rule of the three styles, he reverts to the view that the poet should adjust his style to the level of the audience.[15]

The early medieval tendency to equate poetry with rhetoric was carried forth in the twelfth and thirteenth centuries by commentators on poetry almost without exception.[16] Poetry was still taught as a part of grammar, but although many writers, like John of Salisbury, Alexander of Villedieu, and

Éverard of Béthune, discuss it under the rubric of grammar, they conceive of it in rhetorical terms. [17] And it is analyzed in rhetorical terms even by authors who treat it as an art in its own right. This approach has been noted in Vincent of Beauvais. Despite the fact that he devotes a separate section of his *Speculum doctrinale* to poetry, Vincent affirms that its function is to rouse the minds of its readers to emulate or to reject the ideas which the poet puts forth in images. [18] The ethical emphasis of a Vincent of Beauvais or a John of Salisbury, however, is not always typical of this period. In the numerous *artes poeticae* which now begin to appear, there is a marked tendency to move away from a didactic interpretation of poetry toward an almost preclusive stress on technique, which leads most of the poetic theorists to underline the stylistic and decorative applications of rhetoric to poetry rather than its moral or educational functions. A transition figure in this regard is Alain de Lille. Alain was a product of the school of Chartres, whose members in the twelfth century looked at poetry as a vehicle for philosophy. [19] Alain himself is well known for his lengthy, allegorical, didactic poems. In uniting poetics to rhetoric, however, it is not the didactic side of rhetoric which he stresses. Rather, he sees rhetoric primarily from the point of view of adornment. [20] Allegory is a kind of rhetorical trope, and Alain's rhetoric, in the words of Charles Sears Baldwin, "is not operative as composition, but only as style after the fact. . . . His diffuseness arises from the idea that *poetica* involves decorative dilation by those *colores* of which Cicero and Vergil are equally patterns."[21] The idea, prevalent in the twelfth and thirteenth centuries, that the chief concern of poetic theory was to communicate the technique of decorative dilation by applying the *colores rhetorici* to poetry is traced by Baldwin through the *artes poeticae* of Matthew of Vendôme, Geoffrey of Vinsauf, Éverard the German, and John of Garland. [22] The only significant modification of this approach occurs in the *Poetria* of John of Garland. John appears to be the only figure on Baldwin's list who takes account of the contemporary revision of rhetoric in the *ars dictaminis*. This, however, does not prevent him from giving both poetry and *dictamen* surveillance over the three styles, illustrated from Vergil and sanctioned by citations from Horace's *Ars poetica* and the *Rhetorica ad Herennium*. The only distinction John draws between *dictamen* and poetry is one of quantity. The style of *dictamen*, he says, should be brief; that of poetry should be diffused by means of coloristic dilation. [23]

In the tradition we have been describing, two basic applications of rhetoric to poetry have emerged. Some writers carry over antisophistic principles to poetry, thus endowing the poet with the power and the duty to express the true and the good and to move the reader toward them. Others concentrate instead on the technical aspects of poetic decoration, borrowing from rhetoric its figures, allegories, tropes, and colors and applying them to poetry as canons of adornment. The members of this latter group manifest comparatively little interest in the uses of poetry; they are preoccupied mainly with establishing rules on how to write it. These two approaches rarely occur unmixed with each other between the seventh and the thirteenth centuries. However, in the twelfth and thirteenth centuries they seem to be drawing further apart. During these two centuries, the school tradition, as represented by the *artes poeticae*, tends to emphasize a poetics of purely decorative technique, while the contemporary proponents of a poetics joined in some way to wisdom or virtue are drawn on the whole from the ranks of the practicing poets or the critics and summarizers of culture.

The rhetorical idea of poetry as a medium of education and as a moral stimulus was also retained by medieval commentators who, following the Platonic tradition, thought that the truth of poetry was either covered with fictitious veils or nonexistent. This view can often be found paralleling the more technical or positive attitudes toward poetry described above, and sometimes these divergent approaches coexist in the writings of the same author. Thus Isidore of Seville, in analyzing poets and rhetors as stylists, describes them in the same breath as fabricators of fables. In so doing he cites the standard classical criticisms of the truth of poetry, derived from Platonism, that are put forth by Victorinus, Priscian, Diomedes, and Varro. Poems, according to Isidore, contain fables. Yet they may also contain some truths and may serve a didactic function. Poetic fictions are a way of making delightful to the reader moral or natural truths which he might otherwise find distasteful. Thus the role of the poet is to present these truths obliquely, by decorating his works with rhetorical figures. Poetry, for Isidore, is a method of indirect discourse; poetic fictions, figures, and coloristic decorations are a decoy to the reader and are extrinsic to the poet's message.[24]

Carolingian scholars perpetuated the theory of poetic fiction. The Carolingian anonymous, in commenting on Horace's *Ars poetica*, takes as his point of departure the view that Horace's intention is to treat poetry as the art of composing fables. The author makes a strong effort to relate this idea to his didactic theory of poetry. He thinks, as we have seen above, that the poem should communicate truths and that its pleasing character depends on the truth and goodness of its content. Although poetry is fiction, he argues, it is the kind of fiction that imitates truth, for the best fictions are those possessing verisimilitude.[25] In this way the commentator tries to prevent poetic fable from undermining poetic truth, by stressing a mimetic rather than an imaginative conception of fiction. John the Scot reiterates the idea of poetry as fiction, arguing that although it is not really right for an author to depict deliberate falsehoods, poetic fictions are admissible because they may contain natural or moral truths. John thus agrees with the Carolingian anonymous that the poet must be learned in these matters as well as artful.[26]

In the twelfth and thirteenth centuries the idea of poetic fiction underwent some modifications and was supplemented by a strong scholastic stress on the falsity of poetry. Many twelfth-century writers expressed the view that poetic fiction should be true to life, a tradition deriving from the Horatian principle *ut pictura poesis*.[27] The question of poetic allegory also excited a good deal of attention during these two centuries. Allegory was viewed not merely as a mode of decoration, correlated or not with the didactic and moral aims of poetry, but also as a method of literary criticism. Thus John of Garland, in his *Poetria,* argues that the Christian reader can neutralize the dangerous falsehoods he encounters in pagan literature by allegorizing the offending doctrines.[28] Even more noticeable in the thirteenth century is the tendency to treat allegory as a scriptural and theological method that is incompatible with profane literature, an idea linked with the general denigration of poetry on the part of the scholastics. The view that poetry has no claims to truth was quite popular. It can be found in the works of Robert Grosseteste and the Franciscan Bonaventura as well as in the works of the Dominicans Albert the Great and Thomas Aquinas. However, it is usually Aquinas's dicta on poetry that have been cited to illustrate this scholastic position. Aquinas places poetry on the lowest plane of logic. Poetry is regarded as subrational, as incapable of signifying truth. Poems cannot be grasped by the discursive reason because they deal with fables and illusions, not with realities. Hence, he says, poets use an allegorical or symbolic method. This allegorical method, as used by poets, is by no means to be confused with the symbolic language and techniques employed by theologians and exegetes. Speculative theology may use a symbolic method because its object transcends discursive reason. Scriptural exegesis may use the allegorical method because God himself has placed several levels of meaning in the Bible, and allegory is simply the way in which exegetes discover what is already in the inspired text. On the other hand, concludes the scholastic argument, when similar techniques are applied to poetry, they are being used either improperly or by default, because of the false and infrarational nature of this art.[29]

Despite its relatively late appearance on the medieval scene and the fact that it was professed mainly by scholastic theologians rather than by practicing poets or textbook writers in the school tradition, this depreciation of poetry has achieved the status among many modern scholars of a representative or even a normative medieval poetics. The net effect of this interpretation has been the conclusion that Dante was forced to sever himself radically from the tradition of medieval poetics, for a poetics so conceived could give no place to a professedly theological poem in which the allegorical method of the theologians is deliberately adopted as a principle of construction. This theory fails to take into account the antisophistic didacticism of much of medieval poetic theory or the existence of figures like Peter Riga, who wrote biblical poetry in the late twelfth and early thirteenth centuries in the belief that God was inspiring him.[30] Some scholars, in their desire to prove that Dante was not a Thomist, feel it sufficient to rest their case on the very fact that he was a poet.[31]

Poetics in the Middle Ages can be derived not only from the school tradition and the scholastic theologians. One must also take into account the religious poetry that was produced in abundance during this period. Religious poetry was, on the whole, detached from the decorative canons of the school tradition and from the scholastic derogation of the truth of poetry. The religious poets would not have written so much and with such unabashed confidence unless they had thought that poetry was capable of communicating theological and moral truths and of moving the hearer toward God. Ernst R. Curtius has made the point that the poetics of Dante is best understood in terms of the literature of the Middle Ages, not through its scholastic philosophy.[32] Baldwin adds that the school tradition, preoccupied as it was with style, gives us little insight into the *Divine Comedy*. Rather, he urges, it is medieval hymnody which provides the best introduction to Dante's view of poetry.[33] Baldwin dates the emergence of a specifically Christian poetic in the fourth century, with the hymns of Ambrose, and sees it as a direct analogue of Augustine's Christianization of Ciceronian oratory. "As Augustine redeemed rhetoric," he states, "so Ambrose transformed poetic, by new motives."[34] According to Baldwin, this new Christian poetic has two main characteristics. In the first place, Christian hymns are lyrics, but their authors expand lyricism from the expression of individual emotions to the expression of a shared faith, aspiration, worship, and fellowship. This communal orientation stems from the fact that Christian hymns were written to be used in public worship and to instruct and inspire a congregation. A second new feature of hymnody is its treatment of physical reality as the first step toward eternity; it aims at an expansion of human consciousness, beginning in the here and now, which is to culminate in the beatific vision. This point of view of course reflects the theological and devotional content of the hymns. But, out of these practical, communal, theological necessities there developed a new literary aesthetic. Poetry, in the hymns, is not regarded as a means to an end. The hymn is not regarded as theology in verse. Rather, the theological aspirations and corporate ideals of the poet coalesce with the form of the poem. The content, style, and function of the poem become an aesthetic unit.[35]

In the twelfth and thirteenth centuries, religious poetry retained the communal character of early medieval hymnody, as well as its aesthetic unity, while developing a number of stylistic modifications. Symbolism is used extensively, particularly by the Victorines. But the symbols of an Adam of Saint Victor differ from the figures of poetry as conceived by the textbook writers. They are "not decoration, not epithets or paraphrases used instead of proper names, but immediate lyrical approaches" to the theological realities presented by the author.[36] Some religious poets in this period, like Thomas Aquinas, apply a more intense level of contemplation to the subject matter of their hymns than is evident in early medieval hymnody, while the Franciscans develop a technique of sublimation, starting from concrete images with a high emotional content.[37] The Franciscan style was carried over into the vernacular in the thirteenth century, and its chief Italian exponent, Jacopone da Todi, is thought to have influenced Dante.[38]

In considering the various influences which affected Dante and in terms of which he forged his own poetics, accepting some aspects of his background and rejecting others, we may take a clue from Dante himself and address ourselves to the figures and traditions to which he avows his indebtedness. At the head of this list we must place Vergil, whom Dante acknowledges in the *Comedy* as the light and honor of the other poets, his master and author, and the source of his own style, and whom he takes as his guide through Hell and Purgatory. As we shall have occasion to note below in another connection, Vergil enjoyed an extensive and variegated reputation in the Middle Ages. This stemmed in part from popular legendary tradition and in part from the frequency with which his works were cited as poetic exemplars in the grammatical curriculum. Dante was familiar with both aspects of the medieval tradition of Vergil. In the *Comedy* he freely borrows Vergilian characters, topographical details, and even phrases. Far more important than this, however, is the fact that Dante thinks of himself as a second Vergil. His conception of himself as a poet is thus based to a significant degree on his conception of Vergil as a poet. Whether or not Dante's conception of Vergil actually corresponds with Vergil's poetic theory, that conception is highly relevant to any study of Dante's poetics, for Vergil provided him with an authoritative classical model which he believed he was following in writing the *Divine Comedy*. Dante sees in Vergil the singer of the glory of the Roman Empire, whose medieval analogue he himself was trying to refurbish and restore. He sees Vergil as the reformer and unifier of the Italian dialects of his time, a burden which Dante lays on his own shoulders. He sees Vergil as a prophet of Christ, serving, in this capacity, as a link between the Rome of Caesar and the Rome of Peter. The image of Vergil as a prophet, seer, and sage, instructing his audience through the story of a hero who takes a pilgrimage through the other world, is one that Dante adopts for himself. He has but to translate the wisdom and inspiration expressed through the poet's prophetic voice into Christian terms and to make himself the hero of his own didactic epic.

Vergil, as we have noted, was available to Dante partly through the school tradition. This tradition was represented for Dante more fully by the *ars dictaminis* and by the rhetoric of Brunetto Latini, whom he greets in the *Inferno* as a father and of whom he says, "You taught me how man makes himself eternal."[39] The *ars dictaminis* taught Dante the canons of approved Latin style, to which his Latin works adhere.[40] Though attached to jurisprudence and public affairs, and hence strongly concerned with persuasion, the *ars dictaminis* of Dante's day had also recovered the Ciceronian correlation between eloquence, wisdom, and virtue.[41] Brunetto Latini was thoroughly familiar with the *ars dictaminis,* and in his *Trésor* he reiterates and intensifies its union of ethics, politics, and rhetoric. At the same time, he draws upon the contemporary *artes poeticae* in elaborating the techniques of rhetoric, applying rhetorical canons of decoration to poetry as well as to *dictamen.*[42] Thus several strands of medieval poetics converge in Brunetto's *Trésor.*

Brunetto indicates his debt to Cicero not only by his heavy reliance on the latter's *De inventione* and *De officiis*[43] and in his repetition of Cicero's definition of signs but also in his arrangement of the contents of the *Trésor.*[44] The *Trésor* is divided into three books. The first contains a mélange of subjects, including cosmology, theology, history, astronomy, geography, economics, and natural history. The second deals with ethics, while the third treats rhetoric and politics.[45] Brunetto follows Cicero in insisting the eloquence is necessary for the proper conduct of political life: "Tully says that the highest science of governing the city is rhetoric, that is, the science of speech. For if there were no speech, neither cities, justice, nor human society would be established; it was for these things that speech was given to all men."[46] Rhetoric, Brunetto continues, deals not merely with the science of speaking but with the art of speaking well. It is "full of noble teaching; and teaching is nothing but wisdom; and wisdom is the understanding of things as they are." Wisdom joined to eloquence engenders goodness.[47] In primitive times, Brunetto explains, when men were devoid of civic institutions, there were certain wise and well-spoken men, who taught and counseled their fellows about the greatness of the soul and the dignity of reason. These sage, eloquent men were the first to promote law and justice and to restrain the savagery of primitive man; it was through their leadership that civil society was established.[48]

In discussing the competence of rhetoric, Brunetto states that it has cognizance of matters both private and public. It is used "to induce belief (*por faire croire*), to praise and to blame, and to hold counsel on any needful matter, or about anything that requires judgment."[49] Anything can be dealt with by rhetoric so long as it is written or spoken; thus rhetoric covers prose, poetry, and the *ars dictaminis*.[50] In setting forth the technique of rhetoric, thus broadly conceived, Brunetto follows the Ciceronian sequence of invention, organization, decoration, memorization, and delivery. Decoration consists in applying ornamental figures to one's speech, letter, or poem. In this connection Brunetto cites the Horatian dictum *ut pictura poesis,* while altering its usual emphasis. Rhetoric is like painting, he says, not because they both aim at the imitation of nature, but because both are colorful, rhetoric adding its *colores* to prose and poetry alike.[51]

In the second part of book 3 of the *Trésor,* which deals with politics, Brunetto defines his subject as "the noblest and highest science and the noblest office on earth, for politics generally comprehends all the arts necessary for human society."[52] All political dominion and honor, he says, come from God. God ordains that human governments be firmly established on the three pillars of justice, reverence, and love. By justice, the ruler gives to each subject his due; by reverence, the subjects give honor to the ruler; and by love, the ruler and the ruled give their mutual attention to the needs of the common weal.[53] After laying down these general definitions, Brunetto devotes the rest of this part of book 3 to the two kinds of commonwealths, those with officials elected by the people and those with permanent rulers who appoint the officials.[54] He places greater emphasis on and gives more space to the former kind of commonwealth, since it is more directly applicable to the situation in contemporary Italy. He goes into considerable detail in outlining the qualities that the electorate should seek in candidates for public office,[55] the method of their election,[56] and the ways in which the officials should receive and administer their public charge.[57]

Brunetto's *Trésor* is an important work which exerted considerable influence on Dante. While he adheres to a poetics concerned with decoration, derived from the medieval school tradition, Brunetto also combines poetics with a rhetoric firmly attached to didactic, ethical, and political concerns.[58] The Middle Ages, as we have seen, had a tradition of didactic poetry, carried on side by side with the tradition of poetic decoration. But none of the medieval exponents of didactic poetry had detailed its moral mission in so broad and yet so explicit a sense as Brunetto. Brunetto links rhetoric, including poetry, to wisdom and virtue, and also to a specific kind of political morality which flows from a specific set of political institutions, those of the Italian city-state of his own day. What Dante takes from Brunetto is his didactic, rhetorical idea of poetry and some of its particular political connotations. The idea of poetry as decoration, however, he abandons. Nevertheless, Dante did not have to break away from all of the poetic theory available at his time in order to write didactic poetry.[59]

In addition to the inflluences put forth by Vergil and by the school tradition, as represented by the writings of Brunetto Latini, contemporary vernacular lyric poetry must also be taken into account as part of Dante's immediate background. It is a well-known fact that Dante made a contribution of fundamental importance to this tradition, which encompasses the Provençal lyrics of southern France and their Italian sequels in the *dolce stil nuovo*. Dante is well aware of his links to this movement. In the *Purgatorio* he greets with obvious respect two eminent practitioners of the vernacular lyric, the Provençal Arnaut Daniel and the Italian Guido Guinizelli.[60] At another point he speaks with an earlier author of Italian lyrics, Bonagiunta, explaining to him how the art of poetry has been transformed since his day.[61] Dante also places two lyric poets in the *Comedy* for political reasons—Sordello, in whose mouth he puts a series of judgments on the princes in his circle of Purgatory after his own eloquent diatribe against the current corruption of Italy,[62] and Bertran de Born, whom he consigns to the *Inferno* as an evil counselor and a fomenter of rebellion.[63]

At this point it may be well to set forth some of the main features of troubadour and *dolce stil nuovo* poetry. Both employ rhyme, meter, and a refined and elaborate stanza structure. This latter characteristic is particularly marked in the intellectualistic and even recondite Provençal *trobar clus*. The obscurity of *trobar clus* is replaced in the *dolce stil nuovo* by a more logical method of organizing the stanza and a firm grasp of syntactical connections between words.[64] Although the troubadours present a range of attitudes toward both love and women, including even the cynicism and misogyny of Marcabru, the principal troubadour themes which the *dolce stilnovisti* appropriated were the celebration of the virtues of an ideal lady, the praise of the ennobling effects of love upon the lover, and the lament over the sufferings of unrequited love. The idealized lady is sometimes treated as an inaccessible *princesse lointaine;* she is also often compared with God. The Provençal authors frequently apply feudal terminology to the lady, describing her as a *domina* who commands the loyalty and service of the lover. The Italians further rarefy the image of the lady, treating her as a quasi-celestial figure.[65] This particular idea is not original. It reflects a tradition visible in medieval lyrics from the Carolingian period onward, in which tropes drawn from Christian Latin hymns are applied to the objects of love poems.[66] Thus the tendency of thirteenth-century lyricists to analogize the lady and the emotions that she inspires in the lover to biblical concepts and states of mind and their treatment of her virtues as secularized versions of the biblical counsels of perfection should be seen as the formalization of existing practices.

Dante adopts many of these ideas in his early love poems, and they are evident in his *Vita nuova*. At the same time, this work reflects a modification of the *dolce stil nuovo* attitude toward the lady, and it is the first attempt on Dante's part to make a statement about the nature of poetry. His effort to clarify what he is doing in the *Vita nuova* can be seen by examining the structure of the work, which is composed of poems followed by explanatory prose passages. This genre derives immediately from Provençal poetry, especially that of Bertran de Born, but it is taken ultimately from the style of Boethius's *Consolation of Philosophy*.[67] The incisiveness and power of Dante's lyrics is enhanced by the fact that he expresses his state of mind through a concrete event rather than through a rhetorical mood.[68] His treatment of the lady, Beatrice, shares in the tendency of his school to attribute almost a divine or salvific quality to the lady, a point underlined by Dante in his playing on the verbal similarity between Beatrice's name and beatitude. Scholars interpreting the Beatrice of the *Vita nuova* from the point of view of the Beatrice of the *Divine Comedy* have argued that Beatrice is a Christ figure for Dante from the very first.[69] This interpretation is an error of anticipation, since it applies a later idea retroactively to an earlier period of Dante's thought. It also fails to take sufficient account of the traditional use of religious tropes in medieval lyrics and the refinement of this technique by Provençal and *dolce stil nuovo* poets. A far more significant shift in Dante's treatment of the lady is the fact that in the *Vita nuova* he always portrays Beatrice in a social context, in the company of other people. This is a major departure from the ordinary Provençal and *dolce stil nuovo* practice, where the lady is always alone.[70]

In the *Vita nuova* Dante is also interested in setting forth an idea of poetry. This poetic theory contains certain features which remain permanent in Dante's poetics and which he retains up through the *Divine Comedy*. Other aspects of the view of poetry which he expresses in the *Vita nuova* he later modifies or drops altogether, as his conception of poetry changes and develops. As we have seen in discussing the Augustinian theory of signs in earlier portions of this study, its exponents hold that speech is capable of signifying real objects truly and also that verbal signs are not identical with their significata. Words are thus accurate but imperfect indices of their objects. Further, they hold that speech has a necessary but a purely instrumental role in teaching and moving its audience. Dante reiterates both of these points in the *Vita nuova*. He seeks an authority outside of himself to validate what he is saying; his words, he notes, are dictated by love, a force which he personifies and converses with in the body of the work.[71] Outside of the truthfulness which his words derive from love's inspiration, speech in general, according to Dante, is an authentic sign of preexisting realities. In a frequently quoted statement, he cites the maxim "Nomina sunt consequentia rerum."[72] This dictum has been identified as a commonplace of Roman law.[73] More important, it is a clear expression of the Augustinian principle that the object is prior to its verbal sign, and that the sign must be judged true or false in terms of its object. This principle must be grasped in order to understand Dante's attitude toward poetic style. To speak, for Dante, means to write poetry.[74] Poetic language and form must thus be commensurate with the subject matter of a poem in order for the poem to possess rectitude and to be able to move its readers toward true and worthy ends. According to Dante, it is clear in the *Vita nuova* that words which signify worthy objects have persuasive force and moral power. His praise of his lady, he says, possesses beatitude.[75] One who speaks with her, he adds, cannot come to a bad end.[76] Putting the idea more strongly still, he affirms that his love poems have the power to make people feel love and thus to acquire its ennobling virtues.[77]

In describing how the beloved lady communicates these ennobling virtues to the lover, Dante effects an important change in a standard lyric trope, the eyes and smile of the lady. *Dolce stil nuovo* poets advert frequently to these features of the beloved. The eyes, traditionally, are the windows of the soul. By looking into the lady's eyes, the *dolce stil nuovo* poet sought to discern whether she possessed a gentle heart, whether she was a fitting object of his love and of his song. The lady's smile is a sign of her regard for the poet. Dante also treats the lady's eyes and smile as signs, but he interprets them metaphorically as means of verbal communication. Love's words are smiles, he says.[78] The lady's eyes are bearers of love, of pity; her smile is love's image.[79] The eyes and smile of the lady are thus, for Dante, actual channels through which she transmits to the poet the goodness, truth, and moral power of love, of which she is a messenger.

While words, in the literal sense of speech and poetry, and in the figurative sense of the lady's eyes and smile, are true and persuasive for Dante, he does not neglect the other side of the Augustinian theory. He observes in the *Vita nuova* that speech and poetry also have limitations as signs of their objects. On several occasions in this work he notes that his words are too weak to convey the true glory of his lady and that they are defective signs of his own feelings about her as well.[80] The marvel of Beatrice's smile cannot be grasped fully by his mind or expressed fully by his words; her very salutation makes the tongue fall silent.[81] Dante's best known statement of the limits of poetry in the *Vita nuova* comes at the end of the work, where he says that he must hold his peace until he is able to write a poem truly worthy of Beatrice, a task which he regards his art as now inadequate to perform.[82]

Above and beyond Dante's interest in specifying the powers and limits of poetry, he is also concerned in the *Vita nuova* with describing the uses of vernacular poetry. In this work, Dante takes the position that the sole function of poetry in the *volgare* is to speak of love. In fact he vigorously opposes those who argue that it can serve in any other capacity.[83] Vernacular love poetry, he adds, is patterned after Latin lyrics, both in terms of its subject matter and in terms of its style. It is necessary to use the vernacular for love poetry, he states, because this poetry is addressed to women who cannot be expected to understand Latin.[84] However, since vernacular love poetry has the same aims as Latin love poetry, it may be accorded the same stylistic usages; any rhetorical figures or colors conceded to the Latin "poets" must also be conceded to the vernacular "rhymesters." In the *Vita nuova,* Dante thus remains within the decorative approach to poetry, viewing the style of vernacular lyrics in the context of a poetics of ornamentation.[85] His justification of the vernacular in this work is a purely rhetorical one, going back to the principle that one must choose the style that one's audience can best understand. There is also present in the *Vita nuova* a trace of the medieval view that poetry contains an inner core of truth hidden by poetic veils. In the course of the work, Dante sets before the reader a series of enigmatic or metaphorical statements and situations, which he gradually explains as the work progresses. He regards this technique as an extension of the right of the vernacular poet to use personification and other rhetorical tropes, but he feels it necessary to explain their meaning himself.[86] The most interesting feature of this method is that the reader's enlightenment is provided both through Dante's exegesis of his lyrics and through Dante's own progressive enlightenment as the protagonist of the *Vita nuova.* He thus takes a twofold point of view — that of the central character in a series of events, who learns and grows through his experience, and that of a commentator analyzing his previous states of mind retrospectively.

The *Vita nuova* presents us with a theory of poetry that is inchoate and not entirely consistent. On the one hand, Dante adopts a didactic view of poetry. Poetic speech and its metaphors, such as the lady's eyes and smile, convey information and moral benefits to the lover and, through him, are capable of teaching and moving the reader. Along with the intrinsic significance of language and the authority which the poet derives from love's inspiration go the significative limitations which apply to speech. On the other hand, Dante tends to derogate the didactic function of poetry by confining its vernacular use to love poetry alone and by contrasting the vernacular "rhymesters" in a derogatory sense with the Latin "poets." His view of poetic style as essentially ornamental is ill assorted with his careful construction of the *Vita nuova,* with its shifts in tone as he first speaks in his poems to Beatrice and then about her, an approach which reflects the idea that his poetic style at any given point in the work must correspond to his level of understanding of Beatrice's importance for him.

The features of Dante's poetic in the *Vita nuova* which he retains in his later works are the idea of language as an accurate yet inadequate sign, the notion that poetry is didactic and persuasive, the view that style must reflect the content of the poem and must be adjusted to the audience, and the technique of instructing the reader through the development of the poet as a character within the work. The limitations that Dante places on the use of the vernacular and the ornamental approach to poetry in the *Vita nuova,* however, tend to drop from view in Dante's later works.

In Dante's next work, the *Convivio,* he develops the idea of poetry expressed in his *Vita nuova* and broadens its context considerably. The *Convivio* follows the same general pattern as the *Vita nuova.* It is composed of four books, the last three of which are commentaries on canzoni at their heads. The influence of Boethius's *Consolation of Philosophy* is visible not only in its structure but also in the fact that the lady whose praises the poet sings is Philosophy. Dante employs Boethian terms in describing Philosophy and tells us that he was moved to become her dévoté by reading Boethius and Cicero.[87] By orienting his art to the love of wisdom, Dante is here clearly enlarging the scope of his literary didacticism; he widens it still further to include the Ciceronian correlation of wisdom, virtue, and eloquence by devoting a large portion of the work to the nature of true nobility, which he analyzes in a moral and a political context.

Dante also makes use of the Ciceronian triad of teaching, persuasion, and pleasure in elaborating the powers and limitations of speech. In the *Convivio,* even more than in the *Vita nuova,* he stresses the didactic strand of medieval rhetorical poetics. He also expands the scope of the vernacular. The *Convivio,* Dante tells us, aims to move men to wisdom and virtue; to this end the author

sets forth his knowledge of these subjects for the benefit of others who may have
been deflected from seeking them by public and private cares.[88] He has no
doubts that literature is capable of bringing errant humanity back to the right
path (*diritto calle*); he states in tractate 4 that this is the purpose of the canzone
preceding it, and that the canzone not only presents the truth but refutes
error.[89] Speech, affirms Dante, can transform the behavior of the hearer;
"Words . . . are like seeds of action."[90] This power is based on the fact that
language is the means by which one man expresses his thoughts to others.[91]
The particular language that Dante chooses for this purpose is Italian. He
justifies his use of the vernacular on the rhetorical grounds that it enables him
to reach a wider audience than Latin.[92] He also stresses that the vernacular is
the pathway to the knowledge which is man's final perfection and that it allies
one with his family and his fellow citizens.[93]

In describing the importance he attaches to his own work, Dante analogizes
his tractates to the sun, the symbol of God, and does not scruple at comparing
his own literary efforts to Christ's miraculous multiplication of the loaves:

This commentary shall be that bread . . . with which thousands shall be filled; and
baskets full of it shall remain over. . . . This shall be a new light and a new sun, which
shall rise when the old sun shall set, and shall shine on those who are in darkness and
mist because of the old sun which gives no light to them.[94]

Dante attributes to the vernacular rhetoric of his *Convivio* a political significance
and a moral and an almost religious power. The importance of his objectives,
he says, justifies the mention which he makes of his own life in the work, since
this is done strictly for didactic purposes, as in Augustine's *Confessions*.[95] His
style involves persuasion and pleasure. Dante does not subordinate his task of
teaching and convincing his readers to the task of pleasing them. The two, he
indicates, go hand in hand. In his analysis of the canzone "Voi che 'ntendendo il
terzo ciel movete" in tractate 2, he states that the third heaven of the canzone
corresponds to Venus and to rhetoric, for rhetoric is "the pleasantest of all the
Sciences, inasmuch as its chief aim is to please."[96] By pleasing the reader, the
author can convince him: "In every kind of discourse the speaker ought chiefly
to be intent upon persuasion, that is on charming his audience, for this is that
kind of persuasion which is the beginning of all others, as every rhetorician
knows."[97]

Dante clearly agrees with Augustine that rhetoric can have a potent effect on
man's knowledge and moral behavior, and he applies this view to poetry along
with a variety of rhetorical tropes.[98] He also expresses the Augustinian view
that one's ability to learn through speech is conditioned by one's moral state.[99]

In the *Convivio*, as in the *Vita nuova*, Dante treats speech in a figurative as well as in a literal sense, and, when he does so, he fastens on the same metaphors, the eyes and smile of the lady. The lady in the case of the *Convivio* is an abstraction, Philosophy, which heightens the metaphorical character of her eyes and smile in contrast to those of Beatrice in the *Vita nuova*. In the *Convivio*, however, Dante is more precise about the nature and functions of the lady's eyes and smile than he is in the *Vita nuova*. He defines the eyes of the lady as "her demonstrations, which, when directed into the eyes of the intellect fill with love a soul that is free in her conditions."[100] The mouth, like the eyes, reflects the soul of the lady; laughter is the "coruscation of the soul's delight," and the smiles of the lady are her persuasions.[101] Dante's addition of another level of metaphor to his description of the lady's eyes and smile does not alter the fact that the lady is assuming for him an increasingly didactic role in the *Convivio*, in accordance with the change in her nature from a real person, as in the *Vita nuova*, to a personalized abstraction. While Dante has before his eyes the figure of Boethius's Lady Philosophy, and while he can explain his own personification of Philosophy as the application of a rhetorical figure to poetry,[102] he still describes her in *dolce stil nuovo* terms as "the beatitude of the intellect."[103] More significantly, he still tends to see a love relationship between himself and a lady, symbolic or otherwise, as the context in which he, and by extension, the reader, acquires wisdom and virtue.

Dante, as we can see, retains and amplifies in the *Convivio* the ideas on the powers of speech which he expresses in the *Vita nuova;* this is no less true for his treatment of the limitations of speech. At various points in the *Convivio* he states that his mind is not able to grasp nor his tongue express the things to which he is currently referring.[104] More importantly, Dante limits the truth of poetry in a way that breaks down his previously stated rhetorical union of didacticism and pleasure by recourse to an ornamental view of poetry. He does this by distinguishing the beauty of the first canzone from its goodness. Its beauty, he says, consists in its stylistic adornments, while its goodness consists in its meaning. Dante does not regard the meaning and the way in which it is expressed as two inseparable functions of a unitary work of art; rather, he urges the reader to enjoy the beauty even if he does not understand the meaning.[105] Furthermore, he derogates the truth content of such beautiful poetic decorations as allegories. In his discussion of the fourfold method of literary analysis, he distinguishes the theological use of allegory from the poetic:

Writings can be understood and ought to be expounded chiefly in four senses. The first is called literal, and this is that sense which does not go beyond the strict limits of the letter, the second is called allegorical, and this is disguised under the cloak of . . . stories, and is a truth hidden under a beautiful fiction (*bella menzogna*). . . . Theologians indeed do not apprehend this sense in the same fashion as poets; but inasmuch as my intention is to follow here the custom of poets, I will take the allegorical sense after the manner which poets use.

The third sense is called moral; and this sense is that for which teachers ought as they go through writings intently to watch for their own profit and that of their hearers. . . .

The fourth sense is called anagogic, that is, above the senses; and this occurs when a writing is spiritually expounded, which even in the literal sense by the things signified likewise gives intimation of higher matters belonging to the eternal glory.[106]

He adds that the literal sense should always be established first, since the other three senses depend on it.[107] Dante's definition of the literal, moral, and anagogical senses is perfectly traditional. What he has done with the allegorical sense has been to replace it with the theory of the poetic veils. While poetry still has a core of truth, according to this view, the figures through which this truth is put forth are lies, although beautiful ones. This theory widens the gap Dante posits between his canzone's good inner meaning and its beautiful exterior style. It reinforces the poetic of decoration and undermines the aesthetic and didactic unity which Dante sees as a feature of rhetoric and, by extension, of poetry. Thus the limitations he applies to poetic speech in the *Convivio* do not square with the powers he grants it in the same work.

Notwithstanding this inconsistency, Dante goes on in the fourth tractate to explore the connections between eloquence, wisdom, and virtue. He does this largely by discussing at some length the nature of true nobility. In order to prove his own position and to refute the reverse, Dante also includes a long section on political theory, centering on the need for a universal empire and the nature of its authority. The political ideas that Dante expresses in the *Convivio* present us in germ with his later position in the *De monarchia*. But this is not their only importance. They must not be regarded as a digression in the *Convivio*. Dante begins with a definition of nobility attributed to the emperor Frederick II, who, he says, described nobility as consisting in inherited wealth and fine manners.[108] In order to disprove this definition Dante finds it necessary to define the authority of the emperor, with the aim of showing that the emperor has no right to define nobility. Also, the juxtaposition of nobility and political theory indicates Dante's view that morality and political life cannot be divorced, an Aristotelian principle which he affirms obliquely by referring to Aristotle several times in the tractate as the "master of human life,"[109] the leader of human reason,[110] whose philosophy must be considered as "almost Catholic opinion."[111]

With this orientation of the problem in mind, Dante proceeds to outline the need for a universal empire. Human life, he begins, is ordered toward the end of happiness. No one can achieve this end by himself, since man is by nature social; he cannot attain happiness, nor can he satisfy his needs without the family, the neighborhood, and civil society at all its levels from the city to the empire. If man is naturally social, continues Dante, he is also naturally greedy. This tendency leads men to develop territorial ambitions, which in turn lead to wars among kingdoms, a situation which has a deleterious effect on all aspects of social life and which prevents men from reaching the goal of happiness. But, Dante argues, if there were one empire, wars and their causes would cease, for if one man possessed all territorial dominion, there would be nothing left for him to covet. Omitting to notice that this would not prevent other men from being jealous of the emperor, he concludes that if there were one universal ruler, he would be able to institute a lasting peace. Thus men would be able to live happily and to achieve their end.[112]

Having made this point, it remains for Dante to explain why this universal dominion should be vested in the Holy Roman emperor rather than in some other prince, especially since the power of Rome was initially acquired by force. Dante argues that the choice of the Holy Roman emperor as the one best prince was ordained by God. Thus the empire gained its power by providence, not by force; force was only the instrumental cause. God chose the Romans, whom Dante does not distinguish from the current German emperors, on account of their virtues, since these virtues were needed in order for the empire to fulfill the mission assigned to it by God.[113] This mission is the reconciliation of God and man. It is for this reason that God become incarnate during the Roman era. As further proof of Rome's authority, he states that the birth of David and the foundation of Rome occurred simultaneously, which clearly reveals God's special interest in the establishment of the Roman Empire. God, for Dante no less than for Augustine, oversaw the entire history of Rome, inspired its rulers and citizens with virtues human and divine, and is responsible for its most outstanding accomplishment, universal peace. Thus, Dante concludes, Rome is worthy of special reverence.[114]

Dante now moves to the discussion of the nature of imperial and philosophical authority. The imperial authority derives, as Dante has indicated, from God. But he is also interested in the etymological derivation of the term from the Latin and Greek. Authority, he states, flows from the activity proper to an *auctor;* it also bespeaks the quality of being worthy of trust and obedience, an idea which Dante extracts from the Greek by way of the contemporary jurist Uguccione. He has comparatively little to say about philosophical authority, contenting himself with the judgment that it pertains above all to Aristotle. Dante advocates the cooperation of philosophical and imperial authorities for the good of the commonwealth, a piece of advice which he urges the Italians to take to heart.[115]

With these principles before the reader, Dante now rebuts the view that true nobility is based on wealth, ancestry, and manners. He begins his attack on Frederick II's definition by discussing briefly the nature of worthiness. Worthiness, he says, entails reverence, which he defines as the acknowledgment of one's subjection to both princely and philosophical authority.[116] This reverence, however, is not unlimited, particularly as it applies to the emperor. The empire, argues Dante, was invented for the perfection of human life. Thus the emperor's jurisdiction extends justly over all those human activities which can be described as voluntary, since it is in terms of man's voluntary choices that he achieves or rejects his end. The emperor justly regulates these activities by law, and his authority also covers certain technical matters like marriage, slavery, military affairs, and the laws of succession. But God has imposed limits upon the jurisdiction of the emperor. The emperor has no authority over those things which the human will does not direct, such as nature, supernature, and mathematics. Since true nobility is a natural faculty,[117] whose ultimate source is God alone,[118] it follows for Dante that the emperor does not have a legitimate right to define the nature of true nobility.[119]

This disposes of the right by which Frederick II issued his dictum on the subject. Dante now proceeds to criticize the content of Frederick's definition. The difficulties that Dante sees in attributing nobility to lineage and inherited wealth are manifold. Riches are irrelevant to nobility, he argues, since a man who is noble remains noble even after he loses his wealth.[120] In any case, riches produce worldly cares and corrupt their owner, making him greedy for more. Greed promotes conflict and instills in the wealthy the irrational desire for perfect wealth, which is self-defeating since it cannot be achieved. Riches thus cause evil and deprive their owner of good. They make him envious, fearful of loss, and insecure. Furthermore, these attitudes distract men from their chief end, God.[121] Ancestry is no key to nobility either. The fact that the men of one generation may be noble should not lead us to extend this judgment uncritically and automatically to their descendants.[122] This view is erroneous, according to Dante, because it assumes that people cannot change for better or for worse, an idea which forces us to posit two aboriginal ancestors of the human race, one base and one noble, from whom two different breeds of men are descended, instead of one common ancestor, Adam. [123] Neither are manners a criterion of nobility; they are the effects, not the causes, of nobility. [124]

Moving to the positive side of his argument, Dante now defines nobility as anything perfect in its own nature. [125] Since perfection is the end of the moral life, nobility is related to virtue. Dante cites with approval several classical virtues derived from Aristotle, reserving highest honors for justice as the most distinctively human of them. [126] Each virtue, he says, is subject to two vices, on the side of excess and on the side of defect; virtue can be described as the mean between the two. The virtuous life may be active or contemplative, although Dante voices an Aristotelian and biblical preference for the latter. [127] Nobility, Dante adds, is wider and more inclusive than the moral virtues. It also encompasses the intellectual virtues, piety, and religion, praiseworthy emotions like shame and pity, and physical excellences like health, strength, and beauty. Still, none of these is the sine qua non of nobility, since it can be found in persons like women and children who do not possess all of these characteristics. [128] The addition of these qualifications may appear to muddy the waters of Dante's analysis, but, in any event, he ends by making the covering statement that it is God alone who confers true nobility and that it is beyond the range of human reason to know precisely how he does this. [129] Finally, Dante applies his idea of nobility to the three Aristotelian divisions of the soul—the vegetative, animate, and intellectual—and to the four stages of life—adolescence, youth, old age, and decline—illustrating each aspect of the soul and each age with its appropriate virtues. [130]

The *Convivio* is a rather disjointed and unbalanced work, the result, probably, of the fact that Dante never completed it. Nevertheless, it is interesting for several reasons. It presents a theory of poetry stressing didacticism intertwined with aesthetic pleasure. It adds much weight to Dante's growing stress on the vernacular and on the powers of poetic speech. In it he employs his favorite device, an idealized lady, as the channel through whom he acquires the insights which he sets before the reader. While somewhat inconsistently linked to a view of the limits of poetry which treats its aesthetic strategy as a *bella menzogna*, Dante's poetics in this work shows his increasing tendency to envision eloquence in the context of ethics and politics. Although his treatment of nobility in the *Convivio* is neither particularly orginal[131] nor entirely lucid, Dante relates it, along with the discussion of the Holy Roman Empire which it entails, to the love of wisdom and to an elevated view of literature as a vehicle of truth and a spur to moral action.

Dante's most elaborate theoretical statement on the subject of poetry is found in his *De vulgari eloquentia*. This work, which sets the disussion in the context of an analysis of the nature and origin of language, includes an extensive treatment of Italian dialects and the norms of poetic style. In it Dante joins verbal epistemology and literary theory to his ethical and political concerns in the quest for a new Italian vernacular capable of unifying Italy linguistically and of serving the ideals of wisdom, virtue, and eloquence. [132] Dante begins by pointing out that speech is distinctively human and essential to men, since they require a discursive mode of knowing and of expressing their thoughts to others. [133] "A dialect," he says, "is no less a necessary instrument for [the expression of] our thoughts than a horse is to a soldier." [134] Men, according to Dante, need language because speech, like human nature itself, is both rational and sensible. Words are signs in both their sensible and their rational aspects. They are sensible signs of things insofar as they are sounds; Dante, in the tradition of classical sign theory, stresses the sonic character of language. [135] Language is also a rational sign insofar as it signifies the ideas or intentions of the speaker and communicates them to the hearer, but it must do this through a sensible medium. [136] Dante's emphasis on the need for a sensible medium reflects the view that sense perception is the beginning of human knowledge[137] and the idea that sensible signs can represent nonsensible referents adequately.

In surveying the current linguistic situation, Dante notes that there are many different languages. He interprets the fact of linguistic diversity in a moral context. The variety of languages is a consequence of man's sin. Following a lengthy patristic and medieval tradition which had been reiterated by Brunetto Latini, [138] Dante holds that speech originated in the garden of Eden. Unlike speech after the Fall, which was a cry of woe, Adam's first statement was an act of worship, the recognition of God's sovereignty. [139] The harmony between man and the rest of creation in the Earthly Paradise is also symbolized by Adam's naming of the animals in the garden, which shows in turn the natural affinity between rightly ordered speech and reality. According to Dante, all men spoke the same language, Hebrew, until they built the tower of Babel. The building of the tower was an act of human presumption against God and was the occasion for the division of tongues. But here Dante introduces a distinction between linguistic stasis as an ideal and the natural alteration of languages as a function of usage. Once the building of the tower was set in train, he notes, the different groups of craftsmen who worked on its construction developed specialized vocabularies to refer to their own profession-al activities. [140] Such terminological changes, like the growth of neologisms and the obsolescence of words over time, are conventional, stemming from the ways that language is actually used within a particular community or occupational group. But, beginning with the emergence of technical vocabularies in Hebrew among the workmen of Babel as the result of their specialization of functions, divergences in the use of a single common tongue grew into distinct dialects after mankind was dispersed in the sequel. On the one hand, for Dante, "language could not either endure or be uniform, but like other of our characteristics, such as manners and fashions, it necessarily differs with the change of time or place."[141] On the other hand, the dispersal of mankind, God's punishment for sin, turned these natural linguistic changes into language barriers impeding human communication. Once that state was reached, the languages of the earth, with their own internal rules and usages and their own natural tendency to change, divided men increasingly from each other.

In the present stage of linguistic history the issue, for Dante, is not the elimination of the European languages as currently spoken in favor of a return to the primordial and prelapsarian Hebrew tongue. Rather, he focuses on the relationship between grammar and the vernacular, and in particular, the Italian vernacular. By grammar he means the classical rules governing the use of Latin. Although Latin may be seen as one of the many tongues resulting from the building of the tower of Babel, it alone has managed to consolidate its conventions and to make of them a uniform criterion of stylistic and linguistic decorum.[142] The vernacular, however, lacks a similar set of rules that would enable it to rival Latin as a literary language capable of expressing important subjects of all kinds. The dignity and preeminence of grammar, Dante explains, lie in the fact that it lays down unchanging concepts of language, in contrast to the fluctuating character of the vernacular, which permit people to translate other languages into their own and hence to maintain contact with their past and with other men who live outside of their immediate locality. Despite the commanding position possessed by Latin, Dante holds that the vernacular is intrinsically nobler than grammar. It is natural, not artificial; it is the first speech that men employ; and it is used by everyone, although in different forms.[143] Notwithstanding the natural superiority of the vernacular, it labors under a cultural disadvantage. This being the case, Dante takes as his mission the raising of the vernacular, especially that of Italy, to the dignity of grammar, and he invokes Christ the Word at the beginning of the *De vulgari eloquentia* to aid him in this task.[144] The establishment of the unified Italian language which Dante projects in this work is linked to moral and intellectual rectitude, the pursuit of the good and the true. A unified Italian vernacular, he thinks, will also foster a sense of community among all Italians. In addition, the erection of stylistic norms in the Italian language will enhance the literary culture of the country, as well as serve Dante's own needs as a poet. [145] This fusion of Dante's personal aims with his broader ethical and political objectives, which we have noted in Dante's earlier works, is his underlying motive in the *De vulgari eloquentia.*

The work now moves rapidly into a technical discussion of dialects. Dante subdivides the languages of Europe into three groups, those of the north, which use *iò* for yes, those of the south, which use *oc, oïl,* and *sì,* and those of eastern Europe and parts of Asia, which Dante associates with Greek. [146] He confines himself to the southern group, and within it, to Italian, enumerating fourteen different Italian dialects and discussing their regional peculiarities. [147] Dante thinks that each of these dialects is flawed in some way, which prevents it from serving as his ideal vernacular. The very fact that Dante finds it possible to judge each of these dialects presupposes that there is a normative Italian language which can be used as a criterion. Dante explains that this criterion may be established according to the principle of simplicity: "Each individual thing, insofar as it belongs to a category of things, can be measured against the simplest thing in that category." [148] Thus, the ideal vernacular is somehow present in all the Italian dialects and can be derived from them by abstraction. However, this normative Italian language cannot be identified with the Italian spoken anywhere in contemporary Italy. The ideal vernacular is simultaneously everywhere and nowhere. Dante does not hesitate to analogize the simplicity and omnipresence of his linguistic ideal to God:

And surely these, the most noble standards against which the actions of Latins are measured, do not belong to any particular Italian cities, and are common to them all; and among these we can now discern that vernacular we have been tracking above, which suffuses its perfume in every city, but has its lair in none. It could, however, be stronger in one than another, just as the most simple substance, which is God, is more perceptible in man than in brute animals, in brute animals than in plants, in these more than in minerals. . . .

Having thus found what I have been searching for, I declare that the illustrious, cardinal, courtly, and curial vernacular of Latium is that which belongs to all the Latian cities and seems to belong to none, against which all the Latin municipal vernaculars are measured, weighed, and compared. [149]

The pan-Italian yet nonfunctional description of the ideal vernacular is carried over by Dante into his discussion of its four attributes. In exploring the nature of the illustrious, cardinal, courtly, and curial vernacular, the *De vulgari eloquentia* shows a marked expansion of the competence of the vernacular in comparison with the *Convivio* and the *Vita nuova.* The ideal vernacular is called cardinal, explains Dante, because it is the head, chief, and father of all the

Italian dialects. It is called courtly because it pertains to the common ruler and meeting place of the people. "If we Italians had a royal court, this vernacular would be spoken in the palace." Since no such court exists, the courtly vernacular wanders about homelessly. For its part, the curial vernacular pertains to ethics in general and to the supreme court of justice in particular. It is called curial, says Dante, "because 'curiality' is nothing other than a balanced rule for things which must be done. And . . . we have come to call all of our actions which are well-balanced, curial." While the balancing of man's ethical life is presumably possible under any circumstances, Dante points out that Italy has no supreme court. Although the members of such a court currently exist, he notes, at present they can be unified only by abstracting them rationally from their local institutional settings; they are not unified by the existence of a single prince or governmental system.[150] Dante's distinction of the vernacular into cardinal, courtly, and curial shows that he regards it as a suitable medium for the handling of ethics, law, and public affairs, which he in turn sees as correlatives of each other. Yet his definitions of these three forms of the vernacular place an implicit limitation on it; it appears to be either a hypothetical Romance *Ursprache* or a technical legal and administrative vocabulary which does not exist in fact because the institutions that it might serve do not exist.

However, in discussing the illustrious vernacular, Dante gives the distinct impression that his ideal vernacular does exist. In fact, he names several famous authors who use it, including Cino da Pistoia, Bertran de Born, Arnaut Daniel, and Giraut Borneil,[151] and asserts that it can be found in all parts of Italy.[152] Furthermore, he attributes to the illustrious vernacular a range of topics which enable it to subsume and outstrip the other subdivisions of the *volgare*. The illustrious vernacular is the language of literature, and it is no accident that its powers are so broad. Literature, for Dante, is capable of encompassing the problems of ethics, public life, and religion and is thereby capable of reforming and unifying the Italian people even in the absence of the institutional and legal unity upon which the courtly and curial vernacular depend.

In explaining the nature of the illustrious vernacular, Dante draws upon the literary theory which he expresses in his earlier works, but carries it much further. The literary theory of the *De vulgari eloquentia* includes both prose and poetry. Thus we find in Dante's treatment of the illustrious vernacular his predictable identification of rhetoric and poetics.[153] Dante applies many rhetorical norms, derived both from classical rhetoric and from the *ars dictaminis*, to his treatment of poetic technique[154] and cites Vergil as a stylistic authority in the manner of the school tradition.[155] The rhetorical approach, both sophistic and Ciceronian, is visible in his definition of the illustrious vernacular. It is illustrious, he says, because of the skill it demands, because of its power to move men's hearts, and because it confers fame on authors who use it. [156] He indicates that in poetry, as in prose, there are levels of style and form and that each has its appropriate subject matter. [157] He goes so far as to say that vernacular poets truly merit the title "poet," for their writing is "expressed in verse according to [the arts of] rhetoric and music."[158]

Still more important is Dante's inversion of the traditional assimilation of poetics to rhetoric. Dante's poetics, to be sure, results from the absorption of certain rhetorical aims and techniques by poetry. But, in his handling of the relationship between prose and poetry in the *De vulgari eloquentia*, Dante insists that poetry is prior to prose and that prose should be patterned after the norms that he lays down for verse. [159] Thus the stylistic counsels and the epistemological and didactic functions which poetry once borrowed from rhetoric have become so identified with poetry in Dante's mind that he thinks that prose style can model itself after the strategies of poetry, which he delineates in some detail. In point of fact, Dante does not delineate prose style in the same detail. The *De vulgari eloquentia* is an unfinished work, which leaves off before the author gets up to prose. While of course circumstantial, the truncation of the work can, however, be justified in terms of Dante's poetic priorities. Considering the manner in which rhetoric and poetics originally came together in classical Rome, one might say that Dante has out-Ciceroed Cicero.

The essential characteristic of poetry in the illustrious vernacular is rectitude. Rectitude, for Dante, has the same implications that it has for Anselm. It entails an adequate intellectual and moral attitude on the part of the poet, which is related to the subject that he is writing about. Concerned as he is with literary style, Dante adds to these canons a series of formal, aesthetic, and linguistic norms in terms of which the fitness of a poem vis-à-vis its object can be assessed. He begins by defining the kinds of persons who should use the illustrious vernacular and the kinds of subject matter they may treat. The illustrious vernacular entails skill and poetic power; therefore, says Dante, it should be used only by men possessing poetic genius and knowledge who will use it to express the worthiest thoughts. There are degrees of worthiness, he points out, analogous to the three Aristotelian divisions of the soul: the vegetative, the animate, and the rational. The subjects which pertain to these three aspects of the soul are the useful (*utile*), the pleasant (*delectabile*), and the right (*honestum, rectum*). Each of these categories provides subject matter in its own right. Although the *honestum*, or *rectum*, might seem to be the most specifically human of the three, the *delectabile* and the *utile* are seen as ends in themselves, not as means to other ends. The worthiest thoughts of all are those directed toward rectitude, which man seeks insofar as he is rational; virtue is hence the most fitting subject for poetry, which may also deal with the other two parts of the soul, the animate and the vegetative. Worthy thoughts may be directed to the pleasant, which man seeks insofar as he is animate and which finds as its subject love. Finally, the poet may direct himself worthily to the useful, which man seeks insofar as he is vegetative and which finds as its subject matter safety, by which Dante means warfare and the exercise of arms. He notes that the best poets have written on rectitude, love, and war, citing several Provençal troubadours and practitioners of the *dolce stil nuovo* as examples. [160]

By defining the scope of poetry written in the illustrious vernacular in this fashion, the *De vulgari eloquentia* shows Dante in the process of developing a theory of poetry going far beyond his ideas on this subject in the *Convivio* and the *Vita nuova,* a theory which is beginning to look capable of sustaining a work like the *Divine Comedy.* Safety, love, and virtue may sound quite narrow as topics suitable for vernacular poetry, but they are potentially quite broad. They have both personal and community characteristics. Safety can be expanded to include the peaceful as well as the warlike aspects of civic life. Love can address itself to a beloved who supplies the lover with eternal as well as earthly delights. Virtue can take in the natural and the theological virtues, thus linking earthly love and civic life to the love of God and the community of saints. Moreover, this is a theory containing built-in ethical and philosophical dimensions. Since it is rooted in the soul of man, as Dante understands it, it is thus as wide and deep in its scope as human nature itself.

Since words must correspond to things, the excellent subject matter expressed in the illustrious vernacular is worthy of an equally excellent form. This leads Dante to address himself to the canzone, which he thinks is the noblest of poetic forms. It should therefore be used for the worthiest subjects; indeed, he notes, it has been so used by the best poets. [161] The canzone has a set form, which can be learned and produced as an act of good literary craftsmanship. Dante places much stress on craftsmanship, and in fact devotes a sizable part of the *De vulgari eloquentia* to the formal and linguistic rules for good canzoni, including such topics as meter, the length of lines, syllables, sentence structure, vocabulary, stanza structure, rhyme, and musical setting, and lists abuses to be avoided as well as good examples to be emulated. [162] Perhaps most interesting in Dante's assortment of rules, for our purposes, is his discussion of different kinds of words, the childish, feminine, masculine, sylvan, and urban, the urban being further subdivided into glossy, rumpled, combed-out, and shaggy. Dante places words in one or another of these categories on the basis of how they sound. Feminine words, for example, have many liquid vowels, while sylvan words have harsh consonants, often doubled. [163] This stress on the way words sound as the basis for the appropriateness of their use in particular literary contexts underlines Dante's interest in the sensible quality of language. It brings man's physical nature as well as his soul into the framework of literary theory, while indicating the need for a fitting sensible medium in the process by which words communicate the things they signify.

Literary craftsmanship also involves the selection of a subject that the poet is capable of handling, an insight which Dante borrows from Horace's *Ars poetica,* and the choice of an appropriate genre, which is related both to content and to style. Dante defines three basic genres: elegy, comedy, and tragedy. Elegy is written in the style of the wretched and may use only the lowly vernacular. Comedy is written in a mean-to-low style and should use the middle or low vernacular. Tragedy is written in an elevated style; it employs the illustrious vernacular and should use the canzone form. It alone is worthy of dealing with the most elevated subjects: safety, love, and virtue. [164] These subjects, Dante insists, demand unflagging effort, practice, and craft, and not merely poetic genius. By supplying poets with the rules of their craft, he hopes to make the vernacular a truly literary language and its poetry the equal of Latin poetry. Returning to the theme struck at the beginning of the *De vulgari eloquentia,* he argues that the main difference between the Latin and the vernacular poets is that the former proceed according to rules and the later proceed haphazardly. [165] To reform the vernacular, to make it a medium truly fitted for the discussion of great questions, vernacular poets should imitate the regularity of classical poetry by developing and applying to their own art rules appropriate to their own native language.

In the *De vulgari eloquentia,* Dante goes a long way toward working out the theory of poetry which he ultimately expresses in the *Divine Comedy.* As we have seen, he broadens extensively the scope of the vernacular. The linguistic reform that he projects is closely related to ethical and political reform, involving as it does the healing of at least some of the linguistic breaches caused by human sin as well as promoting a more unified Italy. Dante's quest for the ideal Italian vernacular is also closely related to literary reform and the development of a theory of literature stressing the priority of poetry while according to it the significative functions attributed to rhetoric by the Augustinian tradition. Dante bases his theory, as we have noted, on the nature of man and, from this vantage point, makes it competent to deal with the major problems and interests of mankind. There are two aspects of the poetics of the *De vulgari eloquentia* that Dante later alters in the interests of the *Divine Comedy*. One is his position on the immutability of Latin, which removes any obstacle in the path of his claims for the superiority of the vernacular. The second is his limitation of the worthiest subjects—war, love, and virtue—to the tragic style and his insistence that the canzone is the only suitable form in which to write about them. He is forced to change his mind on this point in order to make the treatment of the theme of salvation in the *Comedy* plausible. Nevertheless, his notion that the comic genre may use a moderate style containing a mixed vocabulary is one that Dante does carry over into the *Comedy*. Certainly the *Comedy* vindicates Dante's argument in the *De vulgari eloquentia* that both craftsmanship based on rules and poetic genius are necessary if the vernacular is to assume its rightful place by the side of Latin as a literary language.

The development of Dante's linguistic and literary answers to current problems in the *De vulgari eloquentia* is matched by his elaboration of a political solution to the same problems in his *De monarchia* and political letters. Dante's political ideas have excited a good deal of interest on the part of scholars.[166] Outside of a brief interlude in the twentieth century, during which the exigencies of the moment inspired Fascist and anti-Fascist interpretations of them,[167] the prevailing approaches have been two in number, paralleling the critical treatments of the *De vulgari eloquentia*. Some scholars are content to abstract Dante's strictly political ideas from his works,[168] while others take account of the fact that Dante's political ideas occur in an ethical and religious context.[169] This latter point of view is by far the more plausible, since Dante's arguments throughout the *De monarchia* and in other works where he treats political questions make much use of biblical authority and the insights of Aristotelian moral philosophy, and he is quite concerned with specifying the relationships between political, ethical, and religious life.

The *De monarchia* is divided into three books, in which Dante attempts to prove the need for a universal empire, the justification for the possession of imperial authority on the part of the ancient Romans, and by extension the current Holy Roman Empire, and the invalidity of papal claims to temporal authority over the emperor. Indeed, the *De monarchia* may be regarded as part of the ongoing debate among medieval publicists on the respective powers of popes and emperors in the Christian commonwealth.[170] In dealing with these questions, Dante recapitulates the basic points that he sets forth in the *Convivio* but expands the discussion considerably, having recourse to arguments drawn from scriptural authority, the authority of classical antiquity, reason (or his own deductions and definitions), and experience (or historical facts as he understands them). An ethical and religious, no less than a strictly political, motivation is evident throughout. This motivation underlies Dante's stated reason for writing about politics and his definition of the nature of his subject. He writes, he tells us, because the learned have a duty to serve the common weal.[171] His intention is to stimulate political reform; unlike mathematics, physics, and theology, he reminds the reader, politics is a matter subject to human control. Its aim is action, which falls under the jurisdiction of the virtue of prudence.[172]

Dante's basic justification for politics, as well as his arguments for a single universal empire, further underlines his association of civic life and ethics. His rationale for this association is the Aristotelian principle that political society is conducive to the good life, and that in a good society the good citizen and the good man are the same.[173] This being the case, Dante offers three main arguments in book 1 of the *De monarchia* designed to identify a universal empire with the good society. Two of these are positive arguments; the third is partly positive and partly negative. He begins by agreeing with Aristotle that the end of man, both personal and social, is the perfection of the intellect. The perfection of the intellect, then, is the end toward which political life is directed. As a basic precondition of his intellectual development man needs peace, and the best means to achieve peace is one universal government.[174] Next Dante takes up the theme of unity, toward which, he thinks, agreeing with Aristotle on this point as well, all things tend. Man, he states, is made in the image of God. Mankind thus resembles God, and, since God is one, mankind should have one universal government and ruler. Dante thinks that unity is better than multiplicity on general principles, an idea which he regards as self-evident in the light of the convertibility of unity, as a metaphysical transcendental, with being and goodness.[175] Finally, he agrees with Augustine, noting that good order in the world is characterized by justice. He defines justice as rectitude (*rectitudo*), "or a rule which drives out obliquity."[176] In the abstract, he goes on, justice is a quality which admits of no degrees. But in concrete terms, justice is found mixed with other things contrary to it. In particular, it is found mixed with human sin and selfishness, as expressed by the vice of greed. Repeating his argument in the *Convivio,* Dante asserts that the only way to remove greed, the cause of wars and contentions, from political life on a permanent basis is to have one universal ruler who possesses everything and who therefore lacks anything to covet. Once the possibility for greed is disposed of, greed itself will vanish, and, since it is the major obstacle to justice, justice will prevail. In this third argument Dante moves from a positive justification for a universal empire, the promotion of justice, to a negative justification, government as a remedy for sin, a point which he repeats in the third book of the *De monarchia*.[177]

Dante's next problem is to demonstrate that universal dominion is rightly vested in the Roman Empire. He adds very little here that is not already present in the *Convivio* in his efforts to show that human reason, divine authority, and history support his case. Starting from the proposition that the basis of political right (*ius*) is the will of God, which, like the intentions of men, can be detected only through visible signs,[178] he argues that the nobility or virtue of the Romans is attested by their own history[179] and by their self-sacrificing concern for the common good.[180] Their natural capacity for world rule is also proved by the justice and prudence of their laws.[181] God, furthermore, sanctioned the power of Rome by his miracles,[182] by permitting the Romans to conquer their enemies on the field of battle,[183] and, finally, by virtue of the fact that Christ chose to become incarnate during Roman imperial times and submitted himself to Roman law.[184] Perhaps the most interesting point that Dante makes in the second book of the *De monarchia* is his association of the emperor with Christ and of his own argument with the sun, the symbol of divinity:

I . . . cry out in behalf of the glorious people and of Caesar in the words of him who cried out in behalf of the Prince of Heaven: "Why have the nations raged and the peoples devised vain things? The kings of the earth stood up and the princes met together against the Lord, and against his Christ" [Ps. 2:1–2]. But as love naturally does not permit derision to endure, and as the summer sun in his rising scatters the morning mists and bathes all in light, so I cease deriding and prefer to throw a correcting light upon the clouds of ignorance, to free from such clouds those raving kings and princes and to reveal a mankind free from the yoke of such rulers.[185]

Finally, Dante, in the tradition of medieval imperialists, addresses himself to combating the idea that the papacy should possess temporal power. Dante does not challenge the pope's spiritual authority, which, he holds, is vested in the papal office by Christ and is a correlative of the fact that man and society have spiritual ends.[186] He uses the sun-and-moon theory of Innocent III and the two-swords theory adumbrated by Gelasius I and Gregory VII and defined by Bernard of Clairvaux as touchstones of the position that he wishes to refute, beginning with an attack on the papalists' technique of arguing their case from ecclesiastical tradition. Tradition flows from the church, he asserts, and therefore it cannot be used to establish the church's powers. Nor does he hesitate to resort to *ad hominem* arguments against various proponents of the papalist position, whom he excoriates as fanatical, greedy for power, and ignorant of anything but the decretals, which, though authoritative, should be subordinated to the Bible, the church fathers, and the decrees of general councils. [187] Next he deals with the sun-and-moon and the two-swords theories in particular. He has two major criticisms of them. Concerning the sun-and-moon theory, he says that it is illogical to deduce the nature of governments, which are accidental creations designed to deal with the circumstantial problems of men, from astronomical phenomena, which are permanent and essential parts of the creation[188]—a strange argument in the light of Dante's own interest in grounding governments in the natural and supernatural orders. Both the sun-and-moon theory and the two-swords theory, he adds, are fallacious because they are based on arbitrary, erroneous, or noncontextual interpretations of the Bible. [189]

Turning to what he regards as correct theory, Dante states that both papacy and empire have an authentic basis. The source of the pope's office, which is limited to spiritual matters, is Christ's will, as revealed by the Bible, and the life of Christ is the norm and pattern of ecclesiastical life. [190] The sources of the emperor's office, which is concerned with temporal matters and which does not derive from papal authority, are natural and supernatural. They flow from God's express mandate[191] and from human right, [192] the nature and needs of men, which, since they are aspects of the law of nature, may be assumed to be in conformity with the will of God. [193] The divine and natural sanctions of the empire, independent of ecclesiastical authorization, are further proved by history; the Roman Empire, Dante notes, predates the church and thus cannot be dependent upon it. [194]

Dante draws several conclusions from these principles. Neither the papacy nor the empire can be the common denominator of the other. [195] No cession of temporal powers to popes by emperors is truly legitimate, and the usurpation of such powers by popes does not confer a right to them. [196] Rather, Dante insists, man has two ends, natural and supernatural. His own nature and the will of God ordain that there should be two institutions, the empire and the papacy, to guide men to these ends. These two institutions have distinct means appropriate to them. The empire employs philosophy, which operates in terms of man's moral and intellectual capacities, to lead man to the Earthly Paradise by means of reason. The church employs religion, which operates in terms of man's theological capacities—faith, hope, and charity—to lead man to eternal bliss by means of revelation and grace. [197]

The *De monarchia* stresses the autonomy of imperial sanctions and functions from the papacy; at the same time, Dante sees religious and political life as inextricably bound together. Reason, philosophy, and ethics are placed within the purview of politics; and politics, like language, is seen as springing from the needs of human nature as well as from the ordinance of God. The empire appears to be the more essential of the two institutions, since peace, which it alone can provide, is the prerequisite for the fulfillment of both the natural and the supernatural ends of man. Yet, politics is finally subordinated, as well as related, to religion, since life on earth is the means to the end of eternal beatitude in heaven.[198]

It is in the light of these priorities and functions that Dante views politics, ethics, religion, and literature, and his letters further cement the close ties which he establishes among them in his other works. Dante's letters bemoan the conditions of both church and state. Christendom, he observes, is plagued with heresies; the cardinals have failed in their responsibility to guide the chariot of the Spouse of Christ and to enlighten the faithful. Rome is a widow, says Dante, adverting to the Babylonian Captivity. Rome has both religious and political significance for him. It is at once the rightful center of the church and the source of Italian civil life.[199] Political life too is beset by abuses, all of which can be traced to lack of respect for imperial authority. Here, as in the *Convivio* and the *De monarchia,* he argues that only a single universal emperor can provide peace and justice, supporting his case with the Bible, reason, and history.[200] In the face of his ardent hope that the emperor Henry VII would succeed in enforcing his claims to Italy and would effect the desired reforms, Dante's letters grow resonant with classical and biblical rhetoric. He describes or addresses Henry as the sun,[201] the bridegroom,[202] the lion of Judah, the new Moses,[203] the sign of God's will,[204] the elect of God,[205] the minister of God, the scion of Jesse, and the Lamb of God.[206] These Christological metaphors are combined with appeals to the classics. The descent of the emperor into Italy, says Dante, will initiate the return of the Saturnian age prophesied by Vergil;[207] Henry is the imperial eagle,[208] the shepherd descended from Hector.[209] Florence, claims Dante, referring to a lengthy urban tradition, has particular cause to support the emperor, since the city, like the empire, is descended from Troy.[210] Yet, he fulminates, the Florentines shamefully reject their Roman traditions, sinfully opposing the will of God by turning their backs on the emperor.[211] Dante's association of politics with ethics and religion is so strong here that he virtually equates failure to support the emperor's claims in Italy with sin before God. Dante relates the classical and biblical aspects of the imperial office and the union of Florence with a Rome symbolizing both political and religious ideals to his blend of language, politics, and morality in a passage in which he compares the Florentines' rejection of the emperor with the arrogance of the builders of the tower of Babel: "Wherefore, then, being disabused of such an idle conceit, do you abandon the Holy Empire, and, like the men of Babel once more, seek to found new kingdoms, so that there shall be one polity of Florence, and another of Rome?"[212] Political and linguistic disintegration go hand in hand with sin, and they are all a deviation from the ideal Rome. Rome, for Dante, stands for Florence, the empire, and the church, purified, working correctly, and revealed in their true glory, for moral regeneration and for linguistic and literary reform, for the classical and the Christian traditions. He carries over this complex of ideas to the *Divine Comedy*, and the component parts cannot be detached from each other without severely distorting it.[213]

Dante deals more expressly with literature in his letters as well. His tenth letter, written to his patron Can Grande della Scala, to whom he dedicated the *Paradiso*, in fact supplies us with his most fully developed statement on the subject of literary theory in its outline of how the *Divine Comedy* is to be understood.[214] He prefaces his remarks by asserting that the *Comedy* is a didactic work (*doctrinale opus*),[215] thereby affirming that poetry is capable of serving as a medium of instruction on the most exalted subjects. The truth of poetry, he observes, is dependent on its conformity to things as they are;[216] elsewhere in his letters he restates the principle that words, although they are accurate signs, fall short of the realities which they are designed to express.[217] Dante's explanation of the *Comedy* in the letter to Can Grande utilizes the rhetorical approach to poetry found in his previous works, but here, in his discussion of six basic characteristics of the work—its subject, author, form, aim, title, and the branch of philosophy to which it pertains—he expands this notion and removes some of his earlier theoretical inconsistencies.[218]

Before doing this, however, he notes that the *Comedy* is polysemous. It contains four levels of meaning: the literal, allegorical, moral, and anagogical. The three latter levels, taken together, may be called allegorical in general. Dante illustrates this idea by analyzing the psalm "In exitu Israel de Aegypto," following the standard fourfold method of scriptural exegesis.[219] It will be remembered that Dante also advocates this method in the *Convivio*, but his treatment of it in the letter to Can Grande represents a major theoretical departure. In the *Convivio*, Dante distinguishes between the allegory of theologians and the allegory of poets. He describes poetic allegory as a *bella menzogna*, a beautiful lie, masking the truth beneath it. The *Convivio* thus shows Dante tied to the theory of poetic fiction, which derogates from the truth of poetry by drawing a distinction between its true content and its fictive form. In the letter to Can Grande, however, Dante drops the *bella menzogna* attitude toward poetic form. He draws no distinction between the allegory of poets and the allegory of theologians, thereby assimilating to poetry the technique as well as the mission of theology. This point is essential to his conception of his role as the author of the *Comedy*. Dante arrogates to himself as a poet the tasks, methods, and powers of theology, and indicates his view that the *Comedy* can be understood in precisely the same way as Holy Scripture.

This thought has led to a good deal of debate among commentators. Some of them do not accept the idea that Dante really regarded himself as a theologian in the *Divine Comedy* and thus view the work according to the critical principles of the *Convivio*, applying the *bella menzogna* idea to the *Comedy* or seeing no difference between the poetic theory in the *Convivio* and that in the letter to Can Grande.[220] Others perceive the differences between these two works and regard the letter to Can Grande, which makes possible a truly theological poetic, as an authentic guide to the understanding of the *Comedy*.[221] This latter group presents by far the more plausible case. Even if the letter to Can Grande should prove to be a forgery, it is, all agree, a contemporary document, and, what is equally important, the theory that it contains does explain the method of the *Comedy* in a far more complete, consistent, and convincing manner than the *Convivio* does.

Furthermore, the critical principles set forth in the letter to Can Grande find support in the ideas of some of Dante's contemporaries and in the earliest commentators on the *Divine Comedy*. Giovanni del Virgilio, a friend of Dante with whom he exchanged eclogues and correspondence, wrote an epitaph on him which aptly expresses the attitude toward poetry found in the letter to Can Grande:

Dante, the theologian, skilled in every branch of knowledge that philosophy may cherish in her illustrious bosom, glory of the muses, author most acceptable to the vulgar, here lieth and smiteth either pole with his fame; who assigned their places to the defunct and their respective places to the twin swords, in laic and rhetoric fashion.[222]

The idea of the poet as theologian is also found in Mussato.[223] Benvenuto da Imola, one of the earliest commentators on the *Comedy*, sees Dante as a theologian whose style resembles that of Holy Scripture in that it presents an elevated subject in a readily accessible form.[224] Pietro Alighieri, Dante's son, who wrote a commentary on the *Divine Comedy* in 1340–41, adheres to the principles of the letter to Can Grande closely, calling his father a "glorious theologian, philosopher, and poet";[225] he uses the polysemous method as well in analyzing the work.

Later on in the fourteenth century, Boccaccio repeats and extends this idea, relating the contribution of Dante to his own humanistic conception of poetry. Boccaccio sees Dante as a poet, philosopher, and theologian, learned in all the arts including that of divinity,[226] as a truly Christian poet, and as an innovator, in that no work on such a grand scale as the *Comedy* had been essayed in the vernacular by a layman before.[227] Dante wrote in the vernacular, according to Boccaccio, in order to teach and to delight his audience more effectively, out of the motive of service to those less learned than himself, as well as because it was the modern thing to do.[228] Dante's didacticism is adopted happily by Boccaccio, who develops it into the view that poetry is the supreme mode of knowledge, communication, and instruction. Poetry, he says, subsumes all the other arts, including theology; it is the most powerful way to move men's minds and hearts; and it is aided in its tasks by divine inspiration.[229] While this theory goes farther than Dante's, it does not go very much farther. In his *Commento sopra il Dante,* a work deriving from the lectureship on Dante which Boccaccio held in Florence from 1373 to 1375, he applies the fourfold method to the *Comedy* in the manner of the letter to Can Grande.[230] All in all, Boccaccio strikes a note repeated by many Florentines of his period in praising Dante as the restorer of good poetry, the genius by whom the Muses returned to Italy.[231] Although some modern scholars may have had trouble with the point, Dante's contemporaries and immediate successors clearly had little difficulty in accepting the theological poetic of the letter to Can Grande and in applying it to the *Divine Comedy.*

Taking the letter to Can Grande at its word, then, let us return to Dante's analysis of the *Comedy*'s subject, author, form, aim, title, and philosophical type. The subject, says Dante, is twofold, depending on whether one looks at the poem literally or allegorically. Literally speaking, the poem is about "the state of souls after death, pure and simple." Allegorically speaking, "the subject is man according as by his merits or demerits in the exercise of his free will he is deserving of reward or punishment by justice."[232] Both of these levels must be taken into account, since, according to the fourfold method, all senses of the text are present in it simultaneously. While the literal level is the foundation upon which the allegorical meanings are based and must be established first, the allegorical levels of meaning do not subsume or obliterate the literal level.

This point is of major importance in understanding Dante's use of allegory in the *Divine Comedy.* It means, in the first place, that allegory is never extrinsic to the poem, but is built into it. This is a notion which may need to be restated in the light of the debate on Dante between the followers of Benedetto Croce and his opponents. Croce and his followers maintain that all poetry is essentially lyrical, the expression of the inner emotions of the poet. They tend to regard didacticism and the allegories by means of which it operates in the *Divine*

Comedy as obstructive, devoid of artistic merit. Whatever truly poetic qualities the poem contains, they argue, spring from a succession of lyric moments, all but hidden in the interstices of its allegorical superstructure.[233] Opponents of Croce's position and its recent variants have stressed, on the other hand, that allegory is an integral part of the *Comedy* and that one must submit oneself to the aesthetic of the poem in order to understand it.[234]

This latter interpretation is supported by the scriptural attitude which Dante takes toward his own poem,[235] an attitude that he puts into practice within the *Comedy*. The symbolic point of view that he adopts toward his characters, like the fourfold method of biblical exegesis, may be described as typological.[236] Most of the figures whom Dante places in the poem, with the exception of a number of classical monsters, had a real, historical existence. This real, earthly existence is the literal level; Dante's personnel, with the exception of those in Purgatory, are frozen eternally in the other world in precisely the moral condition in which they died. In the most obvious sense of the word, they represent themselves. At the same time, Dante's characters represent various ethical, political, intellectual, and religious types from which the reader can infer lessons for his own benefit and for the reform of Christian society. Since the poem depicts life after death, the characters in the *Comedy* also possess an anagogical dimension, pointing to the future, to the condition of the human soul and of Christian society at the end of time. Each character thus contains several levels of meaning, all of which are designed to instruct the reader. The historical existence of Dante's characters comes first; it is the foundation upon which their allegorical meanings are based. Virtues and vices do not exist in the abstract; they can only be found in the context of a concrete, human life.

Thus allegory in the *Comedy* does not blot out historicity. The literal meaning points toward a profounder meaning; at the same time, the profounder meaning is present in, consistent with, and expressed through the literal meaning. The higher and the lower do not stand over against each other. If one reads the *Comedy* rightly, there is no such thing as a character whose vivid humanity distracts one's eyes from his moral significance in the work, and there is no such thing as a character who is purely symbolic. In accordance with the contemporary theory of biblical typology, the literal meaning may never be discarded as irrelevant or as merely ancillary to the allegorical meaning, even after the reader has grasped the symbolic reference. Dante's symbolism of personalities has a twofold thrust. There is a movement of sublimation, as the mind of the reader proceeds from the most concrete level of meaning to the most universal. At the same time, there is a movement of descent, in which the universal is realized in the concrete. The theoretical basis for this twofold process is the Incarnation,[237] which has corollaries for Dante in aesthetics as well as in ethics and epistemology. The Incarnation, for Dante no less than for Augustine, transforms the sensible world. As a result, concrete, material things, individual persons as moral ends, and earthly beauties as objects of authentic aesthetic experience become means by which God chooses to descend to man, in and through the conditions of human life. They are not merely rungs of a ladder by means of which man can transcend the world in order to get to God. The motive of Dantean typology is not to transcend human existence by using the world as a vehicle to God and then leaving it behind. Rather, its motive is to infuse the world and human existence with divine wisdom, power, and love, to transform it from within. Only thus may the selfish and disintegrative tendencies of mankind be righted and men achieve a relation of rectitude to other men and to God.

An important corollary of this idea is Dante's recognition of the cumulative nature of experience. He resists a simplistic presentation of individuals, including himself as a character in the *Comedy*. This can be seen by considering any number of characters in the poem, but it is particularly evident in the case of Dante's three guides in the *Comedy*, Vergil, Beatrice, and Bernard of Clairvaux. There are a variety of reasons why these three personages are important to Dante. While efforts have been made to narrow their significance to one dimension, it is more accurate to say that each of them has several layers of meaning. These layers represent the stages of Dante's development or the various facets of ethics, politics, religion, literature, and public and private life which make up his central theme. It is worth keeping in mind, as Thomas G. Bergin has observed, that "temperamentally Dante was reluctant to admit any inconsistencies in his life; he had an almost obsessive drive for unity of pattern; superseded opinions or altered attitudes are never suppressed but always assimilated."[238]

This point particularly true in the case of Beatrice. There is a progression in Dante's attitude toward Beatrice from the *Vita nuova* to the *Divine Comedy*.[239] Within the *Vita nuova*, Dante chronicles his shifting view of his lady as the purveyor of a purely secular type of ennoblement, according to the canons of the *dolce stil nuovo*, to the cause of the poet's religious conversion. While Beatrice drops from view in the *Convivo*, Dante chooses there to apostrophize philosophy in the image of a lady, which permits him to apply to her the stylistic conventions of his earlier lyrics while using them to denote a broader set of functions. In the *Comedy*, Beatrice is usually taken to represent grace, theology, the church, Christ;[240] she is treated by Dante as a means of salvation in a clearly religious sense. Yet, for all this, she remains a real person.[241] All of the meanings that she has had for Dante during the course of his life are present in the Beatrice of the *Comedy*.[242]

The fusion of past and present is set forth by Dante in the emotion-charged scene where he first sets eyes upon Beatrice in the Earthly Paradise at the top of the mountain of Purgatory. Beatrice, like Dante's other guides, teaches, admonishes, and counsels him, illustrating through her conversation and behavior the attitude which she wants Dante to take to the sights and personages he encounters in the realms through which she leads him. But before she can do this, Dante must recognize the theological role she plays in the *Comedy*, which he does not do at once. In *Purgatorio* 30 and 31, Dante rehearses all his previous attitudes toward Beatrice and summarizes the change that he must undergo in order to perceive her current significance.

In the earlier portions of the *Comedy* Beatrice is described as an emissary from heaven, sent to assist Dante in the moral struggles which have led him into the dark wood of *Inferno* 1.[243] Vergil occasionally invokes her mission in explaining Dante's presence in Hell and Purgatory to the souls or guardians of those realms;[244] he spurs on Dante's lagging spirit by reminding him that Beatrice is presiding over their journey and that Dante can hope to see her at the top of the mountain of Purgatory.[245] The reader is thus prepared early in the work for a Beatrice whose function has become expressly religious. Dante contrasts this view of Beatrice, with which he has already supplied the reader, with the reaction to Beatrice that he experiences as a character in the poem. When Dante first sees the veiled lady clothed in red, white, and green, he recognizes her as the lady of the *Vita nuova:*

And my spirit, which now for so long a time trembling with awe in her presence had not been overcome, without having more knowledge by the eyes, through occult virtue that proceeded from her, felt old love's great power. As soon as on my sight the lofty virtue smote that had already pierced me before I was out of my boyhood, I turned to the left with the confidence of a little child that runs to his mother when he is frightened or in distress, to say to Virgil, "Not a drop of blood is left in me that does not tremble: I know the tokens of the ancient flame."[246]

Vergil has, however, departed, and Dante weeps bitterly. Beatrice chides Dante, both for his seeking of a guide whom he no longer needs and for his response to her, a response indicating an unsatisfactory grasp of her current meaning. Standing "royally and ever stern in her mien," she addresses Dante by name—the only point in the *Comedy* where his name is mentioned—and underlines her words by repetition:

Dante, because Virgil leaves you, do not weep yet, do not weep yet,
for you must weep for another sword!

and

Look at me well: indeed I am, indeed I am Beatrice![247]

Straightaway the angels, "who ever sing in harmony with the eternal
spheres," begin to sing, "In te, Domine, speravi," and Dante is deeply moved:
"The ice that was bound tight around my heart became breath and water."[248]
Beatrice, however, tells the angels that she is inflicting suffering on Dante as a
penance for having abandoned her. She notes that Dante has neglected his gifts
of nature and grace and that, after her death, he had failed to appreciate the
deepening inspiration which she gave him in life, until he had virtually lost
himself. This, she explains, is why she sponsored his descent into Hell and his
ascent of the mountain of Purgatory:

Not only through the working of the great wheels, which direct every seed to some
end, . . . but through largess of divine graces, which have for their rain vapors so lofty
that our sight goes not near thereto, this man was such in his new life, virtually, that
every right disposition would have made marvellous proof in him. But so much the
more rank and wild becomes the land, ill-sown and untilled, as it has more of good
strength of soil. For a time I sustained him with my countenance: showing him my
youthful eyes I led him with me turned toward the right goal. So soon as I was on the
threshold of my second age and had changed life, this one took himself from me and
gave himself to others. When from flesh to spirit I had ascended, and beauty and virtue
were increased in me, I was less dear and less pleasing to him and he turned his steps
along a way not true, following false images of good, which pay no promise in full. Nor
did it avail me to obtain inspirations with which, both in dreams and otherwise, I called
him back, so little did he heed them. He fell so low that all means for his salvation were
now short, save to show him the lost people. For this I visited the gate of the dead, and
to him who conducted him up hither my prayers are offered with tears. The high decree
of God would be broken if Lethe were passed and such viands were tasted without some
scot of penitence that may pour forth tears.[249]

Beatrice than adjures Dante to confess his sins, asking him what drew him
away from the desire for her which had once led him to love the good. Dante
tells of his pursuit of false pleasures. Beatrice once more reminds him that, if
her earthly state drew him to the good, so much more should her risen state
have inspired him toward heavenly delights. To emphasize the point, she looks
at the Griffon, the symbol of Christ, which Dante sees reflected in her eyes,
from which, the angels note, "Love once shot his darts at you." This sight
makes Dante recognize the exalted state of Beatrice:

Beneath her veil and beyond the stream she seemed to surpass more her former self than she surpassed the others here when she was among us; and the nettle of remorse so stung me there that of all other things, that which had most turned to me to love became most hateful to me. Such contrition stung my heart that I felt overcome; and what I then became she knows who was the cause of it.[250]

The vision of the Griffon, reflected in Beatrice's eyes, in which Dante strives to quench his own eyes' "ten-year thirst,"[251] momentarily blinds him. But, having grasped the present function of Beatrice, he is now ready to pass through Lethe and Eunoë and to acquire, through Beatrice, the progressive strengthening of his sight which eventually enables him to look directly at Beatrice and then to move beyond her.

Dante's summary of the theme of the *dolce stil nuovo* lady whose meaning acquires transcendent proportions in the *Comedy* is matched by his frequent use of the *dolce stil nuovo* tropes of the lady's eyes and smile to denote the process of his religious enlightenment. It will be recalled that Dante retains these devices as he moves from the *Vita nuova* to the *Convivio* and that he broadens their epistemological meaning in the latter work, the eyes and smile standing there for the lady's demonstrations and persuasions, respectively. In the *Comedy*, Dante exploits the demonstrative and persuasive functions of Beatrice's eyes and smile thoroughly, using them as metaphors of speech and as a means of describing Beatrice's mediation of wisdom and love to him. In addition, he integrates these tropes with his symbolism of light and darkness, which has frequently been noted in the *Comedy* as a metaphor of spiritual illumination or obfuscation, and which has been related to the symbol of God as light as manifested in medieval light metaphysics.[252] A full appreciation of the functions of Beatrice's eyes and smile in the *Comedy* can be gained only by viewing the sense of sight in the wider context of pleasant and unpleasant sensible environments as tokens of the spiritual atmospheres of the three realms, a context which embraces colors, sounds, smells, and the general physical comfort or discomfort experienced by Dante the traveler.

Dante makes clear the synaesthetic blending of the senses in his first statement about the atmosphere of Hell. He characterizes Hell as the realm "where the sun is silent"[253] and where the souls manifest their grief through their eyes.[254] What colors there are in Hell are dark and depressing, with the exception of the Limbo of virtuous pagans, which is bright with an enamel-green lawn.[255] Dante notes the "dark air" of Hell[256] and its light from below as he descends into it. Charon, the ferryman of the Styx, informs Dante and Vergil that he is taking them into "eternal darkness," and the topography of the river and its environs displays a "livid marsh," "dark water," and a "gloomy plain."[257] As they go farther into the "blind world" of Hell,[258] Dante comments repeatedly on the dark and heavy air[259] and the fetid odors[260] that they encounter. Specific areas of Hell are given particularly unappetizing visual characteristics. The avaricious and prodigal are depicted as so dark as to be scarcely recognizable; having lived undiscerning lives, they have become difficult to discern in death.[261] The marsh of sloth, complete with "black mire" and "murky waves," has waters "far darker than perse" that bathe its "malign gray slopes."[262] The wood of the suicides is uncharted; it is dusky, not green, and is filled with distorted trees bearing gnarled branches on which withered, poisonous thorns grow instead of fruit.[263] Malebolge is dark from end to end,[264] and the only colors which Dante notes there are livid and iron gray[265] and harsh, punishing flame.[266] At the very bottom of the pit of Hell, in Giudecca, where it is "less than night and less than day," Dante comments on the "want of light," and the reader heaves a sigh of relief with him as he at last leaves the Inferno to return to the "bright world."[267]

The move from Hell to Purgatory is at once marked by a distinct improvement in the sensible qualities of the atmosphere. The pleasing music of psalms and hymns is heard throughout this realm, and from time to time Dante mentions ambrosial fragrances.[268] As Dante approaches Purgatory, the morning star is rising; the sky reveals the "sweet hue of oriental sapphire;" the heavens rejoice—a sight which, he observes, "to my eyes restored delight."[269] In general Dante finds it easy to see in Purgatory, except on the ledge of the wrathful, where smoke obscures his sight.[270] Angels appear occasionally in Purgatory. One of them is described as a light on the sea, a whiteness too bright to look at;[271] another is depicted as a beauteous creature, robed in white, with a face like the morning star.[272] Their clothing is not always white; in *Purgatorio* 8, their raiment was "green as newborn leaves."[273]

Dante's physical surroundings in Purgatory are also bright and colorful. The colors may have specific symbolic meanings, as in the case of the white, black, and red steps of contrition, confession, and love, which Dante must ascend in order to enter Purgatory;[274] the white, green, and red garb of Beatrice, signifying faith, hope and charity;[275] and the purple foliage on the imperial tree, signifying royalty.[276] The Eagle which Dante sees in a dream has golden plumage,[277] and the trees which counsel abstinence and warn against gluttony have flourishing green leaves.[278] In other instances, however, brightness and color mainly designate the spiritual optimism and confidence in God which pervade this realm. Even in the ante-Purgatory, Dante and Vergil can find a spot to spend the night decorated with brilliantly colored grass and flowers:

Gold and fine silver, cochineal and white lead, Indian wood bright and clear, fresh emerald at the moment it is split, would all be surpassed in color, if placed within that valley, by the grass and by the flowers growing there, as the less is surpassed by the greater. Nature had not only painted there, but of the sweetness of a thousand scents she made there one unknown to us and blended.[279]

The Earthly Paradise at the top of the mountain, manifesting the characteristics of the classical *locus amoenus,* is even more replete with pleasing sights. In *Purgatorio* 27 Dante finds himself in a grassy clearing in a lush and verdant forest containing bright-hued and fragrant flowers, a stream, a sweet breeze, and singing birds.[280] Flowers are frequently mentioned in the Earthly Paradise, as are the colors gold, red, white, green, rose, and purple.[281] Significantly, the chariot symbolizing the corrupt church is not given color.[282]

In Paradise, the variegated hues of Purgatory give way for the most part to pure light. Light is treated by Dante as a metaphysical principle, an epistemological principle, and an index of blessedness, and it grows increasingly brilliant as he advances farther and farther into Heaven. He describes colors where they occur as the scintillations of jewels; thus he compares a cloud to a "diamond smitten by the sun," and describes the moon as the "eternal pearl"[283] and the Virgin Mary as a "sapphire."[284] The blessed souls form a river of light in *Paradiso* 30, and they are further depicted as blossoms, as topazes, and as rubies set in gold.[285] The angels hovering above the Empyrean Rose like bees are red, gold, and white.[286] However, it is not so much color as candlepower that characterizes the sights in Paradise. On arriving in Heaven, Dante's first reaction is to notice that there is much more light here than elsewhere: "And suddenly day seemed added to day, as if He who has the power had adorned heaven with another sun."[287] He invokes God as "O Love that rulest the heavens, . . . who with thy light didst lift me," and he hears the harmony of the spheres, noting that "the novelty of the sound and the great light kindled in me a desire to know their cause."[288]

In Paradise, as elsewhere, sight and sound are joined. Dante hears many songs of unearthly beauty. The souls whom he meets above the Moon are described as lights, and they grow more brilliant and more beautiful the more perfectly they exemplify the love of God and man.[289] Both light and melody are analogized to joy.[290] The union of light, sound, and joy reveals Dante's acceptance of the Augustinian correlation of love and knowledge. He notes this correlation repeatedly throughout the *Comedy*[291] and underlines the point by reinterpreting his earlier lyric, "Luce intelletual, piena d'amore," in terms of heavenly vision in the Empyrean.[292] Dante's eyes are opened gradually as he moves through Heaven, and at many points he is dazzled because his eyes are not yet strong enough to perceive the objects before them. But at other points he notes that he is now able to see things that he previously could not see.[293] He must use various created lights, including Beatrice, as "mirrors" of the relected glory of God;[294] but he must also learn to transcend them. As Beatrice observes in *Paradiso* 18, "Not only in my eyes is Paradise."[295] At the point when Beatrice is fast approaching the end of her tutelage of Dante, she directs him to "behold now the height and breadth of the Eternal Goodness, since it has made so many mirrors wherein it is reflected."[296] Under the guidance of Bernard, Dante is once more instructed to develop his sight gradually in preparation for the vision of God,[297] which is finally depicted as three concentric circles of light.[298]

In the context of this symbolism of light and sound, related as it is to the interaction of love and knowledge, the eyes and smile of Beatrice retain, yet go far beyond, their *dolce stil nuovo* significance and are reinterpreted as tokens of her commission to guide Dante through the demonstrations of divine wisdom and the persuasions of Christian charity. Beatrice's eyes and smile are sometimes treated separately. Dante describes her eyes as "the beautiful eyes wherein Love made the cord to capture me."[299] They are sometimes turned upward, as a means of directing Dante's gaze to the things of Heaven.[300] At other times, they are turned at Dante himself and convey Beatrice's instruction, forgiveness, and permission to speak, and generally manifest her joy and holiness.[301] Dante notes that she looks at him, "to take the eye so as to possess the mind."[302] The smile, when referred to separately, is generally a manifestation of the love which persuades; the souls in *Paradiso* 31 have faces "all given to love, adorned by the light of Another, and by their own smile."[303] Usually Beatrice's smiles precede or are concurrent with her discourses; she smiles before or while speaking so that her words may move Dante's heart and mind.[304]

For Dante, Beatrice's eyes and smile are the chief characteristics of her beauty;[305] and beauty is a means of knowing and loving God. The union of love and knowledge and the Ciceronian ideals of delight, instruction, and persuasion are further reflected in the numerous passages where Dante blends Beatrice's eyes and smile or where he refers to one of them in terms of the other. Thus Beatrice's eyes glow or sparkle as she smiles;[306] her eyes laugh and smile;[307] her smile is a light.[308] The integration of love and knowledge, vision and hearing, is further shown at the point when Beatrice removes all the scales from Dante's eyes after he has successfully described the nature of love to John the evangelist.[309] Finally, to emphasize the idea still more, Dante states in the Heaven of the Fixed Stars, "What I saw seemed to me a smile of the universe, so that my rapture entered both by hearing and by sight."[310]

The fact that Dante can present Beatrice's earlier meanings for him while expanding them in a new theological perspective indicates the many-layered significance that she possesses in the *Comedy*. An analogous variety of meanings is also visible in the case of Vergil and Bernard. Bernard represents mystical vision. Dante describes Bernard in *Paradiso* 31 as a man "who, in this world, in contemplation tasted of that peace,"[311] thus qualifying him to guide Dante by stages through the Empyrean. Yet mystic vision based on a series of steps is not all that Bernard represents. If it were, there would be no particular reason for Dante to have chosen Bernard as his guide, rather than some other eminent mystic, and Dante places a number of them in Paradise, including Richard of Saint Victor, "who in contemplation was more than man."[312] Bernard is particularly dear to Dante for two other reasons. He was a fervent proponent of the cult of the Virgin Mary, which he did much to popularize in the twelfth century. In his instructions to Dante in Heaven, he stresses devotion to the Virgin, observing that "the Queen of Heaven, for whom I am all afire with love, will grant us every grace, since I am her faithful Bernard."[313] He tells Dante to look upon Mary's face, "which most resembles Christ, for only its brightness can prepare you to see Christ."[314] A sizable portion of the last canto of the *Paradiso* consists of Bernard's lengthy prayer to the Virgin, which immediately precedes Dante's vision of God.[315]

A less obvious but equally important reason why Dante selects Bernard as his guide is that Bernard combined the contemplative life of the mystic with the active life of the ecclesiastical statesman and reformer. Famed for his mellifluous oratory, he preached the Second Crusade in 1144; he mediated the conflicts of the crowned heads of Europe; he combated heresy in the Petrobrusian movement and in the person of Peter Abelard. Bernard was also a strong proponent of ecclesiastical reform. The most dynamic leader of the Cistercian order, he founded the abbey of Clairvaux and was the leading spokesman of the monastic revival of the twelfth century. He also encouraged an even more innovative vocation by lending his influential support to one of the new military orders that fought in the Crusades, the Knights Templars. In his *De consideratione* he denounced both the current worldliness of the papacy and its political aims.[316] He rejected the claims of the papacy to feudal suzerainty over the Norman kingdom of Naples and Sicily; he condemned the political ambitions of the popes in Italy and corresponded with various emperors, urging them to recover their claims in the peninsula. His devotion to the Virgin, his public-spirited oratory, and his specific political views correspond thoroughly with Dante's views on these subjects. The saint alludes to them in Paradise, contrasting by implication the leaders of a corrupt Christian society with "the great patricians of this most just and pious empire"[317] in the Empyrean, where Mary rules as Augusta. Thus the personality and significance of Bernard possess several dimensions for Dante.

Of all the three guides in the *Comedy,* Vergil tutors Dante the longest, and he, like Bernard and Beatrice, has several meanings for the poet.[318] Vergil is usually taken to represent human reason unaided by grace. If one adheres exclusively to this interpretation of Vergil's significance, however, there would be no particular reason for Dante to have chosen him as a guide in preference to a philosopher exemplifying human wisdom, such as Aristotle, "the master of those who know."[319] Vergil has a host of meanings besides that of human reason. He also represents the poet of empire, the reformer of the Roman vernacular of his day, the portrayer of a hero who takes an allegorical journey to the other world, a prophet of the coming of Christ, the bridge between pagan and Christian Rome, a seer, and a repository of literary craft and of poetic genius.[320] Throughout Hell and Purgatory Vergil displays his knowledge of matters both philosophical and theological. Dante addresses him by a wide variety of titles, including poet, master, guide, sage, sea of all intelligence, lord, father, virtue supreme, teacher, escort, leader, comfort, light, and faithful comrade. Of all Vergil's functions, however, his role as poet is the one that Dante returns to most repeatedly and with the most evident interest.[321]

Students of the *Comedy* and the *Aeneid* are well aware of Dante's numerous borrowings from Vergil. More important for our purposes are the scenes where Dante permits himself and Vergil to advert specifically to Vergil's writings. They begin in *Inferno* 1, when the two poets first meet. After encountering the Leopard, the Lion, and the She-wolf, Dante sees "one who seemed faint through long silence"[322] and asks who he is. Vergil acknowledges his place of birth, his Roman citizenship, the time when he lived, and his paganism. He describes his profession in the words, "I was a poet, and I sang of that just son of Anchises who came from Troy after proud Ilium was burned."[323] Dante immediately recognizes Vergil, addresses him as "that fount which pours forth so broad a stream of speech," and praises Vergil as his poetic mentor:

O glory and light of other poets, may the long study and the great love that have made me search your volume avail me! You are my master and my author. You alone are he from whom I took the fair style that has done me honor.[324]

Dante's recognition of Vergil's poetic superiority, bracketed with his allusions to his own literary eminence, is amplified in the Limbo of the virtuous pagans, where Dante meets the shades of Homer, Horace, Ovid, and Lucan. The poets are separated from the other virtuous pagans, Vergil explains, because the name of poet "wins grace in heaven, which thus advances them."[325] The four shades exclaim, "Honor the great Poet!" as Vergil appears on the scene. This greeting Vergil takes as his due: "Since each shares with me the name, . . . they do me honor, and in that they do well,"[326] he observes. Dante is fully prepared to revere the classical poets and to extend the honor to himself:

Thus I saw assembled the fair school of that lord of highest song who, like an eagle, soars above the rest. After they had talked awhile together, they turned to me with a sign of salutation, at which my master smiled; and far more honor still they showed me, for they made of me one of their company, so that I was sixth amid so much wisdom.[327]

In the *Comedy* Vergil acknowledges his authorship of the *Aeneid* and his literary accomplishments as a poet; he also at times refers to the contents of his epic in more detail. He describes the *Aeneid* as "my high Tragedy"[328] and invokes the shade of Ulysses in the name of the "lofty lines"[329] which he wrote on earth. Speaking to Pier delle Vigne in the wood of the suicides, he tells him that Dante would not have broken a twig off Pier's tree-body had he (Dante) paid closer attention to the episode of Aeneas and Polydorus in *Aeneid* 3.[330]

Other characters in the *Comedy* also testify to Vergil's poetic art. In the speech in which Beatrice enlists Vergil to guide Dante through Hell and Purgatory, she praises him in somewhat courtly language. Addressing Vergil as the "courteous Mantuan spirit," whose fame is immortal, she tells him that she has confidence in the power of his "noble speech, which honors you and all who have heard it," to help Dante out of the dark wood.[331] In Purgatory, the poet Sordello addresses Vergil as "O glory of the Latins, . . . through whom our tongue showed forth its power,"[332] thereby manifesting Dante's bias in favor of continuity between the classical past and the medieval present. Still more effusive is Statius. Introducing himself as the poet who "sang of Thebes, and then of the great Achilles," he notes that "the sparks which warmed me from the divine flame whereby more than a thousand have been kindled were the seeds of my poetic fire: I mean the *Aeneid,* which in poetry was both mother and nurse to me."[333] He attributes to Vergil his Christian faith as well as his art:

You it was who first sent me toward Parnassus to drink in its caves and you who first did light me on to God. You were like one who goes by night and carries the light behind him and profits not himself, but who makes those wise who follow him, when you said "the ages are renewed; Justice returns and the first age of man, and a new progeny descends from heaven." Through you I was a poet, through you a Christian.[334]

Vergil, in keeping with the medieval interpretation of his fourth *Eclogue*, thus functions as the prophet of Christ; in his brotherly reunion with his Mantuan compatriot Sordello, he exemplifies good citizenship;[335] and, in his first speech to Dante, he refers to the evils besetting Italy and prophesies the appearance of its savior, the Greyhound.[336] It is precisely in Vergil's capacity as a great poet that Dante credits him with ethical, religious, and political insights. This does not mean, however, that he sees Vergil in one dimension. Dante himself was striving to convey his own ethical, religious, and political insights to his contemporaries by raising Italian to the level of a literary language and by writing a poetic masterpiece embodying these very ideas. As the author of the *Comedy*, Dante sees himself as a second Vergil. Thus by reading back into the historical Vergil his own conception of the role of the poet and his own views on current Italian and European problems, Dante can use Vergil's status as a poet as a sun from which his other meanings radiate.

The evidence could be multiplied to show that many other characters in the *Comedy* besides Dante's three guides possess typological significance. The fact that Dante fully intends the fourfold method of scriptural exegesis which he describes in the letter to Can Grande to be applied to the *Divine Comedy* is further revealed by the words that he puts into Beatrice's mouth as she explains Dante's trip to the other world to the apostle James in Paradise:

The Church Militant has not any child possessed of more hope, as is written in the Sun which irradiates our host; therefore it is granted him to come from Egypt to Jerusalem, that he may see, before his term of warfare is completed.[337]

Dante's choice of the psalm "In exitu Israel de Aegypto" as a biblical text to analyze in order to explain the fourfold method in the letter to Can Grande is not fortuitous. Nor is his placement of the same psalm in the *Comedy*. It is the first psalm that he hears sung in Purgatory.[338] He inserts it into the poem at this juncture to indicate the time of year; the passage of the Israelites from Egypt and their celebration of the Passover are types of the Christian feast of Easter and the celebration of the Eucharist. But the bondage of the Israelites to the Egyptians is also a type of the bondage of the sinner to sin, a moral state which Dante has just symbolically abandoned by leaving Hell, and the wanderings of the Israelites in the desert after their departure from Egypt are a type of the temporal punishment for sin which Dante is symbolically about to undergo in Purgatory.

Dante's conception of the *Comedy* as a work of art capable of being treated critically in the same manner as the Bible is paralleled by his conception of himself, the poet, as a man who writes under the inspiration of God for didactic purposes.[339] Dante illustrates his idea of the poet as prophet in a number of ways in the *Comedy*. He frequently invokes God, as well as the Muses, for inspiration,[340] describing himself as "one who, when Love inspires me, takes note, and goes setting it forth after the fashion which he dictates within me."[341] Dante refers to his poem as "sacred,"[342] a distinction it possesses in virtue of its sublime subject matter[343] and because it is a work "to which heaven and earth have . . . set hand."[344] Dante issues numerous jeremiads throughout the *Comedy* directed against the corruption he sees in contemporary ethics, religion, and politics, and places in the mouths of various heavenly personages, from Cacciaguida[345] and Beatrice[346] to Peter Damien,[347] John the evangelist,[348] and Peter the apostle,[349] warrants for his writing of a poem designed to instruct his fellow men. His frequent addresses to the reader, as a number of scholars have noted, indicate that Dante takes his didactic role quite seriously,[350] as do his requests to souls in Hell and Purgatory to explain their state so that he can report it back to others after his pilgrimage to the other world is over and he returns to earth.[351]

Dante's view of himself in the *Comedy* as an inspired, prophetic teacher is explained in the letter to Can Grande under the rubrics of the aim of the *Comedy* and the branch of philosophy to which it pertains. "The aim of the whole and of the part," says Dante, "is to remove those living in this life from a state of misery, and to bring them to a state of happiness."[352] The branch of philosophy to which the poem pertains is ethics.[353] Ethics is a practical science; it is a means to an end, the end in this case being the eternal bliss of Dante's readers. Dante clearly believes that his work has this sort of public utility[354] and so relates his didacticism to a Ciceronian-Augustinian rhetoric, whose blend of instruction, persuasion, and delight is oriented to the common weal. Dante intends the *Comedy* to be useful and pleasant at the same time. The experience of aesthetic pleasure will draw the reader toward God.[355] Poetry is useful only if it is beautiful; the pleasing function of literature is not expendable for Dante, but integral to his rhetorical poetics. The instruction of the intellect by the poet must be matched by the movement of the will; as Baldwin has well put it, the *Divine Comedy* "arrives not at a demonstration, but at a catharsis."[356]

This is a procedure that depends on God. In the letter to Can Grande the inadequacy of language to express Dante's vision of the other world is acknowledged,[357] the need for God's assistance is affirmed,[358] and poetry is described as "almost in the nature of a divine gift."[359] But the catharsis of the reader also depends on the poet's literary craft. The letter to Can Grande also makes much of this point. In the realm of literary tactics no less than in his moral orientation, Ciceronian-Augustinian rhetoric is Dante's touchstone. Thus, the letter advises, the exordium of the poem should make the audience "favorably disposed, attentive, and willing to learn."[360] With respect to the *Paradiso*, the moral profit which the reader can hope to acquire makes him favorably disposed to the work, the extraordinary nature of the subject matter catches his attention, and the fact that the objective of the poem, beatitude, is within the realm of possibility for the reader, makes him ready to learn.[361]

The orderly structure of the poem and its variegated literary texture will also appeal to the reader, and these aspects of the *Comedy* are discussed in the letter to Can Grande under the rubric of the form of the work, in turn subdivided into the form of the treatise and the form of the treatment. The form of the treatise is threefold: the poem is divided into three cantiche, each of which is divided into thirty-three cantos with the exception of the *Inferno,* which contains an additional prefatory canto, and the rhyme scheme is terza rima. The form of the treatment is "poetic, fictive, descriptive, digressive, and figurative; and further it is definitive, analytical, probative, refutative, and exemplificative."[362] This statement leaves no doubt as to the epistemological force which Dante attributes to his poetry. It is also noteworthy that he distinguishes the poetic from the fictive and that he assimilates philosophy to poetry here just as he has assimilated poetry to theology in his application of the fourfold method to the *Comedy*.

From a stylistic point of view, the letter to Can Grande also takes a major step in expanding Dante's notion of the genre and diction appropriate to a work on an exalted subject. The letter defines the author and title of the *Comedy* as "Incipit Comoedia Dantis Alagherii, Florentine natione, non moribus."[363] Outside of contrasting Dante, the "true Florentine," with his decadent and unappreciative compatriots, this title also leads into a discussion of the nature of comedy and tragedy, which indicates an important shift in his conception of these genres. In the *De vulgari eloquentia,* Dante assigns to tragedy alone the prerogative of dealing with the most elevated subjects and insists that it must use the illustrious vernacular and the canzone form, while elegy uses an abject style and comedy employs moderate or lowly diction.[364] The letter to Can Grande and, of course, the *Divine Comedy* itself, however, indicate that Dante regards comedy as capable of dealing with an extremely exalted subject, human salvation. The distinction between tragedy and comedy posed in the letter to Can Grande is based on the idea that a tragedy begins happily and ends horribly, and that a comedy begins adversely and ends happily. The letter still maintains that tragic diction should be elevated and that comic diction should be humble, but, following Horace, adds that each genre may use the language of the other. [365] This attitude toward diction is manifested in the *Comedy*, where Dante employs a wide range of styles of diction, from the burlesque to the sublime. Examples could be drawn from the *Comedy* to illustrate all the vocabulary types which he enumerates in the *De vulgari eloquentia*. Dante's high subject no longer demands the most refined diction or the canzone form. The author of the *Comedy*, like the Christian orator of Augustine's *De doctrina christiana*, does not hesitate to be popular in order to reach the widest possible audience.

The literary theory of the letter to Can Grande represents the full-blown theological poetics that underlies and explains Dante's *Divine Comedy*. In developing this theory, Dante adheres to some features of medieval poetics, particularly the rhetorical-didactic tradition. However, Dante elevates poetry above rhetoric while maintaining the unification of the two disciplines begun in classical times. He rejects the "falsity of poetry" tradition and its modification in the form of the theory of poetic veils which must be removed in order to acquire the nugget of doctrine within. For Dante the style of poetry is integrally related to its truth. Regarding himself as an inspired poet-theologian, he uses a wide variety of techniques to delight, instruct, and move the reader toward the goal of beatitude. He considers his literary craftsmanship essential but is aware of the limits of language in conveying theological truths to the reader. His poetry celebrates a private vision put to the service of the community and reflecting the interdependence of the individual and the group. Dante's conception of himself as a poet reveals his thorough assimilation of Augustine's redefinition of Ciceronian rhetoric. It is expressed in the Italian vernacular; it reflects Dante's specific views on the ethical, religious, and political reforms which he thinks are needed by his age in order to promote a relationship of rectitude between man and God. This is the poetic theory which is exemplified in the *Divine Comedy*.

It is now our task to show that the verbal theory of knowledge formulated by Augustine and employed by the other thinkers with whom this study has been concerned is expressed by Dante in the theological poetics of the *Divine Comedy*. It may be well to recall to mind the salient aspects of the Augustinian theory of knowledge before examining the *Comedy* further for evidence of its existence in this work. In the first place, Augustine, blending classical sign theory and biblical doctrines of religious knowledge, conceives of words as the basic symbolic intermediaries in the process of knowledge. This conception of words as the fundamental kind of epistemic signs, to which other kinds of signs can be reduced, springs from his preoccupation with religious knowledge, with the doctrine of Christ the Word as God's revelation to man, and with the biblical mandate to preach the Word. The doctrine of the Incarnation is a key idea for all the proponents of Augustine's verbal epistemology in the Middle Ages, whether, like Augustine and Anselm, they see its implications primarily in the redemption of human language and thought processes, or whether, as in Aquinas, its implications lie primarily in the realm of natural theology, in which Christ functions as the Logos of creation as well as the illuminator of the human mind. They all hold that human powers of speech and conceptualization are capable of signifying divine truths accurately although incompletely. They also maintain that human words may turn the nonbeliever in the direction of God or help a believer to deepen his understanding of what he believes, but that the words of the speaker act in an instrumental rather than a heuristic manner in both of these cases. God, they assert, always remains the measure of the accuracy of human signs which refer to him; he thus controls what may be known about him, dictating the moral as well as the intellectual conditions of this knowledge.

Dante reflects thoroughly the Augustinian combination of diffidence and enthusiasm with respect to the powers and limits of poetic language to signify the vision of the other world which his *Comedy* relates. Dante's firm conviction of his prophetic and didactic role as a poet, his repeated stress on the idea that he possesses heavenly warrant for what he writes,[366] and the progressive dissociation of his poetics from the doctrine of poetry as falsehood all show that he doubts neither the truth of poetry nor its unique aptitude for expressing divine realities. He assimilates speech to poetry in his use of the word *dire*, to speak, to mean, "to write poetry."[367] For Dante the truth of poetry depends on its rectitude, its correspondence to realities as they are, as well as on a right moral attitude on the poet's part toward these realities. At the same time that Dante adverts to the powers of poetry, he fills the *Comedy* with statements pointing to its inadequacies.[368] Dante repeatedly notes that his mind cannot conceive nor his memory retain what he has experienced in Hell, Purgatory, and Paradise, and, with growing frequency, he confesses the poverty of his poetic art to express what he has seen in the other world.[369] This confession reaches its climax at the end of the *Paradiso,* where he acknowledges that Beatrice has become so ineffably beautiful that he must terminate his lifelong career of speaking about her.[370] And, ultimately, the vision of God in the last canto of the poem is so overwhelming that he feels forced to fall silent.[371] Dante's numerous appeals for supernatural assistance in relating his experiences to the reader underline the view that God endows the speaker with power to signify divine truths which he would not ordinarily possess.[372] He recognizes the instrumental character of his poetry in the reader's instruction; the divine gifts of faith and grace are needed to fill the gaps between language and reality. Thus he notes that only a believer can picture the heaven of the sun[373] and observes, at the beginning of the *Paradiso,* that "the passing beyond humanity may not be set forth in words: therefore let the example suffice any for whom grace reserves that experience."[374]

As a teacher, Dante instructs the reader through what he, as the author, describes, and through what he, as a character in the work, learns and experiences in the course of the *Comedy.* Discourse or conversation is the primary means that he uses to illustrate the right relations which he thinks should obtain among men and between man and God. Dante employs other media of communication, such as visual art, music, the sensory environment of the other world, dreams, the eyes and smile of Beatrice and others, as well as specific symbols. Like Augustine, he treats nonverbal signs as metaphors of speech and thus interprets signification as such in a preeminently verbal manner.

There are several ways in which conversation functions in the *Comedy.* A large proportion of the poem is composed of Dante's conversations with his guides. Vergil, Beatrice, and Bernard continually explain the nature of the other world to Dante and give him permission to speak to the souls whom he meets. They set forth numerous philosophical and theological doctrines, forming Dante's will and enlightening his intellect through their instruction. Dante's guides do not aim merely at instruction. They aim also at persuasion and delight, which they achieve through the love and confidence which they inspire in Dante. Dante's progressive growth in love and knowledge is illustrated by the shifts in his use of dialogue in the *Comedy.* In Hell we find many more brief interchanges of questions and answers between Dante and his guide than we do in Purgatory or Paradise. Dante's questions in Hell are much more naïve than in the later portions of the poem. In the earlier cantos of the *Comedy* Dante sometimes depicts himself as embarrassed by the prospect that he may have asked a stupid question, and he is often upset and bewildered by Vergil's explanations.[375] All of this shows that Dante the traveler has much to learn at the outset of his journey. As the *Inferno* proceeds, however, Vergil speaks for longer and longer stretches of time, a tendency on the part of Vergil and Beatrice which increases in the *Purgatorio* and *Paradiso.* As Dante grows more enlightened and oriented toward God, he depends less and less on his guides to intercede on his behalf with the souls whom he wants to address, and, after finding his bearings within each of the realms of the other world, he requires fewer detailed explanations. As a token of the ending of his tutelage over Dante, Vergil tells him, "No longer expect word or sign from me," at the top of the mountain of Purgatory.[376] Dante's guides often signify their recognition of his progress by registering their approval of the kinds of questions he has learned to ask and the attitude which he has learned to adopt toward the souls with whom he speaks.[377] They adjure him to speak briefly with the souls in Hell,[378] but to attend and to believe the souls in Paradise.[379]

The souls in the other world also have much to say, and they illustrate their own moral states and the character of the realms in which they are located through their conversation no less than through their appearance and the punishments and rewards they exemplify. Speech, for Dante, is a way of expressing oneself to others; it is therefore the means by which people interact in society. Each of the three realms of the other world is a society. Both vice and virtue have social consequences, and what the souls have to say reveals their attitude toward their fellow man as well as toward God. In Hell, the prevailing tendency on the part of the souls is to deny God, their own humanity, and other men. Verbal expression in Hell frequently takes the form of moans, whines, shrieks, curses, blasphemies, lamentations, and vituperations.[380] Speech in this realm is often perverted and is represented as bestial, incomprehensible, or as otherwise distorted and inhuman. The gluttonous howl like dogs;[381] Vergil compares the voices of the avaricious and prodigal to barking.[382] The words of the false counselors must struggle through the flames which envelop their speakers;[383] "Thus, having at first no course or outlet in the fire, the doleful words were changed into its language."[384] Only after this process can the false counselors speak normally. Plutus speaks gibberish in the meaningless statement, "Pape Satan! Pape Satan aleppe,"[385] as does Nimrod, whom Dante holds responsible for the tower of Babel and the separation of tongues; he is incomprehensible to others and they to him.[386] The slothful "gurgle in their throats, for they cannot speak . . . in full words."[387] Curio's tongue is split so that he cannot speak at all;[388] the thieves' voices are "ill-suited for forming words."[389] Most horrible are the suicides changed to trees. Their words are empty air, like the wind in their branches, and when Pier delle Vigne speaks, "from that broken twig came out words and blood together."[390]

The guardians of the sinners and the sinners themselves are vicious and hostile; they do not welcome Dante and rarely have anything pleasant to say to him. The first soul whom Dante meets in Hell, after Vergil, is Charon, the boatman of the Styx, who greets Dante and Vergil with the words, "Woe to you, wicked souls!"[391] Minos, who assigns the souls to their places in Hell, addresses Dante harshly as "you who come to the abode of pain."[392] Plutus, as we have seen, speaks to Dante in gibberish; Phlegyas cries, "Now you are caught, fell spirit!"[393] The Centaurs are belligerent, and one attacks Dante with the words: "To what torment do you come, you who descend the slope? Tell us from there; if not, I draw my bow!"[394] This hostile reception occurs even though the Centaur Nessus is the first monster in Hell to act in a friendly manner to Dante. The souls are often hostile, too. Argenti asks resentfully, "Who are you that come before your time?"; and his companions in Dis, angry that Dante should be permitted to travel through the other world before his death, are disdainful and curse him.[395] The usurer Rinaldo de' Scrovegni asks Dante: "What are you doing in this ditch? Now get you gone!"[396] Venedico Caccianimico tries to hide from Dante, and when asked why he is in Hell, replies, "Unwillingly I tell it." Alessio Interminei shuns Dante with the words, "Why are you so greedy to look more at me than at the other filthy ones?"[397] Vanni Fucci prophesies that the whites of Florence will suffer defeat purely out of malice toward Dante: "I have said this that it may grieve you," he observes,[398] concluding his speech with an obscenity.[399] In *Inferno* 28, a soul rudely accuses Dante of being a sinner trying to escape his own punishment.[400] The hypocrites look askance at Dante and discuss him invidiously among themselves before talking to him.[401] Bocca degli Abati is easily the most belligerent and uncommunicative soul whom Dante meets in Hell; he refuses to tell who he is or to speak with Dante at all, and instead picks a fight with him.[402]

With a few exceptions, the souls in Hell who do speak attempt to disavow responsibility for their sins and to blame others as equally bad as or worse than themselves. While the blasphemer Capaneus revels in his sin, saying "What I was living, that am I dead,"[403] Francesca da Rimini rejects her freedom of will, excusing her adultery by arguing that she and her lover Paolo had no choice but to sin:

Love, which is quickly kindled in a gentle heart, seized this one for the fair form that was taken from me—and the way of it still afflicts me. Love, which absolves no loved one from loving, seized me so strongly with delight in him, that as you see, it does not leave me even now. Love brought us to one death.[404]

Pier delle Vigne, the suicide, excuses his injustice to himself by adverting to his justice to his master, the emperor Frederick II.[405] The simoniac pope Nicholas III contrasts his own lapses with the vices of Boniface VIII and Clement V.[406] The barrator Ciampolo accuses his fellow sinners, one of whom, Friar Gomita, he characterizes as "no petty barrator, but sovereign."[407] The souls grow more and more malicious and hostile toward each other the farther into Hell Dante goes, a condition symbolized by the fact that their torments result increasingly from their punishment of each other. The hypocrite Malacoda deliberately gives Dante and Vergil false directions when asked the way.[408] When Dante asks rhetorically whether there is anyone as vain as the Sienese, the alchemist Capocchio responds by enumerating a list of sinners, and after commenting on his own virtuosity as a falsifier of nature, complains about the viciousness of another soul, Gianni Schicchi.[409] Adam of Brescia, wallowing in self-pity, says that he yearns to see the punishment of his partners in the crime of forgery; it is on them, not himself, that the blame for his sin rests. Then he picks a fight with another soul, and Dante leaves them hurling vituperations at each other.[410] Ugolino, whom Dante finds gnawing Archbishop Ruggieri of Pisa, curses his victim as a traitor and an evildoer,[411] and Alberigo is so thoroughly obnoxious that Dante says, "To be rude to him was courtesy!"[412]

After the maliciousness of the souls in Hell, the souls in Purgatory are noteworthy for their friendliness to Dante and to each other. The first group of souls whom Dante meets in this realm gather around him as if to hear a messenger bearing news of peace, and embrace him affectionately. The first words spoken by a soul in Purgatory express love. The poet Casella tells Dante, "Even as I loved you in my mortal body, so do I love you freed," and when Dante asks him to sing, he responds graciously by offering one of Dante's poems.[413] This welcome is paralleled by Statius's greeting, "O my brothers, may God give you peace," and his quotation of a line from Vergil's fourth *Eclogue,* as well as by Forese Donati's reception of Dante in the words, "What a grace is this to me!"[414] The souls in Purgatory give directions graciously. They freely acknowledge their sins and the goodness of God.[415] Exchanging courteous greetings with Dante, they speak to him readily and ask him only to pray for them.[416] Sordello tells Dante that it will give the souls joy to speak with him.[417] In contrast to the souls in Hell, the souls in Purgatory welcome their punishments.[418] They do not exalt themselves but are modest about their own accomplishments. When Dante praises the painting of the illuminator Oderisi, he replies by praising in turn the work of Franco Bolognese and by noting the transience of earthly fame.[419] The avaricious explain their state by contrasting themselves with examples of voluntary poverty and generosity.[420] The poet Bonagiunta da Lucca questions Dante about the *dolce stil nuovo,* quoting a line from one of Dante's poems, and when Dante explains the methods of the new style, he accepts it as better than his own.[421] Dante warmly praises the *dolce stil nuovo* poet Guido Guinizelli, whom he calls "the father of me and of others my betters," proclaiming that his works "will make dear their very ink."[422] Guido responds by pointing out the Provençal poet Arnaut Daniel, describing him as "a better craftsman of the mother tongue."[423] The souls in Purgatory express their good fellowship by their courtesy toward Dante and each other. Their good citizenship is reflected in their willingness to embrace compatriots even without knowing who they are, as in the case of the Mantuan Sordello and Vergil.[424] Moreover, they are capable of transcending Italian political conflicts in favor of a wider vision of citizenship; the Sienese Sapia, whose city was at war with Dante's Florence, greets him with the words, "O my brother, each one here is a citizen of a true city."[425] Furthermore, the souls in Purgatory share a sense of religious community. They indicate the mutuality of their moral strivings by joining in common song. In virtually every canto of the *Purgatorio* there are hymns, psalms, and prayers drawn from the liturgy of the church. They express a common worship of God; to the extent that they are drawn from the canonical hours, they indicate the time of day; and they reflect the moral characteristics of the various ledges of the mountain of Purgatory as they move from songs of penitence through the Beatitudes to songs of joy. The sense of community is perhaps most strongly revealed in the *Gloria in excelsis Deo,* which all the souls sing to celebrate the completion of the penance of any one of their number.[426]

We find hymns and psalms sung in Paradise for similar reasons,[427] and, in the main, conversation in this realm functions much as it does in Purgatory, on a more intense level. Long, courteous speeches packed with doctrine are the rule in Paradise, expressing the intellectual and moral power which the saints possess and which Dante is acquiring. The fluency and charity of the souls in Paradise are matched by their willingness to take the conversational initiative. Like Piccarda Donati, they are "eager to speak"[428] to Dante and often perceive what he wants to ask before he asks it.[429] Good fellowship is reflected throughout Paradise. The numerous souls in the Heaven of Jupiter express their sense of community by speaking as one.[430] All earthly rivalries are stilled in Paradise. Souls usually praise the virtues of others when they themselves are praised[431] and live harmoniously with those with whom they have quarreled in life. This latter aspect of Paradise is best expressed in the Heaven of the Sun, where the Dominican Thomas Aquinas and the Franciscan Bonaventura exchange praises of the founders of each other's order. They do not merely magnify the founders of rival orders of friars; they are also capable of sharing their heaven peaceably with Siger of Brabant and Joachim of Flora, men whose ideas were anathema to Thomas and Bonaventura, respectively, during their lifetime.[432] Aquinas's graciousness to his former opponents is further shown when he explains the creation in terms of the doctrine of exemplarism, an idea far more characteristic of the teaching of Bonaventura than of his own.[433] Much has been written on the question of whether Dante was a Thomist,[434] an Averroist or Islamicizer,[435] a Joachite,[436] and even a Scotist,[437] on the basis of the personnel of his Heaven of the Sun as well as on the basis of the philosophical doctrines which he is deemed to have expressed in the *Comedy*. It would seem more plausible, however, to see his assortment of philosophers and theologians in the Heaven of the Sun as a token of the virtue of courage that they manifest in being intellectual innovators and as a reflection of the idea that, in Heaven, all earthly controversies and enmities cease.

In Paradise Dante supplies further insight into the role of speech in drawing the individual toward God and in building a good society. The gracious and voluble reception which Dante is accorded by the saints reveals his notion of the functional interrelations between love and knowledge. The souls greet him so that they may converse, so that information may be exchanged. But this verbal interchange is not merely informative. It is also productive of joy; what the souls and Dante learn from each other increases their mutual love.[438] Love, in turn, is expressed verbally. Cacciaguida, who, according to Dante reflects a perfect balance between love and knowledge, speaks "in clear words and with precise discourse (*latino*)."[439] The passage in which his discourse is placed does indeed include Latin as well as Italian and runs the full gamut of the types of diction used by Dante throughout the *Comedy*. The fact that the poet uses the word *latino* in this context suggests that he has now completely assimilated all the dignities, rigidities, and functions of Latin as a literary language into the Tuscan vernacular. Speech, for Dante as for Augustine, is a form of prayer, a confession of faith, hope, and charity.[440] Furthermore, discourse communicates both wisdom and power.[441] In the *Paradiso* Dante reaffirms the link between speech and moral action which he established in his earlier works by placing a discussion of nobility, which recapitulates his ideas on this subject in the *Convivio*, in the Heaven of Venus. The third heaven signifies love and rhetoric, Dante tells us in the *Convivio*, whose second tractate is given over to an analysis of the canzone "Voi che 'ntendendo il terzo ciel movete," and whose fourth tractate goes into the problem of nobility and other aspects of public morality. This association of ideas is carried over into the *Paradiso*, where Charles Martel, the chief speaker in the Heaven of Venus, quotes Dante's canzone and goes on to discuss nobility and civic virtue.[442] In the *Comedy*, no less than in his earlier works, Dante connects eloquence to wisdom and virtue and therefore relates the state of language to the state of Christian society. Thus, near the end of his heavenly journey, after he has been tested on faith, hope, and charity, Dante encounters Adam, who explains the origin of speech and the *Ursprache* of Eden. In Dante's last conversation with a soul before he ascends to the Empyrean, he takes occasion in this way to reaffirm the connection between language and ethics by having Adam allude to the division of tongues springing from the presumption of Babel. But Adam also affirms that his own Hebraic speech had itself been altered to the point of extinction, by the same process of natural linguistic change to which Dante had referred in the *De vulgari eloquentia,* even before the building of the tower.[443] Thus at this point Dante removes the claims that any language might be able to make to superiority over the vernacular, which he can now treat as the equal of the Hebrew of Eden as well as the Latin of the classical authors.

Dante uses discourse in the literal sense, both spoken and written,[444] to reveal the moral and intellectual status of the souls whom he meets and to show how he, as a character in the *Comedy,* advances in love and knowledge. He also uses a number of nonverbal signs for these purposes, and, like Augustine, he tends to treat them in verbal terms. Music, as we have seen, is found frequently in Purgatory and Paradise. Its impact derives as much from its lyrics, drawn from the Bible and from liturgical texts, as from its melody. Dante treats the eyes and smile of Beatrice, prominent instruments in his enlightenment and motivation, as figures of speech, retaining his *Convivio* interpretation of these devices as the demonstrations and persuasions of the lady. It is true that, on one level, seeing in the *Comedy* may be contrasted with speaking, as vision may be contrasted with knowledge of God by faith, through a glass darkly. This view is substantiated by Dante's increasing tendency in the poem to confess his linguistic ineptitude as his eyes grow progressively stronger, until the vision of God at the end of the *Paradiso* inspires the reaction of silence on the part of the poet. On the other hand, or on another level, it is also possible to regard the senses, particularly sight, as figurative of or correlative with sound and hence as reducible to linguistic signs. Dante indicates his intention of treating vision in sonic, linguistic terms at the outset of the *Inferno,* which he describes as the realm "where the sun is silent."[445] He continues this treatment up through the *Paradiso,* where the order and beauty of the heavens are manifested in the harmony of the celestial spheres.[446] While Dante frequently describes the created intermediaries of knowledge as a series of mirrors reflecting the divine light,[447] in his final vision when he sees the universe as it exists in God, he has recourse to a verbal symbol, the book of nature, "bound by love in one single volume."[448]

Dreams and visual art are other nonverbal devices which Dante treats verbally in explaining the process of his instruction in the other world. The personages whom he meets in dreams do not merely present themselves to be seen but speak or sing.[449] In *Purgatorio* 10 and 12, Dante tells the reader of the sculptures he sees on the wall and pavement as he walks up the mountain. This sculpture is didactic, as it contains figures illustrating types of humility and pride. Dante judges the sculpture excellent and marvelous because of the skill and craftsmanship that went into it and because the figures correspond so graphically to the persons they are designed to signify:

What master was he of brush or of pencil who drew the forms and lineaments which there would make every subtle genius wonder? Dead the dead, and the living seemed alive. He who saw the reality of all I trod upon, while I went bent down, saw no better than I![450]

Dante specifies the realism of the sculpture by interpreting it in verbal terms; he describes it as a "story set in the rock," stating that the figures are so vivid that one can almost hear them speaking.[451] Expressing his inversion of Horace's dictum, *ut pictura poesis,* he calls the sculpture "visible speech."[452] Dante also stresses the connections between morality and knowledge in this passage by placing the sculptures counseling humility on the wall and those illustrating pride on the pavement; the humble are exalted, while the proud are cast down. The viewer who has seen the images of humility and has absorbed their message proceeds with downcast head; it is only in this position that he is able to see the images of pride and to learn from them as well.

Dante also employs a number of symbols as key words. By repeating them in several different contexts and by linking them to several different concepts and persons, he achieves an economical association in the reader's mind among these concepts and persons. The *Comedy* expresses Dante's unification of social, political, religious, personal, and literary concerns,[453] and the repetition of these key symbolic terms is one of the ways in which he reveals this unification. Let us content ourselves with three examples. The richest symbol which Dante uses in this manner is the eagle. The eagle symbolizes the empire, the just ruler, and the supremely social virtue of justice, as well as the rapacity and injustice of a depraved church and empire.[454] At the same time, the eagle, the only creature that can look directly at the sun, signifies Beatrice.[455] The eagle which, in Dante's dream, carries him to the steps of the gate of Purgatory, where he experiences penitence, can be taken to represent grace, or the Holy Spirit, which inspires contrition in the soul of the sinner,[456] while John, the evangelist of charity, is described in Paradise as "the Eagle of Christ,"[457] tying John's Dantean significance with his traditional Apocalyptic symbolism as the eagle in the tetragrammaton. The craft of poetry also participates in this symbol. As Dante avers after joining the classical poets in the Limbo of the virtuous pagans, the lord of highest song, variously identified as Homer or Vergil, transcends the others like the eagle.[458]

Dante uses the symbol of the sun in a similar fashion. The sun traditionally symbolizes God,[459] "the planet that leads man aright by every path,"[460] the Christ whom Vergil was born too late to know.[461] The reflection of the Christ-Griffon in Beatrice's eyes is like the sun in a mirror.[462] But the sun also symbolizes Beatrice herself.[463] It is Apollo, the sun god, the leader of the Muses, whom Dante invokes for poetic aid,[464] and, in the Convivio and the De monarchia, he describes his own writing as the sun dispersing the surrounding darkness.[465] The sun signifies divine illumination,[466] but it also signifies political and ecclesiastical power and their proper relationships. Adverting to a prominent theme of his De monarchia, Dante places in the mouth of Marco Lombardo a speech observing that the church and the empire are ideally equal, independent, and divinely sanctioned, like two suns.[467] A third highly connotative symbol is the tree. The image of the tree in itself conjures up associations of the tree of the knowledge of good and evil in the garden of Eden and the cross of the Crucifixion. Dante uses two speaking trees in Purgatory to express the virtue of moderation, as opposed to avarice and prodigality.[468] He describes the French monarchy, the current threat disturbing the right political and ecclesiastical order of Europe, as an "evil plant."[469] In the Earthly Paradise, Beatrice shows Dante a barren tree, despoiled of its foliage, representing the empire. Then she shows him the same tree blossoming again with leaves and flowers of imperial purple, inviting him to sit with her at its roots, saying, "Here shall you be short time a forester, and you shall be with me forever a citizen of that Rome whereof Christ is Roman."[470] The tree also signifies the laurel, emblem of poetic distinction. In his invocation to Apollo, Dante affirms, "You shall see me come to your beloved tree and crown me with the leaves of which the matter and you shall make me worthy."[471] Finally, Dante uses the symbol of the tree to express his own moral regeneration after passing through Eunoë at the top of Purgatory: "I came forth from the most holy waves, renovated even as a new tree is renewed with new foliage, pure and ready to rise to the stars."[472] Thus Dante binds together his own personal morality, his poetry, Beatrice, his ideal of the Christian society, and God, by applying the same literary symbols to all of them.

Dante's aesthetic of poetic rectitude leads him to strive to make his words and images correspond to their significata. If they did not, his poetry would not possess rectitude. It would lack truth, and hence would be incapable of instructing the reader in the truth. At the same time, the Incarnational point of view which Dante shares with other proponents of Augustinian sign theory as well as his typological approach to symbolism lead him to strive to express spiritual realities in tangible, material, earthly terms, in the terms of daily life. These two objectives interact to produce one of the most distinctive and most frequently noted features of Dante's style. His language, vocabulary, diction, and syntax, the phonetic devices and sonic effects that he uses, are highly concrete, mimetic, and precise. The *Comedy*'s linguistic structure and its variety of linguistic styles always clearly reflect the significative and didactic functions which Dante applies to language.[473]

Let one major example suffice to underline this point. One of Dante's chief means of communicating doctrine to the reader is through persons.[474] Persons, in turn, are delineated through their conversation. What Dante's characters say and the way in which they say it express their own, unique, historical personalities, no less than the moral states they represent in the poem.[475] This fact has both ethical and epistemological importance. Dante wishes to stress the idea that vices and virtues do not exist in the abstract, but only in the context of actual human lives. The human context, therefore, acquires crucial significance. Suicide, for instance, cannot be understood simply as an abstract category of sin, which invariably draws the same response from God. There are several characters in the *Comedy* who are guilty of suicide, but they are not all treated in the same way. Dante places Dido and Cleopatra in the circle of lust in Hell, since they killed themselves in despair over the termination of their passionate, adulterous love affairs, in both cases, it might be noted, at the expense of their political obligations as ruling queens. Pier delle Vigne, the minister of Frederick II, is also in Hell, in the circle of violence. Dante subdivides this circle into four categories: violence against others, violence against oneself, violence against God, and violence against nature and art. He classifies Pier as violent against himself. This classification is based not merely on the fact that Pier took his own life. It is also based on the reasons for his behavior. As Pier explains it, he killed himself in despair at false accusations of disloyalty to Frederick, which led to his imprisonment and blinding on the orders of the prince. Pier maintains that he remained faithful and just to Frederick throughout. But, Dante emphasizes, it is impossible to be just to others if one is unjust to himself. Dante contrasts Pier's self-destruction in the face of unjust treatment by his prince with the case of Romeo of Villeneuve, chamberlain to Raymond Berengar IV of Provence. On losing his office after years of faithful service, Romeo became a wandering beggar and holy man.[476] There is another suicide in the *Comedy*, Cato of Utica. Far from being punished in Hell for having taken his own life, Cato represents the infused cardinal virtues and guards the gate of Purgatory. An opponent of Caesar, Cato committed suicide so as not to have to live under the rule of a usurper after the defeat of the Roman Republican cause. Dante regards Cato's suicide as a supreme sacrifice for the sake of liberty. As such, it is a virtue, not a vice, and hence the position of eminence that he gives to Cato in the *Comedy*.

It is clear from this example that the location of the suicides in the other world depends on the reasons why they killed themselves and involves a concrete knowledge of their lives and personalities on the part of the reader. A concrete projection of his characters thus becomes an important task of the writer, because, as Dante notes through the words of Beatrice, the didactic function of the poem depends on the ability of the reader to recognize the persons who are being rewarded or punished for their actions on earth.[477] It is therefore essential for Dante to choose characters who are historical personages well known to his audience and to put speeches into their mouths capable of expressing their personalities with realism and precision.

Dante's imagery and figures of speech, too, are highly concrete and realistic. His similes and metaphors always play a clarifying role and are never merely coloristic or ornamental.[478] As Bergin has so aptly put it, "For Dante the beginning was the word"; Dante's imagery, no less than his diction, reveals "a richness of objective correlatives."[479] Dante uses a comparatively small number of figures of speech drawn from allusions to literature.[480] He also draws few of his similes from the vegetable world.[481] Many images, however, are taken from the behavior or appearance of animals,[482] from climatic conditions and specific landscapes,[483] from quotidian human activities, reactions, attitudes, and experiences,[484] from familiar objects undergoing common chemical and physical processes,[485] and from a host of miscellaneous everyday things.[486] The keynote in Dante's figurative comparisons is always on the commonplace and the familiar. Dante aims at expressing the strange and wondrous things which he experiences in the other world of the spirit in the terms of this world so that they will be immediately and utterly recognizable to his audience. His motive is didactic, and the underlying rationale of his imagery is Incarnational typology.

It can be seen from this inspection of Dante's poetics, as exemplified in the *Divine Comedy*, that Dante is in full possession of Augustine's linguistic epistemology and that he applies this theory to his poem while shifting Augustine's emphasis in some respects. Dante develops his own poetic theory gradually, drawing upon some aspects of the classical and medieval tradition of literary criticism and rejecting others. His theory is explained fully only in the letter to Can Grande, and he illustrates it fully only in the *Divine Comedy*. Dante, like the other proponents of medieval verbal epistemology treated in this study, conceives of the signs which mediate knowledge in fundamentally linguistic and sensible terms, whether these verbal signs be conceived literally or figuratively. He holds that poetic language can signify God truly, and, in fact, that poetry is the discipline best suited to this purpose but that its power to represent divine realities always remains partial. The significata of his poem are the norm of the rectitude of the terms in which he expresses them, a principle that requires the use of evocative images and a variety of specific stylistic devices. For Dante, the plausibility of representing spiritual truths in highly concrete, material, and temporal terms is a corollary of the Aristotelian element latent in the Augustinian sign theory, the doctrine of the Incarnation, and the typological method allegory transposed from Scripture to Christian poetry.

On the subjective level Dante's poem is designed to teach, to delight, and to persuade the reader, to orient him toward virtue. It assumes the functions of Christian rhetoric as defined by Augustine. Yet, in specifying the nature and aims of rhetorical Christian poetry, Dante introduces an emphasis characteristically his own. The rectitude that Dante seeks to inspire in the reader is an amalgam of personal ethics, religion, and civic virtue, modeled on the Dantean pattern of a regenerated Christian commonwealth, which will restore the cultural and political centrality of Italy to the Holy Roman Empire and to the church and which will bring back the ancient nonpartisan virtues of the Florentines, in addition to integrating Christian Europe, depressing the political currency of France, and eliminating greed and war. Didactic poetry written according to rules in a unified Italian vernacular is to be the means of moving the reader toward these goals. Within the didactic poem there are a variety of stylistic strategies through which the author hopes to teach, delight, and persuade his audience, ranging from the content of the poem, which he thinks will evoke general interest, to a host of specific characters and images designed to make the message immediate to the reader.

Pleasure, for Dante, is never a subordinate aim in rhetorical poetry. The reader cannot internalize the intellectual content of the *Comedy* unless he appropriates it aesthetically. Dante stresses this point by making the chief character in the *Comedy* himself, an initially bewildered pilgrim through Hell, Purgatory, and Heaven who learns through conversation, observation, experience, and human love. By casting himself as a character with whom the reader can identify, Dante the author creates the possibility of the reader's vicariously experiencing what Dante the character experiences. The ultimate objective of Dante the author, outside of winning fame, is to reproduce in the reader a conversion similar to the series of catharses and illuminations which Dante the traveler undergoes. Dante stands for the reader at the same time that he stands above the reader and instructs him; the reader of the *Comedy*, like the reader of Augustine's *Confessions*, shares the spiritual state of the author, if not his knowledge, talent, or sanctity. The traveler, and by extension, the reader, grows in knowledge as he grows in love and as his aesthetic senses are strengthened. Dante illustrates this idea in his use of the theme of light, in his stress on visual and aural perception, and by the important role that he assigns to the emotional relationships between Dante the character and his guides. In this way he underlines the notion that love and beauty are ways of knowing. Joy, for Dante, is not the consequence of knowledge but its concomitant.

Both as author and character, Dante frequently expresses his need for God's grace. The mediation of grace, through other human beings, is the crucial factor in the traveler's progressive enlightenment and, by extension, the enlightenment of the reader. God is revealed in man, for Dante, not in the vestiges of the Trinity impressed in the human soul, but in the total human personality and in the context of complete human relationships, both personal and social. For these media to function as channels of love and knowledge, however, God must deliberately choose to act through them on specific occasions. Thus Dante reveals his adherence to the Augustinian notion that signs play an instrumental, not a heuristic, role in conveying knowledge to the subject.

In assessing whether Dante posits both commemorative and indicative functions for his *Comedy*, in determining whether he wrote the poem for an audience composed of both believers and nonbelievers, the student of Dante faces an interesting paradox. Dante's heavy reliance on traditional Christian doctrines, characters, and images, his equally heavy reliance on characters and figurative allusions familiar only to his contemporaries, and his great stress on linguistic reform manifested in his use of the Tuscan dialect in the *Comedy* indicate that he conceives of himself as addressing a specific audience existing in a specific time and place. This audience is composed of Italians who are at least nominal Christian believers. The function of the poem vis-à-vis this audience is hence commemorative. Dante aims at bringing to the minds of his contemporaries truths, both divine and human, which they already hold, but which they have pushed aside and ceased to use as guides to life. He wants to help this kind of reader deepen his appreciation of these truths. Charles S. Singleton is therefore quite correct in describing the epistemological character of the *Comedy* in the terms of *fides quarens intellectum*.[487] This Anselmian principle, like the moral and epistemological norm of rectitude, indeed provides us with a fitting framework in which to view the poem. However, unlike Anselm, Dante does not pay much attention, even in theory, to the presumptive needs of a nonbelieving audience or to the reader who, unlike an early fourteenth-century Italian, would not be able to recognize all of his scenic descriptions, figurative allusions, or characters. Yet the history of the reception of the *Comedy* indicates that Dante's masterpiece has found a wide audience among readers who do not share his theological, philosophical, or political views. This fact amply testifies to the inadvertent indicative power of the *Comedy*, although it has also produced some interpretative distortions of the work, in which Dante's *bello stile* and the aesthetic pleasure to be derived from the *Comedy* have been occasionally divorced from the poem's doctrinal content and from the poet's didactic poetics. In any event, of the four thinkers discussed in this study, Dante certainly is the one who devotes the least attention to the problem of communicating religious knowledge to the nonbeliever, and he makes the fewest ostensible attempts to speak comprehensibly to him. Yet such is the power of Dante's art that he has probably communicated to the nonbeliever, as well as to the believer, more effectively through the centuries than Augustine, Anselm, or Aquinas.

Conclusion

This study of the theory of signs in religious knowledge in the thought of Augustine, Anselm, Thomas Aquinas, and Dante Alighieri has shown that there are powerful links binding the four together as well as many points of difference among them. Their basic similarities derive from the fact that they possess a common core of Christian ideas on the ways in which man may know God by faith, *per speculum in aenigmate*. All four of them believe that religious knowledge is always mediated through Christ the Word in this life. All four combine this belief with a verbal species of sign theory derived from classical antiquity by way of the trivium. This classical sign theory provides them with their mental tools, with the Stoic conviction that words are accurate signs of the things they signify, and with the Aristotelian certainty that sense data conduce authentically to a knowledge of prior and nonsensible realities. The differences among the four thinkers are dictated largely by the fact that each inherits, and in some cases helps to crystallize, a stress on one or the other of the disciplines of the trivium.

Thus Augustine conceives of human modes of knowing God as literal or figurative statements about him. The specific shape of these statements is determined by their objective reference, the need to represent an object of knowledge that is intrinsically mysterious, and by their function in Christian rhetoric of instructing and persuading an audience. Anselm seeks an accurate grammatical denomination of God, a name of God that takes into account the knower's need for an intellectual and moral attitude appropriate to him. Rectitude is the idea which describes the name of God that satisfies these requirements. He bases the arguments which he uses to support the view that his name of God possesses rectitude upon the uses of eleventh-century grammar. Aquinas approaches the problem of knowing God by the avenue of scholastic logic, with its principles of demonstration and dialectic, its syllogistic structure, and its empirical foundations. This orientation leads him to work out an epistemology of the hidden God through the knowledge of the natural world. Dante adverts once again to rhetoric, but he reexpresses Augustinian rhetoric in the form of Christian poetics. In this poetic theory, the poet's creation of a didactic work of art is his means of expressing the Word; and the reader's aesthetic appreciation of the poem is the means of his moral and intellectual instruction, persuasion, and delight. The differences in the ways by which these four thinkers approach the same problem reflect the varying milieux in which they labored and to which they spoke. They also reflect their variations in professional emphasis and personal style.

Yet, Augustine, Anselm, Aquinas, and Dante all adhere to the same doctrine of words as signs in the knowledge of God. In the theory of signification they all employ, being is prior to knowing. This presupposition is consistent both with the metaphysical bias of the classical philosophy from which they derived the theory and with their concentration on God as the object of knowledge and the intellectual light par excellence. They warrant their search for signs and analogues of God in nature, history, and human psychology with scriptural assertions proclaiming that the creation bears witness to God, and that it is a way of knowing him. At the same time, their reading of the Bible and their sensitivity to the technicalities of the verbal disciplines that supplied them with epistemological guidelines and criteria encourage them to place limits on the significative and communicative powers of signs. Their frequent avowal of literary and conceptual ineptitude in the face of the mystery of God underlines their belief that God always transcends anything that men can think or say about him. Their stress on the extrinsic effectiveness of signs in the acquisition and transmission of religious knowledge flows from their belief that the normative knowledge of God is a knowledge by faith. Faith, they hold, is a gift of God. God gives it to men on his own initiative, irrespective of human efforts. Their interest in the moral as well as the intellectual character of knowledge reflects their conviction that faith is both a moral and an intellectual state. Faith, they affirm, is, not a static mental relationship between God and man, but a dynamic condition in which the believer moves toward the vision of God, a beatitude which perfects the whole man and which transforms all of his human relationships.

These Christian precepts combine with classical doctrines on the functions and values of signs in the cognitive process to form the verbal sign theory basic to the epistemology of the four thinkers examined in this study. In this theory, signs represent things truly but partially. They are never identical with their objects and their accuracy is always judged by reference to these objects. Signs never produce knowledge in the subject in the first instance. The subjective function of signs in helping to communicate knowledge depends on the knower's previous relationship to the object. If he is already a believer, he can recognize the sign as a sign of God and can judge how Godlike it is; the sign in turn can deepen his awareness of God. If he is not a believer, the sign can merely indicate the direction in which he should turn in order to orient himself toward God. Signs are instrumental in the subject's acquisition of belief or of a deeper insight into it only when God wills this to occur in the case of a particular subject at a particular time. For the thinkers here studied, the primary objects of knowledge are God and, to a lesser extent, man and the universe seen in a God-related perspective. The principal signs of God, in a literal sense, are the verbal testimonies of teachers of the Word, whether they be scriptural writers, preachers, theologians, or poets. In a figurative sense, the principal sign of God is the creation and, above all, the human soul, in which the vestiges of the Trinity have been impressed.

Augustine frames this theory for the western Middle Ages in its first and most explicit form. He is also the best example of its expression in the mode of rhetoric. Both of these facts are direct consequences of his conversion from pagan rhetoric to Christian eloquence, an event which forced him to reshuffle his previous views on verbal signs in order to explain how they worked in a Christian epistemology. One may also attribute Augustine's stress on the bond between the Incarnation and the Christian use of words in the knowledge of God to the nature of his intellectual voyage to Christianity and the dangerous, yet tempting, obstacles which he encountered on his way. The Incarnation, to be sure, is central in any Christian theology. In Augustine's thought it is not merely prominent, it also plays a distinctive role. On the level of metaphysics, the Incarnation serves as a compass by means of which he charts his course around the shoals of Manicheism and Neoplatonism. On the level of rhetoric, the immediate implication that Augustine perceives in the Word made flesh is the redemption of human speech. Since he is a rhetorician after his conversion as well as before it, he therefore interprets the theologian's role as a participation in the Incarnational task of expressing the Word to the world.

For Anselm, the Incarnational dimensions of theological statements are implicit rather than explicit. On the whole, despite his extensive borrowings from Augustine, his approach to theology is quite different from that of the bishop of Hippo. While Anselm, like Augustine, can be thought of as a pastoral theologian, he has far fewer problems of communication than Augustine. He is not a bishop faced regularly with the task of addressing a heterogeneous congregation in his cathedral. Nor is he an apologist faced with combating a diverse series of heresies. Instead, Anselm's task is to edify a small group of Benedictine monks, who can be regarded as fairly homogeneous in terms of their education, their intellectual methods, and their vocation. He strives not to extract a theory of signs from the amplitude of classical culture but to translate a spiritually oriented form of meditation on God into a grammatical style of theological speculation. Working with a very limited number of classical sources in an environment not especially fraught with spiritual turmoil, he develops a way of speaking about God which provides for its audience the heightened tang of old wine poured from new bottles. His accomplishment reflects both the sophistication and the limitations of his grammatical tools. Anselm is aware of the capacity of grammatical analysis to refine and reformulate and enrich the devotional approach to the contemplation of God typical of monastic theology. He is also sensitive to the fact that the philosophical linguistics of his day lacked the precision needed to resolve some of the semantic and theological dilemmas he addressed.

While the logical issues that Anselm's questions raise connect him with his scholastic successors, in some ways the arch-scholastic Aquinas resembles Augustine more than he does Anselm. Aquinas, like Augustine, is in possession of a fairly wide range of classical materials, although he channels them through logic as inexorably as Augustine appropriates his own sources in rhetorical terms. Aquinas, too, is faced with the problem of intellectual diversity and apologetic dispute. His works, both in their structure and in the arrangement of their contents, are occasion pieces, despite their ostensibly systematic character; his emphasis is often dictated as much by the nature and extent of the objections that he has set himself to answer as by the intrinsic importance of a given subject to his teachings. However, despite the fact that Thomas has to address a variety of points of view, he can speak to them all in the same intellectual language, the language of the thirteenth-century university. He expects his opponents to engage him in debate at the academic level and in the technical terminology of the professional scholastic theologian. Thomas's adherence to Aristotelianism dictates an approach to religious epistemology which makes the natural world its point of departure and which concentrates on the question of how knowledge enters the human mind. There are points at which this method appears to set Thomas off from Augustine and Anselm, neither of whom is interested in analyzing the process of conceptualization in detail, and both of whom manifest only the most transitory concern with nature as a source of signs of God. While he reflects the contemporary thirteenth-century emphasis on cosmology, Thomas does not always manage to fuse it with complete success to the conventional stress on the mind of man as the most fruitful source of signs of God. His empiricism, deep-rooted though it is, in no way prescinds from his acknowledgment that it is God who guarantees the truth of what men may think about him through his signs. The important place that Christology holds in Augustine's expression of the theory of verbal signs takes a form in Thomas's thought corresponding to the Dominican's emphasis on the natural world. For Aquinas, God's self-revelation through signs resides preeminently in Christ as the Logos of the creation. The restoration of man to God takes place through the redemption of nature and of man's knowledge of it.

The fact that the Augustinian theory of signs can be, and was, applied to religious literature as well as to technical theology is amply demonstrated by Dante. With the zeal of a reformer and the aesthetic convictions of a supreme artist, Dante formulates a theory of literature, put into practice in his *Divine Comedy*, which provides a rationale for a layman to teach the truth about God, man, and Christian society through a work of vernacular poetry. Dante develops this theory gradually. In the process of doing so, he draws upon the various strands of medieval poetics, some of which he rejects and some of which he accepts and reorients. In particular, he receives from his medieval and classical predecessors a conflation of rhetoric and poetics, in which rhetoric absorbs poetry. As Dante appropriates this tradition, however, he changes it in two ways. He understands rhetoric in a Christian sense, according to the Augustinian model, and conceives of it in a political and social context. Also, he stands the conflation of poetics and rhetoric on its head by assimilating rhetoric to poetry. Thus, for Dante, poetic language acquires all the epistemological and moral powers and limitations which Augustine attributes to rhetoric and which Anselm and Aquinas, following Augustine, attribute to grammar and logic, and for exactly the same reasons. Dante's verbal signs encompass the full repertoire of poetic technique, from syntax and vocabulary to similes and symbols. His objective is to express divine truths perceived in a fictional other-worldly vision in language that possesses rectitude. Rectitude implies accuracy and humility vis-à-vis his subject matter and a delightful and convincing mode of expression vis-à-vis his audience. This in turn entails a concrete, precise, and realistic style. Dante's interest in expressing spiritual realities in highly sensible and tangible terms reflects his certainty that sensible signs can convey authentic information about nonsensible significata. Language is itself a sensible sign; but above and beyond this, Dante's poetic style focuses on aurally pleasing sonic effects and vivid visual images. This focus reveals the Christological dimensions of Dante's theory; a work on a transcendent theme expressed concretely and tangibly is the poetic corollary of the Incarnation. Dante selects man above all other creatures as the principal source of signs of God. But, unlike Augustine, Anselm, or Aquinas, he does not stress the vestiges of the Trinity in the human soul. Man, for Dante, participates in the mission of Christ; he signifies and mediates God to his fellow men through a just and peaceful social life in the divinely sanctioned human institutions, the church and the empire, through idealized human love, and through inspired Christian poetry.

Each of these four thinkers employs a characteristic mode of expression; yet none of them is completely at liberty to choose his own theological language. Before the fact, Augustine, Anselm, Aquinas, and Dante are committed to the classical disciplines of thought and expression which have been engrained in their minds by their education and which provide them with their intellectual tools. But to the extent that Augustine, Anselm, Aquinas, and Dante are conscious of current options, they make their choices with an eye to the fitness of given classical or medieval epistemological doctrines to the task of expressing the knowledge of God and of expressing it to the times which they each address. All of them are sensitive to the theologian's simultaneous responsibility to be true and to be meaningful, and all of them are bold in their acceptance of the innovations of their day and in their willingness to convert them to Christian purposes.

Notes

Abbreviations in the Notes and Bibliography

CC   *Corpus christianorum,* series latina.

CSEL *Corpus scriptorum ecclesiasticorum latinorum.*

LCL   Loeb Classical Library.

PL   *Patrologiae cursus completus, series latina.*
      Edited by J. P. Migne.

Notes

Introduction

1. Plato *Meno* 80e–87c (trans. Jowett).

2. The arguments of the iconodules at the Seventh Ecumenical Council at Nicea, 787, at which iconoclasm was formally condemned, sum up the theory of the icon, emphasizing the distinction between significance and identity, the commemorative function of icons, and their link with the doctrine of the Incarnation. See Joannes Dominicus Mansi, ed., *Sacrorum conciliorum,* 12:1069B, D; 1072A; 1080A–D. For an excellent discussion of these points, see Léonide Ouspensky and Vladimir Lossky, *The Meaning of Icons,* pp. 16, 24, 27–34, 37–38, 42–43; also Léonide Ouspensky, *L'icone,* pp. 5–6, 12–15, 17–26; Gervase Mathew, *Byzantine Aesthetics,* pp. 7, 38–47, 95–107, 124–25; Paul J. Alexander, *The Patriarch Nicephorus of Constantinople,* pp. 23–53, 189–213, 217–24; Otto Demus, *Byzantine Mosaic Decoration,* pp. 5–6.

Chapter One

1. See references cited below, p. 232, n. 49.

2. Plato *Phaedrus* 275d–77b, 278b (trans. Jowett).

3. Plato *Timaeus* 29b–c (trans. Jowett).

4. Plato *Cratylus* 391b ff., 428e, 435d–38d (trans. Jowett).

5. Ibid., 429b ff.

6. Ibid., 392d ff., 423b ff., 427c–d, 428e, 434b.

7. Ibid., 434d–35b.

8. Ibid., 432b, 439c–40d.

9. Ibid., 440c. See also 438e–39b.

10. Aristotle *De sophisticis elenchis* 1.165a4–19 (ed. Ross, trans. Pickard-Cambridge); *Rhetoric* 1.1357a24–1357b21, 3.1404a20–23, 1405a9–12, 1410b10–21 (trans. Roberts).

11. Aristotle *Analytica priora* 2.27.70a7–9 (ed. Ross, trans. Jenkinson).

12. Aristotle *Analytica posteriora* 1.2.71b14–18 (ed. Ross, trans. Mure).

13. *Rhet.* 1.1355a4–10, 1356a32–34, 1357a24–1357b21.

14. *De soph. el.* 1.165a4–19; *Rhet.* 3.1404a20–23, 1405a9–12, 1410b10–21.

15. For the physical background, see Hans F. A. von Arnim, ed., *Stoicorum veterum fragmenta*, 1:85, 87, 89–90, 102, 153–54, 162, 493, 495; 2:299–328, 341, 346a, 358–59, 467, 526, 665, 797, 848; 3:34 (cited hereafter as *SVF*). A standard account is S. Sambursky, *Physics of the Stoics*. For the psychological background, see *SVF*, 1:134–43, 216–23, 518–26; 2:773–89, 832–49; 3:544–656. Basic treatments include Ludwig Stein, *Die Psychologie der Stoa*, vol. 1; Gérard Verbeke, *L'évolution de la doctrine du pneuma*, chap. 1; André-Jean Voelke, "L'unité de l'âme dans l'ancien stoïcisme," *Studia philosophica* 2 (1965): 154–81.

16. On Stoic linguistic theory, see *SVF*, 1:74; 2:140–44a; Diogenes Laertius *Lives of the Eminent Philosophers* 7.57–58. For bibliography, see Marcia L. Colish, "The Stoic Theory of Verbal Signification and the Problem of Lies and False Statements from Antiquity to St. Anselm," *L'archéologie de signe*, ed. Lucie Brind 'Amour and Eugene Vance, pp. 17–19.

17. On the Stoic doctrine of cognition and judgment, see *SVF*, 1:53–73, especially 60–61, 63, 66, 68c, 69, 73d; 2:52–71, 74, 78, 84, 90, 91, 105, 107, 141, 850, 858, 862, 871–72; Diogenes Laertius 7.52–54. Basic treatments include Émile Bréhier, *Chrysippe et l'ancien stoïcisme*, 2d ed., pp. 80–107; Antoinette Virieux-Reymond, *La logique et l'épistémologie des stoïciens*; Gerard Watson, *The Stoic Theory of Knowledge*. The terms "extramission" and "intromission" in this context are borrowed from David. C. Lindberg, *Theories of Vision from Al-Kindi to Kepler*, pp. 9–11.

18. On *lekta* and related topics, see *SVF*, 1:93–95, 488; 2:132, 166, 170, 181, 183, 331, 335, 501–2, 511, 514; Diogenes Laertius 7.63–81. For secondary literature, see Colish, "Verbal Signification," pp. 20–21.

19. Cicero *De inventione* 1.30.48 (ed. and trans. Hubbell). See also *Rhetorica ad Herennium* 2.7.10–11 (ed. and trans. Caplan). While the *Ad Herennium* is not known with complete certainty to have been Cicero's own work, it will be included here as a good index of the Ciceronian position.

20. Cicero *Orator* 32.14 (ed. and trans. Hubbell); *De invent.* 1.30.48; *De divinatione* (ed. and trans. Falconer); *Ad Herennium*, especially 2.5.8; *De partitione oratoria* 2.5–7 (ed. and trans. Rackham); *Topica* 8.35 (ed. and trans. Hubbell).

21. For a particularly clear example of this tendency, found throughout Cicero's works, see *Ad Herennium* 2.4.6. This would seem to indicate that the early medieval tendency to conceive of logic in rhetorical terms, noted by Richard McKeon, "Rhetoric in the Middle Ages," *Speculum* 17 (1942): 7–10, had begun as early as Cicero.

22. Cicero *Orator* 21.69.

23. Cicero *De optimo genere oratorum* 1.3–4 (ed. and trans. Hubbell).

24. Cicero *De oratore* 3.52.199 (ed. and trans. Sutton and Rackham).

25. Cicero *Academica* 2.20.64–48.148 (trans. Rackham).

26. For these and other Latin authors as transmitters of Stoic sign theory, logic, and epistemology, see Colish, "Verbal Signification," pp. 19–24, 41–42. On the broader

question of Augustine's sources, see Aimé Solignac, "Doxographies et manuels dans la formation philosophique de saint Augustin," *Recherches augustiniennes* 1 (1958): 113–48.

27. Cicero *De orat.* 3.41.166–42.167.

28. Aegidius Forcellini, *Totius latinitatis lexicon,* vol. 1, s.v. "Aenigma"; *Thesaurus linguae latinae,* vol. 1, s.v. "Aenigma." Cf. C. Du Cange, *Glossarium mediae et infimae latinitatis,* vol. 1, s.v. "Aenigma."

29. Augustine *Soliloquia* 1.2.7. (*PL* 32). In connection with the structure of the *Solil.* it is important to note the observation of John Burnaby, *Amor Dei,* p. 55: "It is never to be forgotten that the Augustinian 'intellect' is not the discursive reason but the mind at worship." This idea has also been developed with considerable insight by Roger Hazelton, "The Devotional Life," *A Companion to the Study of St. Augustine,* ed. Roy W. Battenhouse, pp. 400–403.

30. Cf. Pierre Courcelle, *Recherches sur les Confessions de saint Augustin,* pp. 20 ff., who states first that the *Confessions* is an *oeuvre de circonstance* devoid of plan, but who notes a few paragraphs later that its autobiographical structure is shot through with doctrinal passages of progressive difficulty. Two recent studies with able treatments of Augustine's interpretation of his autobiography in terms of the redemption and rediscovery of language are Ralph Flores, "Reading and Speech in St. Augustine's *Confessions,*" *Augustinian Studies* 6 (1975): 1–13; and Euguene Vance, "Augustine's *Confessions* and the Grammar of Selfhood," *Genre* 6 (1973): 1–28. Cornelius Petrus Mayer, *Die Zeichen in der geistigen Entwicklung und in der Theologie des jungen Augustinus,* however, treats this question in exclusively Platonic terms.

31. Augustine *Confessiones* 1.4.4. (ed. Verheijen, *CC* 27). See also 13.10.11. The idea that the most man can do is to state that God is inexpressible is found in *Enarrationes in Psalmos* 35.4, 99.6 (ed. Dekkers and Fraipont, *CC* 38–39); *Epistula* 242 (ed. Goldbacher, *CSEL* 34:4); *De doctrina christiana* 1.6.6. (ed. Martin and Daur, *CC* 32).

32. *Conf.* 1.1.1.

33. Ibid., 1.5.7.

34. Ibid., 1.6.7–8.

35. Ibid., 1.6.8.

36. Ibid., 1.6.10.

37. Ibid., 1.7.11–12. For further discussion of the moral state of the infant in terms of speech and consciousness, see *Ep.* 177.7.24–8.26.

38. *Conf.* 1.8.13. The formula *puer loquens* which Augustine uses here also denotes the age of seven years in Roman law, at which a child's testimony was admissible in court, as noted by Mayer, *Die Zeichen,* 1:52 n. 12.

39. *Conf.* 1.8.13.

40. Ibid., 1.9.14.

41. Ibid., 1.10.15, 1.19.30.

42. Ibid., 1.10.16, 1.19.30.

43. Ibid., 1.9.14.

44. Ibid., 1.10.15.

45. Ibid., 1.13.20–1.16.26. Augustine states elsewhere that the use of words by pagan authors to signify things which have no existence is a falsification of speech; fictitous statements of this type denote nothing except insofar as they imitate the grammatical structure of true statements. He adds that it is important to know the intention of the author before judging his statements. Poems and tales which aim only to amuse are not false; they are false only when they aim to instruct. See *Solil.* 2.9.16, 2.15.29. Augustine frequently uses the same kind of verbal argument in his attacks on heretics in order to support the contention that an orthodox confession of faith is necessary for truly moral actions. See for example, *In Ioannis Evangelium* 102.1 (ed. Willems, *CC* 36). Augustine develops the same theme in another direction in his full-blown analysis of the semantic and moral significance of lying found in his *De magistro, De doctrina christiana, De mendacio,* and *Contra mendacium.* See Colish, "Verbal Signification," pp. 26–36.

46. *Conf.* 1.18.29–1.19.30.

47. Ibid., 1.20.31.

48. Ibid., 2.1.1, 4.16.31.

49. Ibid., 2.2.4–2.3.5. As Charles Sears Baldwin has pointed out in *Medieval Rhetoric and Poetic (to 1400),* pp. viii, 6, 51, 54–55, 60, 71, Augustine is reacting away from the sophistic rhetoric current in his own day in the direction of an antisophistic rhetoric which would stress the union of wisdom, virtue, and eloquence. This antisophistic tradition has a long history in classical thought. It runs through the work of Plato; see, in particular, *Gorgias,* especially 456b–58b, 464c–65e, 523b–27e; *Phaedrus* 275d–79b. Cicero repeats the same idea frequently; see *De orat.* 1.5.16–18, 1.6.20–22, 1.7.28, 1.14.60–1.16.70, 2.2.6, 3.5.30, 3.6.24, 4.14.54–4.20.77; *De invent.* 1.1.1–1.3.5; *Orator* 4.14, 22.72. Cicero's antisophistic criticism is repeated by Quintilian *Institutiones oratoriae* 1.1.9–20, 1.12.1–2.1.10. Aristotle discusses rhetoric principally in relation to truth, touching on ethics only in the sense that the orator should be aware of his own ethos and that of his audience (*Rhet.* 1. 1356a20–26, 32–34). See also Charles Sears Baldwin, *Ancient Rhetoric and Poetic,* pp. 5, 9–12, 53–55, 247.

50. *Conf.* 2.4.9–2.5.11.

51. Ibid., 2.4.9, 2.6.12, 2.7.15.

52. Ibid., 2.6.13–2.7.15.

53. Ibid., 2.1.1.

54. Ibid., 2.2.2, 2.2.4, 3.1.1.

55. Ibid., 3.2.2–4.

56. Ibid., 2.3.7.

57. Ibid., 3.3.6.

58. Ibid., 3.4.7.

59. Ibid., 3.6.10.

60. Ibid., 3.6.11.

61. Ibid., 3.7.12–3.10.18.

62. Ibid., 2.3.7.

63. Ibid., 3.11.19.

64. Ibid., 3.5.9.

65. Ibid., 3.12.21. Augustine also discusses the importance of moral states in the reception of knowledge in *De fide et symbolo* 9.19 (ed. Zycha, *CSEL* 40); *De doct. christ.* 2.7.11.

66. *Conf.* 4.1.1–4.2.2.

67. This fact has been brought out with clarity and sensitivity by Peter Brown, *Augustine of Hippo*, pp. 61–64, 67–68, 199.

68. *Conf.* 4.4.7–4.9.14.

69. Ibid., 4.4.7, 4.7.12, 4.9.14.

70. Ibid., 4.6.11.

71. Ibid., 4.10.15–4.11.17.

72. Augustine *De catechizandis rudibus* 2.3–4 (*PL* 40).

73. *Conf.* 4.11.19. See also *De civitate dei* 11.2–3 (ed. Dombart and Kalb, *CC* 48). The centrality of the Incarnation in Augustine's theory of redeemed speech as a bridge between the transient and eternal worlds has been brought out by Douglas W. Johnson, "*Verbum* in the Early Augustine," *Recherches augustiniennes* 8 (1972): 25–53.

74. *Enar. in Ps.* 99.6.

75. *Conf.* 4.11.19. On words as vehicles of God's Word, communicated to men through men, see also *De vera religione* 50.99 (ed. Martin and Daur, *CC* 32); *Civ. dei* 10.15; *Enar. in Ps.* 48.5, 77.5; *In Ioan. Ev.* 1.4, 29.4, 54.8; *De fid. et sym.* 2.3–3.4. Cf. Rudolph Berlinger, *Augustins dialogische Metaphysik,* who treats the Incarnational aspect of Augustine's thought from a strictly metaphysical point of view.

76. *Conf.* 4.13.20–4.15.27.

77. Ibid., 4.16.28–29.

78. Ibid., 4.16.30–31.

79. Ibid., 5.3.3, 5.6.10–5.7.13.

80. Ibid., 5.10.19–5.11.21.

81. Ibid., 5.13.23, 6.3.3.

82. Ibid., 5.14.24. The integration of style and content is another of Augustine's antisophistic Ciceronian ideas; see Baldwin, *Medieval Rhetoric,* p. 60.

83. *Conf.* 5.14.25. On the function of preaching, see *De doct. christ.* prooemium, 5–6, 8; bk. 4, especially 16.33–27.59; *De cat. rud.* 4.8, 5.9, 15.23; *In Ioan. Ev.* 1.4, 17.2. On episcopal instruction, see *Ep.* 209.

84. *Conf.* 6.7.12. On conversation, oral and written, see *Ep.* 189, 233.

85. *Conf.* 6.3.4–6.5.8, 7.7.11. Courcelle, *Recherches,* pp. 106–36, thinks that Ambrose was also Augustine's chief source of Platonism at this time. This view is repeated by Maurice Testard, *Saint Augustin et Cicéron,* 1:81–82, 119 ff., who adds that Ambrose converted Augustine from sophistry to Ciceronianism. More recently, Courcelle, *Les Confessions de saint Augustin dans la tradition littéraire,* pp. 26–31, has restated

his view, citing supporters of it. While there is unquestionably a strand of Platonism in Ambrose's thought, it seems overly gallant to give him the major credit for having introduced Augustine to these ideas, particularly since Augustine was currently reading Platonic philosophy on his own. Courcelle himself notes, *Les Confessions*, p. 31, that there was a Christian Neoplatonic group in Milan, including Simplicianus, Theodorus, and others Augustine knew in addition to Ambrose. Cf. Johannes Hessen, *Augustins Metaphysik der Erkenntnis*, pp. 13–14.

86. *Conf.* 7.1.1–7.2.3, 7.6.8–10. On the function of argument and discussion, see *Solil.* 2.7.14. For Augustine's rejection of Academic probabilism on similar verbal grounds, see *Contra academicos* 2.11.26 (ed. Knöll, *CSEL* 63).

87. *Conf.* 7.3.4–7.5.7.

88. Ibid., 7.9.13–15.

89. Ibid., 7.10.16, 7.11.17, 7.14.20, 7.17.23, 12.10.10–12.11.12. On intuition as a verbal medium of cognition, see *Ep.* 4, 147.1.3, 147.1.5–147.2.7; *Civ. dei* 22.29. On the difference between Augustine's intuitive cognition of God and mystical experience, see Burnaby, *Amor Dei*, pp. 31–37.

90. *Conf.* 7.10.16.

91. Ibid., 7.9.13–7.17.23. On God speaking through the natural universe, an argument rarely used by Augustine, see *Civ. dei* 11.4; *In Ioan. Ev.* 1.8–10.

92. *Conf.* 7.9.13–14, 7.18.24. Courcelle, *Les Confessions*, pp. 33–37.

93. *Conf.* 7.18.24–7.20.26. Courcelle, *Les Confessions*, pp. 64–65.

94. *Conf.* 7.20.26–8.1.1. On the Bible as a moral *speculum*, see *Enar. in Ps.* 16.5, 30 exp. 2, serm. 2.1, 46.1, 102.4, 106.1; *In Ioan. Ev.* 10.7, 21.2; *Ep.* 189, 229. Ritamary Bradley, "Backgrounds of the Title *Speculum* in Mediaeval Literature," *Speculum* 29 (1954): 100–115, notes this use of the Bible in Augustine, but confines the idea of *speculum* to it.

95. *Conf.* 8.4.9.

96. Ibid., 8.6.13.

97. Ibid., 8.5.10. On the eloquence of moral example, see also *Ep.* 108.

98. *Conf.* 6.6.9, 6.11.20–6.13.23.

99. Ibid., 8.5.11–8.6.13.

100. Ibid., 8.6.14–15.

101. Ibid., 8.7.17, 8.9.21, 8.11.25–27.

102. Ibid., 8.12.29. Professor Roland H. Bainton has brought to my attention that the child's cry, "Tolle, lege," is another instance, like Augustine's chance remark to Alypius, in which a speaker expresses God's will involuntarily. See Courcelle, *Les Confessions*, pp. 133–63, for an illuminating discussion of the *tolle, lege* theme as a literary topos in classical and early Christian writings, a discussion which forms part of an extended analysis of the stylistic influence of the Platonists on the style of the *Confessions*, pp. 17–197.

103. Cf. Prosper Alfaric, *L'évolution intellectuelle de saint Augustin*, who holds that Augustine was successively a Manichee and a Neoplatonist until the age of forty-six,

when he finally became a Christian. Alfaric seems content to locate Manichean and Neoplatonic ideas in the writings of Augustine, without discussing the uses he made of them in their respective contexts. This latter approach is also found in Henri-Irénée Marrou, *Saint Augustin et la fin de la culture antique,* pp. 242 ff., with respect to Augustine's style. Marrou thinks that Augustine's use of verbal arguments in his early works is a reflection of his classical education and indicates an incomplete grasp of Christian theology in the first few years after his conversion. This use, however, is quite relevant to Augustine's theology and is found in his later works also. In more recent years the debate over whether Augustine became a Christian in 386 or remained a Neoplatonist for some years afterwards has moved to the question of whether his Neoplatonism after that time was a philosophy of life or a form of *intellectus fidei* and whether Porphyry or Plotinus was the chief member of that school on whom he drew. For a useful review of the literature on these points, see Robert J. O'Connell, *St. Augustine's Early Theory of Man,* pp. 26–27. The most judicious recent treatment of the whole issue is Anton C. Pegis, "The Second Conversion of St. Augustine," in *Gesellschaft, Kultur, Literatur,* ed. Karl Bosl, pp. 79–93.

104. *Conf.* 9.1.1. See also 1.7.12, 2.7.15, 5.1.1, 9.8.17, 9.13.36; 11.2.3, 12.2.2, 12.24.33. This use of the word *confessio* was first noted by Courcelle, *Recherches,* p. 14.

105. *Conf.* 9.1.1.

106. Ibid., 9.2.2, 9.5.13.

107. Ibid., 9.4.8–12, 9.12.32. See also 12.13.16, 12.23.32, 12.27.37, 13.29.44.

108. Ibid., 9.4.7.

109. Courcelle, *Recherches,* p. 36.

110. *Conf.* 9.10.23–24.

111. Ibid., 9.10.25. Cf. Joseph A. Mazzeo, "St. Augustine's Rhetoric of Silence," *Journal of the History of Ideas* 23 (1962): 175–96, who stresses the Platonic, while neglecting the biblical, sources of Augustine's doctrine of the mimetic transience of language. Conversely, Burnaby, *Amor Dei,* pp. 78–79, stresses Augustine's biblical sources to the exclusion of all others. For a more balanced view, see Marcia L. Colish, "St. Augustine's Rhetoric of Silence Revisited," *Augustinian Studies* 9 (1978): 15–24.

112. *Conf.* 9.11.29–9.13.37. Note the parallel here to the death of Augustine's friend in book 4.

113. Ibid., 9.13.37, 10.3.3–4, 10.3.6.

114. Ibid., 10.2.2. See also *De trinitate* 15.10.18 (ed. Mountain and Glorie, *CC* 16:1–2).

115. *Conf.* 10.5.7.

116. Ibid., 10.6.8–10.

117. Ibid., 10.8.12 ff.

118. Ibid., 10.24.35–10.26.37.

119. See above, p. 4; *De trin.* 12.15.24.

120. See Colish, "Augustine's Rhetoric," pp. 22−24, for the relevant passage of Aristoxenus and related literature. An otherwise competent summary of Augustine on memory which omits its Aristotelian underpinnings is John F. Callahan, *Four Views of Time in Ancient Philosophy,* pp. 148−87, 200−204.

121. *Conf.* 10.20.29−10.23.33.

122. Ibid., 10.5.7, 10.28.39 ff.

123. Ibid., 10.30.41 ff.

124. Ibid., 10.43.68−70.

125. Ibid., 11.2.1, 11.30.40, 12.17.24−25, 12.25.34.

126. Ibid., 9.4.8.

127. Ibid., 10.3.3, 10.6.10, 11.3.5, 11.8.10, 11.11.13. Good recent treatments of Augustine's sense of the limits as well as the powers of language in theological discourse are Battista Mondin, "Il problema del linguaggio teologico in sant'Agostino," *Augustinianum* 11 (1971): 269−80; Raffaele Simone, "Semiologia agostiniana," *La cultura* 7 (1969): 89−97; Ulrich Wienbruch, " 'Signum,' 'Significatio,' und 'Illuminatio' bei Augustin," in *Der Begriff der Repraesentatio im Mittelalters,* ed. Albert Zimmerman, pp. 76−93, although the last does not discuss the sources of Augustine's doctrine.

128. *De dialectica* 5, 7.9, 7.11, 9 (ed. Pinborg; trans. Jackson). The ascription of this treatise to Augustine has been debated, and Pinborg, ibid., pp. 138−42, reviews the controversial literature. The best studies of this work are Jean Pépin, *Saint Augustin et la dialectique,* pp. 21−60; and Jan Pinborg, "Das Sprachdenken der Stoa und Augustins Dialektik," *Classica et mediaevalia* 22 (1962): 148−77. For other references, see Colish, "Verbal Signification," pp. 25−26. See also Robert H. Ayers, *Language, Logic, and Reason,* pp. 69−74; Jean Collart, "Saint Augustin grammarien dans le *De magistro,*" *Revue des études augustiniennes* 17 (1971): 290; Ulrich Duchrow, *Sprachverständnis und biblisches Hören bei Augustin,* pp. 42−62.

129. For recent literature on the *De mag.,* see Colish, "Verbal Signification," pp. 26−28. Connections between the *De dial.* and *De mag.* have also been noted by Collart, "Saint Augustin," pp. 279−92; Duchrow, *Sprachverständnis,* pp. 62−66, 71−73; Louis G. Kelly, "Saint Augustine and Saussurean Linguistics," *Augustinian Studies* 6 (1975): 50; Simone, "Semiologia agostiniana," pp. 106−9. Luigi Alici, *Il linguaggio come segno e come testimonianza,* chap. 1; and Goulven Madec, "Analyse du *De magistro,*" *Revue des études augustiniennes* 21 (1975): 63−71, give good summaries of the *De mag.* without considering its sources.

130. Mary Sirridge, "Augustine: Every Word Is a Name," *New Scholasticism* 50 (1976): 183−92, argues that Augustine is reaching here for a proto-definition of syncategorematic terms. On the other hand, Simone, "Semiologia agostiniana," pp. 108−9, rightly notes that Augustine is discussing words in this context from a functional, not a metalinguistic standpoint.

131. *De mag.* 2.3−4.10, 7.19−20, 9.28−10.30, 13.41 (ed. Weigel, *CSEL* 77).

See also *Ep.* 7, 147.17.43; *Enar. in Ps.* 3.5, 4.2, 4.4, 36 serm. 1.1, 77.3, 80.2, 97.3, 103 serm. 1.13; *De fid. et sym.* 9.17; *Solil.* 2.11.20.

132. *De mag.* 11.36 (*The Teacher,* trans. Colleran, pp. 175–76). See also 8.22, 10.33–35. The idea that speech, for Augustine, has both indicative and commemorative functions has been noted by Paolo Rotta, *La filosofia del linguaggio nella patristica e nella scolastica,* pp. 112–13. Irwin Lee Glatstein, "Semantics, Too, Has a Past," *Quarterly Journal of Speech* 32 (1946): 49–50, sees this function as solely indicative; K. Kuypers, *Der Zeichen- und Wortbegriff im Denken Augustins,* p. 18; and Alberto Caturelli, *La doctrina agustiniana sobre el maestro,* p. 24, see it as solely commemorative. Ronald H. Nash, *The Light of the Mind,* pp. 84–93, sees the sign theory of the *De mag.* as a reductio ad absurdum.

133. *De mag.* 1.2.

134. Noted also by Caturelli, *La doctrina agustiniana,* pp. 23–24. See also *In Epistolam Ioannis ad Parthos* 13 (PL 25); *Enchiridion de fide, spe, et charitate* 31.9 (PL 40).

135. *De mag.* 11.37–38; see also 13.41.

136. Ibid., 10.33–35. See also *Enar. in Ps.* 87.10, 87.13; *De utilitate credendi* 13.28–14.30 (ed. Zycha, *CSEL* 25); *Ep.* 147.1.5, 147.2.7–147.3.9, 147.6.18, 147.8.20–147.9.21, 147.11.27, 147.14.35.

137. *De mag.* 12.39–40, 13.41.

138. *De doct. christ.* 1.2.3–1.9.9.

139. Ibid., 1.10.10–1.21.19.

140. Ibid., 1.22.20–1.40–44. A good discussion of the moral aspect of Augustine's theory of biblical exegesis can be found in T. S. K. Scott–Craig, "On Christian Instruction," in *A Companion to the Study of St. Augustine,* ed. Roy W. Battenhouse, pp. 128–29, 139–42.

141. *De doct. christ.* 2.1.1.

142. On this point, see Colish, "Verbal Signification," pp. 28–31; Duchrow, *Sprachverständnis,* pp. 153–59; B. Darrell Jackson, "The Theory of Signs in St. Augustine's *De Doctrina Christiana,*" in *Augustine: A Collection of Critical Essays,* ed. R. A. Markus, pp. 92–147; Simone, "Semiologia agostiniana," pp. 99–102. Mayer, *Die Zeichen,* 2:95–104, sees this sign theory as Platonic. Alici, *Il linguaggio,* chap. 1, gives a good summary of the work, but does not discuss its sources. R. A. Markus, "St. Augustine on Signs," *Phronesis* 2 (1957): 60–83, is weakened by the author's effort to try to convert the sign theory in *De doct. christ.* into a general semantics.

143. *De doct. christ.* 2.1.2–2.3.4.

144. Ibid., 1.2.2, 2.10.15. See also *Civ. dei* 10.13; *De vera relig.* 50.98. A useful summary of this part of the *De doct. christ.* is provided by Johan Chydenius, *The Theory of Medieval Symbolism,* pp. 5–8.

145. *De doct. christ.* 2.11.16–2.15.22, 3.1.1–3.4.8.

146. Ibid., 2.16.23–2.41.62.

147. Ibid., 3.10.14–3.37.56.

148. Ibid., 4.7.11–4.11.26, 4.17.34–4.26.58.

149. Ibid., 4.4.6–10, 4.12.27–4.14.31. As it has been well put by Baldwin, *Medieval Rhetoric,* p. 60, "In the pulpit the sophistic heresy of art for art's sake becomes intolerable."

150. *De doct. christ.* 4.15.32–4.16.33, 4.27.59–4.31.64. Baldwin, *Medieval Rhetoric,* p. 67, has noted Augustine's tendency to play on the word *oratio,* using it to mean "speech" and "prayer" at the same time.

151. Baldwin, *Medieval Rhetoric,* pp. ix, 54–55; Marrou, *Saint Augustin,* especially p. 407; Testard, *Saint Augustin et Cicéron.* Hessen, *Augustins Metaphysik der Erkenntnis,* pp. 13–14, is, however, overly gallant in crediting to Cicero all the Platonic and Aristotelian philosophy at Augustine's command.

152. Pierre Courcelle, *Late Latin Writers and Their Greek Sources,* pp. 165–96; Solignac, "Doxographies et manuels," pp. 113–48.

153. The debate is summed up conveniently by Gerald Bonner, *St. Augustine of Hippo,* pp. 394–95. While more recently Harald Hagendahl, *Augustine and the Latin Classics,* 1:9, has reiterated the claim that Augustine's sources were exclusively Latin, Courcelle, *Late Latin Writers,* pp. 149–65, and *Les Confessions,* p. 51, has shown that he was conversant with Greek biblical, literary, and theological materials that were not available in Latin.

154. Kuypers, *Zeichen- und Wortbegriff,* p. 29; Markus, "St. Augustine on Signs," p. 65.

155. Cf., on the contrary, Markus, "St. Augustine on Signs," pp. 69–70; Glatstein, "Semantics, Too," p. 50; Caturelli, *La doctrina agustiniana,* pp. 35 ff.

156. See Maurice Pontet, *L'exégèse de s. Augustin prédicateur;* Charles Donahue, "Patristic Exegesis: Summation," in *Critical Approaches to Medieval Literature,* ed. Dorothy Bethurum, pp. 67–68.

157. *Conf.* 12.25.34–12.31.42. See also *De doct. christ.* 3.26.37; P. J. Llamas, "San Agustín y la multiplicidad de sentidos literales en la Escritura," *Religión y cultura* 15 (1931): 238–74.

158. *Conf.* 11.1.1, 12.15.18, 12.16.23, 12.18.27, 12.20.29.

159. Ibid., 11.12.14–11.27.36.

160. See, in general, Jean Daniélou, *From Shadows to Reality;* Henri de Lubac, "'Typologie' et 'Allegorisme,'" *Recherches de science religieuse* 34 (1947): 180–226, and the same author's magisterial *Exégèse médiévale,* 4 vols. in 2, especially 1, pt. 1; Beryl Smalley, *The Study of the Bible in the Middle Ages.*

161. *De cat. rud.* 3.6.

162. *De libero arbitrio* 2.14.38–2.15.39 (ed. Green, *CSEL* 74); *Ep.* 140.9.25–140.10.27, 147.22.51; *In Ioan. Ev.* 1.2.17–19, 101.5, 124.5.

163. *Conf.* 13.12.13.

164. *Enar. in Ps.* 71.8.

165. *De fid. et sym.* 1.1.

166. *Conf.* 13.23.34.

167. Ibid., 13.23.34, 13.27.42; *Civ. dei* 10.9; *De lib. arb.* 3.10.30. On sacraments in general, see *De doct. christ.* 2.3.4, 3.9.13; *Enar. in Ps.* 16.5; *Ep.* 140.10.27.

168. *Conf.* 13.17.20–13.22.32.

169. Ibid., 13.23.33.

170. *Enar. in Ps.* 37.15, 46.1, 48 serm. 1.5; *Sermo LIII in Mattheum V:3–8* 6.6, 10.10–11 (*PL* 38); *In Ioan. Ev.* 1.4, 14.8, 98.1, 102.3, 124.6; *De spiritu et littera* 23.38, 24.41, 28.49 (ed. Urba and Zycha, *CSEL* 60); *Retractationum* 1.13.3 (ed. Knöll, *CSEL* 36); *Civ. dei* 19.27; *Ep.* 92.

171. *Conf.* 13.5.6–13.11.12. See also *De doct. christ.* 1.12.12; *Civ. dei* 11.26–28; *Sermo LXXX in Matt. XVII:18–20; In Ep. Ioan.* 3.7.9; *In Ioan. Ev.* 14.7. For a well-informed discussion of the pure or purified soul as a mirror of God in Greek patristic thought, with its classical and biblical sources, see Gerhart B. Ladner, *The Idea of Reform*, pp. 92–102; and, less recently, Hans Leisegang, "La connaissance de Dieu au miroir de l'âme et de la nature," *Revue d'histoire et de philosophie religieuses* 17 (1937): 145–71; Johannes Behm, "Das Bildwort vom Spiegel I. Korinther, 13, 12," in *Reinhold-Seeberg-Festschrift*, ed. Wilhelm Koepp, 1:315–42.

172. See, on the contrary, Chydenius, *Theory of Medieval Symbolism*, pp. 8–9; Markus, "St. Augustine on Signs," pp. 76 ff. Caturelli, *La doctrina agustiniana*, pp. 12–15, provides an accurate summary of book 15 of *De trin.* Alfred Schindler, *Wort und Analogie in Augustins Trinitätslehre*, provides the most recent summary of the entire work and notes its sources in Neoplatonism, Stoicism, Greek patristic thought, and Augustine's earlier works, pp. 44–53, 86–118, 119–28, 188–95.

173. *De trin.* 1.1.3, 1.2.4; see also 8.4.6–8.6.9.

174. Ibid., 8.10.14.

175. Ibid., 9.2.2–9.5.8.

176. Ibid., 9.6.9–9.12.18, 10.1.1–10.4.6. Excellent background is given by Schindler in the references cited in n.172. He lists the various terms Augustine uses for this idea elsewhere in appendix 2, pp. 250–51. See also Duchrow, *Sprachverständnis*, pp. 122–27, 137–48; Kelly, "Saint Augustine," pp. 51–52; Fernando Soria, "La teoría del signo en San Agustín," *La ciencia tomista* 92 (1965): 28–92. Augustine's idea of *verbum mentis* should not be confused with that term as used by Thomas Aquinas. See below pp. 119–20.

177. *De trin.* 10.11.17–18.

178. Ibid., 11.5.8.

179. The best treatment of this question is Verbeke, *L'évolution*, pp. 502–7. Also useful if less vigorously argued is Duchrow, *Sprachverständnis*, p. 10. Nash, *The Light of the Mind*, pp. 43–45, 51, ascribes this theory to Plotinus and sees it as an express rejection of Stoicism on Augustine's part. Mary Ann Ida Gannon, "The Active Theory of Sensation in St. Augustine," *New Scholasticism* 30 (1956): 162–65, thinks that Augustine is expressing his independence of Plotinus at this point, although she does not ascribe the theory to the Stoics. George Howie, *Educational Theory and Practice in St.*

Augustine, pp. 73–74, 80–81; and Leonardo R. Patanè, *Il pensiero pedagogico di s. Agostino*, 2d ed., p. 102, think that he is making his own conflation of Aristotle and Plotinus. Neither F.-J. Thonnard, "Les fonctions sensibles de l'âme humaine selon s. Augustin," *L'année théologique augustinienne* 12 (1952): 335–45, nor Sofia Vanni Rovighi, "La fenomenologia della sensazione in s. Agostino," *Rivista de filosofia neo-scolastica* 54 (1962): 18–32, discusses Augustine's sources.

180. *De trin.* 11.1.1–11.2.5, 11.5.9–11.6.10.

181. Ibid., 11.3.6–7, 11.7.11–11.8.15.

182. Ibid., 12.14.21–23, 13.1.1–2.

183. Ibid., 13.19.24.

184. An excellent treatment of this point can be found in Walter H. Principe, "The Dynamism of Augustine's Terms for Describing the Highest Trinitarian Image in the Human Person," in press. I am indebted to Father Principe for permission to consult this text in proof.

185. *De trin.* 14.2.4–14.4.7, 14.12.15–14.19.26. As Burnaby, *Amor Dei*, pp. 80–81, has observed, the fact that Augustine sees the end of man as the vision of God in no way implies that the will is subordinate to the intellect or vice versa. Since Augustine uses the interrelationships of the faculties of the human soul to suggest the Trinity, his "absolutely co-equal Trinity imposes upon him a refusal of all 'subordinationism' in dealing with the spirit of man and its destiny."

186. *De trin.* 15.9.15–16.

187. Ibid., 15.9.16. Donald E. Daniels, "The Argument of the *De trinitate* and Augustine's Theory of Signs," *Augustinian Studies* 8 (1977): 33–54, ignores the limitations of verbal signs reflected in Augustine's breaking down of his Trinitarian analogies at the end of the work, which mars an account that is otherwise consistent with the one given here.

188. *Ep.* 180.

189. *De trin.* 15.10.17–15.11.21, 15.20.39–15.23.49.

190. Ibid., 15.6.9, 15.7.11, 15.7.13, 15.13.22–15.16.26.

191. Ibid., 15.17.27–15.19.37.

192. Ibid., 15.28.50–51.

Chapter Two

1. As Gillian R. Evans, *Anselm and Talking about God*, has rightly said, "No technical skill available to him was so helpful . . . as that of definition" (p. 7).

2. John MacIntyre, "Premises and Conclusions in the System of St. Anselm's Theology," in *Spicilegium Beccense*, 1:95–101.

3. See Alvin Plantinga, ed., *The Ontological Argument, from St. Anselm to Contemporary Philosophers*, for a survey of these arguments.

4. M. T. Antonelli, "Il significato del Proslogion di Anselmo d'Aosta," *Rivista rosminiana* 45 (1951): 260–68; Joseph Clayton, *Saint Anselm*, pp. 136 ff.; Étienne

Gilson, *A History of Christian Philosophy in the Middle Ages*, pp. 130, 139; P. Enrico Rosa, *S. Anselmo di Aosta, arcivescovo Cantuariense e dottore della chiesa*, pp. 135 ff.; A. van Weddington, *Essai critique sur la philosophie de s. Anselme de Cantorbéry*, especially pp. 50 ff.

5. Antonelli, "Il significato del Proslogion," pp. 260–61; D. M. Cappuyns, "L'Argument de s. Anselme," *Recherches de théologie ancienne et médiévale* 6 (1934): 313–30; Clayton, *Saint Anselm*, pp. 136 ff.; F. C. Copleston, *A History of Philosophy*, 2:157–59; Le Comte Domet de Vorges, *Saint Anselme*, p. 134; Gilson, *History of Christian Philosophy*, p. 133; S. A. Grave, "The Ontological Argument of St. Anselm," *Philosophy* 27 (1952): 30–38; Adolf Kolping, *Anselms Proslogion-Beweis der Existenz Gottes im Zusammenhang seines spekulativen Programms Fides quaerens intellectum*.

6. Fr. Spedalieri, "Anselmus an Gaunilo? Seu de recta argumenti sancti Doctoris interpretatione," *Gregorianum* 28 (1947): 54–77; "De intrinseca argumenti s. Anselmi vi et natura," *Gregorianum* 29 (1948): 204–12.

7. Anton Antweiler, "Anselmus von Canterbury, Monologion und Proslogion," *Scholastik* 8 (1933): 551–60; Charles Filliatre, *La philosophie de saint Anselme*, p. 50; Arrigo Levasti, *Sant'Anselmo*, pp. 31–71; Julián Marías Aguilera, *San Anselmo y el insensato*, pp. 5–25; Renato Perino, *La dottrina trinitaria di s. Anselmo*, pp. 28 ff.; Anselm Stolz, *Anselm von Canterbury*, pp. 37–39; "Das *Proslogion* des hl. Anselm," *Revue bénédictine* 47 (1935): 331–47; "'Vere esse' im Proslogion des hl. Anselm," *Scholastik* 9 (1934): 400–406; "Zur Theologie Anselms im Proslogion," *Catholica* 2 (1933): 1–24.

8. Joseph Fischer, *Die Erkenntnislehre Anselms von Canterbury*, pp. 40–42, 66–78; Robert G. Miller, "The Ontological Argument in St. Anselm and Descartes," *Modern Schoolman* 32 (1955): 344; Sofia Vanni Rovighi, *S. Anselmo e la filosofia del secolo undicesimo*, pp. 71–72; Maurice de Wulf, *History of Mediaeval Philosophy*, 1:165.

9. A. Beckaert, "Une justification platonicienne de l'argument a priori?," in *Spicilegium Beccense*, 1:185–90; Filliatre, *La philosophie de saint Anselme*, pp. 20 ff.; Alexandre Koyré, *L'idée de Dieu dans la philosophie de st. Anselme*, pp. vii, 60–99.

10. Paul Evdokimov, "L'aspect apophatique de l'argument de saint Anselme," in *Spicilegium Beccense*, 1:233–58.

11. Ferdinand Bergenthal, "Ist der 'ontologische Gottesbeweis' Anselms von Canterbury ein Trugschluss?," *Philosophisches Jahrbuch* 59, no. 2 (1949): 155–68; Georg Wendschuh, *Verhältnis des Glaubens zum Wissen bei Anselm von Canterbury*.

12. A. E. Davies, "The Problem of Truth and Existence as Treated by Anselm," *Proceedings of the Aristotelian Society*, n.s. 20 (1920): 167–90.

13. Henry G. Wolz, "The Empirical Basis of Anselm's Arguments," *Philosophical Review* 60 (1951): 341–61.

14. Walter Betzendörfer, "Glauben und Wissen bei Anselm von Canterbury," *Zeitschrift für Kirchengeschichte* 48, n.s. 11 (1929): 354–70.

15. Helmut Kimmerle, *Die Gottesbeweise Anselms von Canterbury*.

16. Karl Barth, *Anselm;* Otto Samuel, *Über die Beweisbarkeit der Existenz Gottes*. Support for this position on philosophical grounds is given by Hugh R. Smart,

"Anselm's Ontological Argument: Rationalistic or Apologetic?," *Review of Metaphysics* 3 (1949): 161–66.

17. Robert S. Hartman, "Prolegomena to a Meta-Anselmian Axiomatic," *Review of Metaphysics* 14 (1961): 637–75.

18. R. E. Allen, "The Ontological Argument," *Philosophical Review* 70 (1961): 55–56; William P. Alston, "The Ontological Argument Revisited," *Philosophical Review* 69 (1960): 452–74; Heinz W. Enders, "Die 'quinque viae' des Thomas Aquinas und das Argument aus Anselms Proslogion: Eine bezeichnungstheoretische Analyse," *Wissenschaft und Weisheit* 40 (1977): 158–88; Jules Vuillemin, *Le Dieu d'Anselme et les apparences de la raison.*

19. Mario Dal Pra, "Il problema del fondamento del significato nella controversia fra Anselmo e Gaunilone," *Rivista critica di storia della filosofia* 9 (1954): 132–55; "Studi sul problema logico del linguaggio nella filosofia medioevale, I: 'Cogitatio vocum' e 'cogitatio rerum' nel pensiero di Anselmo," *Rivista critica di storia della filosofia* 9 (1954): 309–43; "Gaunilone e il problema logico del linguaggio," *Rivista critica di storia della filosofia* 9 (1954): 456–84; Wolfgang Leopold Gombocz, *Über E! Zur Semantik des Existenzprädikates und des ontologischen Arguments für Gottes Existenz von Anselm von Canterbury.*

20. Richard Campbell, "Anselm's Theological Method," *Scottish Journal of Theology* 32 (1979): 543–48; *From Belief to Understanding;* Paul Henle, "Uses of the Ontological Argument," *Philosophical Review* 70 (1961): 102–9; Norman Malcolm, "Anselm's Ontological Argument," *Philosophical Review* 69 (1960): 41–62.

21. M. J. Charlesworth, "St. Anselm's Argument," *Sophia* 1 (1962): 25–36.

22. Armando Cicchetti, *L'agostinismo nel pensiero di Anselmo d'Aosta.*

23. Charles Hartshorne, "The Logic of the Ontological Argument," *Journal of Philosophy* 58 (1961): 471–73; "Introduction," St. Anselm, *Basic Writings,* pp. 3–17. Hartshorne's position is most fully expressed in *The Logic of Perfection and Other Essays in Neoclassical Metaphysics,* pp. 3–117; *Man's Vision of God, and the Logic of Theism.*

24. For good bibliographical discussions of this development, see Wolfgang Leopold Gombocz, "Zu neueren Beiträgen zur Interpretation von Anselms Proslogion," *Salzburger Jahrbuch für Philosophie* 20 (1975): 131–35; Arthur C. McGill, "Recent Discussions of Anselm's Argument," in *The Many-Faced Argument,* ed. John Hick and Arthur L. McGill, pp. 33–110; Gregory Schufreider, *An Introduction to Anselm's Argument,* pp. xiii–xv.

25. See, for example, Richard La Croix, *Proslogion II and III;* David A. Pailin, "Credo ut intelligam as the Method of Theology and of Its Verification: A Study of Anselm's Proslogion," in *Analecta anselmiana,* ed. Helmut Kohlenberger, 4, pt. 2: 111–29; Jasper Hopkins, *A Companion to the Study of St. Anselm,* pp. 69–70.

26. See, for example, Desmond Paul Henry, "Proslogion Chapter III," in *Analecta anselmiana,* ed. Helmut Kohlenberger, 1:101–5.

27. See, for example, Schufreider, *Anselm's Argument.*

28. Paul Vignaux, *Philosophy in the Middle Ages,* p. 35.

29. Evans, *Anselm and Talking about God,* p. vii; also pp. 1, 9, 139–43, 208.

30. Charles Sears Baldwin, *Medieval Rhetoric and Poetic (to 1400),* p. 91. Baldwin extends the age of grammar only through the tenth century.

31. Rabanus Maurus *De clericorum institutione* 3.18 (*PL* 107).

32. Martin Grabmann, "Die Entwicklung der mittelalterlichen Sprachlogik," *Mittelalterliches Geistesleben,* 1:109–13; R. W. Hunt, "Studies on Priscian in the Eleventh and Twelfth Century," *Mediaeval and Renaissance Studies* 1 (1941–43): 194–200; Charles Thurot, "Notices et extraits de divers manuscrits latins pour servir à l'histoire des documents grammaticales au moyen âge," *Notices et extraits des manuscrits de la Bibliothèque Impériale et autres bibliothèques* 22, pt. 2: 60–64.

33. *De cler. inst.* prologus.

34. Jean Leclercq, "Smaragde et la grammaire chrétienne," *Revue de moyen âge latin* 4 (1948): 15–22.

35. Jean Leclercq, *The Love of Learning and the Desire for God,* pp. 21–32, 44–56, 76–93, 116–51. This work is an extremely valuable study of literature and spirituality in the medieval monastery.

36. Paschasius Radbertus *Liber de corpore et sanguine Dei* (*PL* 120). Cf. the discussion of Paschasius in Beryl Smalley, *The Study of the Bible in the Middle Ages,* pp. 65–66.

37. On this debate see Leo Donald Davies, "Hincmar of Rheims as a Theologian of the Trinity," *Traditio* 27 (1971): 455–68; Jean Devisse, *Hincmar,* 1:161–70; Jean Jolivet, *Godescalc d'Orbais et la trinité,* esp. pp. 23–31, 173–84; "Quelques cas de 'platonisme grammaticale' du septième au douzième siècle," in *Mélanges offerts à René Crozet,* ed. Pierre Gallais and Yves-Jean Riou, 1:97–98.

38. On Fredigisus, see Concettina Gennaro, *Fridugiso di Tours e il "De substantia nihili et tenebrarum,"* with a good review of the literature, pp. 101–13; John Marenbon, *From the Circle of Alcuin to the School of Auxerre,* pp. 62–64; also Gillian R. Evans, *Anselm and Talking about God,* p. 54 n.4; "The 'Secure Technician': Varieties of Paradox in the Writings of St. Anselm," *Vivarium* 13 (1975): 16–18; Desmond Paul Henry, *Commentary on "De grammatico,"* p. 336; Jolivet, "Platonisme grammaticale," p. 96; Franciscus Salesius Schmitt, ed., *Opera omnia,* by Anselm, 1:249. On John, see especially Gustavo A. Piemonte, "Notas sobre la *creatio ex nihilo* en Juan Escoto Eriugena," *Sapientia* 23 (1968): 37–58; also Donald F. Duclow, "Divine Nothingness and Self-Creation in John Scotus Eriugena," *Journal of Religion* 57 (1977): 110–15; Gillian R. Evans, "The Grammar of Predestination in the Ninth Century," *Journal of Theological Studies,* n. s. 33 (1982): 134–45.

39. Abbo of Fleury *Quaestiones grammaticales* (*PL* 139).

40. Gunzo *Epistola ad Augienses,* ed. Karl Manitius, in *Monumenta Germaniae Historica: Quellen zur Geistesgeschichte des Mittelalters,* vol. 2, bk. 1.

41. Hunt, "Studies on Priscian," pp. 194–231.

42. Osmund Lewry, "Boethian Logic in the Medieval West," in *Boethius,* ed. Margaret Gibson, pp. 90–103; Lorenzo Minio-Paluello, in *Categoriae vel predicamenta,*

in *Aristoteles latinus,* 1, pts. 1—5, pp. x—xxii, li—lii; and his earlier papers reprinted with corrections in *Opuscula,* pp. 1—39, 357—76, 448—58. See also A. van de Vijver, "Les étapes du développement philosophique du haut moyen-âge," *Revue belge de philologie et d'histoire* 8 (1929): 425—52.

43. David Knowles, *The Evolution of Medieval Thought,* p. 100.

44. Donatus *Ars grammatica* (ed. Keil, *Grammatici latini,* 4:373).

45. Priscianus *Institutionum grammaticarum libri XVIII* 2.5.22 (ed. Herz, *Grammatici latini,* 2:56—57).

46. *Inst. gram.* 2.4.15, 2.4.18 (*Gram. lat.* 2:53, 55).

47. Remigius of Auxerre *In Artem Donati minorem commentum* (ed. Fox, pp. 8, 9—10).

48. Alcuin *Grammatica* (PL 101:859).

49. Ibid.

50. Anicius Manlius Severinus Boethius *In Categorias Aristotelis* 4—5, in *Aristoteles latinus,* 1, pts. 1—5 (ed. Minio-Paluello); *In librum Aristotelis De interpretatione* 1 (PL 64). See also Thurot, "Notices et extraits," *Notices et extraits,* 22, pt. 2:166.

51. David C. Douglas, *William the Conqueror,* pp. 86, 116.

52. The best study of Lanfranc as an authority on the liberal arts is Margaret Gibson, *Lanfranc of Bec,* pp. 42—44, 46—50, 57, 71—91. See also R. W. Southern, "Lanfranc of Bec and Berengar of Tours," in *Studies in Medieval History Presented to Frederick Maurice Powicke,* ed. R. W. Hunt, W. A. Pantin, and R. W. Southern, pp. 30, 32—33; *Saint Anselm and His Biographer,* pp. 14, 16.

53. Anselm *Epistola* 19, *Opera omnia* (ed. Schmitt) 3:125—26. All citations to Anselm's works, unless otherwise indicated, will refer to this edition.

54. Ordericus Vitalis *Ecclesiastical History* 3.2.14 (ed. and trans. Chibnall, 2:12). Quotations in English will be taken from Chibnall's translation.

55. Ibid., 4.2.210.

56. Ibid., 4.2.245—46. Henri de Lubac, *Exégèse médiévale,* 1, pt. 1: 94 n.3, gives additional data on the contemporary educational repute enjoyed by Bec.

57. Gibson, *Lanfranc,* pp. 42—44, 46—50, 57, 71—91.

58. The following paragraphs on Lanfranc and Berengarius and the formula for illustrating equipollent argument are based on Southern, "Lanfranc and Berengar," pp. 32, 39—46; *Saint Anselm,* pp. 12—14, 20—26. In more general terms, see also Jos. Ant. Endres, *Forschungen zur Geschichte der frühmittelalterlichen Philosophie,* p. 118.

59. Thurot, "Notices et extraits," pp. 171—76.

60. Lanfranc *Liber de corpore et sanguine Domine* 7 (PL 150:417).

61. Leclercq, *Love of Learning,* pp. 77—83.

62. Knowles, *Evolution of Medieval Thought,* p. 99.

63. Southern, "Lanfranc and Berengar," pp. 35, 46; *Saint Anselm,* pp. 22—23, 25.

64. For the following two paragraphs, see Marcia L. Colish, "St. Anselm's Philosophy of Language Reconsidered," *Anselm Studies,* in press, and the literature cited there; Gillian R. Evans, "*Inopes verborum sunt latini:* Technical Terms in the Writings of St.

Anselm and Some Commentators," *Archives d'histoire doctrinale et littéraire du moyen âge* 43 (1976): 113–34.

65. In addition to the citations in Colish, "Anselm's Philosophy of Language," see Marcia L. Colish, "The Stoic Theory of Verbal Signification and the Problem of Lies and False Statements from Antiquity to St. Anselm," in *L'archéologie du signe,* ed. Lucie Brind'Amour and Eugene Vance, pp. 38–41; Howard L. Dazeley and Wolfgang L. Gombocz, "Interpreting Anselm as a Logician," *Synthese* 40 (1979): 71–96; Evans, "The Secure Technician," pp. 2, 11–14, 21; Desmond Paul Henry, *Medieval Logic and Metaphysics,* pp. 56–88; M. B. Pranger, "Masters of Suspense: Argumentation and Imagination in Anselm, Bernard, and Calvin," *Assays* 1 (1981): 21–27; Eileen Flanigan Serene, "Anselm's *Philosophical Fragments*: A Critical Examination," (Ph.D. diss., Cornell University, 1974). G. Stanley Kane, "*Fides quaerens intellectum* in Anselm's Thought," *Scottish Journal of Theology* 26 (1973): 50–62, argues that this propensity is more marked in Anselm's later than his earlier works, which conclusion is not borne out by the evidence.

66. Anselm *De grammatico* 21.

67. Anselm *De veritate* praefatio.

68. Anselm *Ep.* 208.

69. Eadmer *Life of Anselm* (trans. Southern, p. 28).

70. Filliatre, *La philosophie de saint Anselme,* pp. 18, 147–61; Hunt, "Studies on Priscian," pp. 214–19; Desmond Paul Henry, *Commentary on "De grammatico";* "Saint Anselm's 'De grammatico,'" *Philosophical Quarterly* 10 (1960): 115–26; *The "De grammatico" of St. Anselm;* "Why 'Grammaticus'?," *Archivum latinitatis medii aevi* 28:2–3 (1958): 165–80; Southern, *Saint Anselm,* pp. 14–16; Thurot, "Notices et extraits," p. 166. There are, however, scholars who see the *De gram.* as an exclusively logical work. See Perino, *La dottrina trinitaria,* p. 17 n.15; Jean Rivière, "Saint Anselme logicien," *Recherches de sciences religieuses* 17 (1937): 306–15.

71. Anselm *De gram.* 1.

72. Boethius *In Cat. Arist.* 1.

73. Anselm *De gram.* 13.

74. Ibid., 9, 18.

75. Ibid., 18.

76. Ibid., 12, 15.

77. Anselm *Philosophical Fragments* 23.1–25.1 (ed. Southern and Schmitt, *Memorials of St. Anselm*). This text replaces the earlier edition by Schmitt in *Beiträge,* 33:3.

78. *De potestate et impotentia* 24.16 (trans. Hopkins and Richardson, *Anselm of Canterbury,* 2:4). All Anselm quotations in English, unless otherwise indicated, will be taken from this translation.

79. Ibid., 27.6.

80. Ibid., 34.16.

81. *De ver.* praefatio.

82. Ibid., 1.

83. Martin Grabmann, *Die Geschichte der scholastischen Methode*, 1:314, 320.

84. *De ver.* 2. The first scholar to notice the importance of Anselm's analysis of rectitude in the *De ver.* for his proof of the existence of God has been Étienne Gilson, "Sens et nature de l'argument de saint Anselme," *Archives d'histoire doctrinale et littéraire du moyen âge* 9 (1934): 5–51. Gilson has been followed by Miller, "The Ontological Argument," pp. 341–49. More recently rectitude has been studied as a general key not only to the *De ver.* but also to Anselm's other works. The leading study of this theme is Robert Pouchet, *La rectitudo chez saint Anselme*. See also Donald F. Duclow, "Structure and Meaning in Anselm's *De veritate*," *American Benedictine Review* 26 (1975): 408–9; George S. Heyer, Jr., "*Rectitudo* in the Theology of St. Anselm," (Ph.D. diss., Yale University, 1963); G. Söhngen, "Rectitudo bei Anselm von Canterbury als Oberbegriff von Wahrheit und Gerechtigkeit," in *Sola ratione*, pp. 71–77; Thomas F. Torrance, "The Ethical Implications of Anselm's *De veritate*," *Theologische Zeitschrift* 24 (1968): 309–19.

85. *De ver.* 9.

86. Ibid., 3.

87. Ibid., 4.

88. Ibid., 5.

89. Ibid., 6.

90. Ibid., 7.

91. Ibid., 8.

92. Ibid., 9–12.

93. Ibid., 13.

94. Ibid.

95. Cf. on the contrary, Filliatre, *La philosophie de saint Anselme*, p. 170; Heyer, "Rectitudo," p. 29.

96. Richard McKeon, trans. and ed., *Selections from Medieval Philosophers*, 1:145. See also Barth, *Anselm*, pp. 15 ff.; Filliatre, *La philosophie de saint Anselme*, pp. 435 ff.; Grabmann, *Geschichte*, 1:262–63; Heyer, "Rectitudo," pp. 88 ff., 120 ff.; Gerald B. Phelan, *The Wisdom of Saint Anselm*, pp. 41–42; Vignaux, *Philosophy in the Middle Ages*, pp. 38, 40–41. On the other hand, Copleston, *History of Philosophy*, 2:164, sees only the intellectual implications of rectitude. Anselm explores further the correlation between love and knowledge and their mutual end in beatitude in *Cur deus homo* 2.1.

97. Anselm *Monologion* 1.

98. Anselm *Proslogion* 33; *Contra Gaunilonem* 1, 5.

99. Vignaux, *Philosophy in the Middle Ages*, p. 36.

100. Ibid., p. 40.

101. Knowles, *Evolution of Medieval Thought*, pp. 101–2.

102. Heyer, "Rectitudo," p. 85.

103. A.-M. Jacquin, "Les 'rationes necessariae' de saint Anselme," *Mélanges Mandonnet*, 2:68, 72–73.

104. Ibid., pp. 76, 78; Phelan, *Wisdom of St. Anselm*, pp. 29–32; MacIntyre, "Premises and Conclusions," in *Spicilegium Beccense*, 1:100.

105. *Cur deus homo* 1.10.

106. Ibid., 2.22.

107. *Pros.* prooemium.

108. Anselm *Epistola de incarnatione verbi prior recensio* 2, 4, 11; *Epistola de incarnatione verbi* 1. Precisely the same argument is offered by Saint Bernard and his disciple, William of Saint Thierry, in their objections to Peter Abelard's Trinitarian doctrine at the Council of Sens in 1142. See William of Saint Thierry *Disputatio adversus Petrum Abaelardum ad Gaufridum Carnotensem et Bernardum* 2; *Disputatio catholicorum patrum adversus dogmata Petri Abaelardi* 1 (PL 180).

109. Anselm *Ep.* 129; *Ep. de inc. verb.* 4.

110. *Epistola . . . prior recensio* 10; *Ep. de inc. verb.* 4–5.

111. *Epistola . . . prior recensio* 4. The translation is mine.

112. Ibid., 4; *Ep. de inc. verb.* 1.

113. *Ep. de inc. verb.* 1.

114. Anselm *Ep.* 136.

115. Grabmann, *Geschichte*, 1:282; Desmond Paul Henry, "The Proslogion Proofs," *Philosophical Quarterly* 5 (1955): 147–51; Heyer, "Rectitudo," pp. 80 ff.; Knowles, *Evolution of Medieval Thought*, p. 105; Leclercq, *Love of Learning*, pp. 211–15; Southern, *Saint Anselm*, pp. 6–7, 47–49; "St. Anselm and His English Pupils," *Mediaeval and Renaissance Studies* 1 (1941–43): 29; Vignaux, *Philosophy in the Middle Ages*, pp. 39, 41–42; Gustave Weigel and Arthur G. Madden, *Religion and the Knowledge of God*, pp. 114, 115, 116–17.

116. Weigel and Madden, *Knowledge of God*, p. 117.

117. *Cur deus homo* praefatio. The interpolation is that of the translators.

118. Ibid., 1.1.

119. A similar statement is made in ibid., 1.25, where Boso declares: "I have not come for you to remove from me doubts about my faith but for you to show me the rational basis of my certainty."

120. Ibid., 2.13. See J. Bayart, "The Concept of Mystery according to St. Anselm of Canterbury," *Recherches de théologie ancienne et médiévale* 9 (1937): 165–66.

121. *Cur deus homo* 1.3, 1.10, 1.12, 2.8.

122. Ibid., 1.4.

123. Ibid., 1.1.

124. Ibid., 2.17. Also noted by Bayart, "Concept of Mystery;" Jacquin, "Les 'rationes necessariae,'" p. 70; Vignaux, *Philosophy in the Middle Ages*, p. 38.

125. Hartman, "Prolegomena," pp. 646, 647; Koyré, *L'idée de Dieu*, pp. 24–26; Southern, *Saint Anselm*, p. 30.

126. Heyer, "Rectitudo," pp. 80 ff.; Vignaux, *Philosophy in the Middle Ages,* p. 39.

127. *Cur deus homo* 1.1, 2.1, 2.9, 2.22. See also Grabmann, *Geschichte,* 1:283, 293 ff.; Jacquin, "Les 'rationes necessariae,' " p. 70; Weigel and Madden, *Knowledge of God,* p. 116.

128. The most extensive example is in *Cur deus homo* 1.9.

129. Ibid., 1.24.

130. Evans, *Anselm and Talking about God,* pp. 138, 172, 197; Hopkins, *Companion,* pp. 40–44; Jacquin, "Les 'rationes necessariae,' " p. 71. There has been some confusion on this point, to which Anselm himself contributes. Despite his clear statements in *Cur deus homo* to the effect that he is addressing nonbelievers as well as believers, his foil in the dialogue, Boso, is a Christian. Although Boso attempts to take the part of the man who will not believe unless he is convinced by reason (see for example, 1.10), he is also, and more frequently, found in the role of the believer seeking to understand his faith (see for example, 1.1). As far as scholarly comment on the intended intramural impact of Anselmian argument goes, Weigel and Madden, *Knowledge of God,* pp. 114, 116, think that the force of the proof remains even if faith departs; and Heyer, "Rectitudo," p. 74, thinks that the nonbeliever's willingness to listen testifies to an incipient faith on his part. We do not find anything in Anselm to support either of these interpretations.

131. Southern, *Saint Anselm,* pp. 32–33.

132. *Mon.* prologus.

133. *Pros.* prooemium.

134. Ibid. On the importance of meditation as a mental technique and the changes in the meaning of the term in the eleventh and twelfth centuries, see Southern, *Saint Anselm,* pp. 53–54.

135. *Ep. de inc. verb.* 6. The interpolation is the translators'.

136. Anselm *Ep.* 83.

137. Eadmer *Life of Anselm* 1.19 (trans. Southern, p. 29). Southern, p. 29 n.3, considers this an accurate assessment of Anselm's intention.

138. Ibid., 1.19.

139. Ordericus Vitalis *Eccl. hist.* 4.2.245. The point that the *Mon.* and *Pros.* need to be read as essays in Trinitarian theology has also been made by Henri de Lubac, *Recherches dans la foi,* p. 112; Paul Vignaux, "La méthode de saint Anselme dans le *Monologion* et le *Proslogion,*" *Aquinas* 8 (1965): 110–29; "Structure et sens du *Monologion,*" *Revue des sciences philosophiques et théologiques* 31 (1947): 192–212.

140. *Mon.* prologus.

141. Ibid.

142. Grabmann, *Geschichte,* 1:284 ff.; Heyer, "Rectitudo," pp. 67–69; Southern, *Saint Anselm,* p. 50; Vignaux, *Philosophy in the Middle Ages,* pp. 36, 38; "Structure et sens du *Monologion,*" p. 197.

143. Anselm *Ep.* 72.

144. *Mon.* prologus.

145. Anselm *Ep.* 77.

146. *De ver.* 1. As Southern, *Saint Anselm*, p. 32, points out, definitions play an important role in Anselm's major works.

147. Evans, *Anselm and Talking about God*, pp. 44–49; Heyer, "Rectitudo," p. 71.

148. Vignaux, "Structure et sens," pp. 200–201.

149. *Mon.* prologus.

150. Ibid.

151. Ibid., 4, 6, 8, 22.

152. Ibid., 1.

153. *Pros.* prooemium. The dual function of the *Pros.* has also been noted by Southern, *Saint Anselm*, p. 63.

154. *Ep. de inc. verb.* 6.

155. *Pros.* prooemium. The fact that Anselm is providing one argument in the *Pros.* and that it is developed throughout the work and not merely in chapters 2–4 has been restated recently by de Lubac, *Recherches dans la foi*, p. 112; Evans, *Anselm and Talking about God*, pp. 44–49.

156. *Pros.* 1.

157. *Mon.* prologus.

158. Ibid.

159. Ibid., 1. The interpolation is the translators'.

160. Ibid., 10, 21, 29, 33, 47–50, 59–60, 62, 66–67, 70; *Pros.* 6–7, 13.

161. *Mon.* 11–12, 15–16, 22, 26, 28, 29, 36, 38, 64–65; *Pros.* 15. Noted by de Lubac, *Recherches dans la foi*, pp. 81–124; Evans, *Anselm and Talking about God*, pp. 34–35.

162. *Pros.* 27.

163. Ibid., 17.

164. *Mon.* 55. I have changed the translation and puncutation of this passage slightly. Vignaux, "Structure et sens," pp. 200–201, points out that superlatives in Anselm do not express God substantially, but refer to the relationship between God and not-God. Heyer, "Rectitudo," p. 71, holds that Anselmian statements do not refer to God substantially unless they are in the negative, a point which we find contrary to Anselm.

165. *Mon.* 66–70. See also *Ep. de inc. verb.* 16.

166. *Mon.* 10, 31, 62.

167. Ibid., 1.

168. Ibid., 1.

169. Ibid., 1–3.

170. Ibid., 4.

171. Ibid., 6. I have changed the translation slightly. Noted also by Vignuax, "Structure et sens," p. 202.

172. *Mon.* 8.

173. Ibid., 9–10, 13–14.

174. Ibid., 11–12.

175. Ibid., 15. I have changed the punctuation slightly.

176. Ibid., 15.

177. Ibid., 16–17.

178. Ibid., 18.

179. Ibid., 19.

180. Ibid., 21.

181. Ibid., 22–23.

182. Ibid., 22.

183. Ibid., 25.

184. Ibid., 26.

185. Ibid., 28.

186. Ibid., 26. I have changed "it" to "He" in this translation. The interpolation is the translators'.

187. Ibid., 29, 30, 33, 44.

188. Ibid., 31, 35, 37.

189. Ibid., 47–63.

190. Ibid., 36.

191. Ibid., 38–43.

192. Ibid., 63, 65.

193. Ibid., 66–72.

194. Ibid., 74–76, 78.

195. Ibid., 79.

196. Ibid., 80.

197. It has frequently been suggested that the *Pros.* proof is Augustinian because Anselm's name of God resembles similar formulae found in Augustine's works. Augustine, however, cannot be thought of as Anselm's only probable source on this point. The most detailed treatment of the ancient and early medieval background is Giuseppi Cenacchi, *Il pensiero filosofico di Anselmo d'Aosta.* See also Hopkins, *Companion,* p. 19; Schmitt, ed., *Opera omnia,* by Anselm 1:102; Jules Vergnes, "Les sources de l'argument de saint Anselme," *Revue des sciences religieuses* 4 (1929): 576–79. For the Stoic background of Anselm's use of *nihil* in this formula, see M. Baldassari, "Lo stoicismo antico e l'argomento ontologico," *Rivista di filosofia neo-scolastica* 63 (1971): 391–418, 547–74.

198. *Pros.* 2.

199. Ibid., 2.

200. Ibid., 2.

201. Ibid., 2. According to Southern, *Saint Anselm,* pp. 60–61, and "St. Anselm and His English Pupils," p. 30, the fool uses words without understanding what they mean. It would be more accurate to say that the fool uses words with only a limited truth.

202. *Pros.* 4.

203. Ibid., 3.

204. Ibid., 5.

205. Ibid., 6.

206. Ibid., 7. For a brief summary of other loci where Anselm deals with these questions see Colish, "Anselm's Philosophy of Language."

207. *Pros.* 8–11.

208. Ibid., 12, 18.

209. Ibid., 13.

210. Ibid., 14.

211. Ibid., 15.

212. Anton C. Pegis, "St. Anselm and the Argument of the Proslogion," *Mediaeval Studies* 28 (1966): 248–51.

213. *Pros.* 16.

214. Ibid., 17.

215. Ibid., 19, 21.

216. Ibid., 20.

217. Ibid., 18.

218. Ibid., 22–23.

219. Ibid., 24–26.

220. This point has been made by Henri Bouillard, "La preuve de Dieu et son interpretation par Karl Barth," in *Spicilegium Beccense* 1:191–207; Evans, *Anselm and Talking about God*, pp. 44–49; Pegis, "St. Anselm," pp. 228–67, although none of these scholars relates the idea specifically to the concept of rectitude.

221. Southern, in Eadmer, *Life of Anselm*, p. 31 n.2.

222. Gaunilo *Pro insipiente* 2 (ed. Schmitt, 1).

223. Ibid., 4.

224. Ibid., 6.

225. Ibid., 7.

226. *Contra Gaun.* 1.

227. Ibid.

228. Ibid. Weigel and Madden, *Knowledge of God*, pp. 118–19, are correct in pointing out that Anselm addresses Gaunilo, not as a natural philosopher, but as a Christian. However, they are misleading in saying that he grounds his argument on faith and authority; this overlooks the fact that he argues by necessary reasons in the *Contra Gaun.* Jasper Hopkins, "Anselm's Debate with Gaunilo" in *Anselm of Canterbury*, by Anselm, vol. 4, chap. 4, thinks that Anselm misconstrued Gaunilo's criticism as much as Gaunilo misunderstood Anselm's proof, in that Gaunilo had a purely formal conception of the meaning of the term *intelligere* and used it only with reference to the internal semantic cogency of the *Pros.* formula. This argument is correct for part of Gaunilo's objection, but not for the part where he juxtaposes intramental and extramental verifiability.

229. *Contra Gaun.* 1.

230. Ibid.

231. Ibid., 2, 7–9.

232. Ibid., 3.

233. Ibid., 4.

234. Ibid., 5.

235. Ibid., 6.

236. Ibid., 10.

237. Gillian R. Evans, *Anselm and a New Generation* is the best study of this subject. See also Southern, *Saint Anselm*, pp. 203–17; "St. Anselm and His English Pupils," pp. 3–34.

238. Schmitt, 1:3.

239. Ibid., 1:169.

240. Ibid., 1:91.

241. Evans, *Anselm and a New Generation; Anselm and Talking about God*, p. 202.

242. Hunt, "Studies on Priscian," pp. 220 ff.; Thurot, "Notices et extraits," *Notices et extraits*, 22, pt. 2:129–30.

243. Thurot, "Notices et extraits," pp. 59, 212–14.

244. Grabmann, "Die Entwicklung," *Mittelalterliches Geistesleben*, 1:109–13.

245. Anselm of Besate *Rhetorimachia*, in *Monumenta Germaniae Historica: Quellen zur Geistesgeschichte des Mittelalters*, 2, bk. 2:61–74 (ed. Manitius).

246. Anselm of Besate *Rhet*. p. 61.

247. Anselm of Besate *Epistola ad Droconem magistrum et condiscipulos de logica disputatione in Gallia habita*, in *Rhetorimachia, Monumenta Germaniae Historica*, 2, bk. 2:181.

248. *Ep. ad Droc.; Rhet*. 1.3.

249. *Rhet*. 1.9.

250. Ibid., 1.14.

251. Ibid., 1.15.

252. Ibid., 1.5.

253. Ibid., 2.4, 2.8, 2.12.

254. Anselm of Besate *Epistola ad Drogonem phylosophum*, in *Rhetorimachia, Monumenta Germaniae Historica*, 2, bk. 2:103.

255. Edgar de Bruyne, *Études d'esthétique médiévale*, 2:166, 172 n.2; Grabmann, "Die Entwicklung," *Mittelalterliches Geistesleben*, 1:109–13; Richard McKeon, "Rhetoric in the Middle Ages," *Speculum* 17 (1942): 26–27.

256. M.-D. Chenu, "Grammaire et théologie aux douzième et treizième siècles," *Archives d'histoire doctrinale et littéraire du moyen âge* 10 (1935): 13.

257. Jean Jolivet, *Arts du langage et théologie chez Abélard;* see also Baldwin, *Medieval Rhetoric*, pp. 91–93; Meyrick H. Carré, *Realists and Nominalists*, pp. 42–65; McKeon, "Rhetoric in the Middle Ages," p. 22.

258. Chenu, "Grammaire et théologie," pp. 10–17.

259. Ibid., pp. 19–20.

Chapter Three

1. See above, pp. 106–9. The best general study of the logic of this period is L. M. de Rijk, *Logica Modernorum*, vol. 2, pt. 1. An excellent recent bibliographical guide is A. J. Ashworth, *The Tradition of Medieval Logic and Speculative Grammar*. For the relations between logic and other disciplines, see M.-D. Chenu, "Grammaire et théologie aux douzième et treizième siècles," *Archives d'histoire doctrinale et littéraire du moyen âge* 10 (1935): 19–21; Richard McKeon, "Rhetoric in the Middle Ages," *Speculum* 17 (1942): 22–23; Brother S. Robert, "Rhetoric and Dialectic according to the First Latin Commentary on the Rhetoric of Aristotle," *New Scholasticism* 31 (1957): 484–98.

2. De Rijk, *Logica Modernorum*, vol. 2, pt. 1:124; also chaps. 2, 16. On supposition theory and terminist logic in general, see Philotheus Boehner, *Medieval Logic*, pp. 32–36; Thomas Gilby, *Barbara Celarent*, pp. 50–53; Ernest A. Moody, *Truth and Consequence in Medieval Logic*, pp. 5, 18–25; John E. Murdoch, "Propositional Analysis in Fourteenth-Century Natural Philosophy," *Synthese* 40 (1979): 117–18; Alfons Nehring, "A Note on Functional Linguistics in the Middle Ages," *Traditio* 9 (1953): 433–34; Jan Pinborg, "The English Contribution to Logic before Ockham," *Synthese* 40 (1979): 19–22; C. Prantl, *Geschichte der Logik im Abendlande*, 3:10–18. Prantl seems to be alone in the view that supposition theory derives from the Byzantine philosopher Psellus.

3. De Rijk, *Logica Modernorum*, vol. 2, pt. 1, chap. 2; Sten Ebbesen, "The Dead Man Is Alive," *Synthese* 40 (1979): 43–49; Marjorie Grene, *A Portrait of Aristotle*, pp. 69–70; Gilby, *Barbara Celarent*, p. 32; Ernest A. Moody, "The Medieval Contribution to Logic," *Collected Papers*, pp. 374–76; *Truth and Consequence*, pp. 1, 14–15; Jan Pinborg, *Die Entwicklung der Sprachtheorie im Mittelalter*, chap. 1; "Die Logik der Modistae," *Studia mediewistyczne* 16 (1975): 39–60.

4. Pinborg, "English Contribution," p. 21.

5. Ebbesen, "The Dead Man Is Alive," pp. 47–49; Pinborg, "English Contribution," pp. 21–22; "Die Logik der Modistae," pp. 45–59.

6. Boehner, *Medieval Logic*, p. 4; Prantl, *Geschichte*, 3:92.

7. Étienne Gilson, *A History of Christian Philosophy in the Middle Ages*, pp. 318–19; Gilby, *Barbara Celarent*, pp. 5–6, 33.

8. Boehner, *Medieval Logic*, pp. 19–26, 77–78; Moody, *Truth and Consequence*, pp. 3–5; Prantl, *Geschichte*, 3:19–26.

9. Boehner, *Medieval Logic*, p. 5; Prantl, *Geschichte*, 3:92.

10. Alessandro Ghisalberti, "La fondazione della teologia razionale di s. Tommaso d'Aquino," *Cultura e scuola* 13 (1974): 179–80; L. Lachance, "Saint Thomas dans l'histoire de la logique," in *Études d'histoire littéraire et doctrinale du treizième siècle*, 1:61–103; Battista Mondin, "La logica di s. Tommaso d'Aquino," *Rivista di filosofia neo-scolastica* 60 (1968): 261–71; Michael Ryan, "The Notion and Uses of Dialectic in

St. Thomas Aquinas," (Ph.D. diss., University of Notre Dame, 1962); Robert W. Schmidt, *The Domain of Logic.*

11. Moody, *Truth and Consequence,* pp. 5–6.

12. Fernand van Steenberghen, *Aristote en occident,* pp. 62–63, 98–102.

13. M.-D. Chenu, *Introduction à l'étude de saint Thomas d'Aquin,* pp. 173–75.

14. Boehner, *Medieval Logic,* pp. 2–5.

15. Chenu, *Introduction,* pp. 175–92; Martin Grabmann, "Die Aristoteleskommentar des heiligen Thomas von Aquin," *Mittelalterliches Geistesleben,* 1:266–313; Fernand van Steenberghen, *La philosophie au treizième siècle,* pp. 430–83; James A. Weisheipl, *Friar Thomas d'Aquino,* pp. 263–90.

16. Chenu, *Introduction,* pp. 192–96.

17. George Lindbeck, "Participation and Existence in the Interpretation of St. Thomas Aquinas," *Franciscan Studies* 17 (1957): 108. See also David Knowles, *The Historical Context of the Philosophical Works of St. Thomas Aquinas;* Anton C. Pegis, *The Middle Ages and Philosophy,* pp. viii–xiv, 26–29, 43–60, 69–81; *St. Thomas and Philosophy,* pp. 19, 26–46, 80–82; Josef Pieper, *Introduction to Thomas Aquinas,* pp. 156–59; *The Silence of St. Thomas,* pp. 69–71; Paul Vignaux, *Philosophy in the Middle Ages,* pp. 116–17.

18. Arthur Little, *The Platonic Heritage of Thomism;* Josef Santeler, *Der Platonismus in der Erkenntnislehre des heiligen Thomas von Aquin.* R. J. Henle, *Saint Thomas and Platonism,* cites Platonic epistemological texts mainly to show how extensive Thomas's rejection of them was.

19. Meyrick H. Carré, *Realists and Nominalists,* pp. 79–81, 86; Bernard Lonergan, "The Concept of *Verbum* in the Writings of St. Thomas Aquinas," *Theological Studies* 7 (1946): 349–92; 8 (1947): 35–79, 404–44; 10 (1949): 3–40, 359–93; Richard McKeon, "Thomas Aquinas' Doctrine of Knowledge and Its Historical Setting," *Speculum* 3 (1928): 425–44; Bruno Nardi, *Studi di filosofia medievale,* pp. 193–207; Gaston Rabeau, *Species, verbum: L'activité intellectuelle élémentaire selon s. Thomas d'Aquin;* K. E. Skysgaard, "La connaissance humaine d'après Saint Thomas d'Aquin," *Classica et medievalia* 2, no. 1 (1939): 86–120; Edward F. Talbot, *Knowledge and Object,* pp. 33–49; Viktor Warnach, "Erkennen und Sprechen bei Thomas von Aquin: Ein Deutungsversuch seiner Lehre auf ihrem geistesgeschichtlichen Hintergrund," *Divus Thomas* 15 (1937): 189–218, 263–90; 16 (1938): 161–96; "Das äussere Sprechen und seine Funktionen nach der Lehre des hl. Thomas von Aquin," *Divus Thomas* 16 (1938): 393–419; Paul Wilpert, *Das Problem der Wahrheitssicherung bei Thomas von Aquin;* Paul Wyser, "Die wissenschaftstheoretischen Quaest. V. u. VI in Boethium de Trinitate des hl. Thomas von Aquin," *Divus Thomas* 25 (1947): 437–85; 26 (1948): 74–98. An unusual entry in the class of philosophical comparisons is Alfons Hufnagel, *Intuition und Erkenntnis nach Thomas von Aquin,* who thinks that Thomas was a proto-Husserlian. On Aristotle, see John Herman Randall, Jr., *Aristotle,* pp. 5, 7, 98.

20. The most exaggerated example of this tendency is Pierre Rousselot, *L'intellec-*

tualisme de saint Thomas, especially p. 22. See also Ritamary Bradley, "The Mirror of Truth according to St. Thomas," *Modern Schoolman* 31 (1954): 314; Peter Hoenen, *Reality and Judgment according to St. Thomas;* Hugo Lang, *Die Lehre des hl. Thomas von Aquin von der Gewissheit des übernatürlichen Glaubens,* pp. 18–19; William W. Meissner, "Some Aspects of the *Verbum* in the Texts of St. Thomas Aquinas," *Modern Schoolman* 36 (1958): 1–30; Gerald B. Phelan, "Verum sequitur esse rerum," *Mediaeval Studies* 1 (1939): 17.

21. M. C. D'Arcy, *Thomas Aquinas,* pp. 76–77, 81–84, 88–92, 102–3, 216–17, 224–26; F. C. Copleston, *A History of Philosophy,* 2, pt. 2:109–12; Étienne Gilson, *The Christian Philosophy of St. Thomas Aquinas,* pp. 218–22, 223–34; *The Philosophy of St. Thomas Aquinas,* pp. 57, 250, 263–74; Joseph Moreau, *De la connaissance selon s. Thomas,* chaps. 4–7. The following discussion is based on these references.

22. Thomas Aquinas *Compendium theologiae* 1.37–38, 1.40 (ed. Mandonnet, *Opuscula omnia*); *In duodecim libros Metaphysicorum Aristoteles expositio VII* lect. l.c. 1253 (ed. Cathala); *Quaestiones disputatae de potentia* 1. q.1. a.1. ad 10, q.2. a.1 (ed. Spiazzi et al., *Quaestiones disputatae*); *Quaestiones disputatae de veritate* q.1. a.11–12 (ed. Spiazzi et al., *Quaestiones disputatae*); *Summa theologiae* Ia. q.17. a.2, q.85. a.1 (*Opera omnia*).

23. Cf. above, pp. 50–51.

24. Meissner, "Some Aspects of the *Verbum,*" pp. 1–30; Lonergan, "The Concept of the *Verbum,*" *Theological Studies* 7 (1946): 349–92, 8 (1947): 35–79.

25. Robert H. Ayers, *Language, Logic, and Reason,* pp. 91–93; Benoît Garceau, *Judicium,* pp. 156–59.

26. This point has been brought out clearly by Edward L. Rousseau, "St. Anselm and St. Thomas: A Reconsideration," *New Scholasticism* 54 (1980): 1–24.

27. *De pot.* 1. q.1. a.1. ad 6, q.3. a.17. ad 27–29; *De ver.* q.1. a.1–3, 8–9, 11–12; *In II Met.* lect. 2. c.298; *In IV Met.* lect. 17. c.736; *In IX Met.* lect. 11. c.1896–97; *Scriptum super libros Sententiarum magistri Petri Lombardi episcopi parisiensis* I. d.2. q.1. a.3. ad 2 (ed. Mandonnet and Moos); *Quaestio disputata de anima* a.3. ad 1 (ed. Spiazzi et al., *Quaestiones disputatae*); *ST* Ia. q.5. a.2, q.10. a.3. ad 3, q.16. a.1–2, 5, q.17. a.1, q.21. a.2. On the role of judgment and on the object as the criterion of correct judgments about it, see Ayers, *Language, Logic, and Reason,* pp. 82–90; Garceau, *Judicium;* John Nijenhuis, "The Structure of the Judgment according to Aquinas," *Carmelus* 19 (1972): 3–66; Joseph Owens, "Judgment and Truth in Aquinas," *Mediaeval Studies* 32 (1970): 138–58; Francis Martin Tyrell, *The Role of Assent in Judgment,* pp. 8–21, chap. 3. Xavier Maquart, "La causalité du signe: Réflexions sur la valeur philosophique d'une explication théologique," *Revue thomiste* 32, n.s. 10 (1927): 40–60, notes that Thomas sees signs as measured by their significata, but he thinks that this is relevant primarily to sacraments rather than to theology as a whole or to general epistemology.

28. *De ente et essentia* 2 (ed. Boyer); *In I Met.* lect. 1. c.29, 34; *In III Met.* lect. 6. c.400; *In VII Met.* lect. 2. c.1537, 1541; *ST* IIaIIae. q.9. a.1. ad 1.

29. *De pot.* 1. q.3. a.1. ad 6; *ST* IIaIIae. q.8. a.1, q.9. a.2. See also Phelan, "Verum sequitur esse rerum," pp. 13–14; John K. Ryan, "The Problem of Truth," in *Essays in Thomism,* ed. Robert E. Brennan, pp. 72–73.

30. *Comp. theol.* 2.18; *Summa contra gentiles* 4.1.3 *(Opera omnia).*

31. *De anima* a.16; *In II Met.* lect. 1. c.282–85; *SCG* 3.41–43, 45; *ST* Ia. q.88. a.1–2; IaIIae. q.3. a.6.

32. James F. Anderson, "Is God's Knowledge Scientific? A Study in Thomism," in *An Étienne Gilson Tribute,* ed. C. J. O'Neil, pp. 4–6; Randall, *Aristotle,* p. 98.

33. See, for example, *De ver.* q.19. a.1.

34. See, for example, *In VII Met.* lect. 2. c.1300–1305; the fact that this claim would be impossible to verify if man were confined to a way of knowing from effects to causes has been noted by Victor Preller, *Divine Science,* p. 73, although his study is confined to theological knowledge and he overemphasizes its limits in Thomas.

35. Martin Grabmann, *Thomas Aquinas,* pp. 72–73, 82.

36. *De pot.* 1. q.3. a.17. ad 29.

37. This point has been made by such eminent authorities as Jacques Maritain, *The Angelic Doctor,* p. 51; and Pegis, *The Middle Ages and Philosophy,* pp. viii–xiv, 26–29, 43–60, 69–81; *St. Thomas and Philosophy,* pp. 18–19, 26–46, 80–82; *Saint Thomas and the Greeks,* pp. 1–2. It has been restated recently and pointedly by Inos Biffi, "Prospettive e articolazioni della 'sacra doctrina' nei 'principia' e nel prologo all' 'In Boethium de trinitate' di san Tommaso d'Aquino," *La scuola cattolica* 100 (1972): 290–312; Per Erik Persson, *Sacra doctrina;* James A. Weisheipl, "The Meaning of *sacra doctrina* in *Summa theologiae* I, q.1," *Thomist* 38 (1974): 54–80.

38. Cf. Gilson, *Christian Philosophy of Thomas Aquinas,* p. 9, where he says that conclusions not presupposing revelation may be abstracted from their contexts and treated philosophically, and p. 14, where he states that Thomas was not interested in safeguarding the autonomy of philosophy, but in explaining how theology could use it without destroying the unity of theology; and his *History of Christian Philosophy,* p. 365, where he says: "Thomas changed the water of philosophy into the wine of theology. Thomas always considered himself a theologian."

39. Copleston, *History of Philosophy,* 2, pt. 2:36. This point has been studied in detail by Henri de Lubac, *Augustinisme et théologie moderne,* pp. 136–281; and *Le mystère du surnaturel.* In the first volume, he treats the development of the idea of pure nature, its definition in the sixteenth and seventeenth centuries, and its implications for theologians at that time on the doctrines of man's natural desire for God, beatitude, and man's primal state. In the second volume, he treats the broad theological implications of the idea of pure nature in general.

40. *De pot.* 1. q.3. a.7; *Expositio super librum Boethii de trinitate* q.1. a.1. ad 2 (ed. Decker); *ST* Ia. q.79. a.4, q.89. a.1, q.105. a.3–4, q.117. a.1. ad 1; IaIIae. q.68. a.2, q.109. a.2.

41. *De anima* a.5. ad 6. Also noted by Persson, *Sacra doctrina,* pp. 21–22.

42. *De ver.* q.11. a.1; *ST* Ia. q.117. a.1.

43. Cf. Alberto Caturelli, *La doctrina agustiniana sobre el maestro;* Wilhelm Schneider, *Die Quaestiones Disputatae de Veritate des Thomas von Aquin in ihrer philosophiegeschichtlichen Beziehung zu Augustinus,* pp. 24–26. Thomas does not perceive this distinction between himself and Augustine. See *De ver.* q.11. a.1. ad 6.

44. *Comp. theol.* 1.129; *SCG* 1.60–62; Martin Grabmann, *The Interior Life of St. Thomas Aquinas,* p. 25; Phelan, "Verum sequitur esse rerum," p. 12; Ryan, "The Problem of Truth," p. 67; Schneider, *Die Quaestiones Disputatae,* pp. 6–15.

45. See above, pp. 78–81, 83–84, 88–89, 92–94, 99–100, 105–6.

46. *ST* IaIIae. q.109. a.1. See Ryan, "Notion and Uses of Dialectic," pp. 56–57, chap. 12.

47. *De ver.* q.3. a.1; *In I Sent.* prologus. See Bradley, "Mirror of Truth," pp. 311–12.

48. *SCG* 4.1.3.

49. Ibid., 3.56, 3.57.7, 3.57.9; *ST* IIIa. q.92. a.3.

50. Pieper, *Silence of St. Thomas,* pp. 57–67, 69–71. This point has been studied in detail by Preller, *Divine Science.*

51. *Comp. theol.* 1.3.18–36; *In Boeth. de trin.* prologus; *SCG* 1.3.2, 1.7.2, 2.2.4; *ST* Ia. q.12. a.12; IIaIIae. q.1. a.5. ad 3.

52. See, for example, *ST* Ia. q.2. a.2, q.88. a.3.

53. *In Boeth. de trin.* q.1. a.1. ad 7, a.2, a.4; *In I Sent.* d.2. q.1. a.4, d.3. q.1. a.4; *In III Sent.* d.24. a.3. sol.3; *SCG* 1.1, 1.3.2–3, 1.8.1, 3.38–39; *ST* IaIIae. q.3. a.6, a.8; IIaIIae. q.1. a.5, a.8. ad 1. See also Copleston, *History of Philosophy,* 2, pt. 2: 13–14, 29–31; Gilson, *Christian Philosophy of Thomas Aquinas,* p. 21; *History of Christian Philosophy,* pp. 366–67; *Philosophy of St. Thomas,* pp. 46–48; Grabmann, *Thomas Aquinas,* pp. 90–91; Ghislain Lafont, *Structures et méthode dans la Somme théologique de saint Thomas d'Aquin,* p. 493; Pieper, *Introduction,* pp. 147 ff.: Vignaux, *Philosophy in the Middle Ages,* pp. 123–26; Victor White, *Holy Teaching,* p. 11.

54. See in general, Lang, *Die Gewissheit des übernatürlichen Glaubens,* pp. 34–70, on faith.

55. *De ver.* q.14. a.2; *In III Sent.* d.23. q.3. a.1; *SCG* 3.151.2; *ST* IaIIae. q.62. a.3; IIaIIae. q.2. a.3. ad 2, a.9. ad 3.

56. *In II Met.* lect. 5. c.335–37; *In VI Met.* lect. 1. c.1149; *SCG* 1.3.1; Anthony A. Nemetz, "Logic and the Division of the Sciences in Aristotle and St. Thomas Aquinas," *Modern Schoolman* 33 (1956): 91–109.

57. *Comp. theol.* 1.1.104, 1.1.143, 1.1.149; *De ver.* q.14. a.10; *In Boeth. de trin.* q.6. a.4. ad 5; *SCG* 3.116, 3.118; *ST* Ia. q.12. a.4–5; IaIIae. q.4. a.1–2, q.5. a.6, q.6. a.2; IIaIIae. q.2. a.3.

58. See, on this comparison, *In Boeth. de trin.* q.1. a.1. ad 2, q.3. a.1. ad 4.

59. *SCG* 1.6.1, 3.54.9–13, 3.54.19; *ST* IIaIIae. q.9. a.1. ad 2, q.177, a.1.

60. *In III Sent.* d.23. q.2. a.2. sol.2. ad 3; *SCG* 1.6.1, 3.152.4, 3.154.20; *ST* IIaIIae. q.1. a.9, q.6. a.2.

61. *De anima* a.16. ad 3; *In Boeth. de trin.* q.1. a.2; *ST* IIaIIae. q.6. a.2. ad 1, q.8. a.2, q.9. a.1. ad 2, q.45. a.1. ad 2.

62. *De ver.* q.20. a.1, q.22. a.12; *SCG* 1.5.2; *ST* Ia. q.16. a.4. ad 1, q.82. a.4. See also D'Arcy, *Thomas Aquinas*, p. 130; Lang, *Die Gewissheit des übernatürlichen Glaubens,* pp. 52–53.

63. *In Boeth. de trin.* q.3. a.1. ad 4; *ST* IIaIIae. q.2. a.9. ad 2.

64. *SCG* 1.10–12; *ST* Ia. q.2. a.1.

65. *De ver.* q.14. a.2; *In III Sent.* d.23. q.2. a.2. sol.3. ad 1; *ST* IaIIae. q.67. a.4. ad 1; IIaIIae. q.2. a.1. ad 1, a.3. ad 3, a.5, q.4. a.1, a.8.

66. *De ver.* q.14. a.1; *In Boeth. de trin.* q.1. a.2; *In III Sent.* d.23. q.2. a.2. sol.1–3, d.24. a.1. sol.2; *ST* IIaIIae. q.2. a.9.

67. *In Boeth. de trin.* q.3. a.1. ad 4.

68. Ibid., q.3. a.1. ad 4; *ST* IIaIIae. q.2. a.9. ad 2.

69. *De ver.* q.14. a.3, a.5; *In III Sent.* d.23. q.3. a.1; *ST* IIaIIae. q.4. a.3.

70. M.-D. Chenu, "La psychologie de la foi dans la théologie du treizième siècle," in *Études d'histoire littéraire et doctrinale du treizième siècle,* pp. 163–91.

71. *Comp. theol.* 1.102, 1.106, 1.129; *De pot.* 1. q.1. a.3. ad 7, a.4. ad 5, a.5–7, q.2. a.3. ad 6, q.3. a.19; 2. q.5. a.2; *In III Sent.* d.1. q.1. a.1; *SCG* 1.84; *ST* Ia. q.25. a.3–4; IIIaIIae. q.14. a.4, q.16. a.4. ad 6.

72. Mary Annice Donovan, *The Henological Argument for the Existence of God in the Works of St. Thomas Aquinas;* L.-B. Geiger, *La participation dans la philosophie de s. Thomas d'Aquin,* pp. 152, 295, 360, 373; Gilson, *Christian Philosophy of Thomas Aquinas,* p. 81; *History of Christian Philosophy,* pp. 369–72; Frank R. Harrison, III, "Some Brief Remarks concerning the Quinque Viae of Saint Thomas," *Franciscan Studies* 21 (1961): 80–93; Charles A. Hart, "Participation and the Thomistic Five Ways," *New Scholasticism* 26 (1952): 266–82; Charles Lemaître, "Quarta Via: La preuve de l'existence de Dieu par les degrés de êtres," *Nouvelle revue théologique* 54 (1927): 321–39, 436–68; James B. Nugent, *The Fundamental Theistic Argument in the Metaphysical Doctrine of Saint Thomas Aquinas;* Joseph Owens, "The Conclusion of the *Prima Via*," *Modern Schoolman* 30 (1952–53): 33–53, 109–21, 203–16; "Aquinas and the Proof from the 'Physics,'" *Modern Schoolman* 28 (1966): 119–50; "Actuality in the 'Prima Via' of St. Thomas," *Modern Schoolman* 29 (1967): 26–46; "Immobility and Existence for Aquinas," *Modern Schoolman* 30 (1968): 22–46; E. Rolfes, "Zu dem Gottesbeweise des hl. Thomas aus den Stufen der Vollkommenheit," *Philosophisches Jahrbuch der Görres-Gesellschaft* 26 (1913): 146–59.

The third way has received the most attention from supporters of the proofs, with controversy focused on whether it is a physical or a metaphysical argument. A thorough review of the literature is provided by John F. X. Knasas, "Making Sense of the *Tertia via*," *New Scholasticism* 54 (1980): 476–511, who sees it as a physical proof. Others in the same camp include Joseph Owens, "'Cause of Necessity' in Aquinas' *Tertia via*," *Mediaeval Studies* 33 (1971): 21–45; and John M. Quinn, "The Third Way: A New Approach," *Thomist* 42 (1978): 50–68. Recent defenders of the proof as metaphysical include Anselmo Bianucci dell'Assunta, "La 'Tertia via' di s. Tommaso: Indagine metafisica," *Ephemerides carmeliticae* 16 (1965): 118–72 and Theodore Kondoleon, "The Third Way: 'Encore,'" *Thomist* 44 (1980): 325–56.

73. Mortimer J. Adler, "The Demonstration of God's Existence," *Thomist* 5 (1943): 188–218; Dennis Bonnette, *Aquinas' Proofs for God's Existence;* Patterson Brown, "St. Thomas' Doctrine of Necessary Being," *Philosophical Review* 73 (1964): 76–90; Thomas Kevin Connolly, "The Basis of the Third Proof for the Existence of God," *Thomist* 17 (1954): 280–349; Léon Elders, "Justification des 'cinq voies,'" *Revue thomiste* 61 (1961): 207–25; P. Geny, "À propos des preuves thomistes de l'existence de Dieu," *Revue de philosophie* 24 (1924): 575–601; C. Henry, "Histoire des preuves de l'existence de Dieu au moyen âge, jusqu'à la fin de l'apogée de la scholastique," *Revue thomiste* 19 (1911): 1–24, 141–58; Umberto degl'Innocenti, "L'esistencia di Dio nella prospettiva delle cinque vie de s. Tommaso," *Divinitas* 13 (1969): 77–85; Dermot O'Donoghue, "An Analysis of the *Tertia Via* of St. Thomas," *Irish Theological Quarterly* 20 (1953): 129–51; Joseph Owens, "Aquinas and the Five Ways," *Monist* 58 (1974): 16–35; Jean Paulus, "Le caractère métaphysique des preuves thomistes de l'existence de Dieu," *Archives d'histoire doctrinale et littéraire du moyen âge* 9 (1934): 143–53; José Maria Sánchez-Ruiz, *Las pruebas de la existencia de Dios en el Tomismo;* Matthew Schumacher, *The Knowableness of God;* Fernand van Steenberghen, "La problème de l'existence de Dieu dans le 'Scriptum super Sententiis' de saint Thomas," in *Studia mediaevalia,* pp. 331–49.

Most of the modern philosophers to whom these claims are addressed remain unconvinced. Among the most recent cases, see, for example, George A. Blair, "Another Look at St. Thomas' 'First Way,'" *International Philosophical Quarterly* 19 (1976): 301–14; Anthony Kenny, *The Five Ways;* Lubor Velecky, "'The Five Ways': Proofs of God's Existence?," *Monist* 58 (1974): 38–51.

74. Jan Salamucha, "The Proof 'Ex Motu' for the Existence of God: Logical Analysis of St. Thomas' Arguments," *New Scholasticism* 32 (1958): 334–72.

75. *Comp. theol.* 1.3.

76. *De pot.* 1. q.3. a.5.

77. *SCG* 1.2.3. Good background is provided by Weisheipl, *Friar Thomas,* pp. 130–33.

78. *SCG* 1.3.3.

79. Ibid., 1.3.4–6.

80. Ibid., 1.2.4, 1.2.7–8.

81. Ibid., 1.2.13.

82. Ibid., 1.2.9–12.

83. Ibid., 1.13.2.

84. Ibid., 4.1.

85. Cf. M. B. Crowe, "Saint Thomas against the Gentiles," *Irish Theological Quarterly* 29 (1962): 93–120, who considers the genre of the work problematical on the basis of its organization.

86. *ST* Ia. q. 1. a. 1. See also q. 2. a. 2; IIaIIae. q. 1. a. 5. ad 3.

87. Jean F. Bonnefoy, *La nature de la théologie selon saint Thomas d'Aquin,* pp. 72–79; M.-D. Chenu, *La théologie comme science au treizième siècle,* pp. 26–32; "Les 'Philosophes' dans la philosophie chrétienne médiévale," *Revue des sciences philosophiques et théologiques* 26 (1937): 27–40; P. Hadelin Hoffmans, "Roger Bacon: L'intuition mystique et la science," *Revue néoscolastique* 16 (1909): 370–97.

88. Antoninus Finili, "Is There a Philosophical Approach to God?," *Dominican Studies* 4 (1951): 86–87; Edward Sillem, *Ways of Thinking about God,* pp. 35–39; White, *Holy Teaching,* pp. 7–8; "The Prolegomena to the Five Ways," *Dominican Studies* 5 (1952): 134–58. In this latter work, White sees the didactic aim of the *Summa* as confined only to the training of apologists. Cf. Per Erik Persson, "La plan de la Somme théologique et le rapport 'Ratio-Revelatio,'" *Revue philosophique de Louvain* 56 (1958): 545, who sees no pedagogical importance in the work.

89. *ST* Ia. q. 1. a. 1.

90. Lafont, *Structures et méthode,* p. 41, sees no apologetic aim in the proofs.

91. *ST* Ia. q. 2. a. 1.

92. Ibid., Ia. q. 2. a. 3.

93. Ibid., Ia. q. 2. a. 2.

94. Ibid., Ia. q. 2. a. 1. Cf. *SCG* 1. 10–11.

95. Anton C. Pegis, "St. Anselm and the Argument of the Proslogion," *Mediaeval Studies* 28 (1966): 228–30, 261–67; Gustave Weigel and Arthur G. Madden, *Religion and the Knowledge of God,* p. 124.

96. Sillem, *Ways of Thinking about God,* p. 54, sees the proof for the existence of God as a form of Anselmian *fides quaerens intellectum.* While the *intellectus fidei* approach does pertain to Thomas's theology, as will be seen below, it does not apply to the proofs or to any of the truths about God that Thomas thinks can be known by natural reason.

97. *ST* IaIIae. q. 3. a. 6.

98. Ibid., IIaIIae. q. 2. a. 5, a. 10. ad 2.

99. *Comp. theol.* 2. 8–9; *SCG* 1. 7. 2, 1. 8. 1.

100. *De ver.* q. 24. a. 15; *ST* IaIIae. q. 109. a. 6, q. 112. a. 2.

101. *In Boeth. de trin.* q. 6. a. 3.

102. R. A. Markus, "A Note on the Meaning of the *Via,*" *Dominican Studies* 7 (1954): 241–45.

103. Excellent recent studies of this point include Biffi, "Prospettive e articola-zioni," pp. 290–312; Persson, *Sacra doctrina;* Weisheipl, "The Meaning of *sacra doctrina,*" pp. 49–80. Alexander M. Horváth, "Der wissenschaftliche Charakter der Apologetik," *Divus Thomas* 25 (1947): 29–52, 117–91, 345–408; Siegfried Neumann, *Gegenstand und Methode der theoretischen Wissenschaften nach Thomas von Aquin aufgrund der Expositio super librum Boethii de Trinitate,* p. 66; Gerald F. Van Ackeren, *Sacra Doctrina,* fail to make this distinction.

104. Roy J. Deferrari, *A Latin-English Dictionary of St. Thomas Aquinas,* s.v.

"Scientia"; Gilson, *History of Christian Philosophy*, pp. 316–17.

105. The best work on this subject is Chenu, *La théologie comme science*. See also J.-F. Bonnefoy, "La théologie comme science et l'explication de la foi selon saint Thomas d'Aquin," *Ephemerides theologicae lovanienses* 14 (1937): 412–46, 600–31; 15 (1938): 491–516; A. Gardeil, "Le donné théologique," *Revue thomiste* 17 (1909): 385–405; Gilson, *Christian Philosophy of Thomas Aquinas*, p. 21; *History of Christian Philosophy*, pp. 366–67; *Philosophy of St. Thomas*, pp. 46–48; Grabmann, *Thomas Aquinas*, pp. 90–91; Kuhn, "Glauben und Wissen nach St. Thomas," *Theologische Quartalschrift* 42, no. 2 (1860): 272–340; Lafont, *Structures et méthode*, p. 493; A. R. Motte, "Théodicée et théologie chez s. Thomas d'Aquin," *Revue des sciences philosophiques et théologiques* 26 (1937): 5–26; Pieper, *Introduction*, pp. 147 ff.; Sillem, *Ways of Thinking about God*, pp. 41–48; Vignaux, *Philosophy in the Middle Ages*, pp. 123–26.

106. *In Boeth. de trin.* q. 1. a.4, q.2. a.2–3, q.5. a.2; *In I Sent.* prologus, q. 1. a.3. sol.2, d.2. q. 1. a.4; *ST* Ia. q. 1. a.1–2, a.5. ad 2.

107. *De pot.* 1. q.3. a.17; *SCG* 2.131–38; *ST* Ia. q.46. a.1.

108. The following is dependent on Chenu, *La théologie comme science*, pp. 18–57; Lang, *Die Gewissheit des übernatürlichen Glaubens*, pp. 147 ff.; Weisheipl, *Friar Thomas*, pp. 218–30.

109. *In Boeth. de trin.* q.6. a.1; *In I Sent.* prologus, q. 1. a.3. sol.2; *SCG* 1.8.1; *ST* Ia. q. 1. a.8. ad 2; IIaIIae. q. 1. a.5. ad 2.

110. *SCG* 4.1.10; *ST* Ia. q. 1. a.8; IIaIIae. q.11. a.5. ad 2.

111. *De pot.* 1. q. 1. a.1–2, q.2. a.2, q.3. a.15. ad 16, a.17. ad 8; *In I Sent.* d.8. q.2. a.1–2, d.35. q. 1. a.1, d.37. q.2. a.2–3, d.42. q. 1. a.1; *In III Sent.* d.1. q.2. a.3; *SCG* 1.29.5; *ST* Ia. q.25. a.1.

112. *De pot.* 2. q.5. a.6, q.6. a.6. ad 5, q.9. a.9. ad 1, q.10. a.1. ad 6; *In I Sent.* d.31. q.2. a.1, q.3. a.1; *ST* Ia. q.29. a.3, q.31. a.2, q.36. a.1, q.39. a.7. ad 8, q.43. a.4–5, a.7.

113. *In III Sent.* d.1. q. 1. a.2, a.3. ad 3, a.4, q.2. a.2, d.12. q.3. a.1–2, d.15. q. 1. a.1, d.21. q. 1. a.2–3, q.2. a.1–4, d.22. q.2. a.1; *SCG* 4.42, 4.45–46, 4.54–55; *ST* IIIaIIae. q. 1. a.3, a.5–6, q.3. a.1–2, a.8, q.4. a.5–6, q.5. a.4, q.6. a.3, q.7. a.1, q.8. a.1, q.14. a.1, q.21. a.3, q.22. a.1, q.23. a.1–2, a.4, q.27. a.2, q.28. a.2–3, q.32. a.1, q.45. a.1, q.50. a.1, q.51. a.1, q.52. a.1, q.53. a.2, q.54. a.4, q.55. a.2, q.57. a.1, q.58. a.1. Appropriateness to God as a norm of Thomas's theological proofs is also noted by Chenu, *Introduction*, pp. 153–58; Gilson, *Philosophy of St. Thomas*, pp. 48–49.

114. *In Boeth. de trin.* q. 1. a.1. ad 1–3, a.2. ad 4, q.2. a.3.

115. *SCG* 1.9.2; *ST* IIaIIae. q.2. a.9. ad 1.

116. *In Boeth. de trin.* q.2. a.4; *ST* IIaIIae. q.10. a.7.

117. *In Boeth. de trin.* q.2. a.1. ad 1–3, a.2. ad 4; *In I Sent.* prologus, q. 1. a.3. sol.1; *SCG* 1.1–2; *ST* Ia. q. 1. a.4–6; IIaIIae. q.180. a.4.

118. *ST* IIaIIae. q.2. a.10. ad 2, q.6. a.2. ad 1, q.8. a.1. ad 2.

119. Ibid., IIaIIae. q.9. a.1. ad 2.

120. Ibid., IIaIIae. q.177. a.1. On Thomas's theology as a form of Dominican *sacra praedicatio*, see White, *Holy Teaching*, pp. 21–22.

121. *ST* IIaIIae. q.15. a.3.

122. Bonnefoy, "La théologie comme science," pp. 492–503, 516; Chenu, *La théologie comme science*, pp. 12–13, 37–53, 78; John F. Dedek, *"Quasi experimentalis cognitio:* A Historical Approach to the Meaning of St. Thomas," *Theological Studies* 22 (1961): 357–90; J. Durantel, *Le retour à Dieu par l'intelligence et la volontè dans la philosophie de s. Thomas*, pp. 210–379; A. Gardeil, *Le donné révélé et la théologie*, pp. xxi, 319–58; Martin Grabmann, *The Interior Life of St. Thomas Aquinas*, pp. 12, 29–31; "Scientific Cognition of Truth: Its Characteristic Genius in the Doctrine of St. Thomas Aquinas," *New Scholasticism* 13 (1939): 1–30; *Die theologische Erkenntnis- und Einleitungslehre des hl. Thomas von Aquin auf seiner Schrift "In Boethium de Trinitate,"* pp. 45–100; *Thomas Aquinas*, pp. 50–52; M.-M. Labourdette, "La vie théologale selon s. Thomas," *Revue thomiste* 60 (1960): 364–80; James Coleman Linehan, *The Rational Nature of Man with Particular Reference to the Effects of Immorality on Intelligence according to Saint Thomas Aquinas*. Cf. Reginald Garrigou-Lagrange, "La foi éclairée par les dons," *La vie spirituelle* 64 (1946): 657–66; Dermot O'Keefe, *Theology and Contemplation according to St. Thomas Aquinas;* George van Riet, "Y a-t-il chez saint Thomas une philosophie de la religion?," *Revue philosophique de Louvain* 61 (1963): 44–81, who hold that piety is irrelevant to theology in Thomas. On theology as *fides quaerens intellectum* in Thomas, see Johannes Beumer, "Thomas von Aquin zum Wesen der Theologie," *Scholastik* 30 (1955): 195–214; Pierre Germain, "La théologie de saint Thomas d'Aquin, science de la foi," *Revue de l'Université d'Ottawa*, special section, 28 (1958): 174*; Martin Grabmann, "Il concetto di scienza secondo s. Tommaso d'Aquino e le relazioni della fede e della teologia con la filosofia e le scienze profane," *Rivista di filosofia neo-scolastica* 26 (1934): 127–55; Lafont, *Structures et méthode*, p. 484; White, *Holy Teaching*, pp. 8–9.

123. *Comp. theol.* 1.2.

124. Ibid., 1.105, 2.1; *De ver.* q.10. a.11, a.13, q.14. a.1; *In Boeth. de trin.* q.1. a.2; *ST* Ia. q.12. a.11; IIIaIIae. q.3. a.3. Gilson, *Christian Philosophy of Thomas Aquinas*, pp. 24–25; Grabmann, *Thomas Aquinas*, pp. 137–38.

125. *In Boeth. de trin.* q.2. a.3.

126. Walter J. Ong, "Wit and Mystery: A Revaluation in Mediaeval Latin Hymnody," *Speculum* 22 (1947): 310–41. I would like to thank Father John R. Cavanaugh, C.S.B., for this reference.

127. Some commentators, adhering to the traditional metaphysical emphasis, content themselves with giving an exposition of analogy in order to show its usefulness in systematic philosophy and theology. George P. Klubertanz, *St. Thomas on Analogy*, presents a thorough assemblage of texts and a helpful bibliography on analogy. See also Nicolas Balthasar, *L'abstraction métaphysique et l'analogie des êtres dans l'être;* F. A. Blanche, "L'analogie," *Revue de philosophie* 23 (1923): 248–70; W. Esdaile Byles, "The Analogy of Being," *New Scholasticism* 16 (1942): 331–64; Henry Chavannes, *L'analogie entre*

Dieu et le monde, pp. 21–138; D'Arcy, *Thomas Aquinas,* pp. 125–26, 131–32; J. Fehr, "Offenbarung und Analogie: Ihr Verhältnis in dialektischen und thomistischen Theologie," *Divus Thomas* 15 (1937): 291–307; B. Landry, "L'analogie de proportion chez saint Thomas d'Aquin," *Revue néoscolastique de philosophie* 24 (1922): 257–80; "L'analogie de proportionnalité chez saint Thomas d'Aquin," *Revue néoscolastique de philosophie* 24 (1922): 454–64; *La notion d'analogie chez saint Bonaventure et saint Thomas d'Aquin,* pp. 35–68; Hampus Lyttkens, *The Analogy between God and the World,* pp. 244 ff.; Armand Maurer, "St. Thomas and the Analogy of Genus," *New Scholasticism* 29 (1955): 127–44; George McLean, "Symbol and Analogy: Tillich and Thomas," *Revue de l'Université d'Ottawa,* special section, 28 (1958): 193*–233*; Joseph Owens, "Analogy as a Thomistic Approach to Being," *Mediaeval Studies* 24 (1962): 303–22; Eleuthère Winance, "L'essence divine et la connaissance humaine dans le Commentaire sur les Sentences de saint Thomas," *Revue philosophique de Louvain* 55 (1957): 171–215.

Most commentators spend their time trying to decide which of the various kinds of analogy is "properly Thomistic," which generally involves a dispute over whether Suarez or Cajetan was correct in interpreting Thomas. For the Suarezian approach, see F. A. Blanche, "La notion d'analogie dans la philosophie de s. Thomas d'Aquin," *Revue des sciences philosophiques et théologiques* 10 (1921): 169–93; "Une théorie d'analogie," *Revue de philosophie,* n.s. 3 (1932): 37–78; Thomas A. Fay, "Analogy and the Problem of the Divine Names in the Metaphysics of Thomas Aquinas," *Angelicum* 52 (1975): 69–90; "Analogy: The Key to Man's Knowledge of God in the Metaphysics of Thomas Aquinas," *Divus Thomas* 76 (1973): 343–64; Thomas Marguerite Flanigan, "The Use of Analogy in the *Summa contra gentiles," Modern Schoolman* 35 (1957): 21–37; Ralph J. Masiello, "The Analogy of Proportion according to the Metaphysics of St. Thomas," *Modern Schoolman* 35 (1958): 91–106; Ch. de Moré-Pontgibaud, "Sur l'analogie des noms divins," *Recherches des sciences religieuses* 19 (1929): 481–512; 20 (1930): 193–223.

Some hold a nominally Suarezian position, but on other grounds, usually Platonic. See John S. Dunne, "St. Thomas' Theology of Participation," *Theological Studies* 18 (1957): 487–512; Lindbeck, "Participation and Existence," pp. 1–22, 107–25; Little, *The Platonic Heritage of Thomism;* Thomas Prufer, *Sein und Wort nach Thomas von Aquin.*

The Cajetanians are, on the whole, more numerous, and tend to claim more authority for their position. See James F. Anderson et al., "Some Basic Propositions concerning Metaphysical Analogy," *Review of Metaphysics* 5 (1952): 465–72; Copleston, *History of Philosophy,* 2, pt. 2:73–78; Gilson, *Christian Philosophy of Thomas Aquinas,* p. 106; Antoine van Leeuwen, "L'analogie de l'être: Genèse et contenu du concept d'analogie," *Revue néoscolastique de philosophie* 39 (1936): 293–320; George P. Klubertanz, "The Problem of the Analogy of Being," *Review of Metaphysics* 10 (1957): 553–79; Jacques Maritain, *Distinguish to Unite; or, The Degrees of Knowledge,* appendix 2, pp. 418–21; Ignatius O'Brien, "Analogy and Our Knowledge of God," *Philosophical Studies* 6 (1956): 91–104; M. J. L. Penido, *Le rôle de l'analogie en théologie dogmatique;*

Gerald B. Phelan, *St. Thomas and Analogy;* Schumacher, *The Knowableness of God.*

Lately, some Cajetanians have taken to translating their position into the terminology of modern symbolic logic and linguistic analysis. See. I. M. Bochenski, "On Analogy," *Thomist* 11 (1948): 424–47; William Bryar, *St. Thomas and the Existence of God;* James F. Ross, "Analogy as a Rule of Meaning for Religious Language," *International Philosophical Quarterly* 1 (1961): 468–502.

A recent trend has been for scholars to consider some, or all, of the kinds of analogy logical rather than metaphysical. See David Burrell, "A Note on Analogy," *New Scholasticism* 36 (1962): 225–32; "Religious Language and the Logic of Analogy: Apropos of McInerny's Book and Ross' Review," *International Philosophical Quarterly* 2 (1962): 643–58; Ralph McInerny, "The Logic of Analogy," *New Scholasticism* 31 (1957): 149–71; *The Logic of Analogy;* Robert E. Meagher, "Thomas Aquinas on Analogy: A Textual Analysis," *Thomist* 34 (1970): 230–53; Bernard Montagnes, *La doctrine d'analogie de l'être d'après saint Thomas d'Aquin;* Jan Pinborg, *Logik und Semantik im Mittelalter,* pp. 100–102; Herbert Thomas Schwartz, "Analogy in St. Thomas and Cajetan," *New Scholasticism* 28 (1954): 127–44; Wilbur Marshall Urban, *Language and Reality,* appendix 4, pp. 748–50; C. J. F. Williams, "Existence and the Meaning of the Word 'God,' " *Downside Review* 77 (1958–59): 53–71.

128. M. S. O'Neill, "Some Remarks on the Analogy of God and Creatures in St. Thomas Aquinas," *Mediaeval Studies* 23 (1961): 215.

129. Klubertanz, *St. Thomas on Analogy,* is the fullest and most recent attempt to catalog the various types of analogy in Thomas.

130. D'Arcy, *Thomas Aquinas,* pp. 131–32; Chavannes, *L'analogie,* pp. 21–138.

131. Klubertanz, *St. Thomas on Analogy,* p. 138. See also Lyttkens, *The Analogy between God and the World,* p. 389.

132. Klubertanz, *St. Thomas on Analogy,* p. 3.

133. D'Arcy, *Thomas Aquinas,* p. 127; Lyttkens, *The Analogy between God and the World,* p. 269.

134. For a particularly clear example, see *ST* Ia. q. 13. a. 5; and for some other good examples see *Comp. theol.* 1.27; *In I Sent.* prologus, q. 1. a. 2. ad 2, d. 2. a. 1. a. 3; *ST* Ia. q. 4. a. 3.

135. For a particularly good example, see *De ver.* q. 2. a. 11; and for some others, see *SCG* 1.34; *ST* Ia. q. 3. a. 5. ad 2, q. 13. a. 5.

136. *ST* Ia. q. 88. a. 1; IIIa. suppl. q. 92. a. 1.

137. Cf. William L. Reese, "Analogy, Symbolism, and Linguistic Analysis," *Review of Metaphysics* 13 (1960): 447–68.

138. *ST* Ia. q. 13. a. 10.

139. *De ver.* q. 10. a. 1; *In I Sent.* d. 10. q. 1. a. 1, a. 2–3, d. 12. q. 1. a. 3; *SCG* 4. 11–12, 4. 19; *ST* Ia. q. 14. a. 8, a. 11. ad 1, a. 12, q. 19. a. 1, q. 27. a. 3. ad 3, a. 4, q. 36. a. 1–2, q. 37. a. 1, q. 45. a. 6, a. 7, q. 93. a. 6. ad 4, a. 7, a. 8.

140. *De pot.* 1. q. 2. a. 1, q. 3. a. 16. ad 5–7, ad 10, 3. q. 8. a. 1; *De ver.* q. 4. a. 1. ad 10, a. 2. ad 4–6; *In I Sent.* d. 10. q. 1. a. 4, d. 27. q. 2. a. 1; *SCG* 4. 11–12, 4. 19.

141. *Comp. theol.* 1.216; *De pot.* 1. q.2. a.4. ad 7, a.6. ad 3, 3. q.9. a.5; *De ver.* q.4. a.1. ad 10, a.2. ad 4–6; *SCG* 4.11–12, 4.19; *ST* Ia. q.27. a.1, a.2. ad 2, q.34. a.1. ad 2–3, a.2. ad 1, a.3, q.44. a.3. ad 1.

142. *ST* Ia. q.93. a.1.

Chapter Four

1. Charles Sears Baldwin, *Ancient Rhetoric and Poetic*, pp. 1–3.
2. J. W. H. Atkins, *Literary Criticism in Antiquity*, 2:37.
3. Ibid., p. 100; Mary A. Grant and George Converse Fiske, "Cicero's *Orator* and Horace's *Ars Poetica*," *Harvard Studies in Classical Philology* 35 (1924): 1–74.
4. Baldwin, *Ancient Rhetoric*, p. 246.
5. Ibid., pp. 246–47; Atkins, *Literary Criticism in Antiquity*, 2:76–77.
6. Atkins, *Literary Criticism in Antiquity*, 2:315.
7. Ernst Robert Curtius, "Neue Dantestudien," *Gesammelte Aufsätze zur romanischen Philologie*, pp. 319 ff.
8. Edgar de Bruyne, *Études d'esthétique médiévale*, 1:46.
9. For general statements on this point, see Ernst Robert Curtius, *European Literature and the Latin Middle Ages*, p. 480; Joseph A. Mazzeo, *Medieval Cultural Tradition in Dante's "Comedy,"* p. 3.
10. Charles Sears Baldwin, *Medieval Rhetoric and Poetic*, p. ix; Edmond Faral, *Les arts poétiques du douzième et du treizième siècle*, pp. 55–103.
11. Baldwin, *Medieval Rhetoric*, pp. x, 130–32. See above, pp. 63–65.
12. Michele Barbi, *Life of Dante*, pp. 42–43; Faral, *Les arts poétiques*, pp. 93–97; Edgar de Bruyne, *L'esthétique au moyen âge*, p. 49.
13. De Bruyne, *Études d'esthétique médiévale*, 1:92 ff.
14. Baldwin, *Medieval Rhetoric*, pp. 131–32, 144–45.
15. De Bruyne, *Études d'esthétique médiévale*, 1:223–38.
16. Ibid., 2:14–49; Faral, *Les arts poétiques*. For a good bibliographical overview of this subject, see August Buck, "Gli studi sulla poetica e sulla retorica di Dante e del suo tempo," *Cultura e scuola* 4 (1965): 143–66.
17. Baldwin, *Medieval Rhetoric*, pp. 157–64, 184.
18. Ibid., p. 175.
19. De Bruyne, *Études d'esthétique médiévale*, 2:397; H. H. Glunz, *Die Literaturästhetik des europäischen Mittelalters*, pp. 268–69.
20. Baldwin, *Medieval Rhetoric*, pp. 172–74.
21. Ibid., p. 174.
22. Ibid., pp. 185–96. See also Faral, *Les arts poétiques*.
23. Baldwin, *Medieval Rhetoric*, pp. 191–93.
24. De Bruyne, *Études d'esthétique médiévale*, 1:92–98.
25. Ibid., pp. 223 ff.
26. Ibid., pp. 227–30; de Bruyne, *L'esthétique au moyen âge*, pp. 53–55.

27. De Bruyne, *L'esthétique au moyen âge*, p. 55.

28. De Bruyne, *Études d'esthétique médiévale*, 2:321–27.

29. This idea has been discussed repeatedly. See, for example, ibid., 3:313–18, 344; Ernst Robert Curtius, "The Medieval Basis of Western Thought," *Gesammelte Aufsätze*, pp. 34–35; Glunz, *Die Literaturästhetik*, pp. 189–97; Nancy Lenkeith, *Dante and the Legend of Rome*, pp. 34–36; Johan Chydenius, *The Typological Problem in Dante*, pp. 41–43; Charles Donahue, "Patristic Exegesis," in *Critical Approaches to Medieval Literature*, ed. Dorothy Bethurum, pp. 77–80; Hugh Pope, "St. Thomas as an Interpreter of Holy Scripture," in *St. Thomas Aquinas*, pp. 134–39. These scholastic strictures do not alter the fact that classical poets, especially Ovid and Vergil, were interpreted allegorically during the Middle Ages. See Henri de Lubac, *Exégèse médiévale*, 2, pt. 2:233–62.

30. Curtius, "Medieval Basis of Western Thought," pp. 34–36; Glunz, *Die Literaturästhetik*, pp. 279–81, 372; Lenkeith, *Dante*, pp. 34–42.

31. Ernst Robert Curtius, "Dante und das lateinische Mittelalter," *Romanische Forschungen* 57, nos. 2–3 (1943): 171; "Medieval Basis of Western Thought," p. 36; Cesare Foligno, "Dante: The Poet," *Proceedings of the British Academy* 10 (1921): 3–18; Joseph A. Mazzeo, *Structure and Thought in the "Paradiso,"* pp. 40–41; Daniel Sargent, "Dante and Thomism," *Thomist* 5 (1943): 256–64.

32. Curtius, "Dante und das lateinische Mittelalter," pp. 153–85.

33. Baldwin, *Medieval Rhetoric*, pp. 205, 261, 269–71.

34. Ibid., p. 123. See also F. J. E. Raby, *A History of Christian-Latin Poetry from the Beginnings to the Close of the Middle Ages*, for a general study of Christian hymnody.

35. Baldwin, *Medieval Rhetoric*, pp. 123–25.

36. Ibid., pp. 263–64.

37. Ibid., pp. 204–5; Walter J. Ong, "Wit and Mystery: A Revaluation in Mediaeval Latin Hymnody," *Speculum* 22 (1947): 310–41.

38. Thomas G. Bergin, *Dante*, p. 56; Luigi Tonelli, *Dante e la poesia dell'ineffabile*, p. 213.

39. *Inferno* 15.85 (ed. Chiapelli in *Opere;* trans. Singleton). All quotations from the *Divine Comedy* in English will be taken from this translation, and all references to Dante's works, except where otherwise indicated, will be taken from this edition.

40. See the appendix on the *cursus* in Paget Toynbee's edition of Dante's *Epistolae*, pp. 224–47; also Toynbee's "The Bearing of the *Cursus* on the Text of Dante's *De vulgari eloquentia*," *Proceedings of the British Academy* 11 (1923): 1–19.

41. André Pézard, *Le "Convivio" de Dante*, pp. 51–52; Helene Wieruszowski, "*Ars Dictaminis* in the Time of Dante," *Medievalia et humanistica* 1 (1943): 95–108.

42. Baldwin, *Medieval Rhetoric*, pp. 179–81.

43. The best treatment of Dante's debt to Brunetto is Charles T. Davis, "Brunetto Latini and Dante," *Studi medievali*, 3d ser. 8 (1967): 421–50. See also Thor Sundby, *Della vita e delle opere di Brunetto Latini*, pp. 187, 195.

44. Brunetto Latini *Li Livres dou Trésor* 3.1.50 (ed. Chabaille).

45. Several scholars have argued that the violation of nature implied by Brunetto's placement in the circle of sodomites in Hell is a linguistic and political sin, not a sexual one. André Pézard, *Dante sous la pluie de feu*, pp. 87–130, holds that Brunetto's sin against language consists in his having written the *Trésor* in French and not in his native Italian, a view shared by Giuseppi Mazzotta, *Dante, Poet of the Desert*, pp. 138–40. More broadly, Davis, "Brunetto Latini," pp. 446–47, and Richard Kay, *Dante's Swift and Strong*, chap. 1, see Dante criticizing Brunetto for the application of his rhetorical gifts to improper political ends by serving the regime of Charles of Anjou in Italy while rejecting the authority of the Holy Roman emperor.

46. *Trésor* 3.1.1.

47. Ibid., 3.1.1. See also 3.1.2.

48. Ibid., 3.1.1.

49. Ibid., 3.1.2.

50. Ibid., 3.1.10, 3.1.16–23.

51. Ibid., 3.1.3, 3.1.10.

52. Ibid., 3.2.1.

53. Ibid., 3.2.2.

54. Ibid., 3.2.1. See also Sundby, *Brunetto Latini*, pp. 195–96.

55. *Trésor* 3.2.3.

56. Ibid., 3.2.4–5.

57. Ibid., 3.2.6–33.

58. Bergin, *Dante*, pp. 56–57; Sebastiano Scandura, *L'estetica di Dante, Petrarca e Boccaccio*, pp. 77–78.

59. Cf., on the contrary, Baldwin, *Medieval Rhetoric*, pp. 196, 261, 269–71, 280; Lenkeith, *Dante*, p. 33.

60. *Purgatorio* 26.112–48.

61. Ibid., 24.49–63.

62. Ibid., 6.74–150, 7.85–136.

63. *Inf.* 28.131–42.

64. Erich Auerbach, *Dante*, pp. 38 ff.

65. Bergin, *Dante*, pp. 46–48, 52–55.

66. James J. Wilhelm, *The Cruelest Month*, pp. 88–258; see also Jefferson B. Fletcher, "The Philosophy of Love of Guido Cavalcanti," *Annual Report of the Dante Society, Cambridge, Mass.* 22 (1904): 22–24.

67. Bergin, *Dante*, p. 81; Nicola Zingarelli, *La vita, i tempi e le opere di Dante*, 1:119.

68. Auerbach, *Dante*, pp. 38 ff.

69. See, for example, Jefferson B. Fletcher, "The Allegory of the *Vita Nuova*," *Modern Philology* 11 (1913): 19–37; J. A. Scott, "Dante's 'Sweet New Style' and the *Vita Nuova*," *Italica* 42 (1965): 98–107; James E. Shaw, *Guido Cavalcanti's Theory of Love*, pp. 126–27; Charles S. Singleton, *An Essay on the "Vita Nuova*," pp. 4, 24, 56. This view has been contradicted by E. R. Vincent, "The Crisis in the *Vita Nuova*," in *Centenary Essays on Dante by Members of the Oxford Dante Society*, p. 132–42.

70. Philip H. Wicksteed, *From "Vita Nuova" to "Paradiso,"* p. 76.

71. *Vita nuova* 13.1 (ed. Chiapelli, *Opere*).

72. Ibid., 13.4.

73. Bruno Nardi, *Dante e la cultura medievale,* pp. 218–23; "Due capitoli di filosofia dantesca: I, La conoscenza humana; II, Il linguaggio," *Giornale storico della letteratura italiana,* miscellanea dantesca, suppl. to 19–21 (1921): 246–47; *La filosofia di Dante,* pp. 44 ff. This maxim has also been noted by Bergin, *Dante,* pp. 83–84; Francesco d'Ovidio, *Dante e la filosofia del linguaggio,* p. 6; *Studii sulla Divina Commedia,* pp. 487–88; Paolo Rotta, *La filosofia del linguaggio nella patristica e nella scolastica,* p. 174. Kay, *Dante's Swift and Strong,* chap. 7, interprets this maxim to mean that the names of Dante's characters in the *Comedy* have a specific moral refrence, a theory that seems tenuous.

74. Jefferson B. Fletcher, "The 'True Meaning' of Dante's *Vita Nuova,*" *Romanic Review* 11 (1920): 98–99.

75. *Vita nuova* 18.8.

76. Ibid., 19.10.

77. Ibid., 19.4–5.

78. Ibid., 24.7.

79. Ibid., 19.11–12, 21.2, 37.8, 39.3, 39.10.

80. Ibid., 19.6, 27.2, 28.2, 31.15.

81. Ibid., 21.4, 26.5.

82. Ibid., 42.1–2.

83. Ibid., 25.6.

84. Ibid., 25.6–8; Fletcher, "True Meaning," p. 95.

85. Barbi, *Life of Dante,* p. 42.

86. *Vita nuova* 25.8–10. See also Jefferson B. Fletcher, *Dante,* pp. 33, 36; Domenico de Robertis, *Il libro della "Vita Nuova,"* p. 9.

87. *Convivio* 2.12, 2.15.1–2 (ed. Simonelli). All references to the *Convivio* will be taken from this edition. The influence of Boethius on the *Convivio* has been noted by Vincenzo Grasso, *Il De Consolatione Philosophiae di Boezio in Dante, Petrarca, Chaucer,* pp. 13, 17, 18, 55–56; Edward Moore, *Studies in Dante: First Series,* pp. 282–88; Rocco Murari, *Dante e Boezio,* pp. 211–54; Howard Rollin Patch, *The Tradition of Boethius,* pp. 6, 43, 91–92.

88. *Conv.* 1.1.5–12, 1.9.7, 4.22.1–2.

89. Ibid., 4.1.9, 4.2.14–16.

90. Ibid., 4.2.8.

91. Ibid., 1.5.12.

92. Ibid., 1.7.12–1.9.11.

93. Ibid., 1.12.5, 1.13.5.

94. Ibid., 1.13.13 (trans. Jackson). On God as symbolized by the sun, see 3.12.6–8. On the Eucharistic connotations of this passage, see Glauco Cambon,

"Dante and the Drama of Language," *Dante's Craft*, pp. 25–26; Leo Pollmann, "Vom *Convivio* zur *Epistola a Can Grande*," *Cultura neolatina* 24 (1964): 39–53.

95. *Conv.* 1.2.13–14.

96. Ibid., 1.13.14.

97. Ibid., 2.11.6. On rhetoric as persuasion in the *Conv.*, see Pézard, *Le "Convivio,"* pp. 85–86.

98. James E. Shaw, *The Lady "Philosophy" in the "Convivio,"* p. 17, notices Dante's application of rhetorical tropes to poetry but not his appropriation of didactic rhetoric.

99. *Conv.* 1.1.1–4.

100. Ibid., 2.15.4. See also 3.15.2, 3.15.19–20.

101. Ibid., 3.8.11, 3.15.2, 3.15.19–20.

102. Ibid., 3.9.2, 3.10.6.

103. Ibid., 3.13.2. See also 3.8.20.

104. Ibid. Canzone 2.11.9–18, 3.2.1, 3.3.15, 3.4.1–3, 3.4.4, 3.4.9–12, 3.8.15, 4.21.67.

105. Ibid., 2.11.9.

106. Ibid., 2.1.2–6.

107. Ibid., 2.1.8–15.

108. Ibid., 4.3.6–9.

109. Ibid., 4.23.8.

110. Ibid., 4.2.16, 4.6.6–8.

111. Ibid., 4.6.16.

112. Ibid., 4.4.1–7.

113. Ibid., 4.4.8–14.

114. Ibid., 4.5.

115. Ibid., 4.6.

116. Ibid., 4.8.

117. Ibid., 4.2.11.

118. Ibid., 4.20.

119. Ibid., 4.9.16–17.

120. Ibid., 4.10.

121. Ibid., 4.10–13.

122. Ibid., 4.7.

123. Ibid., 4.14–15.

124. Ibid., 4.8.8–9, 4.10.

125. Ibid., 4.16. For a good summary of Dante's idea of nobility, stressing its Christian and Aristotelian features, see Gino Dallari, "Sul concetto della nobiltà nella terza canzone del 'Convivio' Dantesco," Reale Istituto Lombardo di scienze e lettere, *Rendiconti,* 2d ser. 61 (1928): 572–80. On the other hand, see Eduard Jourdan, "Dante et l'idée de 'virtù,' " in *Mélanges sur Dante,* ed. Maurice Mignon, pp. 79–92, who argues that Dante has a Renaissance idea of virtù.

126. *Conv.* 1.12.5.

127. Ibid., 4.17.

128. Ibid., 4.18–19.

129. Ibid., 4.20–21.

130. Ibid., 4.23–28.

131. Barbi, *Life of Dante*, pp. 47–49; Wieruszowski, *"Ars Dictaminis,"* p. 108. Cf. on the other hand Giovanni Getto, *Aspetti della poesia di Dante*, p. 26.

132. Treatments of the *De vulgari eloquentia* break down into two main types: those which are more or less satisfied with summarizing Dante's ideas on language and those which go on to note the relationship in this work between language, literature, ethics, and politics. The latter approach is best represented by Giorgio Petrocchi's excellent *Il "De vulgari eloquentia" di Dante*. See also Alessandro Passerin d'Entrèves, *Dante politico e altri saggi*, pp. 39, 97–113; Karl Witte, *Essays on Dante*, p. 386; Zingarelli, *La vita*, 1:568. Giulio Bertoni, "La lingua di Dante," *Nuova antologia* 68, no. 1462 (1933): 481–90, retains this view but interprets it in the light of the Fascist sublimation of the individual into the group. Among those summarizing Dante's views on language without setting them in a broader context are Karl Otto Apel, *Die Idee der Sprache in der Tradition des Humanismus*, pp. 98–99, 104–23; J. Cremona, "Dante's Views on Language," in *The Mind of Dante*, ed. U. Limentani, pp. 138–62; Nardi, *Dante*, pp. 235–47; "Due capitoli," pp. 245–64; *La filosofia di Dante*, pp. 44–51; Ovidio, *Dante*, pp. 8–33; Pézard, *Dante*, pp. 151–200, 223–52; Gustavo Vinay, "La teoria linguistica del *De vulgari eloquentia*," *Cultura e scuola* 2 (1962): 30–42; Karl Vossler, *Mediaeval Culture*, 1:162–65.

133. *De vulg. el.* 1.2 (ed. Mengaldo).

134. Ibid., 2.1.8 (trans. Haller, *Literary Criticism of Dante Alighieri*). All quotations from the *De vulg. el.* in English will be taken from this translation. The interpolation in the passage quoted is Haller's.

135. Guglielmo Bilancioni, *Il suono e la voce nell'opera di Dante*, pp. 17–18; Luigi Malagoli, *Linguaggio e poesia nella Divina Commedia*, pp. 104–9.

136. *De vulg. el.* 1.3.2–3.

137. See *Conv.* 2.4.17, 2.5.1–5.

138. *Trésor* 3.1.1. Noted also by Petrocchi, *Il "De vulgari eloquentia,"* pp. 8–10. A thorough analysis of this tradition can be found in Rotta, *La filosofia del linguaggio;* Roger Dragonetti, *Aux frontières du langage poétique*, pp. 7, 9, 10, 17–18, 19 ff., 75, 95; and Willy Krogmann, "Die Mannigfaltigkeit der Sprache in der Sicht Dantes," in *Die Metaphysik im Mittelalter*, pp. 136–43. On the other hand, A. Ewert, "Dante's Theory of Language," *Modern Language Review* 35 (1940): 358, sees this idea as original with Dante.

139. *De vulg. el.* 1.4–5.

140. Ibid., 1.7.6–7. This origin of linguistic differences in the differentiation of social functions among men has been noted by Maria Corti, *Dante a un nuovo crocevia*, pp.

56–60, and Ugo Palmieri, "Appunti di linguistica dantesca," *Studi danteschi* 41 (1964): 48–50. I am indebted to Piero Boitani for the Corti reference.

141. *De vulg. el.* 1.9.6. See also *Conv.* 1.4.7–10.

142. *De vulg. el.* 1.1.11. On the static quality of Latin grammar in Dante's theory of the natural evolution of language, see Palmieri, "Appunti," pp. 50–53. On the other hand, this doctrine is seen as an inconsistency by Cecil Grayson, " 'Nobilior est vulgaris': Latin and Vernacular in Dante's Thought," in *Centenary Essays on Dante*, ed. Cecil Grayson, pp. 54–76, and Pier Vincenzo Mengaldo, *Linguistica e retorica di Dante*, pp. 67–69.

143. *De vulg. el.* 1.1.3–4.

144. Ibid., 1.1.1.

145. Petrocchi, *Il "De vulgari eloquentia,"* pp. 6–7, 35.

146. *De vulg. el.* 1.8. Cf. *Trésor* 3.1.1, where Brunetto Latini sets forth a tripartite subdivision of speech, on somewhat more sophisticated linguistic grounds than Dante, into oriental (guttural), Greek (palatal), and Italian (dental).

147. *De vulg. el.* 1.10–15.

148. Ibid., 1.16.2.

149. Ibid., 1.16.4–6.

150. Ibid., 1.18.1–5. For the two quotations, ibid., 1.18.2 and 1.18.4. See also Petrocchi, *Il "De vulgari eloquentia,"* pp. 55–57.

151. *De vulg. el.* 1.17.3, 2.2.9.

152. Ibid., 1.19.1–2.

153. R. Weiss, "Links between the 'Convivio' and the 'De Vulgari Eloquentia,'" *Modern Language Review* 37 (1942): 156–68.

154. Fletcher, "True Meaning," p. 99; Glunz, *Die Literaturästhetik*, pp. 414–16.

155. Zingarelli, *La vita*, 1:579 ff.

156. *De vulg. el.* 1.17.3; Petrocchi, *Il "De vulgari eloquentia,"* p. 52.

157. *De vulg. el.* 2.3–4.

158. Ibid., 2.4.2. The interpolation is Haller's.

159. Ibid., 2.1.1.

160. Ibid., 2.2; Petrocchi, *Il "De vulgari eloquentia,"* pp. 60–61.

161. *De vulg. el.* 2.3.

162. Ibid., 2.5–13.

163. Ibid., 2.7.

164. Ibid., 2.4.4–9.

165. Ibid., 2.4.1–3.

166. Pino da Prati, *La politica e la filosofia nella "Monarchia" di Dante*, pp. v–xvii, gives a useful survey of criticism on the *De monarchia*.

167. A Fascist interpretation is put forth by Arrigo Solmi, "La 'Monarchia' di Dante," *Nuova antologia* 70:1513 (1935): 321–31, who sees in Dante a precursor of Mussolini's attempted reconstruction of the Roman Empire. This view is expressly

contradicted by Maurice Vallis, "Dante et l'apologie de l'empire," *Mercure de France* 287 (1938): 586–91.

168. See, for example, Barbara Barclay Carter, "Dante's Political Conception," *Hibbert Journal* 35 (1937): 568–79; "Dante's Political Ideas," *Review of Politics* 5 (1943): 338–55; Francesco Ercole, *Il pensiero politico di Dante;* Arturo Graf, *Roma nella memoria e nelle immaginazioni del medio evo,* especially 2:423–69; Hans Kelsen, *Die Staatslehre des Dante Alighieri;* Heinz Löwe, "Dante und das Kaisertum," *Historische Zeitschrift* 190 (1960): 517–52; U. Limentani, "Dante's Political Thought," in *The Mind of Dante,* ed. U. Limentani, pp. 113–37; John Joseph Roebiecki, *The Political Philosophy of Dante Alighieri;* Arrigo Solmi, *Il pensiero politico di Dante.* Some scholars argue that Dante bases his political theory on purely human grounds and that he may thus be regarded as a Renaissance or modern thinker. See Ernst H. Kantorowicz, *The King's Two Bodies,* pp. 451, 459–95; Prati, *La politica;* Theodor Steinbüchel, *Grosse Gestalten des Abendlandes,* p. 217.

169. See, for example, Johannes Jacob, *Die Bedeutung der Führer Dantes in der Divina Commedia;* Fritz Kern, *Humana Civilitas;* P. E. Matheson, "Character and Citizenship in Dante," *Hibbert Journal* 5 (1907): 856–78; A. Meozzi, *L'utopia politica di Dante;* Edward Moore, *Studies in Dante: Second Series,* p. 25; Passerin d'Entrèves, *Dante politico,* pp. 39–113; Luigi Pietrobono, "Dante e Roma," *Giornale dantesco* 33, n.s. 3 (1930): 1–24; Augustin Renaudet, *Dante humaniste,* pp. 55–57, 479–555; Reto Roedel, "Individuo e communità nella Divina Commedia," in *Individuum und Gemeinschaft,* pp. 515–16; Nicolai Rubinstein, "The Beginnings of Political Thought in Florence: A Study in Mediaeval Historiography," *Journal of the Warburg and Courtauld Institutes* 5 (1942): 198–227; Helene Wieruszowski, "Der Reichsgedanke bei Dante," *Deutsches Dante-Jahrbuch* 14, n.s. 5 (1932): 185–209.

170. Kantorowicz, *King's Two Bodies,* pp. 456–58.

171. *De monarchia* 1.1 (ed. Chiapelli, *Opere*).

172. Ibid., 1.2.5–6, 1.3.10.

173. Ibid., 1.12.9–10.

174. Ibid., 1.3–4.

175. Ibid., 1.7–10, 1.14–15.

176. Ibid., 1.11.3. Cf. *Conv.* 1.12.9, where he calls justice the most distinctively human virtue.

177. *De mon.* 1.11.3–20, 1.13, 3.4.14.

178. Ibid., 2.2.

179. Ibid., 2.3.

180. Ibid., 2.5.

181. Ibid., 2.6.

182. Ibid., 2.4.

183. Ibid., 2.7–10.

184. Ibid., 1.16, 2.11–12.

185. Ibid., 2.1.4–6 (trans. Schneider). Cf. *Conv.* 1.13.2, 3.12.6–8.

186. *De mon.* 3.1.8.

187. Ibid., 3.3.

188. Ibid., 3.4.

189. Ibid., 3.4–6, 3.9.

190. Ibid., 3.1, 3.8, 3.15.

191. Ibid., 3.4, 3.16.

192. Ibid., 3.10.

193. Ibid., 3.2.

194. Ibid., 3.13.

195. Ibid., 3.12.

196. Ibid., 3.10–11.

197. Ibid., 3.16.

198. Ibid., 3.16.

199. *Epistola* 8, Dante to the Italian Cardinals, May or June 1314 (ed. and trans. Toynbee). Toynbee's dating and numbering of the letters has been followed throughout.

200. *Ep.* 5, Dante to the princes and peoples of Italy, September or October 1310, pars. 7–10; *Ep.* 6, Dante to the Florentines, 31 March 1311, pars. 1–2; *Ep.* 7, Dante to the Emperor Henry VII, 17 April 1311, pars. 1, 3, 6; *Ep.* 7**, Dante to the Empress Margaret, Countess of Battifolle, April 1311.

201. *Ep.* 5, par. 1; 7, par. 1.

202. Ibid. 5, pars. 1, 2.

203. Ibid., 5, par. 1.

204. Ibid., 5, par. 8.

205. Ibid. 5, par. 2; 6, par. 6.

206. Ibid., 7, pars. 2, 8.

207. Ibid., 7, par. 1.

208. Ibid., 5, par. 4.

209. Ibid., 5, par. 5.

210. Ibid., 5, par. 4; 6, pars. 2, 6. See Rubinstein, "Political Thought in Florence," pp. 198–218, for an excellent discussion of this tradition.

211. *Ep.* 5, pars. 4–6; 6, pars. 2, 3–5.

212. Ibid., 6, par. 2.

213. Thus, Vossler, *Mediaeval Culture,* 1:352–53, sees the moral meaning as primary. Edward Armstrong, *Italian Studies,* pp. 12, 14; and A. M. Pellacani, *Dante vero,* see the natural or human meaning as primary. Charles Allen Dinsmore, *Life of Dante Alighieri,* p. 233; Lenkeith, *Dante,* pp. 71–72; Hanns Lilje, *Dante als christlicher Denker;* Rocco Montano, *Suggerimenti per una lettura di Dante,* p. 36, see the religious meaning as primary. E. G. Parodi, *Poesia e storia nella "Divina Commedia,"* pp. 365–532; Paul Renucci, *Dante,* p. 412; Solmi, "Monarchia," pp. 321–31; Wicksteed, *Vita Nuova to Paradiso,* pp. xi–xii, see the political meaning as primary. A more unified picture is presented by Baldwin, *Medieval Rhetoric,* p. 273; Barbi, *Life of Dante,*

pp. 70–71; Charles Till Davis, *Dante and the Idea of Rome* (the best work on the subject); Graf, *Roma;* Kern, *Humana Civilitas;* Roedel, "Individuo e communità," pp. 515–18.

214. The subject of the authenticity of this letter has been debated extensively. The most useful modern reviews of the literature pro and con are L. Jenaro-MacLennan, *The Trecento Commentaries on the "Divina commedia" and the Epistle to Cangrande,* pp. 1–4; and Friedrich Schneider, "Der Brief an Can Grande," *Deutsches Dante-Jahrbuch* 34–35 (1957): 3–24. Both scholars doubt the authenticity of the letter, and they are joined by C. G. Hardie, "The Epistle to Cangrande Again," *Deutsches Dante-Jahrbuch* 38 (1960): 51–74; Augusto Mancini, "Nuovi dubbi ed ipotesi sulla Epistola a Can Grande," *Atti della Reale Accademia d'Italia: Rendiconti della classe di scienzi morali e storiche,* 7th ser. 4, fascs. 9–12 (1943) 227–42; Luigi Pietrobono, "L'Epistola a Can Grande," *Giornale dantesco* 40, n.s. 10 (1937): 3–51; G. A. Scartazzini, *A Companion to Dante,* pp. 359, 442. Supporters of the authenticity of the letter include Edmund G. Gardner, *Dante,* p. 128; Jacob, *Die Bedeutung der Führer Dantes,* p. 10; Francesco Mazzoni, "L'Epistola a Cangrande," *Accademia nazionale dei Lincei, Rendiconti della classe di scienzi morali, storiche e filologiche,* 8th. ser. 10, fascs. 3–4 (1955): 157–98; Philip McNair, "The Poetry of the 'Comedy,' " in *The Mind of Dante,* ed. U. Limentani, p. 23; Edward Moore, *Studies in Dante: Third Series,* pp. 296–343; Ovidio, *Studii,* pp. 448–85; Hiram Pflaum, "Il 'modus tractandi' della Divina Commedia," *Giornale dantesco* 39, n.s. 9 (1936): 153–78; Francesco Torraca, *Studi danteschi,* pp. 249–304; Ernest Hatch Wilkins, *A History of Italian Literature,* p. 59.

215. *Ep.* 10, Dante to Can Grande della Scala, ca. 1319, par. 6. Toynbee considers the letter authentic, p. 163.

216. *Ep.* 10, par. 5.

217. Ibid., 4, Dante to Lord Moroello, Marquis of Malaspina, 1308–10, pars. 8–9.

218. Ibid., 10, par. 6.

219. Ibid., 10, par. 7. This point is confirmed by de Lubac, *Exégèse médiévale,* 2, pt. 2:319–25.

220. See, for example, Sorrentino Andrea, "La coscienza poetica di Dante," *Giornale dantesco* 30 (1927): 182; de Bruyne, *L'esthétique au moyen âge,* pp. 253–54; Francis Fergusson, *Dante's Drama of the Mind,* pp. 3, 10, 26–27, 29, although he takes the opposite view on p. 103; Allan H. Gilbert, *Dante and His Comedy,* pp. 1–7, 12, 17, 28, 29–30, 42, 43; Charles Hall Grandgent, *The Power of Dante,* pp. 181–82; Richard Hamilton Green, "Dante's 'Allegory of the Poets' and the Mediaeval Theory of Poetic Fiction," *Comparative Literature* 9 (1957): 118–28; Engelbert Krebs, "Erlebnis und Allegorie in Dantes Commedia," *Deutsches Dante-Jahrbuch* 8 (1924): 11–25; 9 (1925): 98–108; P. Mandonnet, *Dante le théologien,* pp. 182–83; Gustav E. Mueller, "Dante's Aesthetics," *Personalist* 27 (1946): 386–98; Luigi Pietrobono, "L'allegorismo e Dante," *Giornale dantesco* 38, n.s. 8 (1935): 86; Scartazzini, *Companion,* p. 441; Emanuele Testa, "Poetica e poesia in Dante," *Archivum Romanicum* 16 (1932): 211–53;

Domenico Vittorini, *High Points in the History of Italian Literature,* p. 26; Charles Williams, *The Figure of Beatrice,* pp. 56–57.

221. See, for example, Barbi, *Life of Dante,* pp. 55–56; R. P. Blackmur, "Dante's Ten Terms for the Treatment of the Treatise," *Kenyon Review* 14 (1952): 291; Morton W. Bloomfield, "Symbolism in Medieval Literature," *Modern Philology* 56 (1958): 79; Curtius, "Medieval Basis of Western Thought," p. 36; Giovanni Fallani, *Poesia e teologia nella Divina Commedia,* 1:5–21; Allan H. Gilbert, *Dante's Conception of Justice,* p. 67; Charles Hall Grandgent, *Dante,* pp. 273–76; Robert Hollander, *Allegory in Dante's Commedia;* Mazzeo, *Medieval Cultural Tradition,* pp. 2–3; *Structure and Thought,* pp. 25–26, 33; Charles Grosvener Osgood, *Poetry as a Means of Grace,* p. 31; Jean Pépin, *Dante et la tradition d'allegorie,* chaps. 1–2; Pollmann, "Vom *Convivio* zur *Epistola a Can Grande,*" pp. 39–53; Dorothy L. Sayers, *Introductory Papers on Dante,* pp. xiv, 2, 7, 8–9, 11, 21–42, 102 ff., 107; Charles S. Singleton, *Commedia,* pp. viii, 1–2, 12, 14–16, 62, 84–98; "Dante and Myth," *Journal of the History of Ideas* 10 (1949): 489–502; *Journey to Beatrice,* p. 6; "The Irreducible Dove," *Comparative Literature* 9 (1957): 129–35; "The Other Journey," *Kenyon Review* 14 (1952): 189–206.

222. Philip H. Wicksteed and Edmund G. Gardner, *Dante and Giovanni del Virgilio,* p. 175. The translation is Wicksteed and Gardner's. See also August Buck, "Dante im Urteil der Literaturästhetik des italienischen Humanismus," *Deutsches Dante-Jahrbuch* 28 (1949): 2–3; Ernst Robert Curtius, "Theologische Poetik im italienischen Trecento," *Zeitschrift für romanische Philologie* 60 (1940): 1.

223. Curtius, "Theologische Poetik," pp. 3–15.

224. Louis B. Rossi, "Dante and the Poetic Tradition in the Commentary of Benvenuto da Imola," *Italica* 32 (1955): 215–21.

225. Pietro Alighieri *Super Dantis ipsius genitoris Comoediam commentarium,* (ed. Nannucci and Vernon, p. 3). The best study of Pietro Alighieri is Jenaro-MacLennan, *Trecento Commentaries,* chap. 3. See also John Paul Bowden, *An Analysis of Pietro Alighieri's Commentary on the Divine Comedy;* Francesco Mazzoni, "Pietro Alighieri interprete di Dante," *Studi danteschi* 40 (1963): 279–360.

226. Giovanni Boccaccio *Genealogie deorum gentilium* 14.10 (ed. Romano); *Vita di Dante e difesa di poesia* 3 (ed. Muscetta).

227. *Vita di Dante* 26.

228. Ibid.

229. Ibid., 21–22; *Genealogie deorum* 14.6–7.

230. Giovanni Boccaccio *Il commento alla Divina Commedia e gli altri scritti intorno di Dante* lez. 5 (ed. Guerri). See also Edward Moore, *Dante and His Early Biographers,* pp. 4–5.

231. *Vita di Dante* 2; Buck, "Dante," p. 4–7.

232. *Ep.* 10, par. 8.

233. A helpful summary of the pro- and anti-Crocean literature may be found in Egidio Guidubaldi, "Poesia e non-poesia negli ultimi quarant'anni di critica dantesca

in Italia," *Civiltà cattolica* 110:4 (1959): 42–52. H. Hatzfeld, "Modern Literary Scholarship as Reflected in Dante Criticism," *Comparative Literature* 3 (1951): 289–309, is also useful. For Croce's position, see Benedetto Croce, *The Poetry of Dante*, pp. 5–6, 11, 14–15, 19–20, 34–36, 91 ff., 296 ff. Croce has been more or less faithfully seconded by Francesco Biondolillo, *Poetica e poesia di Dante;* Getto, *Aspetti*, pp. 125–88; Allan H. Gilbert, "Doctrine and Romance in Dante's *Commedia*," in *Renaissance Papers, 1960*, pp. 104–10; Gioacchino Natoli, "Il valore estetico del simbolo nell'arte di Dante," *Sophia* 23 (1955): 38–52; Francesco De Sanctis, *History of Italian Literature*, 1:67–69, 160, 171, 176–77, 178–263; *Lezioni sulla Divina Commedia*, pp. 11–13, 14, 26, 33, 37–44; Theophil Spoerri, *Dante und die europäische Literatur;* John Addington Symonds, *An Introduction to the Study of Dante*, pp. 103, 112; Tonelli, *Dante*, pp. 19, 20–21, 22–23, 28, 39–40.

234. See, for example, T. S. Eliot, *Dante*, p. 43; Pompeo Giannantonio, *Dante e l'allegorismo;* Mueller, "Dante's Aesthetics," p. 392; Pietrobono, "L'allegorismo e Dante," pp. 85–102; "Per l'allegoria di Dante," *Giornale dantesco* 25 (1922): 206–10; "Struttura allegorica e poesia nella Divina Commedia," *Giornale dantesco* 43, n.s. 13 (1940): 9–45; Luigi Pirandello, "The Poetry of Dante," in *Dante*, ed. John Freccero, pp. 14–22; Singleton, "Dante and Myth," p. 489; Mark Van Doren, "The Divine Comedy," *Sewanee Review* 54 (1946): 349–95; Witte, *Essays on Dante*, p. 17.

235. Freccero, *Dante*, p. 3.

236. Quite a few scholars have noted the typological dimensions of Dante's symbolism. See Auerbach, *Dante*, pp. 86–90; "Figura," *Neue Dantestudien*, pp. 11–71; "Figurative Texts Illustrating Certain Passages of Dante's *Commedia*," *Speculum* 21 (1946): 474–89; "Typological Symbolism in Medieval Literature," *Yale French Studies* 9 (1952): 3–10; Baldwin, *Medieval Rhetoric*, p. 274; Michele Barbi, *Problemi fondamentali per un nuovo commento della Divina Commedia*, pp. 118–19; Salvatore Battaglia, "Introduzione alla teoria del poeta teologo," *Cultura e scuola* 4 (1965): 72–86; Thomas G. Bergin, "On the *Personae* of the *Comedy*," *Italica* 42 (1965): 1–7; Irma Brandeis, *The Ladder of Vision*, pp. 17–18; Chydenius, *The Typological Problem*, especially p. 49; Cecil Grayson, "Dante's Theory and Practice of Poetry," in *The World of Dante*, ed. Cecil Grayson, pp. 146–65; Robert Hollander, "Dante *Theologus-Poeta*," *Dante Studies* 94 (1976): 91–136; W. P. Ker, "Allegory and Myth," in *Dante*, ed. John Freccero, pp. 33–36; M.-J. Lagrange, "Le réalisme et le symbolisme de Dante," *Revue biblique* 46 (1937): 481–505; Mazzeo, *Medieval Cultural Tradition*, p. 7; Passerin d'Entrèves, *Dante politico*, p. 43; Sayers, *Introductory Papers*, pp. xiv, 7, 102–7; *Further Papers*, pp. 56, 58–59; Charles S. Singleton, "In Exitu Israel de Aegypto," in *Dante*, ed. John Freccero, pp. 103, 112; "The Other Journey," pp. 189–206. On the other hand, for the view of allegory as sublimation or as "purely symbolic," see Irma Brandeis, "Metaphor in the Divine Comedy," *Hudson Review* 8 (1956): 557–75; Kenelm Foster, "The Mind in Love: Dante's Philosophy," in *Dante*, ed. John Freccero, p. 48; Eleanor F. Jourdain, *Le symbolisme dans la Divine Comédie de Dante*, p. 3; Mandonnet, *Dante*, pp. 29–65. For the view of allegory in Dante as Jungian archetype, see H. Flanders

Dunbar, *Symbolism in Medieval Thought;* Helen M. Luke, *Dark Wood to White Rose.*

237. This point has been noted by Andrew Bongiorno, "The Divine Comedy," Humanities Lecture, Oberlin College, 6 January 1958, pp. 5–6 (my thanks to Professor Bongiorno for a copy of this lecture) and has been developed most fully, with a recognition of Dante's debt to Augustinian sign theory, by John Freccero, "Dante's *Medusa*: Allegory and Autobiography," in *By Things Seen,* ed. David L. Jeffrey, pp. 33–46. See also Fletcher, *Dante,* p. 99; Freccero, *Dante,* p. 7; Montano, *Suggerimento,* pp. 20–21, 46; Singleton, *Commedia,* pp. 74–75; Williams, *The Figure of Beatrice,* pp. 9–11; Zingarelli, *La vita,* 2:882.

238. Bergin, *Dante,* p. 98.

239. Gilbert, *Dante,* pp. 146–51.

240. As noted by Fletcher, *Dante,* pp. 139–40; Singleton, *Commedia,* pp. 51–59; *Journey to Beatrice,* pp. 86, 88; *Essay on the "Vita Nuova,"* pp. 4, 24, 56 (although he reads the Christ-Beatrice back into the *Vita nuova*); Bernard Stambler, "The Confrontation of Beatrice and Dante: *Purgatorio* XXX," *Italica* 42 (1965): 61–75.

241. Williams, *The Figure of Beatrice,* pp. 7–8. Cf. Gratia Eaton Baldwin, *The New Beatrice;* and Mandonnet, *Dante,* pp. 46–49, 56–65, who regard Beatrice as a purely transcendental figure or as the hypostasis of Dante's inner crises, respectively.

242. Auerbach, *Dante,* pp. 99–100.

243. *Inf.* 2.52–142.

244. Ibid., 12.88–90; *Purg.* 1.52–54, 7.24.

245. *Inf.* 10.130–32; *Purg.* 6.43–48, 9.52–57, 15.76–78, 18.73–75, 27.34–42.

246. *Purg.* 30.34–48. This attitude is also reflected in 27.37–42, where Dante alludes to Pyramus and Thisbe in referring to his attitude toward Beatrice.

247. Ibid., 30.55–57, 30.73.

248. Ibid., 30.92–93, 30.97–98.

249. Ibid., 30.109–45.

250. Ibid., 31.83–90, 31.117.

251. Ibid., 32.2.

252. Brandeis, *Ladder of Vision,* p. 115; Brizio Casciola, *L'enimma dantesco,* p. 62; de Bruyne, *Études d'esthétique médiévale,* 3:3–29; Gilbert, *Dante,* pp. 7–17, 22, 38; Ulrich Leo, *Sehen und Wirklichkeit bei Dante,* p. 84; Mazzeo, *Medieval Cultural Tradition,* pp. 23, 56–132, 170–71; *Structure and Thought,* pp. 1, 7–8, 10–14, 18; Singleton, *Commedia,* pp. 19, 22–23; *Journey to Beatrice,* pp. 15–34; Allen Tate, "The Symbolic Imagination: A Meditation on Dante's Three Mirrors," *Kenyon Review* 14 (1952): 272–77.

253. *Inf.* 1.60.

254. Ibid., 17.46.

255. Ibid., 4.118.

256. Ibid., 2.1.

257. Ibid., 3.87, 3.98, 3.118, 3.130.

258. Ibid., 4.13, 27.25.

259. Ibid., 6.11, 9.82, 16.130, 31.37.

260. Ibid., 6.12, 7.28, 9.31, 10.136, 29.50–51.

261. Ibid., 7.52–54.

262. Ibid., 7.103, 7.104, 7.108, 7.124.

263. Ibid., 13.2–6.

264. Ibid., 21.6, 24.71.

265. Ibid., 18.2, 19.14.

266. Ibid., 19.25, 19.33, 26.31, 26.38–42, 26.47–48, 26.52–54, 26.58, 26.64–65, 26.76, 26.79, 26.85–90, 28.1–2, 28.4–6, 28.13–15, 28.57–59, 28.63, 28.127, 28.130–32.

267. Ibid., 31.10, 34.99, 34.134.

268. *Purg.* 7.80–81, 24.150, 28.6–7, 29.22, 29.36.

269. Ibid., 1.13, 1.16.

270. Ibid., 15.142–17.12.

271. Ibid., 2.17, 2.38–39, 8.34–35.

272. Ibid., 12.88–90.

273. Ibid., 8.28–29.

274. Ibid., 9.94–102.

275. Ibid., 30.31–33.

276. Ibid., 32.58.

277. Ibid., 9.20.

278. Ibid., 23.69, 24.103.

279. Ibid., 7.73–81.

280. Ibid., 28.1–2, 28.6–7, 28.14–18, 28.25–42, 28.55–56.

281. Ibid., 28.36, 28.41, 28.55–56, 29.35, 29.65–66, 29.73–78, 29.84, 29.88, 29.93, 29.113–14, 29.122–31, 29.148, 30.23, 30.28, 30.31–33, 31.16, 32.58; 33.110.

282. Ibid., 32.104–60.

283. *Par.* 2.33, 2.34.

284. Ibid., 23.101.

285. Ibid., 9.69, 15.85, 19.4, 22.29, 30.61–66, 30.76.

286. Ibid., 31.13–14.

287. Ibid., 1.61–63.

288. Ibid., 1.74–75, 1.82–84.

289. Ibid., 8.46–48, 9.13–15, 10.82–84, 11.16–18, 12.31–33, 14.37–42, 18.25–27, 21.43–44.

290. Ibid., 2.28, 5.106–8, 5.133–39, 14.17–24, 21.64–66, 21.88–90.

291. *Inf.* 3.1–9, 3.16–18; *Par.* 7.58–60, 11.28–39, 14.37–42, 15.73–75, 27.88–90, 28.70–72, 30.40–42. Noted also by Steinbüchel, *Grosse Gestalten,* p. 218.

292. *Par.* 30.40–42.

293. *Purg.* 32.1–3; *Par.* 14.76–84, 18.13–21, 21.140–42, 23.16–18, 23.46–48, 30.46–60.

294. *Par.* 21.16–18.

295. Ibid., 18.21. Note also in this connection Beatrice's joy when Dante's love of God eclipses her, 10.55–63.

296. Ibid., 19.142–44.

297. Ibid., 31.94–99, 32.4–87, 32.109–50, 33.49–54.

298. Ibid., 33.115–33.

299. Ibid., 28.11–12.

300. *Purg.* 31.80–81; *Par.* 1.46–47, 2.22, 17.114.

301. *Purg.* 30.66, 31.115–23, 33.16–21; *Par.* 1.100–141, 3.124–30, 4.139–42, 5.1–6, 9.16–18, 18.7–9, 23.46–48, 26.13–15.

302. *Par.* 27.92.

303. Ibid., 31.49–50.

304. *Purg.* 33.95; *Par.* 1.95, 2.52, 7.17, 16.13–16, 17.121–24, 22.10–11, 25.28, 27.103–4.

305. *Par.* 21.4–12, 28.11, 30.14–27.

306. Ibid., 3.24, 3.42, 5.125–26.

307. Ibid., 10.61–63, 15.34.

308. Ibid., 18.19.

309. Ibid., 26.76–78.

310. Ibid., 27.4–6. See also 15.37.

311. Ibid., 31.110–11. See Alexandre Masseron, *Dante et Saint Bernard*, for the fullest discussion of Saint Bernard's role in the *Comedy*, and pp. 40–43 for Saint Bernard as a mystic.

312. *Par.* 10.133.

313. Ibid., 31.100–102; Masseron, *Dante*, pp. 71–143.

314. *Par.* 32.85–87.

315. Ibid., 33.1–39.

316. Masseron, *Dante*, pp. 248–52.

317. *Par.* 32.116–17.

318. The best modern discussions of the literature of this subject include Giannantonio, *Dante*, pp. 258–59 n.2; and Mario Santoro, "Virgilio personaggio della *Divina Commedia*," *Cultura e scuola* 4 (1965): 343–55. For the older literature, see C. Galassi Paluzzi, "Perchè Dante scelse Virgilio a sua guida," *Giornale dantesco*, n.s. 9 (1936): 287–307.

319. *Inf.* 4.131.

320. See above, pp. 162–63. These views have been noted frequently. See Albert R. Bandini, "Virgil and Dante—and Statius," *Thought* 5 (1930): 10; Bergin, *Dante*, p. 59; Domenico Comparetti, *Vergil in the Middle Ages*, especially pp. 195–231; Domenico Consoli, *Significato del Virgilio dantesco*; Davis, *Dante*, pp. 101–38; Dinsmore, *Life of Dante*, p. 229; Fletcher, *Dante*, pp. 175–76; Fortunato Laurenzi, *Ermetica ed ermeneutica*

dantesca, pp. 44–45, 52; Kenneth McKenzie, "Virgil & Dante," *The Tradition of Virgil,* pp. 13–20; Moore, *Studies in Dante: First Series,* pp. 166–97; R. Palgen, "La légende virgilienne dans la *Divine Comédie*," *Romania* 73 (1952): 332–90; Renucci, *Dante,* p. 340; Singleton, *Journey to Beatrice,* pp. 89–92; John Webster Spargo, *Virgil the Necromancer,* p. 335; J. H. Whitfield, *Dante and Virgil,* pp. 31, 68, 73, 93; Vladmiro Zabughin, *Vergilio nel rinascimento italiano da Dante a Torquato Tasso,* 1:6, 7, 15–16.

321. Gilbert, *Dante,* pp. 42–44.

322. *Inf.* 1.63.

323. Ibid., 1.73–75.

324. Ibid., 1.82–87.

325. Ibid., 4.76–78.

326. Ibid., 4.80, 4.91–93.

327. Ibid., 4.94–102.

328. Ibid., 20.113.

329. Ibid., 26.79–84.

330. Ibid., 13.46–49.

331. Ibid., 2.58–60, 2.67, 2.113–14.

332. *Purg.* 7.16–17.

333. Ibid., 21.92, 21.94–98.

334. Ibid., 22.64–73.

335. Ibid., 6.72–75, 7.1–3.

336. *Inf.* 1.91–129.

337. *Par.* 25.52–57.

338. *Purg.* 2.46.

339. This point has been noted frequently. See Andrea, "La coscienza poetica," p. 187; Erich Auerbach, "Dante's Addresses to the Reader," *Romance Philology* 7 (1954): 268–78; Barbi, *Life of Dante,* p. 97; *Problemi,* p. 116; Frédéric Bergmann, *Dante,* pp. 15–25; Curtius, *European Literature,* pp. 328, 359; Dinsmore, *Life of Dante,* p. 235; *The Teachings of Dante,* pp. 47–49; Foligno, "Dante," pp. 3–18; Gilbert, *Dante,* pp. 28–42; Hermann Gmelin, "Die Anrede an den Leser in Dantes Göttlicher Komödie," *Deutsches Dante-Jahrbuch* 29–30, n.s. 20–21 (1951): 130–40; Grandgent, *Power of Dante,* p. 223; A. G. Ferrers Howell, *Dante,* p. 83; Laurenzi, *Ermetica ed ermeneutica,* pp. 8, 44–52; Lenkeith, *Dante,* pp. 64, 71–72; Mazzeo, *Structure and Thought,* pp. 8, 36–37, 45; Moore, *Studies in Dante: Second Series,* pp. 1–78; Nardi, *Dante,* pp. 338, 340–41, 392; Pézard, *Dante,* pp. 253–61; Pietrobono, "Struttura allegorica e poesia," pp. 12–45; Scandura, *L'estetica,* pp. 79–80, 89–90; Vossler, *Mediaeval Culture,* 2:103; Ernest Hatch Wilkins, "Dante as Apostle," in *Symposium,* p. 43; *Dante,* pp. 19, 26, 42, 45–46, 55–56; *History of Italian Literature,* p. 61; Zingarelli, *La vita,* 2:881.

340. *Inf.* 2.7–9; *Purg.* 1.7–12, 29.40–42; *Par.* 1.13–36, 2.8–9, 18.82–87, 22.112–23, 30.97–99, 33.67–75.

341. *Purg.* 24.52–54.

342. *Par.* 23.62, 25.1.

343. Ibid., 1.27.

344. Ibid., 25.2.

345. Ibid., 17.124–42.

346. *Purg.* 32.103–5, 33.52–54.

347. *Par.* 21.97–99.

348. Ibid., 25.129.

349. Ibid., 27.64–66.

350. *Inf.* 9.61–63, 12.49–51, 14.16–18, 16.118–20, 19.1–6, 20.19–20; *Purg.* 8.19–21, 9.70–72, 10.104–11, 12.70–72, 29.97–102; *Par.* 2.1–6; 10.7–9. See Auerbach, "Dante's Addresses," pp. 268–78; Gmelin, "Die Anrede an den Leser," pp. 130–40; Leo Spitzer, "The Addresses to the Reader in the *Commedia*," *Italica* 12 (1935): 143–65. Ernst Robert Curtius relates Dante's didactic conception of the *Comedy* to the symbol of the book in the poem, which represents doctrine, prophesy, and divine revelation, in "Das Buch als Symbol in der Divina Commedia," in *Festschrift zum sechzigsten Geburtstag von Paul Clemen*, pp. 44–54. He supplies more details in his "Schrift- und Buchmetaphorik in der Weltliteratur," in *Neue Beiträge deutscher Forschung*, ed. Erich Fidder, pp. 70–86, where he traces the sources of this idea in early Christian and medieval thought.

351. *Inf.* 29.103–8, 32.133–39; *Purg.* 26.53–66.

352. *Ep.* 10, par. 15.

353. Ibid., 10, par. 16.

354. Ibid., 10, par. 32.

355. Ibid., 10, par. 33.

356. Baldwin, *Medieval Rhetoric*, p. 277.

357. *Ep.* 10, pars. 28–29.

358. Ibid., 10, pars. 18, 31.

359. Ibid., 10, par. 18.

360. Ibid., 10, par. 19.

361. Ibid., 10, par. 19.

362. Ibid., 10, par. 9.

363. Ibid., 10, par. 10.

364. See above, p. 182.

365. *Ep.* 10, par. 10.

366. See citations in notes 339, 341, 345–50, this chapter.

367. Gilbert, *Dante*, p. 42.

368. Ibid., pp. 42–60; Giovanni Chiapparini, "Dante e la poesia dell'ineffabile," *Rassegna nazionale* 3d ser. 22 (1934): 425–29; Dinsmore, *Life of Dante*, p. 236; Robin Kirkpatrick, *Dante's "Paradiso" and the Limitations of Modern Criticism*, pp. 36–43, 86–89; Laurenzi, *Ermetica ed ermeneutica*, p. 3; Mazzeo, *Structure and Thought*, p. 39; Giovanni Pischedda, *L'orrido e l'ineffabile nella tematica dantesca*, pp. 87–89, 99; Tonelli, *Dante;* Van Doren, "The Divine Comedy," p. 370.

369. Dinsmore, *Life of Dante*, p. 236; Van Doren, "The Divine Comedy," p. 370;

Inf. 2.10–36, 4.145–47, 9.34, 28.1–6, 32.1–15, 34.22–24; *Purg.* 12.110–11, 29.40–42, 31.97–99, 31.139–45; *Par.* 1.4–12, 1.70–72, 6.61–63, 10.43–48, 14.103–5, 14.123, 15.76–78, 17.92–93, 18.7–12, 20.11–12, 21.139–42, 23.40–45, 23.49–63, 24.22–27, 27.73–75, 27.100–102, 30.19–36, 31.136–38, 33.55–57, 33.106–8, 33.121–23, 33.142–45.

370. *Par.* 30.19–36.

371. Ibid., 33.142–45.

372. See citations in note 340, this chapter.

373. *Par.* 10.43–48.

374. Ibid., 1.70–72.

375. *Inf.* 3.79–81, 5.70–72.

376. *Purg.* 27.139. On the length of Dante's guides' speeches, see Bergin, *Dante*, p. 265; Fletcher, *Dante*, pp. 91, 93–94, 98.

377. *Inf.* 8.44–45, 14.133, 19.121–23, 26.70–71; *Par.* 10.61–63.

378. *Inf.* 3.45, 3.51, 10.39, 17.40.

379. *Par.* 3.31, 5.122–23.

380. *Inf.* 3.22–24, 3.103–5, 4.25–27, 5.25–27, 6.76, 9.121–23, 12.102, 13.22, 14.27, 15.42, 16.19–20, 17.122, 18.103–4, 20.7–8, 23.58–60, 29.43. Also noted by Joan M. Ferrante, "The Relation of Speech to Sin in the *Inferno*," *Dante Studies* 87 (1969): 33–46, who cites some of the same examples mentioned below.

381. *Inf.* 6.19.

382. Ibid., 7.43.

383. Ibid., 26.85–90, 27.7–15, 27.58–60, 27.130–32.

384. Ibid., 27.13–15.

385. Ibid., 7.1. Notwithstanding the later solutions that have been applied to this phrase, Dante the character in the poem treats it as incomprehensible.

386. Ibid., 31.67, 31.70–75.

387. Ibid., 7.125–26.

388. Ibid., 28.100–102.

389. Ibid., 24.66.

390. Ibid., 13.43–44, 13.91–92, 13.138.

391. Ibid., 3.84.

392. Ibid., 5.16.

393. Ibid., 8.18.

394. Ibid., 12.61–63.

395. Ibid., 8.33, 8.84–93.

396. Ibid., 17.66–67.

397. Ibid., 18.53, 18.118–19.

398. Ibid., 24.151.

399. Ibid., 25.1–3.

400. Ibid., 28.43–45.

401. Ibid., 23.85–90.

402. Ibid., 32.87–123.
403. Ibid., 14.51.
404. Ibid., 5.100–106.
405. Ibid., 13.58–78.
406. Ibid., 19.52–57, 19.66–87.
407. Ibid., 22.87.
408. Ibid., 23.127–44.
409. Ibid., 29.109–30.33.
410. Ibid., 30.58–129.
411. Ibid., 33.13–78.
412. Ibid., 33.150.
413. *Purg.* 2.88–89, 2.112–14.
414. Ibid., 21.13, 22.70–72, 23.43.
415. See for example, ibid., 3.121–23, 5.52–57, 11.58–72, 13.106–14, 14.81–85, 19.106–14, 22.27–54, 23.61–75, 26.83–91.
416. Ibid., 3.136–45, 4.130–35, 5.130–36, 13.147, 26.147.
417. Ibid., 8.43–45.
418. Ibid., 18.103–5, 18.113–17, 19.115–26, 23.61–72, 26.139–48.
419. Ibid., 11.79–117.
420. Ibid., 20.9–33.
421. Ibid., 24.45–62.
422. Ibid., 26.97–98, 26.114.
423. Ibid., 26.117.
424. Ibid., 6.74–75.
425. Ibid., 13.94–95.
426. Hymns, psalms, prayers, scriptural passages, liturgical texts, and allusions to them may be found in *Purg.* in 2.46 ("In exitu Israel de Aegypto"); 5.24 ("Miserere"); 7.82 ("Salve, Regina"); 8.13 ("Te lucis ante"); 9.140 ("Te Deum laudamus"); 10.1 ff. ("Paternoster"); 12.110 ("Beati pauperes spiritu"); 13.29 ("Vinum non habent"); 15.38 ("Beati misericordes"); 16.19 ("Agnus dei"); 17.68–69 ("Beati pacifici"); 19.50, 19.73, 19.137 ("Beati qui lugent," "Adhaesit pavimento anima mea," "Neque nubent"); 20.136 ("Gloria in excelsis Deo"); 22.6 ("Beati qui sitiunt"); 23.11 ("Labia mea, Domine"); 25.121, 25.128 ("Summe Deus clementie," "Virum non cognosco"); 27.8, 27.58 ("Beati mundo corde," "Venite, benedicti Patris mei"); 28.80 ("Delectasti"); 29.3, 29.51, 29.85–87 ("Beati quorum tecta sunt peccata," "Osanna," "Benedicta tue ne le figlie d'Adamo" [cf. "Benedicta tu in mulieribus"]); 30.11, 30.19, 30.83 ("Veni, sponsa de Libano," "Benedictus qui venis," "In te, Domine, speravi"); 31.98 ("Asperges me"); 33.1, 33.10–12 ("Deus, venerunt gentes," "Modicum, et non videbitis me"). The functions of liturgical song in the *Comedy* have been noted by Baldwin, *Medieval Rhetoric,* p. 273; Fallani, *Poesia e teologia,* 2:15–28; Fletcher, *Dante,* pp. 140–41; and Singleton, *Commedia,* pp. 36–38. The whole question of Dante and the liturgy has been studied in detail by Olaf Graf, *Die Divina*

Commedia als Zeugnis des Glaubes. Surprisingly, Gilbert, *Dante,* p. 115, says that there is no evidence of formal worship in the *Comedy.*

427. *Par.* 3.120–21 ("Ave Maria"); 7.1–3 ("Osanna, sanctus Deus sabaoth"); 8.29 ("Osanna"); 18.90–93 ("Diligite justitiam qui judicatis terram"); 24.113 ("Dio laudamo" [cf. "Te Deum laudamus"]); 25.98 ("Sperent in te"); 26.69 ("Santo, santo, santo" [cf. "Sanctus"]); 27.1–2 ("Al Padre, al Figlio, a lo Spirito Santo, gloria" [cf. "Gloria patri"]); 32.95 ("Ave Maria, gratia plena").

428. Ibid., 3.16, 3.42.

429. Ibid., 4.16–18, 7.19–24, 10.90–93, 13.46–48, 15.70–72, 20.88–90, 26.103–5.

430. Ibid., 19.10–21.

431. Ibid., 3.109–20, 11.28–139, 12.31–145.

432. Ibid., 10.136–38, 12.140–41.

433. Ibid., 13.52–81.

434. Fletcher, *Dante,* p. 160; Mandonnet, *Dante le théologien,* pp. 10, 130–31, 137–41, 153–57, 255–61, 263–78; A. J. Waters, "The Poet-Theologian of the Middle Ages," *American Catholic Quarterly Review* 39 (1914): 152–59; and Philip H. Wicksteed, *Dante and Aquinas,* are among the many who regard the *Divine Comedy* as the *Summa theologiae* set to music. This view has been rebutted by Curtius, "Dante," p. 171; *European Literature,* pp. 372, 595; Étienne Gilson, *Dante the Philosopher,* p. 307; Daniel Sargent, "Dante and Thomism," *Thomist* 5 (1943): 256–64; Sayers, *Further Papers,* pp. 38–43; Lydia Pucci de Simone, "Dante poeta della filosofia medievale," *Sapienza* 18 (1965): 465–70; H. L. Stewart, "Dante and the Schoolmen," *Journal of the History of Ideas* 10 (1949): 357–73. A more moderate view, acknowledging that Dante agrees with Thomas at some points and not at others, is Kenelm Foster, "St. Thomas and Dante," *The Two Dantes and Other Studies,* pp. 56–65.

435. Supporters of an Averroistic interpretation of Dante are Miguel Asín y Palacios, *Islam and the Divine Comedy,* pp. 262–64; Bruno Nardi, *Dal "Convivio" alla "Commedia,"* pp. 37–74; "Dante e la filosofia," *Studi danteschi* 25 (1940): 5–42; "Intorno il tomismo di Dante e alla questione di Sigieri," *Giornale dantesco* 22 (1914): 182–97; "L'averroismo del 'primo amico' di Dante," *Studi danteschi* 22 (1940): 43–79; "L'averroismo di Sigieri e Dante," *Studi danteschi* 22 (1938): 83–113.

Although Corti, *Dante,* chaps. 1 and 4, has sought to revive the idea of Dante as an Averroist, the literature after World War II on Dante and Islam stresses instead his putative dependence on the *Libro della Scala,* an eschatological work by an anonymous Muslim author which was discovered in 1946–47. A good review of the bibliography on this question up to 1965 is Vincente Cantarino, "Dante and Islam: History and Analysis of a Controversy," in *A Dante Symposium,* ed. William DeSua and Gino Rizzo, pp. 175–98. More recently, Enrico Cerulli, "Dante e l'Islam," *Atti della Accademia delle scienze di Torino: Classe di scienze morali, storiche e filologiche* 107, no. 1 (1973): 383–402; Silvio Pelosi, *Dante e la cultura islamica;* and Germán Sepúlveda, *Influencia del Islam en la Divina Commedia,* have supported the thesis of Dante's dependence on the *Libro della*

Scala, while it has been opposed by Vincent Cantarino, "Dante and Islam: Theory of Light in the *Paradiso,*" *Kentucky Romance Quarterly* 15 (1968): 3–35; and Edoardo Crema, *La leyenda de un Dante islamizado.* A more recent entry, Egidio Guidubaldi, ed., *Dal "De luce" di R. Grossatesta all'islamico "Libro della scala,"* prints the relevant texts and emphasizes parallels between Dante and his possible sources along the lines of Jungian archetypal theory, rather than arguing for or against genetic influence.

436. R. E. Kaske, "Dante's 'DXV' and 'Veltro,'" *Traditio* 17 (1961): 185–254; Gertrude Leigh, *New Light on the Youth of Dante* and *The Passing of Beatrice* support a Joachite interpretation. The most recent review of the literature on this question is Giannantonio, *Dante,* pp. 148–49 n.5. Davis, *Dante,* pp. 405–54, also reviews the bibliography and concludes that Dante was not a Joachite, a view sustained by Marjorie Reeves, "Dante and the Prophetic View of History," in *The World of Dante,* ed. Cecil Grayson, pp. 44–60.

437. Gertrude Leigh, "Links between Dante and Duns Scotus," *Church Quarterly Review* 96 (1923): 306–31. The literature on the entire question of Dante's alleged philosophical preferences is given a thorough review by Cesare Vasoli, "Filosofia e teologia in Dante," *Cultura e scuola* 4 (1965): 47–71.

438. *Par.* 5.105, 5.119–20, 8.46–48, 21.64–66.

439. Ibid., 17.34–35.

440. Ibid., 14.88–90, 24.106–54, 25.67–139, 26.13–66, 33.1–39.

441. Ibid., 3.1–3, 29.73–75, 30.55–57.

442. Ibid., 8.32–148.

443. Ibid., 26.123–38. See also note 142, this chapter.

444. In addition to the spoken word, Dante uses the written word, as in the message over the gate of Hell, the inscription on Pope Anastasius's tomb identifying the occupant, and the phrase "Diligite justitiam qui judicatis terram" spelled out by the souls in the Heaven of Jupiter (*Inf.* 3.1–9, 11.8–9; *Par.* 18.90, 18.93).

445. *Inf.* 1.60.

446. *Par.* 1.76–78.

447. Ibid., 29.142–44.

448. Ibid., 33.86. See Curtius, "Das Buch als Symbol," pp. 44–54; "Schrift- und Buchmetaphorik," pp. 70–86.

449. *Purg.* 17.34–39, 19.7–33, 27.97–108.

450. Ibid., 12.64–69.

451. Ibid., 10.52, 10.39–45, 10.58–60, 10.82–93.

452. Ibid., 10.95.

453. Noted by Baldwin, *Medieval Rhetoric,* pp. 273, 279; Freccero, *Dante,* pp. 2–3; Gilbert, *Dante's Conception of Justice;* Wilkins, *Dante,* p. 37.

454. *Purg.* 10.79–81; *Par.* 6.1–9, 18.70–136; *Purg.* 32.112–17, 32.124–41.

455. *Par.* 1.48.

456. *Purg.* 9.19–49. In this connection, see Exod. 19:4: "Ye have seen what I did unto the Egyptians and how I bore you on eagle's wings and brought you unto myself."

On the exodus theme in the *Comedy*, see Singleton, "In Exitu Israel de Aegypto," pp. 102–21, and especially 117, 120–21. I am indebted to Professor Andrew Bongiorno for this reference.

457. *Par.* 26.53.

458. *Inf.* 4.94–96.

459. *Par.* 1.47.

460. *Inf.* 1.17–18.

461. *Purg.* 7.25–27.

462. Ibid., 31.121–23.

463. Ibid., 32.1–12; *Par.* 3.1–6.

464. *Par.* 1.13–15.

465. *Conv.* 1.13.12; *De mon.* 2.1.4–6.

466. *Par.* 1.61–63.

467. *Purg.* 16.106–14.

468. Ibid., 22.130–54, 24.100–126.

469. Ibid., 20.43–44.

470. Ibid., 32.100–103, 32.37–60, 32.86–99.

471. *Par.* 1.25–27.

472. *Purg.* 33.142–45.

473. Auerbach, *Dante*, pp. 49, 97–98, 160–73; Barbi, *Life of Dante*, pp. 72, 83; Luigi Cellucci, "La poetica di Dante e la sua poesia," *Cultura neolatina* 10, no. 1 (1950): 89; Gilbert, *Dante*, pp. 62, 64–66; Grandgent, *Power of Dante*, pp. 224–25; Laurenzi, *Ermetica ed ermeneutica*, p. 10; Malagoli, *Linguaggio e poesia*, especially pp. 7–26; Mazzeo, *Medieval Cultural Tradition*, p. 9; *Structure and Thought*, pp. 46–47; Singleton, *Journey to Beatrice*, p. 7; Williams, *Figure of Beatrice*, p. 199; Zingarelli, *La vita*, 2:773–74.

474. Bergin, "On the *Personae* of the *Comedy*," pp. 1–7.

475. As shown by Erich Auerbach's exemplary analysis of the speeches of Farinata and Cavalcanti in *Mimesis*, pp. 151–76; and Renato Poggioli's "Paolo and Franscesca," *Dante*, pp. 61–77. Many other characters in the *Comedy* are susceptible of this kind of analysis, and await their Auerbachs and Poggiolis. It goes without saying that Dante, like other medieval thinkers, regards most of the characters in classical fiction as historical personages.

476. *Par.* 6.127–42.

477. Ibid., 17.124–42.

478. Auerbach, *Dante*, pp. 19–21, 154–55; Barbi, *Life of Dante*, p. 83; Bergin, *Dante*, pp. 252, 279–86; "Hell: Topography and Demography," in *Essays on Dante*, ed. Mark Musa, pp. 77–78; Eliot, *Dante*, p. 24; Gilbert, *Dante*, pp. 84–100; Ker, *Essays*, p. 49; Pischedda, *L'orrido e l'ineffabile*, pp. 100 ff.; Sayers, *Introductory Papers*, pp. 8–9, 121–42; *Further Papers*, p. 55; Scandura, *L'estetica di Dante*, pp. 109 ff.; Vittorino, *High Points*, pp. 10–11.

479. Bergin, *Dante*, pp. 279, 286.

480. *Inf.* 27.7–15, 30.1–27, 31.4–6; *Purg.* 27.37–42, 29.4–7; *Par.* 1.68, 2.16–18, 17.46–48, 33.66.

481. *Inf.* 2.127–32, 3.112–17, 25.58–60; *Purg.* 32.52–60, 33.142–45; *Par.* 4.130–31, 22.52–57, 26.85–90.

482. *Inf.* 2.44–48, 3.115–17, 5.40–49, 5.82–87, 6.28–33, 7.82–84, 8.49–51, 9.76–81, 12.22–25, 13.109–14, 13.124–26, 16.1–3, 17.16–24, 17.48–50, 17.127–35, 22.19–30, 22.127–32, 25.130–32, 26.28–33, 30.25–27, 32.30–36, 32.50–51, 34.46–51; *Purg.* 2.124–33, 9.13–18, 12.1–3, 13.67–72, 13.122–23, 19.64–67, 24.64–69, 25.10–15, 26.34–39, 26.43–48, 26.133–35, 27.76–87, 32.128–35; *Par.* 4.1–6, 4.127–28, 5.82–84, 5.100–105, 8.52–54, 18.73–78, 19.34–39, 19.91–96, 20.73–78, 21.34–45, 23.1–12, 25.19–24, 26.97–102, 31.7–12.

483. *Inf.* 5.28–30, 7.13–17, 9.64–72, 9.112–17, 12.4–10, 13.7–9, 14.28–30, 14.79–81, 15.4–12, 16.94–105, 20.61–93, 24.1–18, 32.22–30, 34.4–7; *Purg.* 3.49–51, 4.25–27, 5.37–42, 5.94–129, 10.7–9, 12.100–108, 14.16–21, 14.130–35, 17.1–12, 24.145–50, 28.7–21, 30.85–99, 33.109–11; *Par.* 8.58–78, 9.25–31, 11.43–54, 16.82–84, 20.19–21, 21.106–11, 22.99, 23.40–45, 27.28–30, 27.67–72, 28.79–87, 30.46–51, 31.118–32.

484. *Inf.* 1.22–27, 1.55–58, 2.37–42, 8.22–24, 15.16–21, 15.120–24, 16.22–27, 16.130–36, 17.85–88, 18.22–23, 19.49–50, 20.7–9, 21.7–18, 23.1–3, 23.37–42, 29.46–51, 30.52–57, 30.91–92, 30.136–41, 31.34–39, 32.32–33, 32.127–29, 34.44–45; *Purg.* 2.10–12, 4.19–24, 4.103–5, 6.1–12, 9.16–18, 9.41–42, 9.64–67, 12.127–29, 13.58–66, 15.3, 16.10–14, 16.85–94, 17.40–45, 23.1–3, 23.16–21, 24.70–74, 24.94–97, 24.106–8, 25.4–7, 26.67–70, 27.44–45, 28.52–57, 30.58–63, 30.79–81, 31.64–67, 32.19–24, 32.67–68, 33.130–34; *Par.* 1.51, 1.101–2, 2.127–29, 2.133–38, 4.1–3, 10.79–81, 18.58–69, 22.1–6, 23.121–26, 24.46–51, 24.148–54, 25.102–8, 25.133–39, 30.82–96, 30.138–41, 31.43–48, 32.139–41, 33.58–61, 33.106–8, 33.133–36.

485. *Inf.* 8.13–18, 14.37–39, 17.135–36, 19.28–30, 23.46–49, 25.57–66, 26.38–39, 26.85–87, 34.10–12; *Purg.* 15.16–24, 17.31–33, 24.136–39, 25.17–18, 25.91–99, 30.85–90, 31.15–21, 31.96, 33.79–81; *Par.* 1.40–42, 1.58–60, 2.22–24, 2.31–36, 2.89–90, 5.91–94, 8.16–21, 9.112–14, 14.1–9, 14.52–57, 15.22–24, 16.28–32, 17.121–23, 18.70–72, 19.4–6, 19.19–21, 20.22–27, 20.79–81, 21.28–29, 24.13–16, 28.4–12, 28.88–93, 29.25–30, 30.109–14.

486. *Inf.* 17.19–20, 17.100–105, 18.10–13, 19.16–18, 28.22–27, 29.73–84, 31.58–59, 31.136–45, 32.49–50, 34.46–48; *Purg.* 1.2, 4.91–93, 10.130–39, 17.77–78, 24.1–3, 32.116–17; *Par.* 2.1–15, 5.37–39, 10.139–48, 14.118–23, 20.142–48, 23.67–69.

487. Singleton, "Dante and Myth," pp. 484–87.

Bibliography

Reference Works

Ashworth, A. J. *The Tradition of Medieval Logic and Speculative Grammar from Anselm to the End of the Seventeenth Century: A Bibliography from 1836 Onwards.* Toronto: Pontifical Institute of Mediaeval Studies, 1978.

Bourke, Vernon J. *Thomistic Bibliography, 1920–1940.* Supplement to *Modern Schoolman,* vol. 21. Saint Louis, Mo.: The Modern Schoolman, 1945.

Deferrari, Roy J. *A Latin-English Dictionary of St. Thomas Aquinas.* Boston: St. Paul Editions, 1960.

Du Cange, C. *Glossarium mediae et infimae latinitatis.* Vol. 1. Graz: Akademische Druck-u. Verlagsanstalt, 1954.

Forcellini, Aegidius. *Totius latinitatis lexicon.* Vol. 1. Prato: Aldini Edenti, 1858.

Mandonnet, P., and Destrez, J. *Bibliographie thomiste.* 2d ed. Revised by M.-D. Chenu. Paris: Vrin, 1960.

Thesaurus linguae latinae. Vol. 1. Leipzig: Teubner, 1900.

Wyser, Paul. *Thomas von Aquin.* Bibliographische Einführungen in das Studium der Philosophie, edited by I. M. Bochenski, vols. 13–14. Bern: A. Francke, 1950.

Primary Sources

Abbo of Fleury. *Quaestiones grammaticales. PL,* vol. 139. Paris, 1853.

Alcuin. *Grammatica. PL,* vol. 101. Paris, 1851.

Anselm of Besate. *Rhetorimachia.* Edited by Karl Manitius. *Monumenta Germaniae Historica: Quellen zur Geistesgeschichte des Mittelalters,* vol. 2, pt. 2. Weimar: Hermann Böhlaus Nachfolger, 1958.

Anselm of Canterbury. *Anselm of Canterbury.* Translated and edited by Jasper Hopkins and Herbert Richardson. 4 vols. Toronto: Edwin Mellen Press, 1975–76.

———. *Basic Writings.* Translated by S. N. Deane. Introduction by Charles Hartshorne. La Salle, Ill.: Open Court, 1962.

———. *Memorials of St. Anselm.* Edited by R. W. Southern and F. S. Schmitt. London: Oxford University Press, 1969.

———. *Ein neues unvollendetes Werk des hl. Anselm von Canterbury.* Edited by Franciscus Salesius Schmitt. *Beiträge zur Geschichte der Philosophie und Theologie des Mittelalters,* edited by Martin Grabmann, vol. 33, pt. 3. Münster in Westphalia: Aschendorffschen Verlagsbuchhandlung, 1936.

———. *Opera omnia.* Edited by Franciscus Salesius Schmitt. 6 vols. Edinburgh: Thomas Nelson & Sons, 1940–61.

Aquinas, Thomas. *De ente et essentia.* Edited by Charles Boyer. Rome: Gregorian University Press, 1933.

———. *Expositio super librum Boethii de trinitate.* Edited by Bruno Decker. Leiden: E. J. Brill, 1955.

———. *In duodecim libros Metaphysicorum Aristotles expositio.* Edited by M. R. Cathala. Revised by R. Spiazzi. Turin: Marietti, 1950.

———. *In librum beati Dionysii de Divinis nominibus expositio.* Edited by Ceslai Pera. Turin: Marietti, 1950.

———. *Opera omnia iussu impensaque Leonis XIII P.M. edita.* 16 vols. Rome: Typographia Polyglotta, 1882–1948.

———. *Opuscula omnia.* Edited by P. Mandonnet. 5 vols. Paris: Lethiellieux, 1927.

———. *Quaestiones disputatae.* 8th ed., rev. Edited by Raymundi Spiazzi, with P. Bazzi, M. Calcaterra, T. S. Centi, E. Odetto, and P. M. Pession. 2 vols. Turin: Marietti, 1949.

———. *Scriptum super libros Sententiarum magistri Petri Lombardi episcopi parisiensis.* Edited by P. Mandonnet and M. F. Moos. 4 vols. Paris: Lethiellieux, 1929–47.

Aristotle. *Categoriae vel praedicamenta.* Edited by Laurentius Minio-Paluello. *Aristoteles latinus,* vol. 1, pts. 1–5. Bruges: Desclée de Brouwer, 1961.

———. *Rhetoric.* Translated by W. Rhys Roberts. New York: Modern Library, 1924.

———. *The Works of Aristotle.* Vol. 1. Edited by W. D. Ross. Oxford: Oxford University Press, Clarendon Press, 1928.

Arnim, Hans F. A. von, ed. *Stoicorum veterum fragmenta.* 4 vols. Leipzig: Teubner, 1903–24.

Augustine. *Confessionum.* Edited by Lucas Verheijen. *CC,* vol. 27. Turnhout: Brepols, 1981.

———. *Contra academicos.* Edited by Pius Knöll. *CSEL,* vol. 63. Vienna: Hölder-Pichler-Tempsky, 1922.

———. *De catechizandis rudibus; Enchiridion de fide, spe, et charitate. PL,* vol. 40. Paris, 1845.

———. *De civitate dei.* Edited by Bernardus Dombart and Alphonsus Kalb. *CC,* vol. 48. Turnhout: Brepols, 1955.

———. *De dialectica.* Edited by Jan Pinborg. Translated by B. Darrell Jackson. Dordrecht: Reidel, 1975.

————. *De doctrina christiana; De vera religione.* Edited by Iosephus Martin and K.-D. Daur. *CC,* vol. 32. Turnhout: Brepols, 1962.

————. *De fide et symbolo.* Edited by Iosephus Zycha. *CSEL,* vol. 40. Vienna: Tempsky, 1900.

————. *De libero arbitrio.* Edited by Guilelmus M. Green. *CSEL,* vol. 74. Vienna: Hölder-Pichler-Tempsky, 1956.

————. *De magistro.* Edited by Guenther Weigel. *CSEL,* vol. 77. Vienna: Hölder-Pichler-Tempsky, 1961.

————. *De spiritu et littera.* Edited by Carolus F. Urba and Iosephus Zycha. *CSEL,* vol. 60. Vienna: Tempsky, 1913.

————. *De trinitate.* Edited by W. J. Mountain and Fr. Glorie. *CC,* vol. 16, pts. 1–2. Turnhout: Brepols, 1968.

————. *De utilitate credendi.* Edited by Iosephus Zycha. *CSEL,* vol. 25. Vienna: Tempsky, 1891.

————. *De vera religione; De doctrina christiana.* Edited by Iosephus Martin and K.-D. Daur. *CC,* vol. 32. Turnhout: Brepols, 1962.

————. *Enarrationes in Psalmos.* Edited by D. Eligius Dekkers and Ioannes Fraipont. *CC,* vols. 38–40. Turnhout: Brepols, 1956.

————. *Enchiridion de fide, spe, et charitate; De catechizandis rudibus. PL,* vol. 40. Paris, 1845.

————. *Epistula.* Edited by Al. Goldbacher, *CSEL,* vol. 34. Vienna: Tempsky, 1895–1923.

————. *The Greatness of the Soul; The Teacher.* Translated by Joseph M. Colleran. Ancient Christian Writers, vol. 9. Westminster, Md.: Newman Press, 1950.

————. *In Epistolam Ioannis ad Parthos tractatus X. PL,* vol. 25. Paris, 1845.

————. *In Ioannis Evangelium tractatus CXXIV.* Edited by D. Radbodus Willems. *CC,* vol. 36. Turnhout: Brepols, 1954.

————. *Retractationum.* Edited by Pius Knöll. *CSEL,* vol. 36. Vienna: Tempsky, 1902.

————. *Sermones de Scripturis. PL,* vol. 38. Paris, 1845.

————. *Soliliquiorum. PL,* vol. 32. Paris, 1845.

Boccaccio, Giovanni. *Il commento alla Divina Commedia e gli altri scritti intorno di Dante.* Edited by Domenico Guerri. 3 vols. Bari: Gius. Laterza & Figli, 1918.

————. *Genealogie deorum gentilium libri.* Edited by Vincenzo Romano. 2 vols. Bari: Gius. Laterza & Figli, 1951.

————. *Vita di Dante e difesa di poesia.* Edited by Carlo Muscetta. Rome: Edizioni dell'Ateneo, 1963.

Boethius, Anicius Manlius Severinus. *Commentaria in Porphyrium; Commentaria in Aristotelem. PL,* vol. 64. Paris, 1847.

Cicero. *Academica; De natura deorum.* Edited and translated by H. Rackham. LCL. London: William Heinemann, 1933.

————. *De divinatione; De senectute; De amicitia.* Edited and translated by William Armistead Falconer. LCL. London: William Heinemann, 1923.

————. *De inventione; De optimo genere oratorum; Topica.* Edited and translated by H. M. Hubbell. LCL. Cambridge, Mass.: Harvard University Press, 1949.

————. *De optimo genere oratorum; De inventione; Topica.* Edited and translated by H. M. Hubbell. LCL. Cambridge, Mass.: Harvard University Press, 1949.

————. *De oratore.* Edited and translated by E. W. Sutton and H. Rackham. LCL. 2 vols. Cambridge, Mass.: Harvard University Press, 1942.

————. *De partitione oratoria; De oratore, Book III; De fato; Paradoxa stoicorum.* Edited and translated by H. Rackham. LCL. Cambridge, Mass.: Harvard University Press, 1943.

————. *Orator.* Edited and translated by H. M. Hubbell. *Brutus.* Edited and translated by G. L. Hendrickson. LCL. Cambridge, Mass.: Harvard University Press, 1942.

————. *Rhetorica ad Herennium.* Translated by Harry Caplan. LCL. Cambridge, Mass.: Harvard University Press, 1954.

Dante Alighieri. *Convivio.* Edited by Maria Simonelli. Bologna: Patròn, 1966.

————. *Convivio.* Translated by William Walrond Jackson. Oxford: Oxford University Press, Clarendon Press, 1909.

————. *De monarchia.* 2d ed. Translated by Herbert W. Schneider. New York: Liberal Arts Press, 1957.

————. *De vulgari eloquentia.* Edited by P. V. Mengaldo. 2 vols. Padua: Antenore, 1967.

————. *The Divine Comedy.* Translated by Charles S. Singleton. 3 vols. Princeton, N.J.: Princeton University Press, 1970–75.

————. *Epistolae.* 2d ed. Edited and translated by Paget Toynbee. Oxford: Oxford University Press, Clarendon Press, 1966.

————. *Literary Criticism of Dante Alighieri.* Translated and edited by Robert S. Haller. Lincoln: University of Nebraska Press, 1973.

————. *Opere.* Edited by Fredi Chiapelli. Milan: Ugo Mursia, 1965.

Diogenes Laertius. *Lives of the Eminent Philosophers.* Vol. 2. Translated by R. D. Hicks. LCL. London: William Heinemann, 1925.

Disputatio catholicorum patrum adversus dogmata Petri Abaelardi. PL, vol. 180. Paris, 1855.

Donatus. *Ars grammatica.* Edited by Heinrich Keil. *Grammatici latini,* edited by Heinrich Keil, vol. 4. Leipzig: Teubner, 1864.

Eadmer. *The Life of St. Anselm, Archbishop of Canterbury.* Edited and translated by R. W. Southern. London: Thomas Nelson & Sons, 1962.

Gunzo. *Epistola ad Augienses.* Edited by Karl Manitius. *Monumenta Germaniae Historica: Quellen zur Geistesgeschichte des Mittelalters,* vol. 2, pt. 1. Weimar: Hermann Böhlaus Nachfolger, 1958.

Lanfranc. *Liber de corpore et sanguine Domini. PL,* vol. 150. Paris, 1854.

Latini, Brunetto. *Li Livres dou Trésor.* Edited by P. Chabaille. Paris: Imprimerie Impériale, 1863.

Mansi, Joannes Dominicus, ed. *Sacrorum conciliorum, nova, et amplissima collectio.* 1st ser. Edited by Phil. Labbeus, Gabr. Cossartius, and Nicolaus Coleti. 31 vols. Florence: Expensis Antonii Zatta Veneti, 1759–98.

Ordericus Vitalis. *Ecclesiastical History.* Vol. 2. Edited and translated by Marjorie Chibnall. Oxford: Oxford University Press, Clarendon Press, 1969.

Paschasius Radbertus, *Liber de corpore et sanguine Dei. PL,* vol. 120. Paris, 1852.

Pietro Alighieri. *Super Dantis ipsius genitoris Comoediam commentarium.* Edited by Vincentio Nannucci and G. J. Bar. Vernon. Florence: Guilielmum Piatti, 1845.

Plato. *The Dialogues.* 4th ed. Translated by Benjamin Jowett. 4 vols. Oxford: Oxford University Press, Clarendon Press, 1953.

Priscianus. *Institutionum grammaticarum libri XVIII.* Edited by Martin Herz. *Grammatici latini,* edited by Heinrich Keil, vols. 2–3. Leipzig: Teubner, 1865–69.

Quintilian. *Institutiones oratoriae.* Edited and translated by H. E. Butler. LCL. 4 vols. London: William Heinemann, 1933–36.

Rabanus Maurus. *De clericorum institutione. PL,* vol. 107. Paris, 1851.

Remigius of Auxerre. *In Artem Donati minorem commentum.* Edited by W. Fox. Leipzig: Teubner, 1902.

William of Saint Thierry. *Disputatio adversus Petrum Abaelardum ad Gaufridum Carnotensem et Bernardum. PL,* vol. 180. Paris, 1855.

Secondary Sources

Abelson, Paul. *The Seven Liberal Arts: A Study in Mediaeval Culture.* New York, 1906.

Adler, Mortimer J. "The Demonstration of God's Existence." *Thomist* 5 (1943): 188–218. Reprint. *The Maritain Volume of the Thomist.* New York: Sheed & Ward, 1943.

Alexander, Paul J. *The Patriarch Nicephorus of Constantinople: Ecclesiastical Policy and Image Worship in the Byzantine Empire.* Oxford: Oxford University Press, Clarendon Press, 1958.

Alfaric, Prosper. *L'évolution intellectuelle de saint Augustin.* Vol. 1. Paris: Émile Nourry, 1918.

Alici, Luigi. *Il linguaggio come segno e come testimonianza: Una rilettura di Agostino.* Rome: Edizioni Studium, 1976.

Allen, R. E. "The Ontological Argument." *Philosophical Review* 70 (1961): 56–66.

Alston, William P. "The Ontological Argument Revisited." *Philosophical Review* 69 (1960): 452–74.

Anderson, James F., et al. "Some Basic Propositions concerning Metaphysical Analogy." *Review of Metaphysics* 5 (1952): 465–72.

Andrea, Sorrentino. "La coscienza poetica di Dante," *Giornale dantesco* 30 (1927): 181–90.

Antonelli, M. T. "Il significato del Proslogion di Anselmo d'Aosta." *Rivista rosminiana* 45 (1951): 260–68; 46 (1952): 35–43.

Antweiler, Anton. "Anselmus von Canterbury, Monologion und Proslogion." *Scholastik* 8 (1933): 551–60.

Apel, Karl Otto. *Die Idee der Sprache in der Tradition des Humanismus von Dante bis Vico.* Bonn: H. Bouvier, 1963.

Armstrong, Edward. *Italian Studies.* Edited by Cecilia M. Ady. London: Macmillan & Co., 1934.

Asín y Palacios, Miguel. *Islam and the Divine Comedy.* Translated and abridged by Harold Sunderland. New York: E. P. Dutton & Co., 1926.

Assunta, Anselmo Bianucci dell'. "La 'Tertia via' di s. Tommaso: Indagine metafisica." *Ephemerides carmeliticae* 16 (1965): 118–72.

Atkins, J. W. H. *Literary Criticism in Antiquity: A Sketch of Its Development.* Vol. 2. New York: Peter Smith, 1952.

Auber, C. *Histoire et théorie du symbolisme religieux avant et depuis le christianisme.* 4 vols. Paris: Féchoz et Letouzey, 1884.

Auerbach, Erich. *Dante: Poet of the Secular World.* Translated by Ralph Manheim. Chicago: University of Chicago Press, 1961.

———. "Dante's Addresses to the Reader." *Romance Philology* 7 (1954): 268–78.

———. "Figura." *Neue Dantestudien.* Istanbuler Schriften, vol. 5. Istanbul, 1944.

———. "Figurative Texts Illustrating Certain Passages of Dante's *Commedia.*" *Speculum* 21 (1946): 474–89.

———. *Mimesis: The Representation of Reality in Western Literature.* Translated by Willard Trask. Garden City, N.Y.: Doubleday Anchor Books, 1957.

———. "Typological Symbolism in Medieval Literature." *Yale French Studies* 9 (1952): 3–10.

Ayers, Robert H. *Language, Logic, and Reason in the Church Fathers: A Study of Tertullian, Augustine, and Aquinas.* Hildesheim: Georg Ohms Verlag, 1979.

Baldassari, M. "Lo stoicismo antico e l'argomento ontologico." *Rivista di filosofia neo-scolastica* 63 (1971): 391–418, 547–74.

Baldwin, Charles Sears. *Ancient Rhetoric and Poetic Interpreted from Representative Works.* New York: Macmillan Co., 1924.

———. *Medieval Rhetoric and Poetic (to 1400) Interpreted from Representative Works.* New York: Macmillan Co., 1928.

———. "St. Augustine and the Rhetoric of Cicero." *Proceedings of the Classical Association* 22 (1925): 24–46.

Baldwin, Gratia Eaton. *The New Beatrice; or, The Virtue That Counsels.* New York: Columbia University Press, 1928.

Ballard, Edward G. "An Augustinian Doctrine of Signs." *New Scholasticism* 23 (1949): 207–11.

Balthasar, Nicholas. *L'abstraction métaphysique et l'analogie des êtres dans l'être.* Louvain: Em. Warny, 1935.

Bandini, Albert R. "Virgil and Dante—and Statius." *Thought* 5 (1930): 209–23.

Barbi, Michele. *Life of Dante.* Edited and translated by Paul G. Ruggiers. Berkeley and Los Angeles: University of California Press, 1954.

———. *Problemi fondamentali per un nuovo commento della Divina Commedia.* Florence: G. C. Sansoni, 1956.

Bardy, Gustave. *Saint Augustin: L'homme et l'oeuvre.* 7th ed. Paris: Desclée de Brouwer, 1948.

Barry, M. Inviolata. *St. Augustine the Orator: A Study of the Rhetorical Qualities of St. Augustine's Sermones ad Populum.* Catholic University of America Patristic Studies, vol. 6. Washington, D.C. Catholic University of America, 1924.

Barth, Karl. *Anselm: Fides quaerens intellectum. Anselm's Proof of the Existence of God in the Context of His Theological Scheme.* Translated by Ian W. Robertson. Richmond, Va.: John Knox Press, 1960.

Battaglia, Salvatore. "Introduzione alla teoria del poeta teologo." *Cultura e scuola* 4 (1965): 72–86.

Battenhouse, Roy W., ed. *A Companion to the Study of St. Augustine.* New York: Oxford University Press, 1955.

Bayart, J. "The Concept of Mystery according to St. Anselm of Canterbury." *Recherches de théologie ancienne et médiévale* 9 (1937): 125–66.

Behm, Johannes. "Das Bildwort vom Spiegel I. Korinther 13, 12." In *Reinhold-Seeberg-Festschrift,* edited by Wilhelm Koepp. Leipzig: A. Diechertsche Verlagsbuchhandlung D. Werner Scholl, 1929.

Bergenthal, Ferdinand. "Ist der 'ontologische Gottesbeweis' Anselms von Canterbury ein Trugschluss?" *Philosophisches Jahrbuch* 59, no. 2 (1949): 155–68.

Bergin, Thomas G. *Dante.* New York: Orion Press, 1965.

———. "On the *Personae* of the *Comedy.*" *Italica* 42 (1965): 1–7.

Bergmann, Frédéric. *Dante: Sa vie et ses oeuvres.* Strasbourg: C. F. Schmidt, 1881.

Berlinger, Rudolph. *Augustins dialogische Metaphysik.* Frankfort on the Main: Vittorio Klostermann, 1962.

Bertoni, Giulio. "La lingua di Dante." *Nuova antologia* 68, fasc. 1462 (1933): 481–90.

Bethurum, Dorothy, ed. *Critical Approaches to Medieval Literature: Selected Papers from the English Institute, 1958–59.* New York: Columbia University Press, 1960.

Betzendörfer, Walter. "Glauben und Wissen bei Anselm von Canterbury." *Zeitschrift für Kirchengeschichte* 48, n.s. 11 (1929): 354–70.

Beumer, Johannes. "Thomas von Aquin zum Wesen der Theologie." *Scholastik* 30 (1955): 196–214.

Biffi, Inos. "Prospettive e articolazioni della 'sacra doctrina' nei 'principia' e nel prologo all' 'In Boethium de trinitate' di san Tommaso d'Aquino." *La scuola cattolica* 100 (1972): 290–312.

Bilancioni, Guglielmo. *Il suono e la voce nell'opera di Dante.* Pisa: Mariotti e Pacini, 1927.

Biondolillo, Francesco. *Poetica e poesia di Dante.* Biblioteca di cultura contemporanea, vol. 19. Messina: G. d'Anna, 1948.

Blackmur, R. P. "Dante's Ten Terms for the Treatment of the Treatise." *Kenyon Review* 14 (1952): 286–300.

Blair, George A. "Another Look at St. Thomas' 'First Way.' " *International Philosophical Quarterly* 16 (1976): 301–14.

Blanche, F. A. "L'analogie." *Revue de philosophie* 23 (1923): 248–70.

———. "La notion d'analogie dans la philosophie de s. Thomas d'Aquin." *Revue des sciences philosophiques et théologiques* 10 (1921): 169–93.

———. "Une théorie de l'analogie." *Revue de philosophie,* n.s. 3 (1932): 37–78.

Bloomfield, Morton W. "Symbolism in Medieval Literature." *Modern Philology* 56 (1958): 73–81.

Bochenski, I. M. "On Analogy." *Thomist* 11 (1948): 424–47.

Boehner, Philotheus. *Medieval Logic: An Outline of Its Development from 1250–c. 1400.* Manchester: Manchester University Press, 1952.

Bonhoeffer, Thomas. *Die Gotteslehre des Thomas von Aquin als Sprachproblem.* Tübingen: J. C. B. Mohr, 1961.

Bonnefoy, Jean F. *La nature de la théologie selon saint Thomas d'Aquin.* Paris: Vrin, 1939.

———. "La théologie comme science et l'explication de la foi selon saint Thomas d'Aquin." *Ephemerides theologicae lovanienses* 14 (1937): 412–46, 600–631; 15 (1938): 491–516.

Bonner, Gerald. *St. Augustine of Hippo: Life and Controversies.* Philadelphia: Westminster Press, 1963.

Bonnette, Dennis. *Aquinas' Proofs for God's Existence: St. Thomas Aquinas on "the 'per accidens' necessarily implies the 'per se.' "* The Hague: Martinus Nijhoff, 1972.

Bourke, Vernon J. *Augustine's Quest of Wisdom: Life and Philosophy of the Bishop of Hippo.* Milwaukee, Wisc.: Bruce Publishing Co., 1945.

Bowden, John Paul. *An Analysis of Pietro Alighieri's Commentary on "The Divine Comedy."* New York, 1951.

Boyer, Charles. *Essais sur la doctrine de saint Augustin.* Paris: Gabriel Beauchesne et ses fils, 1932.

———. *L'idée de vérité dans la philosophie de saint Augustin.* Paris: Gabriel Beauchesne, 1920.

———. "La preuve de Dieu augustinienne." *Archives de philosophie* 7, no. 2 (1930): 105–41.

Bradley, Ritamary. "Backgrounds of the Title *Speculum* in Mediaeval Literature." *Speculum* 29 (1954): 100–115.

———. "The Mirror of Truth according to St. Thomas." *Modern Schoolman* 31 (1954): 307–17.

Brandeis, Irma. *The Ladder of Vision: A Study of Dante's Comedy.* London: Chatto & Windus, 1960.

———. "Metaphor in the Divine Comedy." *Hudson Review* 8 (1956): 557–75.

Bréhier, Émile. *Chrysippe et l'ancien stoïcisme.* 2d ed. Paris: PUF, 1951.

Brown, Patterson. "St. Thomas' Doctrine of Necessary Being." *Philosophical Review* 73 (1964): 76–90.

Brown, Peter. *Augustine of Hippo.* Berkeley and Los Angeles: University of California Press, 1967.

Bruyne, Edgar de. *L'esthétique du moyen âge.* Louvain: Éditions de l'Institut Supérieur de Philosophie, 1947.

———. *Études d'esthétique médiévale.* 3 vols. Bruges: De Tempel, 1946.

Bryar, William. *St. Thomas and the Existence of God: Three Interpretations.* Chicago: Henry Regnery Co., 1951.

Buck, August. "Dante im Urteil der Literaturästhetik des italienischen Humanismus." *Deutsches Dante-Jahrbuch* 28 (1949): 1–15.

———. "Gli studi sulla poetica e sulla retorica di Dante e del suo tempo." *Cultura e scuola* 4 (1965): 143–66.

Burke, Kenneth. *The Rhetoric of Religion: Studies in Logology.* Boston: Beacon Press, 1961.

Burnaby, John. *Amor Dei: A Study of the Religion of St. Augustine.* London: Hodder & Stoughton, 1938.

Burrell, David. "Aquinas on Naming God." *Theological Studies* 24 (1963): 183–212.

———. "A Note on Analogy." *New Scholasticism* 36 (1962): 225–32.

———. "Religious Language and the Logic of Analogy: Apropos of McInerny's Book and Ross' Review." *International Philosophical Quarterly* 2 (1962): 643–58.

Butler, Cuthbert. *Western Mysticism: The Teaching of SS. Augustine, Gregory, and Bernard on Contemplation and the Contemplative Life: Neglected Chapters in the History of Religion.* London: Constable & Co., 1922.

Byles, M. Esdaile. "The Analogy of Being." *New Scholasticism* 16 (1942): 331–64.

Callahan, John F. *Four Views of Time in Ancient Philosophy.* Cambridge, Mass.: Harvard University Press, 1948.

Cambon, Glauco. "Dante and the Drama of Language." *Dante's Craft: Studies in Language and Style.* Minneapolis: University of Minnesota Press, 1969.

Campbell, Richard. "Anselm's Theological Method." *Scottish Journal of Theology* 32 (1979): 541–62.

———. *From Belief to Understanding: A Study of Anselm's Proslogion Argument on the Existence of God.* Canberra: Australian National University, 1976.

Cantarino, Vincente. "Dante and Islam: History and Analysis of a Controversy." In *A Dante Symposium in Commemoration of the Seven-hundredth Anniversary of the Poet's Birth,* edited by William DeSua and Gino Rizzo. Chapel Hill: University of North Carolina Press, 1965.

———. "Dante and Islam: "Theory of Light in the *Paradiso.*" *Kentucky Romance Quarterly* 15 (1968): 3–35.

Caplan, Harry. "Classical Rhetoric and the Mediaeval Theory of Preaching." In *Historical Studies of Rhetoric and Rhetoricians,* edited by Raymond F. Howes. Ithaca,

N.Y.: Cornell University Press, 1961.

Cappuyns, D. M. "L'argument de s. Anselme." *Recherches de théologie ancienne et médiévale* 6 (1934): 313–30.

Carré, Meyrick H. *Realists and Nominalists.* Oxford: Oxford University Press, 1946.

Carter, Barbara Barclay. "Dante's Political Conception." *Hibbert Journal* 35 (1937): 568–79.

————. "Dante's Political Ideas." *Review of Politics* 5 (1943): 338–55.

Casciola, Brizio. *L'enimma dantesco.* Bergamo: Istituto Italiano d'Arti Grafiche, 1950.

Casotti, Mario. "Il 'De magistro' di s. Agostino e il metodo intuitivo." *S. Agostino: Pubblicazione commemorativa del quindicesimo centenario della sua morte.* Supplement to *Rivista di filosofia neo-scolastica* 23 (1931): 57–74.

Caturelli, Alberto. *La doctrina agustiniana sobre el maestro y su desarrollo en Santo Tomás de Aquino.* Córodoba, Argentina: Instituto de Metafísica, 1954.

Cayré, Fulbert. *La contemplation augustinienne: Principes de la spiritualité de saint Augustin.* Paris: André Blot, 1927.

————. *Initiation à la philosophie de saint Augustin.* Paris: Desclée de Brouwer, 1947.

Cellucci, Luigi. "La poetica di Dante e la sua poesia." *Cultura neolatina* 10, no. 1 (1950): 77–97.

Cenacchi, Giuseppe. *Il pensiero filosofico di Anselmo d'Aosta.* Padua: CEDAM, 1974.

Cerulli, Enrico. "Dante e l'Islam." *Atti della Accademia delle scienze di Torino: Classe di scienze morali, storiche e filologiche* 107, no. 1 (1973): 383–402.

Charlesworth, M. J. "St. Anselm's Argument." *Sophia* 1 (1962): 25–36.

Chavannes, Henry. *L'analogie entre Dieu et le monde selon saint Thomas d'Aquin et selon Karl Barth.* Paris: Éditions du Cerf, 1969.

Chenu, M.-D. "Un essai de méthode théologique au douzième siècle." *Revue des sciences philosophiques et théologiques* 24 (1935): 258–67.

————. "Grammaire et théologie aux douzième et treizième siècles." *Archives d'histoire doctrinale et littéraire du moyen âge* 10 (1935): 5–28.

————. *Introduction a l'étude de saint Thomas d'Aquin.* 2d ed. Université de Montréal Publications de l'Institut d'Études Médiévales, vol. 11. Montreal: Institut d'Études Médiévales, 1954.

————. "Les 'Philosophes' dans la philosophie chrétienne médiévale." *Revue des sciences philosophiques et théologiques* 26 (1937): 27–40.

————. "La psychologie de la foi dans la théologie du treizième siècle." In *Études d'histoire littéraire et doctrinale du treizième siècle.* Publications de l'Institut d'Études Médiévales d'Ottawa, vol. 2. Paris: Vrin, 1932.

————. *La théologie au douzième siècle.* Paris: Vrin, 1957.

————. "La théologie comme science au treizième siècle." *Archives d'histoire doctrinale et littéraire du moyen âge* 2 (1927): 31–71.

————. *La théologie comme science au treizième siècle.* 3d ed. Paris: Vrin, 1957.

Chiapparini, Giovanni. "Dante e la poesia dell'ineffabile." *Rassegna nazionale,* 3d ser.

20 (1934): 425–29.

Chydenius, Johan. *The Theory of Medieval Symbolism*. Societas Scientiarum Fennica, Commentationes Humanarum Litterarum, vol. 27, no. 2. Helsinki: Centraltryckeriet, 1960.

———. *The Typological Problem in Dante: A Study in the History of Medieval Ideas*. Societas Scientiarum Fennica, Commentationes Humanarum Litterarum, vol. 25, no. 1. Helsinki: Centraltryckeriet, 1958.

Cicchetti, Armando. *L'agostinismo nel pensiero di Anselmo d'Aosta*. Rome: "Arte e Storia," 1951.

Cippico, Antonio, et al., eds. *Dante: Essays in Commemoration, 1321–1921*. London: University of London Press, 1921.

Clark, Donald Lemen. *Rhetoric in Graeco-Roman Education*. New York: Columbia University Press, 1957.

Clarke, M. L. *Rhetoric at Rome: A Historical Survey*. London: Cohen & West, 1953.

Clayton, Joseph. *Saint Anselm: A Critical Biography*. Milwaukee, Wisc.: Bruce Publishing Co., 1933.

Clements, Robert J., ed. *American Critical Essays on the Divine Comedy*. New York: New York University Press, 1967.

Cochrane, Charles Norris. *Christianity and Classical Culture: A Study of Thought and Action from Augustus to Augustine*. New York: Oxford University Press, 1957.

Colish, Marcia L. "Anselm's Philosophy of Language Reconsidered." *Anselm Studies*, in press.

———. "St. Augustine's Rhetoric of Silence Revisited." *Augustinian Studies* 9 (1978): 15–24.

———. "The Stoic Theory of Verbal Signification and the Problem of Lies and False Statements from Antiquity to St. Anselm." In *L'archéologie du signe*, edited by Lucie Brind'Amour and Eugene Vance. Toronto: Pontifical Institute of Mediaeval Studies, 1983.

Collart, Jean. "Saint Augustin grammarien dans le *De magistro*." *Revue des études augustiniennes* 17 (1971): 279–92.

Combès, Gustave. *Saint Augustin et la culture classique*. Paris: Plon, 1927.

Comeau, Marie. *La rhétorique de saint Augustin d'après les Tractatus in Ioannem*. Paris: Boivin & Cie, 1930.

———. *Saint Augustin: Exégète du quatrième évangile*. Paris: Gabriel Beauchesne, 1930.

Comparetti, Domenico. *Vergil in the Middle Ages*. Translated by E. F. M. Beneke. London: Swan Sonnenschein & Co., 1908.

Conklin, Henry Ernest. "The Aesthetic of Dante." *Rice Institute Pamphlet* 8, no. 2 (1921): 118–38.

Connolly, Thomas Kevin. "The Basis of the Third Proof for the Existence of God." *Thomist* 17 (1954): 280–349.

Consoli, Domenico. *Significato del Virgilio dantesco*. Florence: Le Monnier, 1967.

Contri, Siro. *Il problema della verità in s. Tommaso d'Aquino*. Turin: Società Editrice

Internazionale, 1925.

Copleston, F. C. *Aquinas*. Baltimore: Penguin Books, 1955.

————. *A History of Philosophy*. Vols. 1–2. New and rev. ed. Westminster, Md.: Newman Press, 1957–59.

Corti, Maria. *Dante a un nuovo crocevia*. Florence: Sansoni, 1981.

Cottiaux, Jean. "La conception de la théologie chez Abélard." *Revue d'histoire ecclésiastique* 28 (1932): 247–95, 533–51, 788–828.

Courcelle, Pierre. *Les Confessions de saint Augustin dans la tradition littéraire: Antécédents et posterité*. Paris: Études Augustiniennes, 1963.

————. *Late Latin Writers and Their Greek Sources*. Translated by Harry E. Wedeck. Cambridge, Mass.: Harvard University Press, 1969.

————. *Recherches sur les Confessions de saint Augustin*. Paris: E. de Boccard, 1950.

Creaven, J. A. "Aspects of Analogy," *Philosophical Studies* 8 (1958): 71–88.

Crema, Edoardo. *La leyenda de un Dante islamizado*. Caracas: Editorial Arte, 1966.

Croce, Benedetto. *The Poetry of Dante*. Translated by Douglas Ainslie. New York: Henry Holt & Co., 1922.

Crowe, M. B. "St. Thomas against the Gentiles." *Irish Theological Quarterly* 29 (1962): 93–120.

Curtius, Ernst Robert. "Das Buch als Symbol in der Divina Commedia." In *Festschrift zum sechzigsten Geburtstag von Paul Clemen*. Bonn: Fried. Cohen, 1926.

————. "Dante und das lateinische Mittelalter." *Romanische Forschungen* 57, nos. 2–3 (1943): 153–85.

————. *European Literature and the Latin Middle Ages*. Translated by Willard Trask. New York: Pantheon Books, 1953.

————. "The Medieval Basis of Western Thought." *Gesammelte Aufsätze zur romanischen Philologie*. Bern: Franke Verlag, 1960.

————. "Neue Dantestudien." *Gesammelte Aufsätze zur romanischen Philologie*. Bern: Franke Verlag, 1960.

————. "Schrift- und Buchmetaphorik in der Weltliteratur." In *Neue Beiträge deutscher Forschung: Wilhelm Worringer zum sechzigsten Geburtstag*, edited by Erich Fidder. Königsberg: Kanter-Verlag, 1943.

————. "Theologische Poetik im italienischen Trecento." *Zeitschrift für romanische Philologie* 60 (1940): 1–5.

————. "Zur Geschichte des Wortes Philosophie in Mittelalter." *Romanische Forschungen* 57, nos. 2–3 (1943): 290–309.

Dallari, Gino. "Sul concetto della nobiltà nella terza canzone del 'Convivio' Dantesco." Reale Istituto Lombardo di scienze e lettere. *Rendiconti*, 2d ser. 61 (1928): 572–80.

Dal Pra, Mario. "Gaunilone e il problema logico del linguaggio." *Rivista critica di storia della filosofia* 9 (1954): 456–84.

————. "Il problema del fondamento del significato nella controversia fra Anselmo e Gaunilone." *Rivista critica di storia della filosofia* 9 (1954): 132–55.

————. "Studi sul problema logico del linguaggio nella filosofia medioevale, I:

'Cogitatio vocum' e 'cogitatio rerum' nel pensiero di Anselmo." *Rivista critica di storia della filosofia* 9 (1954): 309–43.

D'Alton, J. F. *Roman Literary Theory and Criticism: A Study in Tendencies.* London: Longmans, Green & Co., 1931.

Damon, Phillip. "The Two Modes of Allegory in Dante's *Convivio.*" *Philosophical Quarterly* 40 (1961): 144–49.

Daniélou, Jean. *From Shadows to Reality: Studies in the Biblical Typology of the Fathers.* Translated by Wulstan Hibberd. London: Burns & Oates, 1960.

————. *God and the Ways of Knowing.* Translated by Walter Roberts. New York: Greenwich Editions, 1957.

Daniels, Donald E. "The Argument of the *De trinitate* and Augustine's Theory of Signs." *Augustinian Studies* 8 (1977): 33–54.

Daniels, P. Augustinus. *Quellenbeiträge und Untersuchungen zur Geschichte der Gottesbeweise im dreizehnten Jahrhundert mit besonderer Berucksichtingung des Arguments im Proslogion des hl. Anselm. Beiträge zur Geschichte der Philosophie des Mittelalters,* edited by Clemens Bauemker, vol. 8, pts. 1–2. Münster in Westphalia: Aschendorffschen Buchhandlung, 1909.

D'Arcy, M. C. *Thomas Aquinas.* London: Ernest Benn, 1930.

————, et al. *St. Augustine.* New York: Meridian Books, 1957.

Davies, A. E. "The Problem of Truth and Existence as Treated by Anselm." *Proceedings of the Aristotelian Society,* n.s. 20 (1920): 167–90.

Davies, Leo Donald. "Hincmar of Rheims as a Theologian of the Trinity." *Traditio* 27 (1971): 455–68.

Davis, Charles Till. "Brunetto Latini and Dante." *Studi medievali,* 3d ser. 8 (1967): 421–50.

————. *Dante and the Idea of Rome.* Oxford: Oxford University Press, Clarendon Press, 1957.

Dazeley, Howard L., and Gombocz, Wolfgang L. "Interpreting Anselm as a Logician." *Synthese* 40 (1979): 71–96.

Dedek, John F. "*Quasi experimentalis cognitio:* A Historical Approach to the Meaning of St. Thomas." *Theological Studies* 22 (1961): 357–90.

Demus, Otto. *Byzantine Mosaic Decoration: Aspects of Monumental Art in Byzantium.* London: Kegan Paul Trench Trubner & Co., 1948.

De Sanctis, Francesco. *History of Italian Literature.* Vol. 1. Translated by Joan Redfern. New York: Basic Books, 1959.

————. *Lezioni sulla Divina Commedia.* Edited by Michele Manfredi. Bari: Gius. Laterza & Figli, 1955.

Devisse, Jean. *Hincmar, archevêque de Reims, 845–882.* 3 vols. Geneva: Librairie Droz, 1975–76.

Diggs, Bernard J. "St. Augustine against the Academicians." *Traditio* 7 (1949–51): 73–93.

Dinsmore, Charles Allen. *Life of Dante Alighieri.* Boston: Houghton Mifflin Co., 1919.

———. *The Teachings of Dante*. Boston: Houghton Mifflin Co., 1901.

Domet de Vorges, le Comte. *Saint Anselme*. Paris: Félix Alcan, 1901.

Dondaine, H. F. *Le corpus dionysien de l'Université de Paris au treizième siècle*. Rome: Storia e Letteratura, 1953.

Donovan, Mary Annice. *The Henological Argument for the Existence of God in the Works of St. Thomas Aquinas*. Notre Dame, Ind., 1946.

Douglas, David C. *William the Conquerer: The Norman Impact upon England*. Berkeley and Los Angeles: University of California Press, 1964.

Dragonetti, Roger. *Aux frontières du langage poétique: Études sur Dante, Mallarmé, Valéry*. Romanica Gandensa, vol. 9. Ghent: Rijksuniversiteit te Gent, Faculteit der Wijsbegeerte en Letteren, 1961.

Duchrow, Ulrich. *Sprachverständnis und biblisches Hören bei Augustin*. Tübingen: J. C. B. Mohr, 1965.

Duclow, Donald F. "Divine Nothingness and Self-Creation in John Scotus Eriugena." *Journal of Religion* 57 (1977): 109–23.

———. "Structure and Meaning in Anselm's *De veritate*." *American Benedictine Review* 26 (1975): 406–17.

Dunbar, H. Flanders. *Symbolism in Medieval Thought and Its Consummation in "The Divine Comedy."* New Haven, Conn.: Yale University Press, 1929.

Dunne, John S. "St. Thomas' Theology of Participation." *Theological Studies* 18 (1957): 487–512.

Durantel, J. *Le retour à Dieu par l'intelligence et la volonté dans la philosophie de s. Thomas*. Paris: Félix Alcan, 1918.

Ebbesen, Sten. "The Dead Man Is Alive." *Synthese* 40 (1979): 43–70.

Elders, Léon. "Justification des 'cinq voies.' " *Revue thomiste* 61 (1961): 207–25.

Eliot, T. S. *Dante*. The Poets on the Poets, no. 2. London: Faber & Faber, 1930.

Enders, Heinz W. "Die 'quinque viae' des Thomas Aquinas und das Argument aus Anselms Proslogion: Eine bezeichnungstheoretische Analyse." *Wissenschaft und Weisheit* 40 (1977): 158–88.

Endres, Jos. Ant. *Forschungen zur Geschichte der frühmittelalterlichen Philosophie. Beiträge zur Geschichte der Philosophie des Mittelalters*, edited by Clemens Bauemker, vol. 17, pts. 2–3. Münster in Westphalia: Aschendorffsche Verlagsbuchhandlung, 1915.

Ercole, Francesco. *Il pensiero politico di Dante*. 2 vols. Milan: Edizioni "Alpes," 1927–28.

Eskridge, James Burnette. *The Influence of Cicero upon Augustine in the Development of His Oratorical Theory for the Training of the Ecclesiastical Orator*. Menasha, Wisc.: Collegiate Press, 1912.

Evans, Gillian R. *Anselm and a New Generation*. Oxford: Oxford University Press, Clarendon Press, 1980.

———. *Anselm and Talking about God*. Oxford: Oxford University Press, Clarendon Press, 1978.

―――. "The Grammar of Predestination in the Ninth Century." *Journal of Theological Studies*, n.s. 33 (1982): 134–45.

―――. "*Inopes verborum sunt latini:* Technical Language and Technical Terms in the Writings of St. Anselm and Some Commentators of the Mid-twelfth Century." *Archives d'histoire doctrinale et littéraire du moyen âge,* 43 (1976): 113–34.

―――. *Old Arts and New Theology: The Beginnings of Theology as an Academic Discipline.* Oxford: Oxford University Press, Clarendon Press, 1980.

―――. "The 'Secure Technician': Varieties of Paradox in the Writings of St. Anselm." *Vivarium* 13 (1975): 1–21.

Ewert, A. "Dante's Theory of Language." *Modern Language Review* 35 (1940): 355–66.

Fallani, Giovanni. *Poesia e teologia nella Divina Commedia.* 2 vols. Milan: Marzorati, 1959–61.

Faral, Edmond. *Les arts poétiques du douzième et du treizième siècle: Recherches et documents sur la technique littéraire du moyen âge.* Bibliothèque de l'École des Hautes Études, fasc. 238. Paris: Champion, 1924.

Fay, Thomas A. "Analogy and the Problem of the Divine Name in the Metaphysics of Thomas Aquinas." *Angelicum* 52 (1975): 69–90.

―――. "Analogy: The Key to Man's Knowledge of God in the Metaphysics of Thomas Aquinas." *Divus Thomas* 76 (1973): 343–64.

Fehr, J. "Offenbarung und Analogie: Ihr Verhältnis in dialektischen und thomistischen Theologie." *Divus Thomas* 15 (1937): 291–307.

Féret, H.-M. "*Sacramentum. Res.* dans la langue théologique de saint Augustin." *Revue des sciences philosophiques et théologiques* 29 (1940): 218–43.

Fergusson, Francis. *Dante's Drama of the Mind: A Modern Reading of the Purgatorio.* Princeton, N.J.: Princeton University Press, 1953.

Ferrante, Joan M. "The Relation of Speech to Sin in the *Inferno.*" *Dante Studies* 87 (1969): 33–46.

Filliatre, Charles. *La philosophie de saint Anselme: Ses principes, sa nature, son influence.* Paris: Félix Alcan, 1920.

Finaert, Joseph. *L'évolution littéraire de saint Augustin.* Paris: Les Belles Lettres, 1939.

―――. *Saint Augustin rhéteur.* Paris: Les Belles Lettres, 1939.

Finili, Antoninus. "Is There a Philosophical Approach to God?" *Dominican Studies* 4 (1951): 80–101.

Fischer, Joseph. *Die Erkenntnislehre Anselms von Canterbury. Beiträge zur Geschichte der Philosophie des Mittelalters,* edited by Clemens Bauemker, vol. 10, pt. 3. Münster in Westphalia: Aschendorffsche Verlagsbuchhandlung, 1911.

Flanigan, Thomas Marguerite. "The Use of Analogy in the *Summa contra gentiles.*" *Modern Schoolman* 35 (1957): 21–37.

Fletcher, Jefferson B. "The Allegory of the *Vita Nuova.*" *Modern Philology* 11 (1913): 19–37.

―――. *Dante.* New York: Henry Holt & Co., 1916.

————. "The Philosophy of Love of Guido Cavalcanti." *Annual Report of the Dante Society, Cambridge, Mass.* 22 (1904): 9–35.

————. "The 'True Meaning' of Dante's *Vita Nuova.*" *Romanic Review* 11 (1920): 95–148.

Flores, Ralph. "Reading and Speech in St. Augustine's *Confessions.*" *Augustinian Studies* 6 (1975): 1–13.

Foligno, Cesare. "Dante: The Poet." *Proceedings of the British Academy* 10 (1921): 3–18.

Foster, Kenelm. "St. Thomas and Dante." *The Two Dantes and Other Studies.* Berkeley and Los Angeles: University of California Press, 1977.

Freccero, John, ed. *Dante: A Collection of Critical Essays.* Englewood Cliffs, N.J.: Prentice-Hall, 1965.

————. "Dante's *Medusa:* Allegory and Autobiography." In *By Things Seen: Reference and Recognition in Medieval Thought,* edited by David L. Jeffrey. Ottawa: University of Ottawa Press, 1979.

Frutos Cortés, Eugenio, et al. *San Agustín: Estudios y coloquios.* Actos de los coloquios convocados por la Institución "Fernando el Católico" para conmemorar el XVI centenario de San Agustín. Zaragoza: "Fernando el Católico," 1960.

Funaioli, Gino. "Dante e il mondo antico." In *Medioevo e rinascimento: Studi in onore di Bruno Nardi.* Vol. 1. Florence: G. C. Sansoni, 1955.

Gannon, Mary Ann Ida. "The Active Theory of Sensation in St. Augustine." *New Scholasticism* 30 (1956): 154–80.

Garceau, Benoît. *Judicium: Vocabulaire, sources, doctrine de saint Thomas d'Aquin.* Université de Montréal Publications de l'Institut d'Études Médiévales, vol. 20. Montreal: Institut d'Études Médiévales; Paris: Vrin, 1968.

Gardeil, A. *Le donné révélé et la théologie.* 2d ed. Juvisy: Les Éditions du Cerf, 1932.

————. "Le donné théologique." *Revue thomiste* 17 (1909): 385–405.

Gardner, Edmund G. *Dante.* New York: E. P. Dutton & Co., 1923.

————. *Dante and the Mystics: A Study of the Mystical Aspects of the "Divina Commedia" and Its Relations with Some of Its Mediaeval Sources.* London: J. M. Dent & Sons, 1913.

Garrigou-Lagrange, Reginald. "La foi éclairée par les dons." *La vie spirituelle* 64 (1946): 657–66.

Garvey, Mary Patricia. *Saint Augustine: Christian or Neoplatonist?* Milwaukee, Wisc.: Marquette University Press, 1939.

Geiger, L.-B. *La participation dans la philosophie des. Thomas d'Aquin.* Paris: Vrin, 1942.

Gennaro, Concettina, *Fridugiso di Tours e il "De substantia nihili et tenebrarum": Edizione critica e studio introduttivo.* Padua: CEDAM, 1963.

Geny, P. "A propos des preuves thomistes de l'existence de Dieu." *Revue de philosophie* 24 (1924): 575–601.

Germain, Pierre. "La théologie de saint Thomas d'Aquin, science de la foi." *Revue de l'Université d'Ottawa,* special section, 28 (1958): 156*–84*.

Getto, Giovanni. *Aspetti della poesia di Dante.* Biblioteca del Leonardo, vol. 37. Florence: G. C. Sansoni, 1947.

Ghellinck, J. de. *L'essor de la littérature latine au douzième siècle*. 2 vols. Brussels: L'Édition Universelle, 1946.

———. *Le mouvement théologique du douzième siècle*. 2d ed. Bruges: De Tempel, 1948.

Ghisalberti, Alessandro. "La fondazione della teologia razionale di s. Tommaso d'Aquino." *Cultura e scuola* 13 (1974): 177–84.

Giannantonio, Pompeo. *Dante e l'allegorismo*. Florence: Leo S. Olschki, 1969.

Gibson, Margaret. *Lanfranc of Bec*. Oxford: Oxford University Press, Clarendon Press, 1978.

Gilbert, Allan H. *Dante and His Comedy*. New York: New York University Press, 1963.

———. *Dante's Conception of Justice*. Durham, N.C.: Duke University Press, 1925.

———. "Doctrine and Romance in Dante's *Commedia*." In *Renaissance Papers, 1960*. The Southeastern Renaissance Conference, 1961.

Gilby, Thomas. *Barbara Celarent: A Description of Scholastic Dialectic*. London: Longmans, Green & Co., 1949.

Gilson, Étienne. *The Christian Philosophy of Saint Augustine*. Translated by L. E. M. Lynch. New York: Random House, 1960.

———. *The Christian Philosophy of St. Thomas Aquinas*. Translated by L. K. Shook. New York: Random House, 1956.

———. *Dante the Philosopher*. Translated by David Moore. New York: Sheed & Ward, 1949.

———. *A History of Christian Philosophy in the Middle Ages*. New York: Random House, 1955.

———. *Philosophie et incarnation selon saint Augustin*. Conférence Albert le Grand, 1947. Montreal: Institut d'Études Médiévales, 1947.

———. *The Philosophy of St. Thomas Aquinas*. 2d ed. Translated by Edward Bullough. Edited by G. A. Elrington. Saint Louis, Mo.: Herder, 1941.

———. "Sens et nature de l'argument de saint Anselme." *Archives d'histoire doctrinale et littéraire du moyen âge* 9 (1934): 5–51.

Giussani, Carlo. "La questione del linguaggio secondo Platone e secondo Epicuro." *Memorie del Reale Istituto Lombardo di scienze e lettere, classe di lettere, scienze storiche e morali*. vol. 20, 3d ser. 11:103–41. Milan: Tipografia Bernardoni di C. Rebeschini e C., 1889.

Glatstein, Irwin Lee. "Semantics, Too, Has a Past." *Quarterly Journal of Speech* 32 (1946): 48–51.

Glover, Terrot Reaveley. *Life and Letters in the Fourth Century*. Cambridge: University Press, 1901.

Glunz, H. H. *Die Literaturästhetik des europäischen Mittelalters*. Bochum: Heinrich Pöppinghaus, 1937.

Gmelin, Hermann. "Die Anrede an den Leser in Dantes Göttlicher Komödie." *Deutsches Dante-Jahrbuch* 29–30, n.s. 20–21 (1951): 130–40.

Gombocz, Wolfgang Leopold. *Über E! Zur Semantik des Existenzprädikates und des ontologischen Argument für Gottes Existenz von Anselm von Canterbury.* Vienna: Verband der Wissenschaftlichen Gesellschaften Österreichs, 1974.

————. "Zu neueren Beiträgen zur Interpretation von Anselms Proslogion." *Salzburger Jahrbuch für Philosophie* 20 (1975): 131–35.

Grabmann, Martin. "Il concetto di scienza secondo s. Tommaso d'Aquino e le relazioni della fede e della teologia con la filosofia e le scienze profane." *Rivista di filosofia neo-scolastica* 26 (1934): 127–55.

————. *Die Geschichte der scholastischen Methode.* 2 vols. Darmstadt: Wissenschaftliche Buchgesellschaft, 1956.

————. "Die geschichtliche Entwicklung der mittelalterlichen Sprachphilosophie und Sprachlogik." In *Mélanges Joseph de Ghellinck.* Vol. 2. Gembloux: J. Duclutot, 1951.

————. *The Interior Life of St. Thomas Aquinas.* Translated by Nicholas Ashenbrenner. Milwaukee, Wisc.: Bruce Publishing Co., 1951.

————. *Mittelalterliches Geistesleben: Abhandlungen zur Geschichte der Scholastik und Mystik.* Vol. 1. Munich: Max Hueber, 1926.

————. "Scientific Cognition of Truth: Its Characteristic Genius in the Doctrine of St. Thomas Aquinas." *New Scholasticism* 13 (1939): 1–30.

————. *Die theologische Erkenntnis- und Einleitungslehre des hl. Thomas von Aquin auf seiner Schrift "In Boethium de Trinitate" im Zusammenhang der Scholastik des dreizehnten und beginnenden vierzehnten Jahrhunderts dargestellt.* Thomistische Studien, Schriftenreihe des *Divus Thomas,* vol. 4. Fribourg: Paulusverlag, 1948.

————. *Thomas Aquinas: His Personality and Thought.* Translated by Virgil Michel. New York: Longmans, Green & Co., 1928.

————, and Mausbach, Joseph, eds. *Aurelius Augustinus: Die Festschrift der Görres-Gesellschaft zum tausendfünfhundertsten Todestag des heiligen Augustinus.* Cologne: J. P. Bachem, 1930.

Graf, Arturo. *Roma nella memoria e nelle immaginazioni del medio evo.* 2 vols. Turin: Ermanno Loescher, 1882–83.

Graf, Olaf. *Die Divina Commedia als Zeugnis des Glaubes: Dante und die Liturgie.* Freiburg: Herder, 1965.

Grandgent, Charles Hall. *Dante.* New York: Duffield & Co., 1916.

————. *The Power of Dante.* Boston: Marshall Jones Co., 1918.

Grandgeorge, L. *Saint Augustin et le néo-Platonisme.* Paris: E. Leroux, 1898.

Grant, Mary A., and Fiske, George Converse. "Cicero's *Orator* and Horace's *Ars Poetica.*" *Harvard Studies in Classical Philology* 35 (1924): 1–74.

Grasso, Vincenzo. *Il De Consolatione Philosophiae di Boezio in Dante, Petrarca, Chaucer: Contributo allo studio delle loro fonti.* Catania: Vincente Muglia, 1923.

Grave, S. A. "The Ontological Argument of St. Anselm." *Philosophy* 27 (1952): 30–38.

Grayson, Cecil. "Dante's Theory and Practice of Poetry." In *The World of Dante: Essays on Dante and His Times,* edited by Cecil Grayson. Oxford: Oxford University Press, Clarendon Press, 1980.

———. *"'Nobilior est vulgaris': Latin and Vernacular in Dante's Thought."* In *Centenary Essays on Dante by Members of the Oxford Dante Society.* Oxford: Oxford University Press, Clarendon Press, 1965.

Green, Richard Hamilton. "Dante's 'Allegory of Poets' and the Mediaeval Theory of Poetic Fiction." *Comparative Literature* 9 (1957): 118–28.

Grene, Marjorie. *A Portrait of Aristotle.* Chicago: University of Chicago Press, 1963.

Guardini, Romano. *The Conversion of Augustine.* Translated by Elinor Briefs. Westminster, Md.: Newman Press, 1960.

———. *Vision und Dichtung: Der Charakter von Dantes göttlicher Komödie.* Tübingen: Rainer Wunderlich, 1946.

Guidubaldi, Egidio, ed. *Dal "De luce" di R. Grossatesta all'islamico "Libro della scala": Il problema delle fonti arabe una volta accettata la mediazione oxfordiana.* Florence: Leo S. Olschki, 1978.

———. "Poesia e non-poesia negli ultimi quarant'anni di critica dantesca in Italia." *Civiltà cattolica* 110: 4 (1959): 42–52.

Hagendahl, Harald. *Augustine and the Latin Classics.* 2 vols. Studia graeca et latina Gothoburgensis, vol. 20, pts. 1–2. Göteborg: Almquist & Wiksell, 1967.

Hardie, C. G. "The Epistle to Cangrande Again." *Deutsches Dante-Jahrbuch* 38 (1960): 51–74.

Harrison, Frank R., III. "Some Brief Remarks concerning the Quinque Viae of Saint Thomas." *Franciscan Studies* 21 (1961): 80–93.

Hart, Charles A. "Participation and the Thomistic Five Ways." *New Scholasticism* 26 (1952): 266–82.

———. *The Thomistic Concept of Mental Faculty.* Washington, D.C.: Catholic University of America, 1930.

Hartford, R. R. "Fides quaerens intellectum." In *Hermathena: A Series of Papers on Literature, Science, and Philosophy by Members of Trinity College, Dublin* 74 (1949): 1–8.

Hartman, Robert S. "Prolegomena to a Meta-Anselmian Axiomatic." *Review of Metaphysics* 14 (1961): 637–75.

Hartshorne, Charles. *The Logic of Perfection and Other Essays in Neoclassical Metaphysics.* La Salle, Ill.: Open Court Publishing Co., 1962.

———. "The Logic of the Ontological Argument." *Journal of Philosophy* 58 (1961): 471–73.

———. *Man's Vision of God, and the Logic of Theism.* Chicago: Willet, Clark & Co., 1941.

Hatzfeld, H. "Modern Literary Scholarship as Reflected in Dante Criticism." *Comparative Literature* 3 (1951): 289–309.

Henle, Paul. "Uses of the Ontological Argument." *Philosophical Review* 70 (1961): 102–9.

Henle, R.J. *Saint Thomas and Platonism: A Study of the "Plato" and "Platonici" Texts in the Writings of Saint Thomas.* The Hague: Martinus Nijhoff, 1956.

Henry, C. "Histoire des preuves de l'existence de Dieu au moyen âge, jusqu'à la fin de l'apogée de la scholastique." *Revue thomiste* 19 (1911): 1–24, 141–58.

Henry, Desmond Paul. *Commentary on "De grammatico:" Historical-Logical Dimensions of a Dialogue of St. Anselm.* Dordrecht: Reidel, 1974.

———. *The "De Grammatico" of St. Anselm: The Theory of Paronymy.* University of Notre Dame Publications in Mediaeval Studies, vol. 18. Notre Dame, Ind.: University of Notre Dame Press, 1964.

———. *The Logic of Saint Anselm.* Oxford: Oxford University Press, Clarendon Press, 1967.

———. *Medieval Logic and Metaphysics: A Modern Introduction.* London: Hutchinson University Library, 1972.

———. "Proslogion Chapter III." In *Analecta anselmiana,* vol. 1, edited by F. S. Schmitt. Frankfort on the Main: Minerva GMBH, 1969.

———. "The Proslogion Proofs." *Philosophical Quarterly* 5 (1955): 147–51.

———. "Saint Anselm's 'De grammatico.' " *Philosophical Quarterly* 10 (1960): 115–26.

———. "Why 'Grammaticus'?" *Archivum latinitatis medii aevi* 28, fascs. 2–3 (1958): 165–80.

Hessen, Johannes. *Augustins Metaphysik der Erkenntnis.* Berlin: Ferd. Dümmlers, 1931.

———. *Die Philosophie des heiligen Augustinus.* Freising: Glock und Lutz, 1948.

Heyer, George S., Jr. *"Rectitudo* in the Theology of St. Anselm." Ph.D. diss., Yale University, 1963.

Hoenen, Peter. *Reality and Judgment according to St. Thomas.* Translated by Henry F. Tiblier. Appendix by Charles Boyer. Chicago: Henry Regnery Co., 1952.

Hoffmann, Ernst. *Platonismus und Christlicher Philosophie.* Zurich: Artemis-Verlag, 1960.

Hoffmans, P. Hadelin. "Roger Bacon: L'intuition mystique et la science." *Revue néoscolastique* 16 (1909): 370–97.

Hollander, Robert. *Allegory in Dante's Commedia.* Princeton, N.J.: Princeton University Press, 1969.

———. "Dante *Theologus-Poeta.*" *Dante Studies* 94 (1976): 91–136.

Hopkins, Jasper. "Anselm's Debate with Gaunilo." In *Anselm of Canterbury,* translated and edited by Jasper Hopkins and Herbert Richardson, vol. 4. Toronto: Edwin Mellen Press, 1976.

———. *A Companion to the Study of St. Anselm.* Minneapolis: University of Minnesota Press, 1972.

Horváth, Alexander M. "Der wissenschaftliche Charakter der Apologetik." *Divus Thomas* 25 (1947): 29–52, 177–91, 395–408.

Howell, A. G. Ferrers. *Dante: His Life and Work.* Rev. ed. London: T. C. & E. C. Jack, 1920.

Howie, George. *Educational Theory and Practice in St. Augustine.* New York: Columbia University Teachers College Press, 1969.

Hufnagel, Alfons. *Intuition und Erkenntnis nach Thomas von Aquin.* Veröffentlichungen des katholischen Institutes für Philosophie, Albertus-Magnus-Akademie zu Köln, vol. 2, pts. 5–6. Münster in Westphalia: Aschendorffschen Verlagsbuchhandlung, 1932.

Hunt, Richard William. "The Introduction to the 'Artes' in the Twelfth Century." In *Studia mediaevalia in honorem admodum Reverendi Patris Raymundi Josephi Martin.* Bruges: De Tempel, 1948.

———. "Studies on Priscian in the Eleventh and Twelfth Century." *Mediaeval and Renaissance Studies* 1 (1941–43): 194–231.

Innocenti, Umberto degl'. "L'esistenza di Dio nella prospettiva delle cinque vie di s. Tommaso." *Divinitas* 13 (1969): 77–85.

Jackson, B. Darrell. "The Theory of Signs in St. Augustine's *De Doctrina Christiana.*" In *Augustine: A Collection of Critical Essays,* edited by R. A. Markus. Garden City, N.Y.: Doubleday, 1972.

Jacob, Johannes. *Die Bedeutung der Führer Dantes in der Divina Commedia: Virgil, Beatrix, St. Bernhard, in Bezug auf den idealen Zweck des Gedichtes und auf Grund der geistigen Lebensentwicklung des Dichters.* Leipzig: J. C. Hinrichs'sche Buchhandlung, 1874.

Jacquin, A.-M. "Les 'rationes necessariae' de saint Anselme." In *Mélanges Mandonnet: Études d'histoire littéraire et doctrinale du moyen âge,* vol. 2. Paris: Vrin, 1930.

Jansen, Bernhard, "Geist und Form der Philosophie des h. Augustinus." In *Miscellanea Augustiniana: Gedenkboek samengesteld uit Verhandelingen over S. Augustinus bij de Viering van Zijn Zalig overlijden vóór 15 Eeuwen CDXXX–MCXXX.* Rotterdam: P. P. Augustijnen der Nederlandsche Provincie, 1930.

Jansen, François. "Saint Augustin et la rhétorique." *Nouvelle revue théologique* 57 (1930): 282–97.

Jenaro-MacLennan, L. *The Trecento Commentaries on the "Divina commedia" and the Epistle to Cangrande.* Oxford: Oxford University Press, Clarendon Press, 1974.

Johnson, Douglas W. "*Verbum* in the Early Augustine (386–397)." *Recherches augustiniennes* 8 (1972): 25–53.

Jolivet, Jean. *Arts du langage et théologie chez Abélard.* Paris: Vrin, 1969.

———. *Godescalc d'Orbais et la trinité: La méthode de la théologie à l'époque carolingienne.* Paris: Vrin, 1958.

———. "Quelques cas de 'platonisme grammatical' du septième au douzième siècle." In *Mélanges offerts à René Crozet,* vol. 1, edited by Pierre Gallais and Yves-Jean Riou. Poitiers: Société d'Études Médiévales, 1966.

Jolivet, Régis. "La doctrine augustinienne de l'illumination." *Revue de philosophie,* n.s. 1, quinzième centenaire de la mort de saint Augustin (1930): 383–502.

Jourdain, Eleanor F. *Le symbolisme dans la Divine Comédie de Dante.* Paris: Alphonse Picard & Fils, 1904.

Jourdan, Eduard. "Dante et l'idée de 'virtù.' " In *Mélanges sur Dante: Publiés par la*

Nouvelle revue d'Italie à l'occasion du sixième centenaire de la mort du poète, edited by Maurice Mignon. Rome: Nouvelle Revue d'Italie, 1924.

Kane, G. Stanley. *"Fides quaerens intellectum* in Anselm's Thought." *Scottish Journal of Theology* 26 (1973): 40–62.

Kantorowicz, Ernst H. *The King's Two Bodies: A Study in Mediaeval Political Theology.* Princeton, N.J.: Princeton University Press, 1957.

Kaske, R. E. "Dante's 'DXV' and 'Veltro.' " *Traditio* 17 (1961): 185–254.

Kay, Richard. *Dante's Swift and Strong: Essays on Inferno XV.* Lawrence: Regents Press of Kansas, 1978.

Kelly, Louis G. "Saint Augustine and Saussurean Linguistics." *Augustinian Studies* 6 (1975): 45–64.

Kelsen, Hans. *Die Staatslehre des Dante Alighieri.* Vienna: Franz Deutiche, 1905.

Kenny, Anthony. *The Five Ways: St. Thomas Aquinas' Proof of God's Existence.* New York: Schocken Books, 1969.

Ker, W. P. *Essays on Medieval Literature.* London: Macmillan & Co., 1905.

Kern, Fritz. *Humana Civilitas: Staat, Kirche und Kultur: Eine Dante-Untersuchung.* Leipzig: K. F. Koehler, 1913.

Kimmerle, Helmut. *Die Gottesbeweis Anselms von Canterbury: Ihre Voraussetzungen und ihre Bedeutung für die philosophische Theologie.* Berlin: Ernst-Reuter-Gesellschaft, 1961.

Kirkpatrick, Robin. *Dante's "Paradiso" and the Limitations of Modern Criticism: A Study of Style and Poetic Theory.* Cambridge: Cambridge University Press, 1978.

Klubertanz, George P. "The Problem of the Analogy of Being." *Review of Metaphysics* 10 (1957): 553–79.

———. *St. Thomas Aquinas on Analogy: A Textual Analysis and Systematic Synthesis.* Chicago: Loyola University Press, 1960.

Knasas, John F. X. "Making Sense of the *Tertia Via.*" *New Scholasticism* 54 (1980): 476–511.

Knowles, David. *The Evolution of Medieval Thought.* London: Longmans, Green & Co., 1962.

———. *The Historical Context of the Philosophical Works of St. Thomas Aquinas.* London: Blackfriars, 1958.

Kolping, Adolf. *Anselms Proslogion-Beweis der Existenz Gottes im Zusammenhang seines spekulativen Programms Fides quaerens intellectum.* Bonn: Hch. Ludwig, 1938.

Kondoleon, Theodore. "The Third Way: 'Encore.' " *Thomist* 44 (1980): 325–56.

Koyré, Alexandre. *L'idée de Dieu dans la philosophe de st. Anselme.* Paris: Ernest Leroux, 1923.

Krebs, Engelbert. "Erlebnis und Allegorie in Dantes Commedia." *Deutsches Dante-Jahrbuch* 8 (1924): 11–25; 9 (1925): 98–103.

Krogmann, Willy. "Die Mannigfaltigkeit der Sprache in der Sicht Dantes." In *Die Metaphysik im Mittelalter: Ihr Ursprung und ihre Bedeutung. Vorträge des zweiten internationalen Kongresses für mittelalterliche Philosophie, Köln, 31. August–6. September 1961.* Miscellanea Mediaevalia: Veroffentlichungen des Thomas-Instituts an der Universität

Köln, edited by Paul Wilpert, vol. 2. Berlin: Walter de Gruyter & Co., 1963.

Kroner, Richard. *Speculation and Revelation in the Age of Christian Philosophy.* Philadelphia: Westminster Press, 1959.

Kuhn. "Glauben und Wissen nach St. Thomas." *Theologische Quartalschrift* 42: 2 (1860): 273–340.

Kuypers, K. *Der Zeichen- und Wortbegriff im Denken Augustins.* Amsterdam: N.V. Swets & Zeitlinger, 1934.

Labourdette, M.-M. "La vie théologale selon s. Thomas." *Revue thomiste* 60 (1960): 364–80.

Lachance, L. "Saint Thomas dans l'histoire de la logique." In *Études d'histoire littéraire et doctrinale du treizième siècle.* Publications de l'Institut d'Études Médiévales d'Ottawa, vol. 1. Paris: Vrin, 1932.

La Croix, Richard. *Proslogion II and III: A Third Interpretation of Anselm's Argument.* Leiden: E. J. Brill, 1972.

Ladner, Gerhart B. *The Idea of Reform: Its Impact on Christian Thought and Action in the Age of the Fathers.* Cambridge, Mass.: Harvard University Press, 1959.

Lafont, Ghislain. *Structures et méthode dans la Somme théologique de saint Thomas d'Aquin.* Paris: Desclée de Brouwer, 1961.

Lagrange, M.-J. "Le réalisme et le symbolisme de Dante." *Revue biblique* 46 (1937): 481–505.

Laistner, M. L. W. "The Christian Attitude toward Pagan Literature." *History,* n.s. 20 (1935): 49–54.

———. *Thought and Letters in Western Europe, A.D. 500 to 900.* 2d ed. London: Methuen & Co., 1957.

Landry, B. "L'analogie de proportion chez saint Thomas d'Aquin." *Revue néoscolastique de philosophie* 24 (1922): 257–80.

———. "L'analogie de proportionnalité chez saint Thomas d'Aquin." *Revue néoscolastique de philosophie* 24 (1922): 454–64.

———. *La notion d'analogie chez saint Bonaventure et saint Thomas d'Aquin.* Louvain: Institut Supérieur de Philosophie, 1922.

Lang, Hugo. *Die Lehre des hl. Thomas von Aquin von der Gewissheit des übernatürlichen Glaubens.* Augsburg: Benno Filser, 1929.

Laurenzi, Fortunato. *Ermetica ed ermeneutica dantesca.* Collezione di opusculi danteschi inediti o rari, vols. 137–39. Città di Castello: S. Lapi, 1931.

Leclercq, Jean. *The Love of Learning and the Desire for God: A Study of Monastic Culture.* Translated by Catherine Misrahi. New York: New American Library, 1962.

———. "Le magistère du prédicateur au treizième siècle." *Archives d'histoire doctrinale et littéraire du moyen âge* 21 (1946): 105–47.

———. "Prédication et rhétorique au temps de saint Augustin." *Revue bénédictine* 57 (1947): 117–31.

———. "Smaragde et la grammaire chrétienne." *Revue du moyen âge latin* 4 (1948): 15–22.

Leder, Hermann. *Untersuchungen über Augustins Erkenntnistheorie in ihren Beziehungen zur antiken Skepsis, zu Plotin, und zu Descartes.* Marburg: N. G. Elwert'sche Verlagsbuchhandlung, 1901.

Leeuwen, Antoine van. "L'analogie de l'être: Genèse et contenu du concept d'analogie." *Revue néoscolastique de philosophie* 39 (1936): 293–320.

Leigh, Gertrude. "Links between Dante and Duns Scotus." *Church Quarterly Review* 96 (1923): 306–31.

————. *New Light on the Youth of Dante.* London: Faber & Faber, 1929.

————. *The Passing of Beatrice: A Study of the Heterodoxy of Dante.* London: Faber & Faber, 1932.

Leisegang, Hans. "La connaissance de Dieu au miroir de l'âme et de la nature." *Revue d'histoire et de philosophie religieuses* 17 (1937): 145–71.

Lemaître, Charles. "Quarta via: La preuve de l'existence de Dieu par les degrés des êtres." *Nouvelle revue théologique* 54 (1927): 321–39, 436–68.

Lenkeith, Nancy. *Dante and the Legend of Rome.* Mediaeval and Renaissance Studies, edited by Richard Hunt and Raymond Klibansky, supplement 2. London: Warburg Institute, 1952.

Leo, Ulrich. *Sehen und Wirklichkeit bei Dante.* Analecta Romanica, supplements to *Romanische Forschungen,* edited by Fritz Schalk, vol. 4. Frankfort on the Main: Vittorio Klostermann, 1957.

Levasti, Arrigo. *Sant'Anselmo: Vita e pensiero.* Bari: Gius. Laterza & Figli, 1929.

Lewry, Osmund. "Boethian Logic in the Medieval West." In *Boethius: His Life, Thought, and Influence,* edited by Margaret Gibson. Oxford: Basil Blackwell, 1981.

Liebeschütz, Hans. "Kosmologische Motive in der Bildungswelt der Frühscholastik." *Vorträge der Bibliothek Warburg* 3 (1923–24): 83–148.

Lilje, Hanns. *Dante als christlicher Denker.* Hamburg: Furche-Verlag, 1955.

Limentani, U., ed. *The Mind of Dante.* Cambridge: University Press, 1965.

Lindbeck, George. "Participation and Existence in the Interpretation of St. Thomas Aquinas." *Franciscan Studies* 17 (1957): 1–22, 107–25.

Lindberg, David C. *Theories of Vision from Al-Kindi to Kepler.* Chicago: University of Chicago Press, 1976.

Linehan, James Coleman. *The Rational Nature of Man with Particular Reference to the Effects of Immorality on Intelligence according to Saint Thomas Aquinas.* Catholic University of America Philosophical Studies, vol. 37. Washington, D.C.: Catholic University of America, 1937.

Little, Arthur. *The Platonic Heritage of Thomism.* Dublin: Golden Eagle Books, 1949.

Llamas, P. J. San Agustín y la multiplicidad de sentidos literales en la Escritura." *Religión y cultura* 15 (1931): 238–74.

Lonergan, Bernard. "The Concept of *Verbum* in the Writings of St. Thomas Aquinas." *Theological Studies* 7 (1946): 349–92; 8 (1947): 35–79, 404–44; 10 (1949): 3–40, 359–93.

Löwe, Heinz. "Dante und das Kaisertum." *Historische Zeitschrift* 190 (1960): 517–52.

Lubac, Henri de. *Augustinisme et théologie moderne*. Paris: Aubier, 1965.

———. *Exégèse médiévale: Les quatre sens de l'Ecriture*. 4 vols. in 2. Paris: Aubier, 1959–64.

———. *Le mystère du surnaturel*. Paris: Aubier, 1965.

———. *Recherches dans la foi: Trois études sur Origène, saint Anselme, et la philosophie chrétienne*. Paris: Beauchesne, 1979.

———. " 'Typologie' et 'Allegorisme.' " *Recherches de science religieuse* 34 (1947): 180–226.

Luke, Helen M. *Dark Wood to White Rose: A Study of Meanings in Dante's Divine Comedy*. Pecos, Tex.: Dove Publications, 1975.

Lyttkens, Hampus. *The Analogy between God and the World: An Investigation of Its Background and Interpretation of Its Use by Thomas of Aquino*. Uppsala: Almqvist & Wiksells, 1952.

McGill, Arthur C. "Recent Discussions of Anselm's Argument." In *The Many-faced Argument: Recent Studies on the Ontological Argument for the Existence of God*, edited by John Hick and Arthur C. McGill. New York: Macmillan Co., 1967.

McInerny, Ralph. "The Logic of Analogy." *New Scholasticism* 31 (1957): 149–71.

———. *The Logic of Analogy: An Interpretation of St. Thomas*. The Hague: Martinus Nijhoff, 1961.

McKenzie, Kenneth. "Virgil & Dante." In *The Tradition of Virgil: Three Papers on the History and Influence of the Poet*, by Junius S. Morgan, Kenneth McKenzie, and Charles Osgood. Princeton, N.J.: Princeton University Press, 1930.

McKeon, Richard. "Medicine and Philosophy in the Eleventh and Twelfth Centuries: The Problem of Elements." *Thomist* 24 (1961): 211–56.

———. "Poetry and Philosophy in the Twelfth Century: The Renaissance of Rhetoric." *Modern Philology* 43 (1946): 217–34.

———. "Renaissance and Method in Philosophy." In *Studies in the History of Ideas*, vol. 3. New York: Columbia University Press, 1935.

———. "Rhetoric in the Middle Ages." *Speculum* 17 (1942): 1–32.

———. "Thomas Aquinas' Doctrine of Knowledge and Its Historical Setting." *Speculum* 3 (1928): 425–44.

———, ed. and trans. *Selections from Medieval Philosophers*. Vol. 1. New York: Charles Scribner's Sons, 1929.

McLean, George. "Symbol and Analogy: Tillich and Thomas." *Revue de l'Université d'Ottawa*, special section, 28 (1958): 193*–233*.

Madec, Goulven. "Analyse du *De magistro*." *Revue des études augustiniennes* 21 (1975): 63–71.

Maier, Franz Georg. *Augustin und das antike Rom*. Stuttgart: W. Kohlhammer, 1955.

Malagoli, Luigi. *Linguaggio e poesia nella Divina Commedia*. Genoa: Briano, 1949.

Malcolm, Norman. "Anselm's Ontological Argument." *Philosophical Review* 69 (1960): 41–62.

Mancini, Augusto. "Nuovi dubbi ed ipotesi sulla Epistola a Can Grande." *Atti della*

Reale Accademia d'Italia: Rendiconti della classe di scienze morali e storiche, 7th ser. 4, fascs. 9–12 (1943): 227–42.

Mandonnet, P. *Dante le théologien: Introduction à l'intelligence de la vie, des oeuvres, et de l'art de Dante Alighieri.* Paris: Desclée de Brouwer, 1935.

Manitius, Max. *Geschichte der lateinischen Literatur des Mittelalters.* 3 vols. Munich: C. H. Beck'sche Verlagsbuchhandlung, 1911–31.

Manthey, Franz. *Die Sprachphilosophie des hl. Thomas von Aquin und ihre Anwendung auf Probleme der Theologie.* Paderborn: Ferdinand Schöningh, 1937.

Maquart, Xavier. "La causalité du signe: Réflexions sur la valeur philosophique d'une explication théologique." *Revue thomiste* 32, n.s. 10 (1947): 40–60.

Marenbon, John. *From the Circle of Alcuin to the School of Auxerre: Logic, Theology, and Philosophy in the Early Middle Ages.* Cambridge: Cambridge University Press, 1981.

Marías Aguilera, Julián. *San Anselmo y el insensato y otros estudios de filosofía.* 2d ed. Madrid: Revista de Occidente, 1954.

Maritain, Jacques. *The Angelic Doctor: The Life and Thought of Saint Thomas Aquinas.* Translated by J. F. Scanlan. New York: Dial Press, 1931.

———. *Distinguish to Unite; or, The Degrees of Knowledge.* 4th ed. Translated by Gerald B. Phelan. New York: Charles Scribner's Sons, 1959.

Markus, R. A. "A Note on the Meaning of *Via.*" *Dominican Studies* 7 (1954): 239–45.

———. "St. Augustine on Signs." *Phronesis* 2 (1957): 60–83.

Marrou, Henri-Irénée. *Saint Augustin et la fin de la culture antique.* Bibliothèque des écoles françaises d'Athènes et de Rome, vol. 145. Paris: E. de Boccard, 1938.

———. *Saint Augustin et la fin de la culture antique: "Retractatio."* Bibliothèque des écoles françaises d'Athènes et de Rome, vol. 145, supplement. Paris: E. de Boccard, 1949.

Martin, Edward James. *A History of the Iconoclastic Controversy.* London: Society for Promoting Christian Knowledge, n.d.

Masiello, Ralph J. "The Analogy of Proportion according to the Metaphysics of St. Thomas." *Modern Schoolman* 35 (1958): 91–106.

Masseron, Alexandre. *Dante et Saint Bernard.* Paris: Albin Michel, 1953.

Masure, E. *Le signe: Le passage du visible à l'invisible.* Paris: Bloud & Gay, 1953.

Matheson, P. E. "Character and Citizenship in Dante." *Hibbert Journal* 5 (1907): 856–78.

Mathew, Gervase. *Byzantine Aesthetics.* New York: Viking Press, 1963.

Maurer, Armand. "St. Thomas and the Analogy of Genus." *New Scholasticism* 29 (1955): 127–44.

May, Rollo, ed. *Symbolism in Religion and Literature.* New York: George Braziller, 1960.

Mayer, Cornelius Petrus. *Die Zeichen in der geistigen Entwicklung und in der Theologie Augustins: Die antimanichäische Epoche.* Würzburg: Augustinus-Verlag, 1974.

———. *Die Zeichen in der geistigen Entwicklung und in der Theologie des jungen Augustinus.* Würzburg: Augustinus-Verlag, 1969.

Mazzeo, Joseph Anthony. *Medieval Cultural Tradition in Dante's "Comedy."* Ithaca, N.Y.: Cornell University Press, 1960.

———. "St. Augustine's Rhetoric of Silence." *Journal of the History of Ideas* 23 (1962): 175–96.

———. *Structure and Thought in the "Paradiso."* Ithaca, N.Y.: Cornell University Press, 1958.

Mazzoni, Francesco. "L'Epistola a Cangrande." *Accademia nazionale dei Lincei: Rendiconti della classe di scienze morali, storiche e filologiche,* 8th ser. 10, fascs. 3–4 (1955): 157–98.

———. "Pietro Alighieri interprete di Dante." *Studi danteschi* 40 (1963): 279–360.

Mazzotta, Giuseppi. *Dante, Poet of the Desert: History and Allegory in the Divine Comedy.* Princeton, N.J.: Princeton University Press, 1979.

Meagher, Robert E. "Thomas Aquinas on Analogy: A Textual Analysis." *Thomist* 34 (1970): 230–53.

Meissner, William W. "Some Aspects of the *Verbum* in the Texts of St. Thomas Aquinas." *Modern Schoolman* 36 (1958): 1–30.

———. "Some Notes on a Figure in St. Thomas." *New Scholasticism* 31 (1957): 68–84.

Mengaldo, Pier Vincenzo. *Linguistica e retorica di Dante.* Pisa: Nistri-Lischi, 1978.

Meozzi, A. *L'utopia politica di Dante.* Milan: Edizioni Athena, 1929.

Meyer, Hans. *The Philosophy of St. Thomas Aquinas.* Translated by Frederic Eckhoff. Saint Louis, Mo.: Herder, 1948.

Miller, Robert G. "The Ontological Argument in St. Anselm and Descartes." *Modern Schoolman* 32 (1955): 341–49.

Minio-Paluello, Lorenzo. "The Genuine Text of Boethius' Translation of Aristotle's *Categories.*" *Mediaeval and Renaissance Studies* 1 (1941–43): 151–77.

———. *Opuscula: The Latin Aristotle.* Amsterdam: Adolf M. Hakkert, 1972.

———. "The Text of the *Categoriae:* The Latin Tradition." *Classical Quarterly* 39 (1945): 63–74.

———. "Les traductions et les commentaires aristotéliciens de Boèce." In *Studia Patristica,* vol. 2. Papers Presented to the Second International Conference on Patristic Studies Held at Christ Church, Oxford, 1955, pt. 2, edited by Kurt Aland and F. L. Cross. Berlin: Akademie-Verlag, 1957.

Mondin, Battista. "La logica di s. Tommaso d'Aquin." *Rivista di filosofia neo-scolastica* 60 (1968): 261–71.

———. "Il problema del linguaggio teologico in sant'Agostino." *Augustinianum* 11 (1971): 263–80.

Montagnes, Bernard. *La doctrine de l'analogie de l'être d'après saint Thomas d'Aquin.* Louvain: Publications Universitaires, 1963.

Montano, Rocco. *Suggerimenti per una lettura di Dante.* Naples: Conte, 1956.

Moody, Ernest A. "The Medieval Contribution to Logic." *Studies in Medieval Philosophy, Science, and Logic: Collected Papers, 1933–1969.* Berkeley and Los Angeles:

University of California Press, 1975.

———. *Truth and Consequence in Medieval Logic.* Amsterdam: North-Holland Publishing Co., 1953.

Moore, Edward. *Dante and His Early Biographers.* London: Rivingtons, 1890.

———. *Studies in Dante: First Series.* Oxford: Oxford University Press, Clarendon Press, 1896.

———. *Studies in Dante: Second Series.* Oxford: Oxford University Press, Clarendon Press, 1899.

———. *Studies in Dante: Third Series.* Oxford: Oxford University Press, Clarendon Press, 1903.

Moreau, Joseph. *De la connaissance selon s. Thomas d'Aquin.* Paris: Beauchesne, 1976.

Moré-Pontgibaud, Ch. de. "Sur l'analogie des noms divins." *Recherches de science religieuse* 19 (1929): 481–512; 20 (1930): 193–223.

Motte, A. R. "Théodicée et théologie chez s. Thomas d'Aquin." *Revue des sciences philosophiques et théologiques* 26 (1937): 5–26.

Mueller, Gustav E. "Dante's Aesthetics." *Personalist* 27 (1946): 386–98.

Mullane, Donald T. *Aristotelianism in St. Thomas.* Washington, D.C.: Catholic University of America, 1929.

Murari, Rocco. *Dante e Boezio: Contributo allo studio delle fonti dantesche.* Bologna: Nicola Zanichelli, 1905.

Murdoch, John E. "Propositional Analysis in Fourteenth-Century Natural Philosophy." *Synthese* 40 (1979): 117–46.

Musa, Mark, ed. *Essays on Dante.* Bloomington: Indiana University Press, 1964.

Nardi, Bruno. "L'averroismo del 'primo amico' di Dante." *Studi danteschi* 25 (1940): 43–79.

———. "L'averroismo di Sigieri e Dante." *Studi danteschi* 22 (1938): 83–113.

———. *Dal "Convivio" alla "Commedia": Sei saggi danteschi.* Istituto storico italiano per il medio evo, studi storici, vols. 35–39. Rome: Palazzo Borromini, 1960.

———. *Dante e la cultura medievale.* 2d ed. Bari: Guis. Laterza & Figli, 1949.

———. "Dante e la filosofia." *Studi danteschi* 25 (1940): 5–42.

———. "Due capitoli di filosofia dantesca: I, La conoscenza humana; II, Il linguaggio." *Giornale storico della letteratura italiana, miscellanea dantesca,* supplement to vols. 19–21, pp. 205–64. Turin: Giovanni Chiantore, 1921.

———. *La filosofia di Dante.* Milan: Carlo Marzorati, 1952.

———. "Intorno al tomismo di Dante e alla questione di Sigieri." *Giornale dantesco* 22 (1914): 182–97.

———. *Nel mondo di Dante.* Rome: Storia e Letteratura, 1944.

———. "Nomina sunt consequentia rerum." *Giornale storica della letteratura italiana* 93 (1929): 101–5.

———. *Studi di filosofia medievale.* Rome: Storia e Letteratura, 1960.

Nash, Ronald H. *The Light of the Mind: St. Augustine's Theory of Knowledge.* Lexington: University Press of Kentucky, 1969.

Natoli, Gioacchino. "Il valore estetico del simbolo nell'arte di Dante." *Sophia* 23 (1955): 38–52.

Nehring, Alfons. "A Note on Functional Linguistics in the Middle Ages." *Traditio* 9 (1953): 430–34.

Nemetz, Anthony A. "Logic and the Division of the Sciences in Aristotle and St. Thomas Aquinas." *Modern Schoolman* 33 (1956): 91–109.

Neumann, Siegfried. *Gegenstand und Methode der theoretischen Wissenschaften nach Thomas von Aquin aufgrund der Expositio super librum Boethii de Trinitate.* Münster in Westphalia: Max Kramer, 1963.

Nijenhuis, John. "The Structure of the Judgment according to Aquinas." *Carmelus* 19 (1972): 3–66.

Norden, Eduard. *Die antike Kunstprosa vom sechsten Jahrhundert v. Chr. bis in die Zeit der Renaissance.* Vol. 2. Leipzig: Teubner, 1898.

Nugent, James B. *The Fundamental Theistic Argument in the Metaphysical Doctrine of Saint Thomas Aquinas.* Catholic University of America, Philosophical Studies, vol. 192, abstract 42. Washington, D.C.: Catholic University of America, 1961.

O'Brien, Ignatius. "Analogy and Our Knowledge of God." *Philosophical Studies* 6 (1956): 91–104.

O'Connell, Robert J. *St. Augustine's Early Theory of Man, A.D. 386–391.* Cambridge, Mass.: Harvard University Press, 1968.

O'Donoghue, Dermot. "An Analysis of the *Tertia Via* of St. Thomas." *Irish Theological Quarterly* 20 (1953): 129–51.

O'Keefe, Dermot L. *Theology and Contemplation according to St. Thomas Aquinas.* Rome: Officium Libri Catholici, 1952.

O'Neil, C. J., ed. *An Étienne Gilson Tribute.* Milwaukee, Wisc.: Bruce Publishing Co., 1959.

O'Neill, M. S. "Some Remarks on the Analogy of God and Creatures in St. Thomas Aquinas." *Mediaeval Studies* 23 (1961): 206–15.

Ong, Walter J. "Wit and Mystery: A Revaluation in Mediaeval Latin Hymnody." *Speculum* 22 (1947): 310–41.

Osgood, Charles Grosvenor. *Poetry as a Means of Grace.* Princeton, N.J.: Princeton University Press, 1941.

Ouspensky, Léonide. *L'icone: Vision du monde spirituel: Quelques mots sur son sens dogmatique.* Paris: Sétor, 1948.

———, and Lossky, Vladimir. *The Meaning of Icons.* Translated by G. E. H. Palmer and E. Kadloubovsky. Edited by Titus Burckhardt. Olten, Switzerland: Urs Graf-Verlag, 1952.

Ovidio, Francesco d'. *Dante e la filosofia del linguaggio.* Naples: Tipografia della Regia Università, 1892.

———. *Studii sulla Divina Commedia.* Milan: Remo Sandron, 1901.

Owens, Joseph. "Actuality in the 'Prima Via' of St. Thomas." *Mediaeval Studies* 29 (1967): 26–46.

————. "Analogy as a Thomistic Approach to Being." *Mediaeval Studies* 24 (1962): 303–22.

————. "Aquinas and the Five Ways." *Monist* 58 (1974): 16–35.

————. "Aquinas and the Proof from the 'Physics.'" *Mediaeval Studies* 28 (1966): 119–50.

————. "'Cause of Necessity' in Aquinas' *Tertia Via*." *Mediaeval Studies* 33 (1971): 21–45.

————. "The Conclusion of the *Prima Via*." *Modern Schoolman* 30 (1952–53): 33–53, 109–21, 203–16.

————. "Immobility and Existence for Aquinas." *Mediaeval Studies* 30 (1968): 22–46.

————. "Judgment and Truth in Aquinas." *Mediaeval Studies* 32 (1970): 138–58.

Pailin, David A. "Credo ut intelligam as the Method of Theology and of Its Verification: A Study in Anselm's 'Proslogion.'" In *Analecta anselmiana*, vol. 4, pt. 2, edited by Helmut Kohlenberger. Frankfort on the Main: Minerva GMBH, 1975.

Palgen, R. "La légende virgilienne dans la *Divine Comédie*." *Romania* 73 (1952): 332–90.

Palmieri, Ugo. "Appunti di linguistica dantesca." *Studi danteschi* 41 (1964): 45–53.

Paluzzi, C. Galassi. "Perchè Dante scelse Virgilio a sua guida." *Giornale dantesco* 39, n.s. 9 (1936): 287–307.

Parker, H. "The Seven Liberal Arts." *English Historical Review* 5 (1890): 417–61.

Parodi, E. G. *Poesia e storia nella "Divina Commedia."* Naples: Francesco Perrella, 1921.

Passerin d'Entrèves, Alessandro. *Dante politico e altri saggi*. Turin: Einaudi, 1955.

Patanè, Leonardo R. *Il pensiero pedagogico di s. Agostino*. 2d ed. Bologna: Patròn, 1969.

Patch, Howard Rollin. *The Tradition of Boethius: A Study of His Importance in Medieval Culture*. New York: Oxford University Press, 1935.

Paulus, Jean. "Le caractère métaphysique des preuves thomistes de l'existence de Dieu." *Archives d'histoire doctrinale et littéraire du moyen âge* 9 (1934): 143–53.

Pegis, Anton C. *The Middle Ages and Philosophy: Some Reflections on the Ambivalence of Modern Scholasticism*. Chicago: Henry Regnery Co., 1963.

————. "St. Anselm and the Argument of the Proslogion." *Mediaeval Studies* 28 (1966): 228–67.

————. *St. Thomas and Philosophy*. Aquinas Lecture, 1964. Milwaukee, Wisc.: Marquette University Press, 1964.

————. *Saint Thomas and the Greeks*. Aquinas Lecture, 1939. Milwaukee, Wisc.: Marquette University Press, 1943.

————. "The Second Conversion of St. Augustine." In *Gesellschaft, Kultur, Literatur: Beiträge Luitpold Wallach gewidmet*, edited by Karl Bosl. Stuttgart: Anton Hiersemann, 1975.

Pellacani, A. M. *Dante vero: Nel poema della grazia l'apologia della ragione*. Padua: CEDAM, 1964.

Pelosi, Silvio. *Dante e la cultura islamica: Analogia tra la Commedia e il Libro della Scala*.

Quaderni dell'Istituto italiano di cultura di Tripoli, vol. 1. Tripoli, 1965.

Penido, M. J. L. *Le rôle de l'analogie en théologie dogmatique.* Paris: Vrin, 1931.

Pépin, Jean. *Dante et la tradition de l'allégorie.* Conférence Albert-le-Grand, 1969. Montréal: Institut d'Études Médiévales, 1970.

————. *Saint Augustin et la dialectique.* Villanova, Pa.: Villanova University Press, 1976.

Perino, Renato. *La dottrina trinitaria di s. Anselmo nel quadro del suo metodo teologico e del suo concetto di Dio.* Rome: Herder, 1952.

Persson, Per Erik. "Le plan de la Somme théologique et la rapport 'Ratio-Revelatio.' " *Revue philosophique de Louvain* 56 (1958): 545–72.

————. *Sacra doctrina: Reason and Revelation in Aquinas.* Translated by Ross Mackenzie. Oxford: Basil Blackwell, 1970.

Petrocchi, Giorgio. *Il "De vulgari eloquentia" di Dante.* Messina: La Editrice Universitaria, 1961.

Pézard, André. *Le "Convivio" de Dante.* Annales de l'Université de Lyon, 3d ser., vol. 9. Paris: Les Belles Lettres, 1940.

————. *Dante sous la pluie de feu.* Paris: Vrin, 1950.

Pflaum, Hiram. "Il 'modus tractandi' della Divina Commedia." *Giornale dantesco* 39, n.s. 9 (1936): 153–78.

Phelan, Gerald B. *St. Thomas and Analogy.* Aquinas Lecture, 1941, Milwaukee, Wisc. Marquette University Press, 1943.

————. "Verum sequitur esse rerum." *Mediaeval Studies* 1 (1939): 11–22.

————. *The Wisdom of Saint Anselm.* Wimmer Lecture, vol. 3. Latrobe, Pa.: Archabbey Press, 1960.

Piemonte, Gustavo A. "Notas sobre la *creatio ex nihilo* en Juan Escoto Eriugena." *Sapientia* 23 (1968): 37–58.

Pieper, Joseph. *Introduction to Thomas Aquinas.* Translated by Richard and Clara Winston. London: Faber & Faber, 1963.

————. *The Silence of St. Thomas: Three Essays.* Translated by John Murray and Daniel O'Connor. New York: Pantheon, 1957.

Pietrobono, Luigi. "Allegoria o arte?" *Giornale dantesco* 37, n.s. 7 (1934): 93–134.

————. "L'allegorismo e Dante." *Giornale dantesco* 38, n.s. 8 (1935): 85–102.

————. "Dante e Roma." *Giornale dantesco* 33, n.s. 3 (1930): 1–24.

————. "L'Epistola a Can Grande." *Giornale dantesco* 40, n.s. 10 (1937): 3–51.

————. "Per l'allegoria di Dante." *Giornale dantesco* 25 (1922): 206–10.

————. "Struttura allegorica e poesia nella Divina Commedia." *Giornale dantesco* 43, n.s. 13 (1940): 9–45.

Pinborg, Jan. "The English Contribution to Logic before Ockham." *Synthese* 40 (1979): 19–42.

————. *Die Entwicklung der Sprachtheorie im Mittelalter. Beiträge zur Geschichte der Philosophie und Theologie des Mittelalters,* vol. 2, pt. 2. Münster in Westphalia: Aschendorffschen Buchhandlung, 1967.

————. "Die Logik der Modistae." *Studia mediewistyczne* 16 (1975): 39–97.

————. *Logik und Semantik im Mittelalter: Ein Überlick.* Stuttgart: Friedrich Frommann Verlag, 1972.

————. "Das Sprachdenken der Stoa und Augustins Dialektik." *Classica et mediaevalia* 23 (1962): 148–77.

Pischedda, Giovanni. *L'orrido e l'ineffabile nella tematica dantesca.* Aquila: La Bodoniana Tipografica, 1958.

Plantinga, Alvin, ed. *The Ontological Argument, from St. Anselm to Contemporary Philosophers.* Garden City, N.Y.: Doubleday Anchor Books, 1965.

Pollmann, Leo. "Vom *Convivio* zur *Epistola a Can Grande.*" *Cultura neolatina* 24 (1964): 39–53.

Pontet, Maurice. *L'exégèse de s. Augustin prédicateur.* Paris: Aubier, 1944.

Pope, Hugh. "St. Thomas as an Interpreter of Holy Scripture." In *St. Thomas Aquinas: Being Papers Read at the Celebration of the Sixth Centenary of the Canonization of Saint Thomas Aquinas, Held at Manchester, 1924.* Oxford: Basil Blackwell, 1925.

Portalié, Eugène. *A Guide to the Thought of Saint Augustine.* Translated by Ralph J. Bastian. Chicago: Henry Regnery Co., 1960.

Pouchet, Robert. *La rectitudo chez saint Anselme: Un itinéraire augustinien de l'âme à Dieu.* Paris: Études Augustiniennes, 1964.

Pranger, M. B. "Masters of Suspense: Argumentation and Imagination in Anselm, Bernard, and Calvin." *Assays* 1 (1981): 15–34.

Prantl, C. *Geschichte der Logik im Abendlande.* Vol. 3. Leipzig: S. Hirzel, 1867.

Prati, Pino da. *La politica e la filosofia nella "Monarchia" di Dante.* 2d ed. Sanremo: Grafiche Bracco, 1963.

Preller, Victor. *Divine Science and the Science of God: A Reformulation of Thomas Aquinas.* Princeton, N.J.: Princeton University Press, 1967.

Principe, Walter H. "The Dynamism of Augustine's Terms for Describing the Highest Trinitarian Image in the Human Person." In press.

Prufer, Thomas. *Sein und Wort nach Thomas von Aquin.* Inaugural Dissertation. Munich, 1959.

Quinn, John M. "The Third Way: A New Approach." *Thomist* 42 (1978): 50–68.

Rabeau, Gaston. *Species, verbum: L'activité intellectuelle élémentaire selon s. Thomas d'Aquin.* Paris: Vrin, 1938.

Raby, F. J. E. *A History of Christian-Latin Poetry from the Beginnings to the Close of the Middle Ages.* 2d ed. Oxford: Oxford University Press, Clarendon Press, 1953.

————. *A History of Secular Latin Poetry in the Middle Ages.* 2 vols. 2d ed. Oxford: Oxford University Press, Clarendon Press, 1957.

Randall, John Herman, Jr. *Aristotle.* New York: Columbia University Press, 1960.

Reese, William L. "Analogy, Symbolism, and Linguistic Analysis." *Review of Metaphysics* 13 (1960): 447–68.

Reeves, Marjorie. "Dante and the Prophetic View of History." In *The World of Dante:*

Essays on Dante and His Times, edited by Cecil Grayson. Oxford: Oxford University Press, Clarendon Press, 1980.

Reiners, Jos. *Der Nominalismus in der Frühscholastik: Ein Beitrag zur Geschichte der Universalienfrage im Mittelalter. Beiträge zur Geschichte der Philosophie des Mittelalters,* edited by Clemens Baeumker, vol. 8, pt. 5. Münster in Westphalia: Aschendorffschen Buchhandlung, 1910.

Reitzenstein, R. "Augustin als antiker und als mittelalterlicher Mensch." *Vorträge der Bibliothek Warburg* 2 (1922–23): 28–65.

Renaudet, Augustin. *Dante humaniste.* Paris: Les Belles Lettres, 1952.

Renucci, Paul. *Dante: Disciple et juge du monde gréco-latin.* Clermont-Ferrand: G. de Bussac, 1954.

Riet, Georges van. "Y a-t-il chez saint Thomas une philosophie de la religion?" *Revue philosophique de Louvain* 61 (1963): 44–81.

Rijk, L. M. de. *Logica Modernorum: A Contribution to the History of Early Terminist Logic.* Vol. 2, pt. 1. Assen: Van Gorcum, 1967.

Rivière, Jean. "Saint Anselme logicien." *Revue des sciences religieuses* 17 (1937): 306–15.

Robert, Brother S. "Rhetoric and Dialectic according to the First Latin Commentary on the 'Rhetoric' of Aristotle." *New Scholasticism* 31 (1957): 484–98.

Robert, Jean-Dominique. "Eléments d'une définition analogique de la connaissance chez s. Thomas." *Revue philosophique de Louvain* 55 (1957): 443–69.

Robertis, Domenico de. *Il libro della "Vita Nuova."* Quaderni degli "Studi danteschi," vol. 1. Florence: G. C. Sansoni, 1961.

Roberts, W. Rhys. *Greek Rhetoric and Literary Criticism.* New York: Longmans, Green & Co., 1928.

Roebiecki, John Joseph. *The Political Philosophy of Dante Alighieri.* Washington, D.C.: Catholic University of America, 1921.

Roedel, Reto. "Individuo e communità nella Divina Commedia." In *Individuum und Gemeinschaft: Festschrift zur fünfzigjahrfeier der Handels-Hochschule St. Gallen.* Saint Gall: Fehr'schen Buchhandlung, 1949.

Rolfes, E. "Zu dem Gottesbeweise des hl. Thomas aus den Stufen der Volkommenheit." *Philosophisches Jahrbuch der Görres-Gesellschaft* 26 (1913): 146–59.

Rosa, P. Enrico. *S. Anselmo di Aosta, archivescovo Cantuariense e dottore della chiesa.* Florence: Libreria Editrice Fiorentina, 1909.

Ross, James F. "Analogy as a Rule of Meaning for Religious Language." *International Philosophical Quarterly* 1 (1961): 468–502.

Rossi, Louis B. "Dante and the Poetic Tradition in the Commentary of Benvenuto da Imola." *Italica* 32 (1955): 215–21.

Rostagni, Augusto. "Risonanze dell'estetica di Filodemo in Cicerone." *Atene e Roma,* n.s. 3 (1922): 28–44.

Rotta, Paolo. *La filosofia del linguaggio nella patristica e nella scolastica.* Turin: Fratelli Bocca, 1909.

Rousseau, Edward L. "St. Anselm and St. Thomas: A Reconsideration." *New Scholasticism* 54 (1980): 1–24.

Rousselot, Pierre. *L'intellectualisme de saint Thomas.* Paris: Félix Alcan, 1908.

Rubinstein, Nicolai. "The Beginnings of Political Thought in Florence: A Study in Mediaeval Historiography." *Journal of the Warburg and Courtauld Institutes* 5 (1942): 198–227.

Rule, Martin. *The Life and Times of St. Anselm, Archbishop of Canterbury and Primate of the Britains.* 2 vols. London: Kegan Paul, Trench, & Co., 1883.

Ryan, John K. "The Problem of Truth." In *Essays in Thomism,* edited by Robert E. Brennan. New York: Sheed & Ward, 1942.

Ryan, Michael. "The Notion and Uses of Dialectic in St. Thomas Aquinas." Ph.D diss., University of Notre Dame, 1962.

Salamucha, Jan. "The Proof 'Ex Motu' for the Existence of God: Logical Analysis of St. Thomas' Arguments." *New Scholasticism* 32 (1958): 334–72.

Sambursky, S. *Physics of the Stoics.* New York: Macmillan Co., 1959.

Samuel, Otto. *Über die Beweisbarkeit der Existenz Gottes: Konsequenzen des anselmischen Beweisverfahrens.* Munich: Chr. Kaiser, 1936.

Sánchez-Ruiz, José Maria. *Las pruebas de la existencia de Dios en el tomismo.* Turin: Pontificio Ateneo Salesiano, 1957.

Santeler, Josef. *Der Platonismus in der Erkenntnislehre des heiligen Thomas von Aquin.* Leipzig: Felizian Rauch, 1939.

Santoro, Mario. "Virgilio personaggio della *Divina Commedia.*" *Cultura e scuola* 4 (1965): 343–55.

Sargent, Daniel. "Dante and Thomism." *Thomist* 5 (1943): 256–64.

Sayers, Dorothy L. *Further Papers on Dante.* New York: Harper & Brothers, 1957.

———. *Introductory Papers on Dante.* New York: Harper & Brothers, 1954.

Scandura, Sebastiano. *L'estetica di Dante, Petrarca, e Boccaccio.* Acireale: Tipografia Edit. XX Secolo, 1928.

Scartazzini, G. A. *A Companion to Dante.* Translated by Arthur John Butler. London: Macmillan & Co., 1893.

Schindler, Alfred. *Wort und Analogie in Augustins Trinitätslehre.* Hermeneutische Untersuchungen zur Theologie, vol. 4. Tübingen: J. C. B. Mohr, 1965.

Schmidt, Robert W. *The Domain of Logic according to Saint Thomas Aquinas.* The Hague: Martinus Nijhoff, 1966.

Schneider, Friedrich. "Der Brief an Can Grande." *Deutsches Dante-Jahrbuch* 34–35 (1957): 3–24.

Schneider, Wilhelm. *Die Quaestiones Disputatae de Veritate des Thomas von Aquin in ihrer philosophiegeschichtlichen Beziehung zu Augustinus.* Beiträge zur Geschichte der Philosophie und Theologie des Mittelalters, edited by Martin Grabmann, vol. 27, pt. 3. Münster in Westphalia: Aschendorffschen Verlagsbuchhandlung, 1930.

Schufreider, Gregory. *An Introduction to Anselm's Argument.* Philadelphia: Temple

University Press, 1978.

Schumacher, Matthew. *The Knowableness of God: Its Relation to the Theory of Knowledge in St. Thomas*. Notre Dame, Ind.: Notre Dame University Press, 1905.

Schwartz, Herbert Thomas. "Analogy in St. Thomas and Cajetan." *New Scholasticism* 28 (1954): 127–44.

Sciacca, M. F. *Saint Augustin et le néoplatonism: La possibilité d'une philosophie chrétienne*. Louvain: Publications Universitaires de Louvain, 1956.

Scott, J. A. "Dante's 'Sweet New Style' and the *Vita Nuova*." *Italica* 42 (1965): 98–107.

Seiferth, Wolfgang. "Zur Kunstlehre Dantes." *Archiv für Kulturgeschichte* 17 (1927): 194–225.

Sepúlveda, Germán. *Influencia del Islam en la Divina Comedia*. Santiago, Chile: Ediciones del Istituto chileno-arabe de cultura, 1965.

Serene, Eileen Flanigan. "Anselm's *Philosophical Fragments*: A Critical Examination." Ph.D. diss., Cornell University, 1974.

Sertillanges, A.-D. *S. Thomas d'Aquin*. 2 vols. Paris: Félix Alcan, 1910.

Shaw, James E. *Guido Cavalcanti's Theory of Love: The Canzoni d'Amore and Other Related Problems*. Toronto: University of Toronto Press, 1949.

———. *The Lady "Philosophy" in the Convivio*. Cambridge, Mass.: Dante Society of Cambridge, Mass., 1938.

Sillem, Edward. *Ways of Thinking about God: Thomas Aquinas and Some Recent Problems*. London: Darton, Longman & Todd, 1961.

Simone, Lydia Pucci de. "Dante poeta della filosofia medievale." *Sapienza* 18 (1965): 465–70.

Simone, Raffaele. "Semiologia agostiniana." *La cultura* 7 (1969): 88–117.

Singleton, Charles S. *Commedia: Elements of Structure*. Dante Studies, vol. 1. Cambridge, Mass.: Harvard University Press, 1954.

———. "Dante and Myth." *Journal of the History of Ideas* 10 (1949): 482–502.

———. *An Essay on the "Vita Nuova."* Published for the Dante Society. Cambridge, Mass.: Harvard University Press, 1949.

———. "The Irreducible Dove." *Comparative Literature* 9 (1957): 129–35.

———. *Journey to Beatrice*. Dante Studies, vol. 2. Cambridge, Mass.: Harvard University Press, 1958.

———. "The Other Journey." *Kenyon Review* 14 (1952): 189–216.

Sirridge, Mary. "Augustine: Every Word Is a Name." *New Scholasticism* 50 (1976): 183–92.

Skysgaard, K. E. "La connaissance humaine d'après saint Thomas d'Aquin." *Classica et medievalia* 2, no. 1 (1939): 86–120.

Smalley, Beryl. *The Study of the Bible in the Middle Ages*. Oxford: Oxford University Press, Clarendon Press, 1941.

Smart, Hugh R. "Anselm's Ontological Argument: Rationalistic or Apologetic?"

Review of Metaphysics 3 (1949): 161–66.

Söhngen, G. "Rectitudo bei Anselm von Canterbury als Oberbegriff von Wahrheit und Gerechtigkeit." In *Sola ratione: Anselm-Studien für Pater Dr. h.c. Franciscus Salesius Schmitt OSB zum fünfundsiebzigsten Geburtstag am 20 Dezember 1969.* Stuttgart: Friedrich Frommann Verlag, 1970.

Solignac, Aimé. "Doxographies et manuels dans la formation philosophique de saint Augustin." *Recherches augustiniennes* 1 (1958): 113–48.

Solmi, Arrigo. "La 'Monarchia' di Dante." *Nuova antologia* 70, fasc. 1513 (1935): 321–31.

———. *Il pensiero politico di Dante: Studi storici.* Florence: La Voce, 1922.

Soria, Fernando. "La teoría del signo en San Agustín." *La ciencia tomista* 92 (1965): 357–96.

Southern, R. W. "Lanfranc of Bec and Berengar of Tours." In *Studies in Medieval History Presented to Frederick Maurice Powicke,* edited by R. W. Hunt, W. A. Pantin, and R. W. Southern. Oxford: Oxford University Press, Clarendon Press, 1948.

———. *Saint Anselm and His Biographer: A Study of Monastic Life and Thought, 1059–c. 1130.* Cambridge: University Press, 1963.

———. "St. Anselm and His English Pupils." *Mediaeval and Renaissance Studies* 1 (1941–43): 3–34.

Spargo, John Webster. *Virgil the Necromancer: Studies in Virgilian Legends.* Cambridge, Mass.: Harvard University Press, 1934.

Spedalieri, Fr. "Anselmus an Gaunilo? Seu de recta argumenti sancti Doctoris interpretatione." *Gregorianum* 28 (1947): 54–77.

———. "De intrinseca argumenti s. Anselmi vi et natura." *Gregorianum* 29 (1948): 204–12.

Spicilegium Beccense. Vol. 1. Congrès Internationale du neuvième centenaire de l'arrivée d'Anselme au Bec. Le Bec-Hellouin: Notre Dame du Bec, 1959.

Spitzer, Leo. "The Addresses to the Reader in the *Commedia.*" *Italica* 12 (1935): 143–65.

Spoerri, Theophil. *Dante und die europäische Literatur.* Stuttgart: W. Kohlhammer, 1963.

Stambler, Bernard. "The Confrontation of Beatrice and Dante: *Purgatorio* XXX." *Italica* 42 (1965): 61–93.

Steenberghen, Fernand van. *Aristote en occident: Les origines de l'aristotélisme parisien.* Louvain: Éditions de l'Institut Supérieur de Philosophie, 1946.

———. *La philosophie au treizième siècle.* Louvain: Publications Universitaires, 1966.

———. "Le problème de l'existence de Dieu dans le 'Scriptum super Sententiis' de saint Thomas." In *Studia mediaevalia in honorem admodum Reverendi Patris Raymundi Josephi Martin.* Bruges: De Tempel, 1948.

Stein, Ludwig. *Die Psychologie der Stoa.* 2 vols. Berlin: S. Calvary, 1886–88.

Steinbüchel, Theodor. *Grosse Gestalten des Abendlandes: Bild und Beispiel christlicher Verwirklichung.* 2d ed. Edited by Alfred Schüler. Trier: Paulinus-Verlag, 1955.

Stewart, H. L. "Dante and the Schoolmen." *Journal of the History of Ideas* 10 (1949): 357–73.

Stolz, Anselm. *Anselm von Canterbury*. Munich: Kösel-Pustet, 1937.

———. "Das *Proslogion* des hl. Anselm." *Révue bénédictine* 47 (1935): 331–47.

———. "'Vere esse' im Proslogion des hl. Anselm." *Scholastik* 9 (1934): 400–406.

———. "Zur Theologie Anselms im Proslogion." *Catholica* 2 (1933): 1–24.

Sundby, Thor. *Della vita e delle opere di Brunetto Latini*. Florence: Succesori Le Monnier, 1884.

Suraci, Antonio. *Il pensiero e l'opere educativa de sant'Anselmo di Aosta (1033–1109)*. Turin: Società/Editrice Internazionale, 1953.

Sweeney, Leo. "Analogy and Being." *Modern Schoolman* 39 (1962): 253–62.

Symonds, John Addington. *An Introduction to the Study of Dante*. 4th ed. London: Adam & Charles Black, 1906.

Talbot, Edward F. *Knowledge and Object*. Washington, D.C.: Catholic University of America, 1932.

Tate, Allen. "The Symbolic Imagination: A Meditation on Dante's Three Mirrors." *Kenyon Review* 14 (1952): 256–77.

Testa, Emanuele. "Poetica e poesia in Dante." *Archivum romanicum* 16 (1932): 211–53.

Testard, Maurice. *Saint Augustin et Cicéron: Cicéron dans la formation et dans l'oeuvre de saint Augustin*. 2 vols. Paris: Études Augustiniennes, 1958.

Thonnard, F.-J. "Les fonctions sensibles de l'âme humaine selon s. Augustin." *L'année théologique augustinienne* 12 (1952): 335–45.

Thurot, Charles. "Notices et extraits de divers manuscrits latins pour servir à l'histoire des doctrines grammaticales au moyen âge." *Notices et extraits des manuscrits de la Bibliothèque Impériale et autres bibliothèques*, vol. 22, pt. 2. Paris: Imprimerie Impériale, 1868.

Tonelli, Luigi. *Dante e la poesia dell'ineffabile*. Florence: G. Barbèra, 1934.

Torraca, Francesco. *Studi danteschi*. Naples: Francesco Perrella, 1912.

Torrance, Thomas F. "The Ethical Implications of Anselm's *De Veritate*." *Theologische Zeitschrift* 24 (1968): 309–19.

Toynbee, Paget. "The Bearing of the *Cursus* on the Text of Dante's *De vulgari eloquentia*." *Proceedings of the British Academy* 11 (1923): 1–19.

Tyrrell, Francis Martin. *The Role of Assent in Judgment: A Thomistic Study*. Catholic University of America Philosophical Series, vol. 100. Washington, D.C.: Catholic University of America Press, 1948.

Ueberweg, Friedrich. *Grundriss der Geschichte der Philosophie*. Vol. 2. 11th ed. Edited by Bernhard Geyer. Berlin: E. S. Mittler & Sohn, 1928.

Urban, Wilbur Marshall. *Language and Reality: The Philosophy of Language and the Principles of Symbolism*. London: George Allen & Unwin, 1939.

Valentini, Giuseppina. "Ricerche intorno al 'De Magistro' di s. Agostino." *Sophia* 4 (1936): 83–89.

Vallis, Maurice. "Dante et l'apologie de l'empire." *Mercure de France* 287 (1938): 586–91.

Van Ackeren, Gerald F. *Sacra Doctrina: The Subject of the First Question of the "Summa Theologica" of St. Thomas Aquinas*. Rome: Officium Libri Catholici, 1952.

Vance, Eugene. "Augustine's *Confessions* and the Grammar of Selfhood." *Genre* 6 (1973): 1–28.

Van Doren, Mark. "The Divine Comedy." *Sewanee Review* 54 (1946): 349–95.

Vanni Rovighi, Sofia. *S. Anselmo e la filosofia del secolo undicesimo*. Milan: Fratelli Bocca, 1949.

———. "La fenomenologia della sensazione in s. Agostino." *Rivista di filosofia neoscolastica* 54 (1962): 18–32.

Vasoli, Cesare. "Filosofia e teologia in Dante." *Cultura e scuola* 4 (1965): 47–71.

Velecky, Lubor. "'The Five Ways': Proofs of God's Existence?" *Monist* 58 (1974): 36–51.

Verbeke, Gérard. *L'évolution de la doctrine du pneuma du stoïcisme à s. Augustin*. Paris: Desclée de Brouwer; Louvain: Éditions de l'Institut Supérieur de Philosophie, 1945.

Vergnes, Jules. "Les sources de l'argument de saint Anselme." *Revue des sciences religieuses* 4 (1924): 576–79.

Vignaux, Paul. "La méthode de saint Anselme dans le *Monologion* et le *Proslogion*." *Aquinas* 8 (1965): 110–29.

———. *Philosophy in the Middle Ages: An Introduction*. Translated by E. C. Hall. New York: Meridian Books, 1959.

———. "Structure et sens du *Monologion*." *Revue des sciences philosophiques et théologiques* 31 (1947): 192–212.

Vijver, A. van de. "Les étapes du développement philosophique du haut moyen-âge." *Revue belge de philologie et d'histoire* 8 (1929): 425–52.

Vinay, Gustave. "La teoria linguistica del *De vulgari eloquentia*." *Cultura e scuola* 2 (1962): 30–42.

Vincent, E. R. "The Crisis in the *Vita Nuova*." In *Centenary Essays on Dante by Members of the Oxford Dante Society*. Oxford: Oxford University Press, Clarendon Press, 1965.

Virieux-Reymond, Antoinette. *La logique et l'épistémologie des stoïciens*. Chambéry: Imprimeries Réunies, 1949.

Vittorini, Domenico. *High Points in the History of Italian Literature*. New York: David McKay Co., 1958.

Voelke, André-Jean. "L'unité de l'âme dans l'ancien stoïcisme." *Studia philosophica* 2 (1965): 154–81.

Vossler, Karl. *Mediaeval Culture: An Introduction to Dante and His Times*. Translated by William Cranston Lawton. 2 vols. New York: Harcourt, Brace & Co., 1929.

Vuillemin, Jules. *Le Dieu d'Anselme et les apparences de la raison*. Paris: Aubier Montaigne, 1971.

Walker, C. R. "St. Anselm: A Revaluation." *Scottish Journal of Theology* 5 (1952): 362–73.

Warnach, Viktor. "Das äussere Sprechen und seine Funktionen nach der Lehre des hl. Thomas von Aquin." *Divus Thomas* 16 (1938): 393–419.

———. "Erkennen und Sprechen bei Thomas von Aquin: Ein Deutungsversuch seiner Lehre auf ihren geistesgeschichtlichen Hintergrund." *Divus Thomas* 15 (1937): 189–218, 263–90; 16 (1938): 161–96.

Waters, A. J. "The Poet-Theologian of the Middle Ages." *American Catholic Quarterly Review* 39 (1914): 152–59.

Watson, Gerard. *The Stoic Theory of Knowledge.* Belfast: The Queen's University, 1966.

Wébert, J. "L'image dans l'oeuvre de saint Thomas." *Revue thomiste* 31, n.s. 9 (1926): 427–45.

Weddington, A. van. *Essai critique sur la philosophie de s. Anselme de Cantorbéry.* Brussels: F. Hayez, 1875.

Weigel, Gustave, and Madden, Arthur G. *Religion and the Knowledge of God.* Englewood Cliffs, N.J.: Prentice-Hall, 1961.

Weisheipl, James A. *Friar Thomas d'Aquino: His Life, Thought, and Work.* Garden City, N.Y.: Doubleday, 1974.

———. "The Meaning of *sacra doctrina* in *Summa theologiae* I, q. 1." *Thomist* 38 (1974): 49–80.

Weiss, R. "Links between the 'Convivio' and the 'De Vulgari Eloquentia.' " *Modern Language Review* 37 (1942): 156–68.

Wendschuh, Georg. *Verhältnis der Glaubens zum Wissen bei Anselm von Canterbury: Ein Beitrag zu Anselms Erkenntnistheorie.* Weida in Thüringia: Thomas & Hubert, 1909.

White, Victor. *Holy Teaching: The Idea of Theology according to St. Thomas Aquinas.* Aquinas Society of London, Aquinas Paper 33. London: Blackfriars, 1958.

———. "The Prolegomena to the Five Ways." *Dominican Studies* 5 (1952): 134–58.

Whitfield, J. H. *Dante and Virgil.* Oxford: Basil Blackwell, 1949.

Wicksteed, Philip H. *Dante and Aquinas.* London: J. M. Dent & Sons, 1913.

———. *From "Vita Nuova" to "Paradiso": Two Essays on the Vital Relations between Dante's Successive Works.* Publications of the University of Manchester, vol. 151. Manchester: Manchester University Press, 1922.

———, and Gardner, Edmund G. *Dante and Giovanni del Virgilio, Including a Critical Edition of the Text of Dante's "Eclogae Latinae" and of the Poetic Remains of Giovanni del Virgilio.* Westminster: Archibald Constable & Co., 1902.

Wienbruch, Ulrich. "'Signum,' 'Significatio,' und 'Illuminatio' bei Augustin." In *Der Begriff der Repraesentatio im Mittelalters: Stellvertretung, Symbol, Zeichen, Bild,* edited by Albert Zimmerman. Berlin: Walter de Gruyter, 1971.

Wieruszowski, Helene. "*Ars Dictaminis* in the Time of Dante." *Medievalia et humanistica* 1 (1943): 95–108.

———. "Der Reichsgedanke bei Dante." *Deutsches Dante-Jahrbuch* 14, n.s. 5 (1932): 185–209.

Wilhelm, James J. *The Cruelest Month: Spring, Nature, and Love in Classical and Medieval Lyrics.* New Haven, Conn.: Yale University Press, 1965.

Wilkins, Ernest Hatch. "Dante as Apostle." In *Symposium: Dante Six Hundred Years After*. Chicago: Chicago Literary Club, 1921.

————. *Dante: Poet and Apostle*. Chicago: University of Chicago Press, 1921.

————. *A History of Italian Literature*. Cambridge, Mass.: Harvard University Press, 1954.

Williams, Charles. *The Figure of Beatrice: A Study in Dante*. New York: Noonday Press, 1961.

Williams, C. J. F. "Existence and the Meaning of the Word 'God.'" *Downside Review* 77 (1958–59): 53–71.

Wilmart, André. "Le premier ouvrage de saint Anselme contre le trithéisme de Roscelin." *Recherches de théologie ancienne et médiévale* 3 (1931): 20–30.

Wilpert, Paul. *Das Problem der Wahrheitssicherung bei Thomas von Aquin: Ein Beitrag zur Geschichte der Evidenzproblems*. *Beiträge zur Geschichte der Philosophie und Theologie des Mittelalters*, edited by Martin Grabmann, vol. 30, pt. 3. Münster in Westphalia: Aschendorffeschen Verlagsbuchhandlung, 1931.

Winance, Eleuthère. "L'essence divine et la connaissance humaine dans le Commentaire sur les Sentences de saint Thomas." *Revue philosophique de Louvain* 55 (1957): 171–215.

Witte, Karl. *Essays on Dante*. Selected, edited, and translated by C. Mabel Lawrence and Philip H. Wicksteed. London: Duckworth & Co., 1910.

Wolz, Henry G. "The Empirical Basis of Anselm's Arguments." *Philosophical Review* 60 (1951): 341–61.

Wulf, Maurice de. "Augustinisme et aristotélisme au treizième siècle." *Revue néoscolastique* 8 (1901): 151–66.

————. *History of Mediaeval Philosophy*. 3d ed. Translated by Ernest C. Messenger. 2 vols. London: Longmans, Green & Co., 1935–38.

————. *The System of Thomas Aquinas*. New York: Dover Publications, 1959.

Wyser, Paul. "Die wissenschaftstheoretischen Quaest. V. u. VI. in Boethium de Trinitate des hl. Thomas von Aquin." *Divus Thomas* 25 (1947): 437–85; 26 (1948): 74–98.

Zabughin, Vladmiro. *Vergilio nel rinascimento italiano da Dante a Torquato Tasso*. Vol. 1. Bologna: Nicola Zanichelli, 1923.

Zingarelli, Nicola. *La vita, i tempi, e le opere di Dante*. 2 vols. Milan: Francesco Vallardi, 1931.

Index

www.ingramcontent.com/pod-product-compliance
Ingram Content Group UK Ltd.
Pitfield, Milton Keynes, MK11 3LW, UK
UKHW032027240225
455518UK00001B/138